Learn How to Create Images,
Set Up a Studio, and Launch
Your Photography Career

LIGHTRIGHT

Joe Lavine | Brad Bartholomew

Peachpit
Press

LIGHT RIGHT

Learn How to Create Images, Set Up a Studio, and Launch Your Photography Career

Joe Lavine and Brad Bartholomew

Peachpit
www.peachpit.com

To report errors, please send a note to errata@peachpit.com.

Peachpit is a division of Pearson Education.

Acquisitions Editor: Ted Waitt
Project Editor: Susan Rimerman
Production Editor: Lisa Brazieal
Development/Copy Editor: Peggy Nauts
Proofreader: Elaine Merrill
Indexer: Karin Arrigoni
Interior Design and Composition: Kim Scott, Bumpy Design
Cover Design: Aren Straiger
Cover Photograph: Joe Lavine

ISBN-10: 0-321-86385-2
ISBN-13: 978-0-321-86385-0

9 8 7 6 5 4 3 2 1

Printed and bound in the United States of America

For my partner, best friend, wife, and voice of reason—Kathleen.
I could never have completed this project without her.
Also, to my father, who made me the man I am today.

—Joe Lavine

This book is dedicated to my lovely wife, Betsy,
who has supported and loved me for over 30 years.
Anything I have done wouldn't have been possible without her.

—Brad Bartholomew

Acknowledgments

Thank you to the many role models that I've had in my career. Throughout my entire life, my father has been an example of the definition of hard work and determination. My sister Helene, who has proven what you can accomplish when you set a goal. In college, Norman Lerner for never letting me settle for simply doing OK; OK was never good enough, and still isn't. I could have never asked for a better mentor and friend than Jan Oswald; she taught me how to be successful in photography and business.

I must thank all the students who have crossed my path during the last 15 years. Each one forced me to learn more about photography and education than I ever could have on my own.

A giant thank-you must go out to the entire team at the MAC Group, especially Bill Gratton. Bill and the MAC Group have supported me as an educator, lecturer, photographer, and author. Thanks to Dan Cuny and Profoto for letting me borrow some incredible lighting equipment, which I may never return. Beth Hawkins was gracious in offering her amazing food styling skills for multiple images. This book would have never been possible without my coauthor, mentor, studio partner, and friend, Brad. Last, and definitely not least, no acknowledgement would be complete without thanking my wife Kathleen (aka Kiki) for putting up with me, and my loving quirks, every day.

—Joe

Let's start at the beginning with my two amazing parents, who taught me the importance of love, patience, and hard work. I love you both. Thanks to all the faculty and fellow classmates at Art Center, especially David Roth, for demanding only the very best work week in and week out. Assisting Richard Noble was a once-in-a-lifetime experience that reinforced my desire to become a commercial photographer. Thanks to Howard Sokol and Frank Varney for being terrific mentors and friends. I appreciate the generosity of all the instructors I have worked with at the Art Institute of Colorado over the years. Trying to emulate them has made me a better teacher.

You can't teach without students. I have received far more from them than they did from me. Thanks in particular to Jake Potts and Jennifer Coudron for their amazing images, and the fact that their drive to succeed inspired me to be a better instructor.

I've been fortunate to work with some amazing, talented, zany designers, art directors, and clients over more than 25 years. Collaborating with Connie Asher, Suzette McKinnon, Dan Ragland, Annie Danielson, and a host of other truly talented people has made this the most enjoyable job I can imagine. It sure beats working for a living. Finally, thanks to my immediate and extended family—Allison, Ian, and Betsy, thanks for putting up with me. I am fortunate to be surrounded by incredibly supportive people, who have made sacrifices to make my life better. Lastly, thanks to Joe for being a generous friend and partner in this project. It never would have happened without you.

—Brad

We have had an incredible group of people guiding this project. Thanks to Peggy Nauts for making us sound more lucid and intelligent, Susan Rimerman for encouraging us while still being able to keep us on track, and Lisa Brazieal and Kim Scott for a beautifully designed book. Thanks to the gifted and generous photographers Howard Sokol, Jan Oswald, Casey Bieker, Jake Potts, Jennifer Coudron, Brian Mark, and Martin Wonnacott for allowing us to use your stunning images throughout the book. It would've suffered greatly without them. The diagrams wouldn't have been possible without the clever program written by Kevin Kertz. Gina lent us her talent and lovely face for several images, and Kathy MacKay contributed her hair and makeup skills and friendship for this project, as she has for many others over the years. You all made this relatively painless and we couldn't be happier with the results.

—Joe and Brad

About the Authors

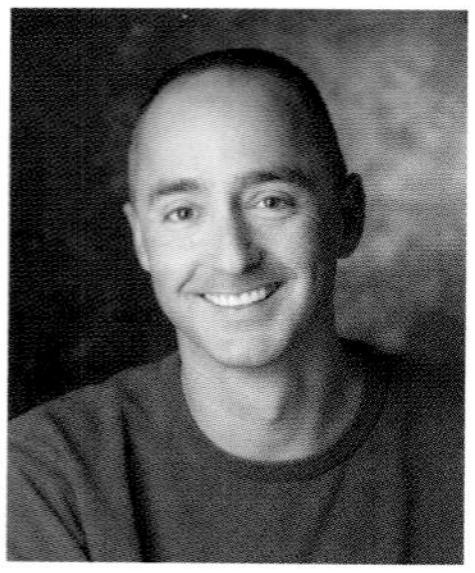

Joe Lavine

Photography has been part of my life for over 30 years. I remember being given a Pentax K1000 SLR camera for my 13th birthday; that day changed my life forever. Truth is, I wish that I still owned that camera.

I am simply one of those people who love photography. I was told early in my life that if you can make your avocation your vocation, you'll have a happy life. This is the premise I have followed throughout my career; whether it was undergraduate and graduate studies, teaching, lecturing, writing, or working as a photographer, I have always believed in doing what makes one happy.

Two of my passions are food and photography. That and an attention to detail have allowed me to build a commercial studio where I specialize as a food and beverage photographer. Years of focusing on the details, which generally involved much experimentation and problem solving, have made me an expert in understanding my subjects and using lighting techniques to bring them to life. My clients range from small restaurants to Fortune 500 companies. A partial client list includes Coors, Betty Crocker, General Mills, Coca-Cola, Pillsbury, Coleman Foods, JBS Swift, and Celestial Seasonings. With the help of my great clients, I have won local and national honors.

Whether as a student or as a young photographer, if it weren't for a handful of mentors, my career would not have been as fruitful. That's why I became an educator and author. I began teaching photography at the collegiate level in 1998 and have held either an adjunct or full-time position ever since. Along with running a studio, teaching, and writing, I am a frequent guest lecturer at colleges and seminars around the country.

I have learned that there is no single method that works for all photographers. Heck, my wife, Kathleen, is a professional photographer, and our approaches and styles are worlds apart, but that is OK; this is what makes photography great. Whether lecturing or writing, I want to give people the tools to achieve their goals in photography.

Brad Bartholomew

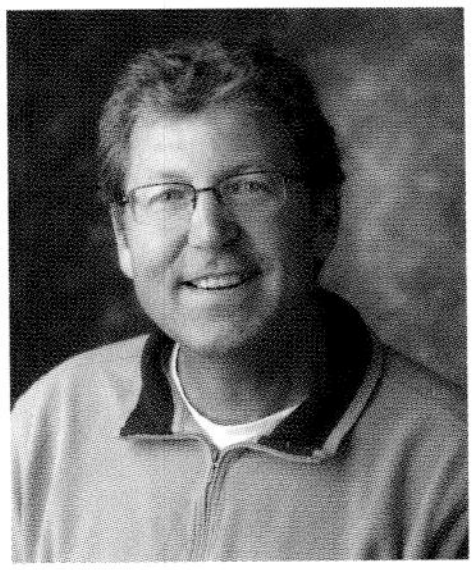

Brad Bartholomew is an award-winning commercial photographer and educator living and working in Denver, Colorado. For over 25 years he has shot a variety of subjects in his studio for a myriad of local and national clients, including Apple Computer, Celestial Seasonings, the Colorado Ballet, JD Edwards, Children's Hospital, Coors Brewing Company, Forest Oil, Head Sports, My Twinn, Pentax, and Qwest.

Brad specializes in not specializing. He photographs products and people both in the studio and on location. Brad works with advertising agencies and design firms as well as directly with clients. Believing in the collaborative nature of commercial photography, he says, "I am pleased when, at the end of the project, the client will say, 'Well, that was fun' as if they are surprised. Pushing to create strong, conceptual, beautiful images can be stressful, but in the end, we're taking pictures. It's supposed to be fun."

Brad has taught a variety of classes at the Colorado Institute of Art for over 25 years. His main emphasis is teaching studio, lighting, portfolio, and advertising photography and the principles classes. He believes it's his obligation to provide students with a challenging and nurturing environment in which they can apply their tremendous energy to reach far and create dynamic, vibrant imagery. Brad encourages students to take risks. Progress cannot be achieved without trying new things, and progress cannot occur without failure. He's come to realize that he gets far more from his students than they get from him. That's one reason he continues to teach.

This book is an extension of the desire to teach more people and give back to a profession that Brad feels passionate about.

Brad has been married for almost 30 years. He and his wife, Betsy, have two wonderful kids, one in college, the other a graduate out in the working world, who are vibrant, interesting individuals. When Brad and Betsy are not gathering with family and friends around the table eating good food and drinking wine, you can find them traveling the West in their 1979 VW camper.

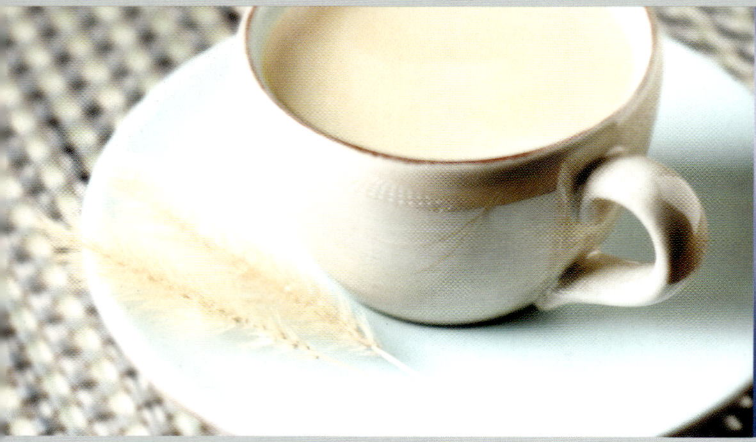
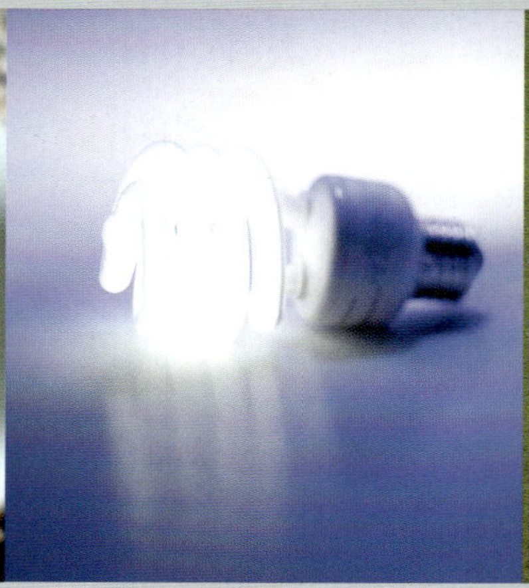
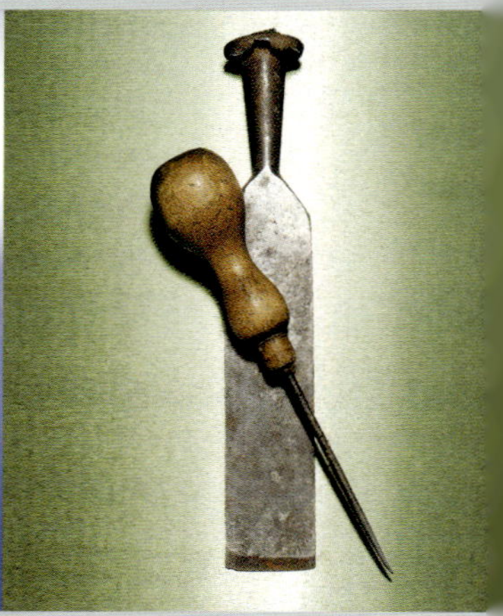

CONTENTS

Introduction xiii

SECTION I Philosophy of Lighting

chapter one
WHAT LIGHT DOES 5

- Lighting Is a Building Process 7
- Dimension 8
  - Point Source vs. Diffused Lighting 9
  - Lighting Ratios 12
- Texture 18
  - Creating Texture 19
  - Controlling Texture 23
- Separation 24
- Drama 30
- interview Howard Sokol 38

chapter two
THE BUILDING PROCESS 43

- Understand Your Subject 46
- What Are You Trying to Say? 49
- Previsualize 54
- Addition and Subtraction 58
  - Addition 59
  - Subtraction 62
- Comparison 65

chapter three
LIGHTING AS PART OF COMPOSITION 71

- Direct the Viewer's Eye 73
  - Jan Oswald, Artist with Light 74
- Subject Hierarchy 80
- Painting with Light 83
  - Different Ways to Light Paint 83
  - Light Painting in the Studio 85
  - The Process 87
  - High-Key Shots 90
  - Exposure 91
- interview Jan Oswald 92

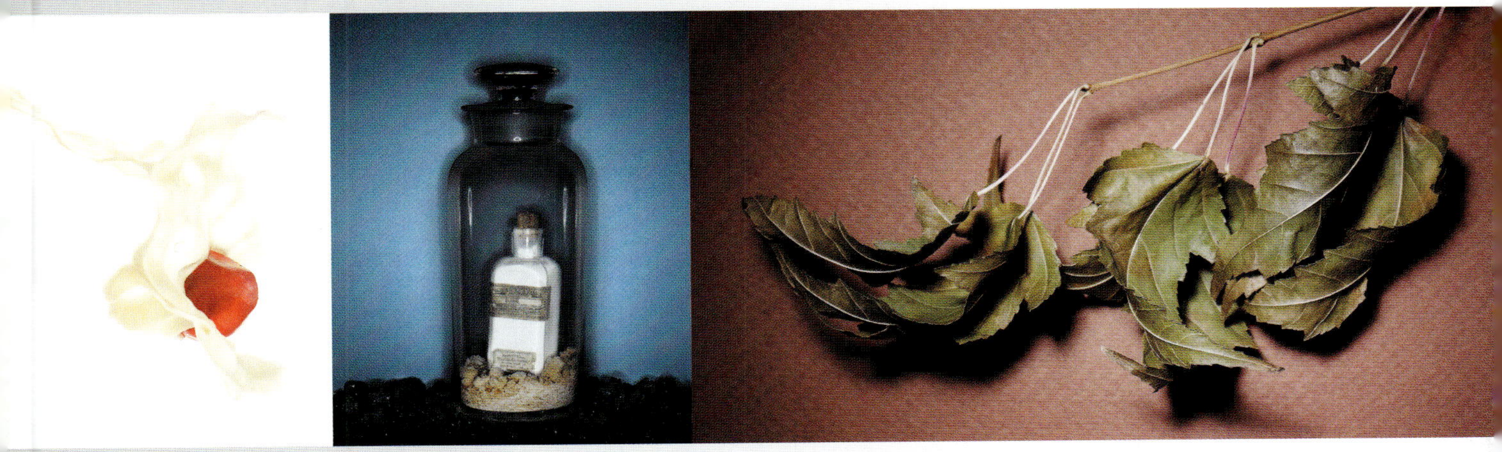

chapter four

EXPERIMENTATION 97

- Don't Settle 99
- No Pat Answers 103
- More Than One Solution 106
- Constantly Grow 110
  - Developing a Personal Style 112
- Comparison 113

SECTION II The Basics

chapter five

LIGHTING EQUIPMENT 121

- Strobe/Flash 123
  - Flash Duration 125
  - Temperature 127
- Continuous 128
- Filtering 131
  - Color Correction 132
  - Creative 133
- Accessories 135
  - Grip (Gear) 136
  - Light Modifiers 136
  - Sync Cords and Radio Slaves 138
- Comparison 141

chapter six

DSLR CAMERAS 145

- Camera Basics 147
  - Sensors 148
  - Features 150
- Lenses 153
  - Aperture/Speed 153
  - Focal Length 154
- Other Options 157
  - Digital Backs 157
  - Medium Format 158
  - Large-Format/View Cameras 159
- interview Jennifer Coudron 162

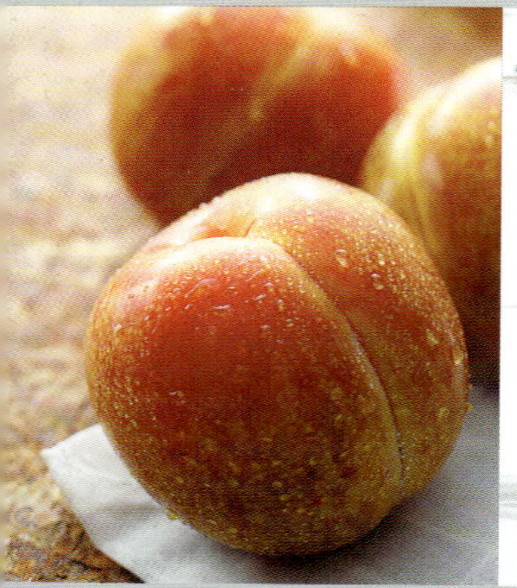
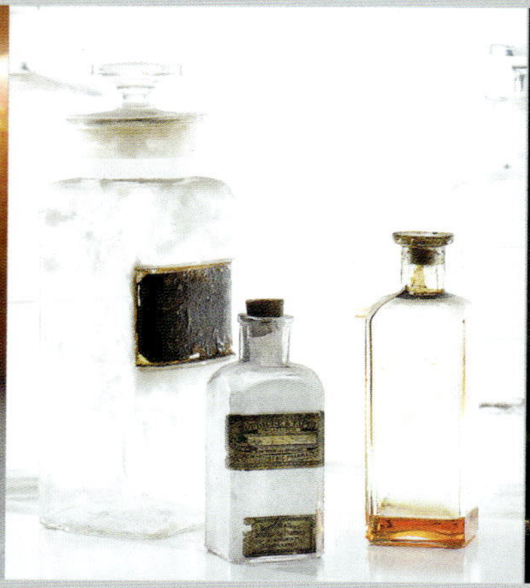
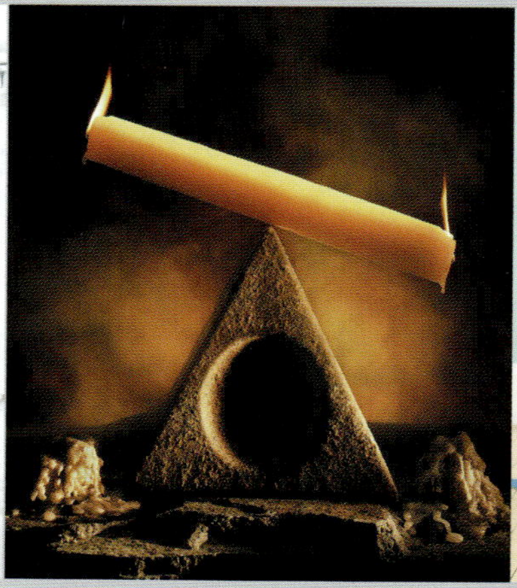
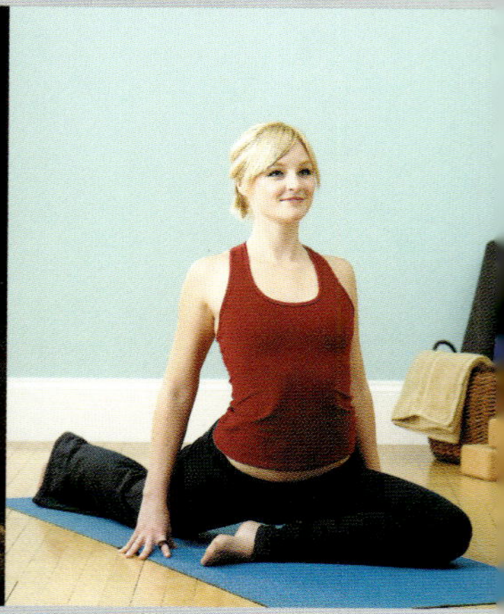

chapter seven
METERING 165

Dynamic Range 167
Determinants of Exposure 168
Available Light 169
ISO 169
Aperture 171
Shutter Speed 171
Equivalent Exposures 171
Bracketing 173
Types of Meters 174
Reflected vs. Incident 175
In-Camera vs. Handheld 176
Priority Modes 178
Comparison 179

chapter eight
READING A HISTOGRAM 185

What Is a Histogram? 187
Why Are Histograms Important? 191
Subject Failure 191
High-Key Scenes 192
Low-Key Scenes 194
Backlit Scenes 194
Maintaining Histogram Integrity 198
interview Brian Mark 202

SECTION III
Building a Studio and Launching a Career

chapter nine
GETTING STARTED WITH $500 207

Equipment 209
Studio 209
Lighting 210
Grip Equipment 214
Stands 214
Budgets 217
Expectations 219
interview Jake Potts 226

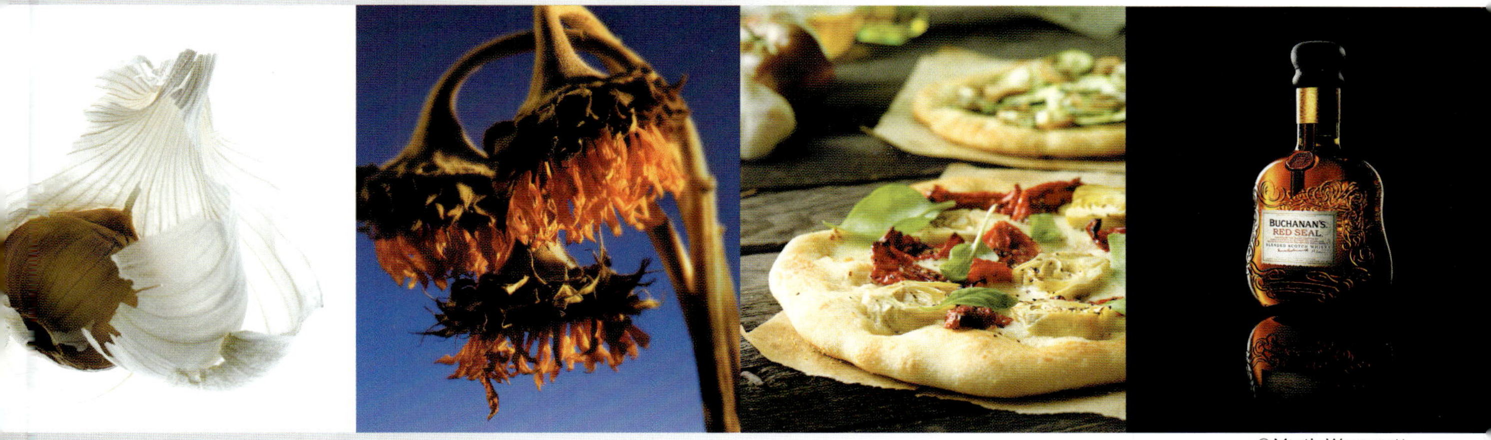

© Martin Wonnacott

chapter ten

A WORKING STUDIO 231

- Equipment 233
  - Studio 233
  - Lighting 237
  - Grip Equipment 244
- Budgets 246
- Expectations 247
  - Self-Imposed Standards 247
  - Working with Clients 248
- Comparison 250

chapter eleven

SUCCESS 257

- Things Are Good 259
  - The Trap 259
- Marketing 264
  - Branding 264
  - Ways to Reach Your Audience 266
- High-End Equipment 274
  - Studio 274
  - Lighting 276
  - Grip Equipment 278
- Budgets 278
  - Representation 280
- Conclusion 280
- interview Martin Wonnacott 282

Index 286

Introduction

In theory, baking a chocolate cake is a simple process. There are a limited number of ingredients that need to be combined in the right proportions. These are then placed in an oven at the right temperature for a prescribed amount of time, and presto, you have the perfect cake. All you have to do is follow the recipe. Yet sometimes the cake is too dry, sometimes it's a soggy mess, and sometimes it's rock hard. The theory is relatively simple, but in practice it's not always easy to get the results you desire.

Lighting a photograph is very much the same kind of endeavor. The theory is simple, but creating beautifully lit images is not an easy thing to do. In theory, light needs to do only a few things. It should create volume in the subject matter; it should separate objects from one another and the background. The light should create texture and perhaps drama. Simply get the light to do those few things and presto, you have a great image. Just follow the recipe.

Many good books have been written about the subject of lighting. Many of them provide the readers with recipes to follow to achieve specific results. They include diagrams with lighting placement and lighting ratios: If you place your subject here and put this kind of light on it in the following amounts, you'll get the following results. There is nothing inherently wrong with this formula except that it's, by nature, formulaic. Lighting a photograph should be anything but formulaic. Lighting is one of the most important creative components of any image. In fact, we'd go so far as to say that it's the most important component. It's what we do as photographers. Lighting is how we create our images. It must be a creative, not a formulaic endeavor.

Returning to the cake analogy—what if we want to make a lemon cake? Can we just substitute the same amount of lemons for the chocolate we were using? Should we use whole lemons, lemon extract, or lemon juice? What about the peels? Why doesn't my recipe tell me these things? Well, I have a recipe for chocolate cake, not lemon cake. Sure, I can probably find a lemon cake recipe, but then my cake will taste just like the cake made by anyone else who uses this recipe.

You do not want your photographs to look like everyone else's photos. That's why this book will rely on few recipes, few diagrams, and few set-in-stone guidelines. To benefit from reading this text, you'll need to do more than simply follow a set of rigid preset rules. You'll need to be willing to experiment; you'll have to be willing to fail as you learn to create images that reflect your own personal taste and style.

Of course, we have to start with some basic principles, principles that you'll be able to apply to your own subjects. We'll give you many examples to help guide you through the process, but it's imperative that you don't think that the exact lighting used in these examples will work for your specific subjects. It won't be as easy as setting up our lighting schemes to duplicate our results. We are showing how to make a chocolate cake, but you may be trying to make a lemon, strawberry, or vanilla cake. The principles are hugely important, and they will help, but you'll need to do your own experimentation to get the results you desire.

OK, then—this book isn't a collection of lighting recipes. It's not a strictly technical how-to book. So what is it? It will be your guide to fully immerse yourself in the ways you can get light to do what you want it to do. Ultimately, you want light to accentuate the positive aspects of what is in front of your camera while it hides or diminishes lesser attributes. The secret is that no simple solutions to solving these problems exist. There are many ways to get from point A to point B; compelling ways in which each of you will decide to light your subjects. The key idea here is that you are making conscious decisions. You're not taking photographs; you are making them. You are constantly analyzing your subjects, and you make a series of choices and decisions to help portray these subjects in the way you wish them to be portrayed.

The entire process starts by thinking—thinking about each individual subject you shoot. You must know exactly what you want to say about what you are about to photograph. Are you trying to minimize or maximize texture? What's good for one subject might be terrible for another. An old sea captain might look great with a hard cross light that brings out the weathered crags in his face, whereas your grandmother might not appreciate the same lighting treatment.

These are your choices as you start the process of lighting your shots. Nothing drives us crazier than watching students set up lights in exactly the same spots with the same light modifiers week after week, with no thought to what they're trying to accomplish with those lights. Using the same lighting schemes for all your images is a sure way to run your career right into the ground.

We'll show you how to use specific tools to create unique and cogent lighting. You'll explore the analytical skills necessary to bring your subject to life through lighting that works for that specific subject and for the way you see it, him, or her. We'll concentrate on lighting within a studio environment, but it's important to realize that these thought processes and techniques can be applied to all types of lighting, both within and outside the studio.

In addition to discussions about lighting in the abstract, we'll examine practical tools and techniques to make your image making easier and more effective. We'll begin with simple, inexpensive equipment options. (Yes, there are ways to create fabulous light that don't cost a lot.) As the book progresses, we'll consider more complicated and more expensive alternatives. As your careers progress and your job assignments become more complicated, clients' and other viewers' expectations of you and your abilities will also grow. This can be both exciting and intimidating.

It's important to understand that you won't have all the equipment you need at the very beginning of your career. Almost all photographers start their careers with relatively simple equipment, and then they add to it as needed. We'll help you get the most out of each piece of lighting equipment that you acquire.

One of the major focuses of this book, in addition to lighting effectively, is the goal of growing your business and all that will entail. While hobbyist photographers might enjoy this book, it's really geared toward those individuals who want to take their photography to a level where it can support them over a long and satisfying career. Photography is a wonderful and vexing mixture of art and science, aesthetics and technology, and creative enterprise and business. Being deficient in any of these areas will keep you from being truly successful. It's our hope that this book will help you to create dramatic and appropriately lit images that will entice others to work with you or hire you, enabling you to grow your business over time.

One of the keys to running a successful photography business is understanding that at its core, it's a customer service business. As your business grows, you'll be using more sophisticated lighting equipment, but you'll also need to use more sophisticated customer service techniques. Fully understanding exactly what your clients want and expect and then being able to deliver on these expectations is an essential part of running a successful commercial photography business—or any other kind of business, for that matter.

The most important thing to remember as you begin reading this book is to keep an open mind. Maintain a willingness to experiment and push yourself outside of your comfort zone, beyond tried-and-true methods, so that you can develop your own unique voice. In the following pages you'll see many different examples of similar subjects lit in various ways. We've done this deliberately to help drive home the point that there is no single solution to any specific lighting problem. There are always multiple approaches, and it'll be up to you to decide on the one that best works for what you're trying to say with each of your images.

After more than 40 years of combined teaching experience, we realize that often students just want to be told the right answer. We also have learned that to do so is not good teaching. The students who are truly successful use fundamental lighting principles as a foundation and then experiment as they build their own unique and compelling images. They light each subject in its own way. In short, they light right.

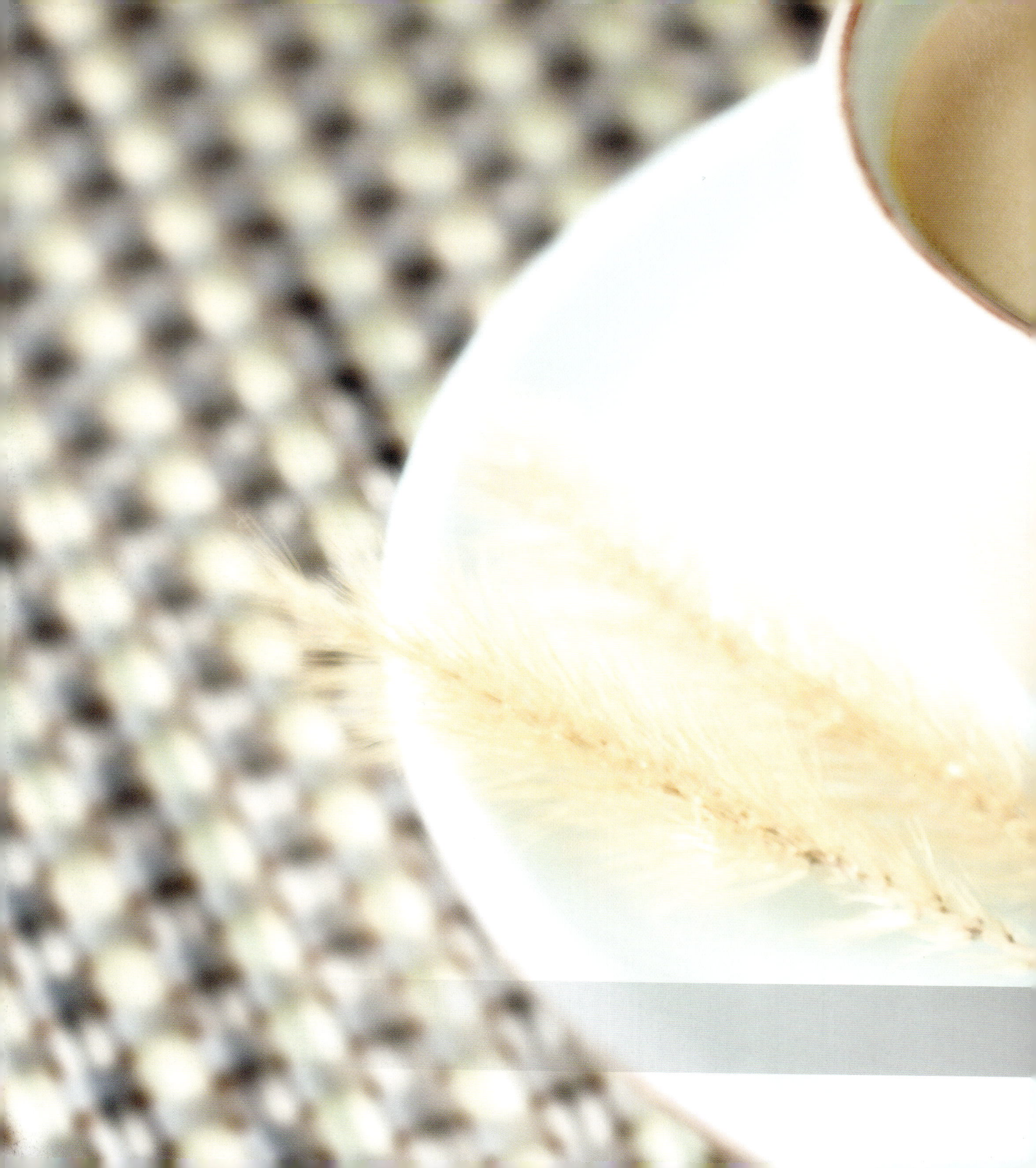

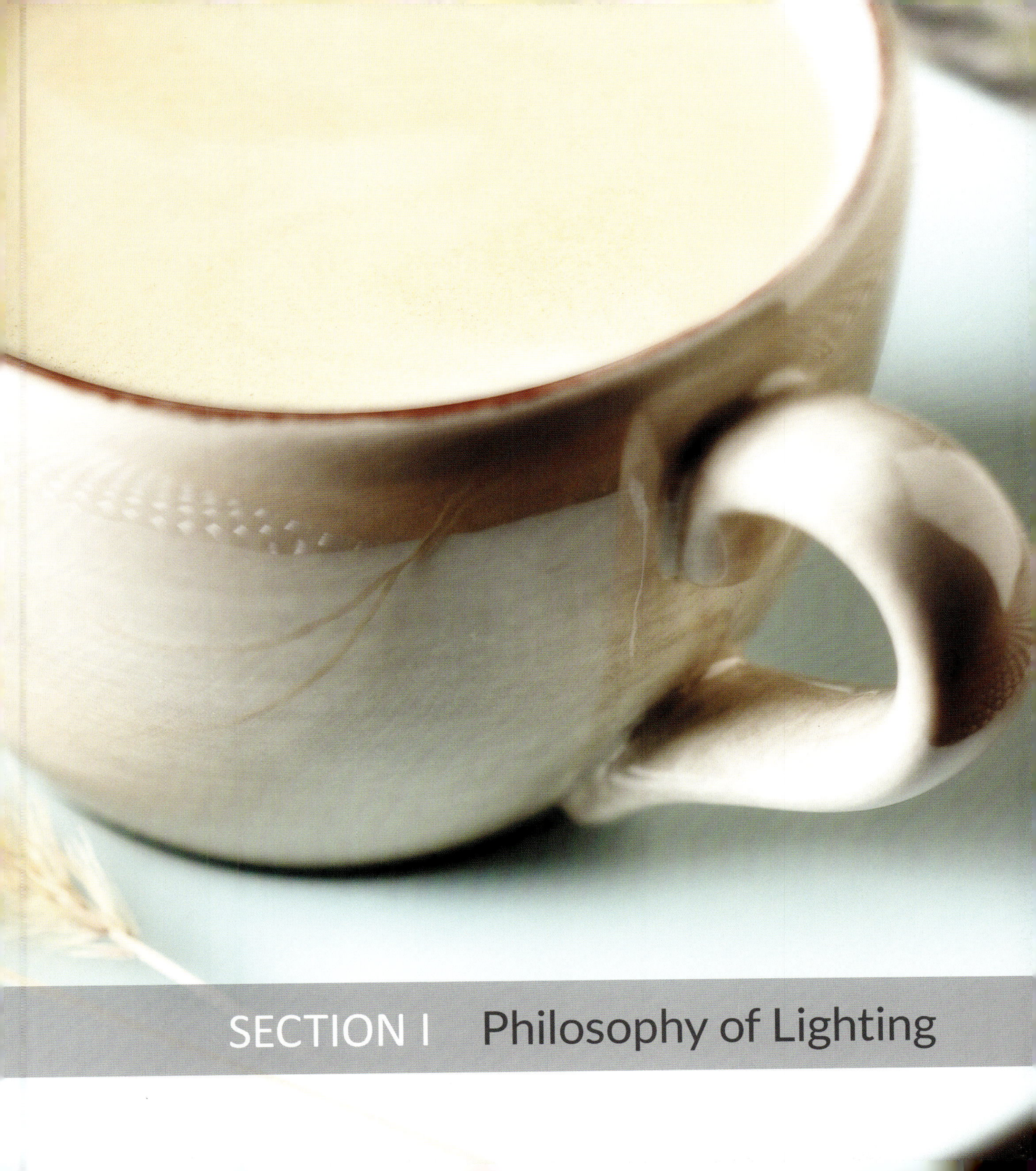

SECTION I Philosophy of Lighting

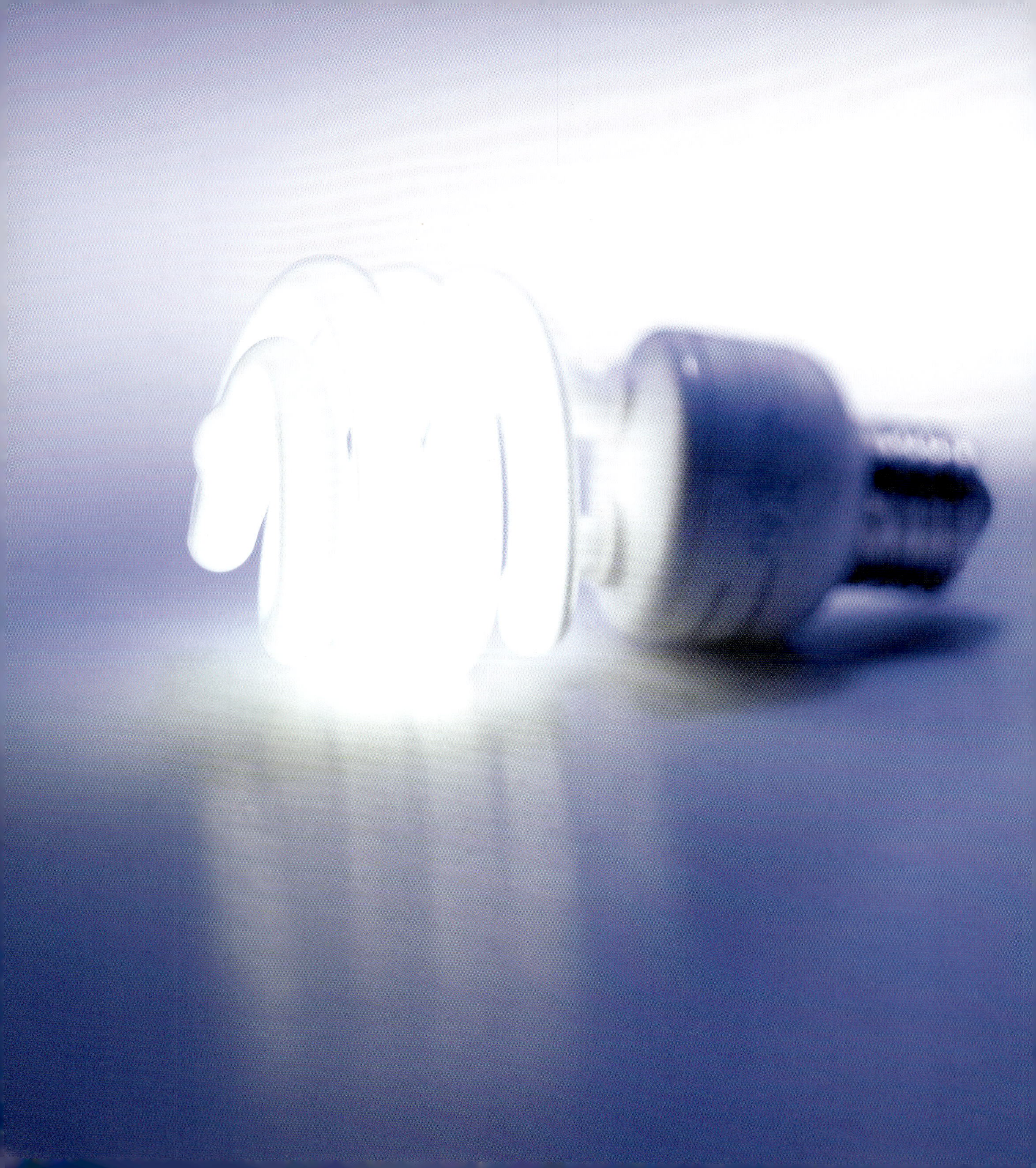

chapter one

WHAT LIGHT DOES

We have all seen gorgeous images of Half Dome that move us, and we have seen photographs of the same Half Dome that have no emotional effect. Why the difference?

In Yosemite Valley, the knowledgeable photographer will wait for the right day, hour, minute, and sometimes even second to capture that perfect moment when Half Dome comes to life. It takes that moment and click of the shutter to make the subject sing. The subject and the light become one to create a unique and moving image. The studio photographer has a somewhat different challenge; he will not need to wait for the perfect moment, but instead creates the light that makes the image work.

ISO 50, 2 sec., f/5.6, 210mm lens

Opening Image: Photographic Equipment

Camera: Sinar 4 x 5 view camera with Leaf Aptus-II digital back

Lens: Nikkor 100mm

Lighting: Profoto Acute2 generator and two strobe heads

Light modifiers: Softbox, grid, and purple gel

The picture of the light bulb on the previous page was relatively easy to produce. It was created for a local real-estate developer. The trickiest part was getting the bulb to glow. I took an extension cord and cut off the female end, and then stripped the insulation off the ends of the two wires. I took an exposure using the two strobe heads to light up the overall scene. I then put one wire against the bottom and one wire on the back of the metal part of the bulb; this makes the bulb light up. I took an exposure with the bulb lit and the strobes working. I then composited the two images in Photoshop and masked out the wires. Just a word of caution—be very careful when working with hot electrical wires!

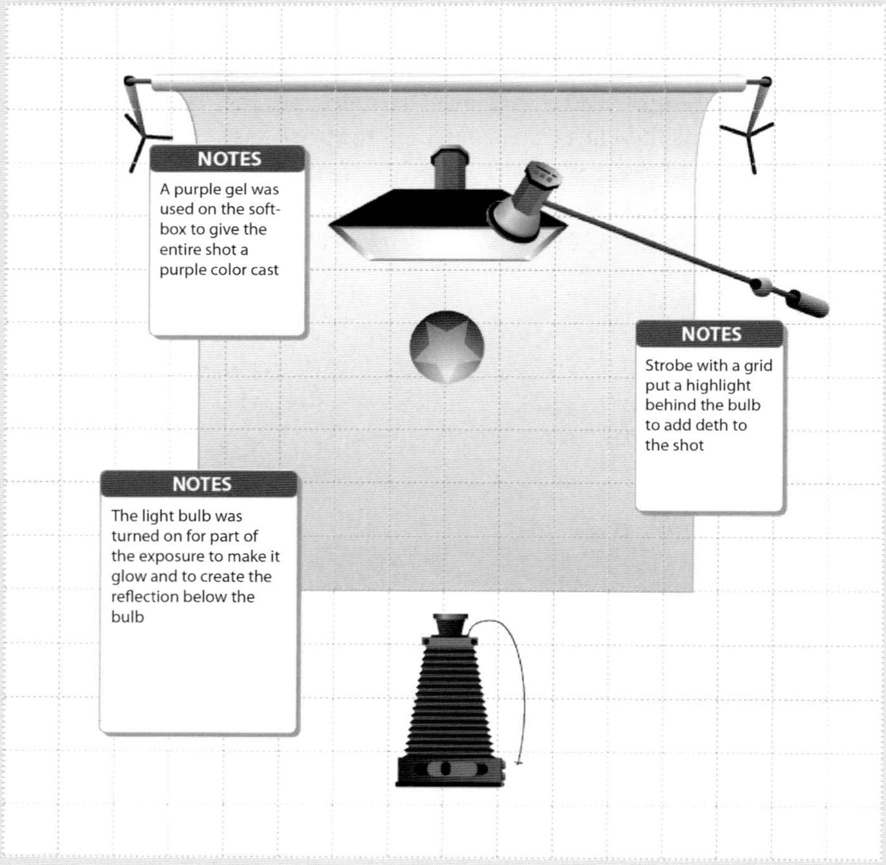

Light brings a subject to life. Many adjectives have been used to describe a subject where there is no quality of light; flat, dull, and dead are just a few. Why is lighting so important? Because subjects are generally three-dimensional, our mind interprets objects as three-dimensional, but photography is a two-dimensional medium. It is through lighting that an image gains life and the illusion of shape and form emerges.

Lighting Is a Building Process

A common error often witnessed when watching a group of photography students or inexperienced photographers is the desire to place a subject on a table and use available light—not the pre-existing light in the environment, but rather every available light the photographers have at their disposal. It is far easier to see the effects of a single light than the sum of many. For this reason, we always begin with a single light, work with it until we achieve the desired result, and then, and only then, move on to adding another light if necessary. Sometimes the single light is all that is needed; sometimes the process is repeated, and we add one light at a time to build on the previous light. Eventually, a developing photographer will inherently understand that certain combinations will not work, but a successful photographer will always experiment with new possibilities. That's how we grow as artists.

Lighting is a relatively simple process. When we look at the subject we're trying to light, it's important to think about exactly what we're trying to say about that subject. Are we trying to make it beautiful? Should it look disturbing? Is it supposed to look peaceful or dramatic? The way we choose to light that subject will go a long way toward determining if we're successful in making the proper statement.

Lighting needs to do only a few things; it needs to create dimension, separation, texture, and drama in our subjects. It's important to remember that lighting doesn't need to do all of these things in all of our shots. It's up to us to pick the right lighting to enhance specific attributes in each individual subject. The key words in that last sentence are *specific* and *individual,* and it's essential that you are constantly aware of the specific things you want your lighting to do for each and every subject.

This chapter will go into greater detail on the ways in which you can create dimension, separation, texture, and drama through your use of various lighting techniques. If you can learn to get your lighting to do these four things, you will be able to light anything. And if you master these four things and apply them in thoughtful ways in all your shots, you'll be well on your way to establishing yourself as a successful commercial photographer.

Dimension

The most basic effect of lighting is dimension. The world we live in has three dimensions, but photographs are two-dimensional, so we must learn how to compress three dimensions into two-dimensional space while still maintaining the illusion of three dimensions. One of the ways to do this is to light objects so that they do not look flat; instead, light them so that they look three-dimensional.

In order to explore this further, we need to grasp a couple of basic concepts and some vocabulary. The first thing to understand is the camera axis and where we place lights in relationship to this axis. The camera axis is a straight line drawn through the camera that runs an infinite distance both in front of and behind the camera (**FIGURE 1.1**).

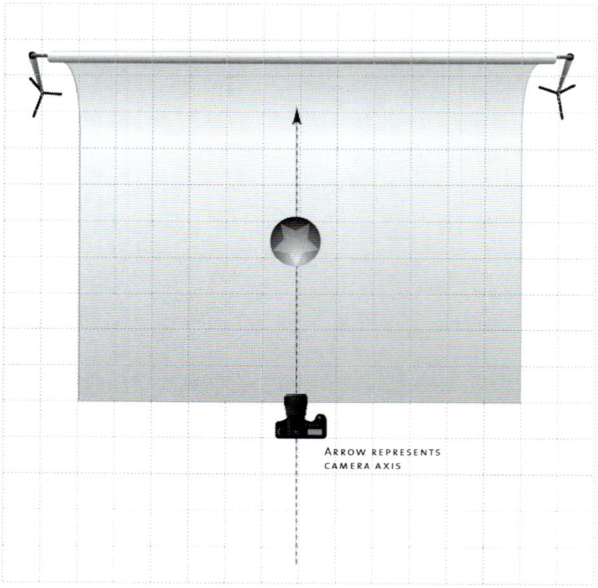

FIGURE 1.1 Camera axis

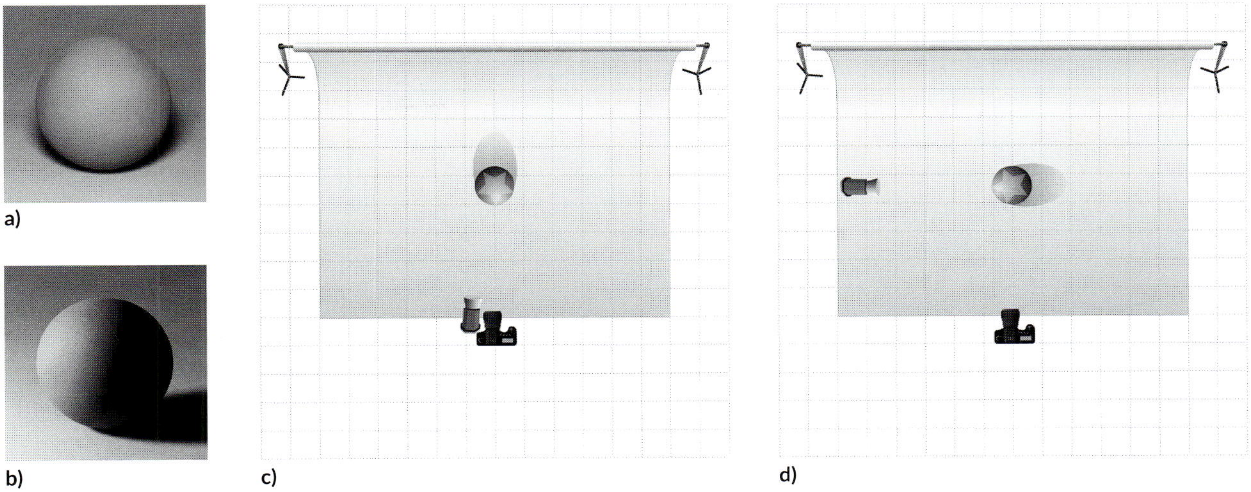

FIGURE 1.2 **a)** Light positioned along the camera axis; **b)** positioned 90 degrees from the camera axis; **c)** positioned along the camera axis; **d)** positioned 90 degrees from the camera axis.

Subjects will be on this line somewhere in front of the camera. We can then draw a perpendicular line to the camera axis through our subject. Bringing the lights closer to the camera axis will reduce the amount of subject dimension created by the lights. Moving the lights either above or below the camera axis or closer to the perpendicular line running through the subject will render more dimension in the subject (FIGURE 1.2).

The examples above clearly illustrate this idea. The shot with the light along the camera axis is not devoid of dimension; it is slightly brighter in the center and then gradates towards the edges, but it has nowhere near the amount of dimension seen in the second image, the one where the light has been moved off the camera axis.

note At times you might want to light images with flat light, times when lighting your subjects so that they appear two-dimensional will enhance your overall concept and what you are trying to say about your subjects. Once you understand the general rules of lighting, you can break them consciously as you experiment with your own solutions.

Point Source vs. Diffused Lighting

The next thing that needs to be understood is the difference between point source and diffused light. The previous photos were all taken using a single point source light. The simplest way to describe the difference between the two is to think of the sun and then compare its light to that of a cloudy day. The sun is a point source light. Clouds spread the sun's light over a large area,

When Two Dimensions Can Be Effective

Composing an image with strong vertical or horizontal lines that run parallel to the picture plane tends to make it feel more static. It appears more two-dimensional, and because of this it may feel more calm and tranquil. Images that have strong diagonal lines running through them appear more three-dimensional and in general are more dynamic in nature.

Joe: When would a two-dimensional look be suitable?

Brad: Lighting a subject or scene so that it appears two-dimensional tends to simplify the image. If you want to create an image that is more static, a flatter and less dimensional lighting scheme helps you achieve this. Reducing dimension also adds a graphic quality (FIGURE 1.3).

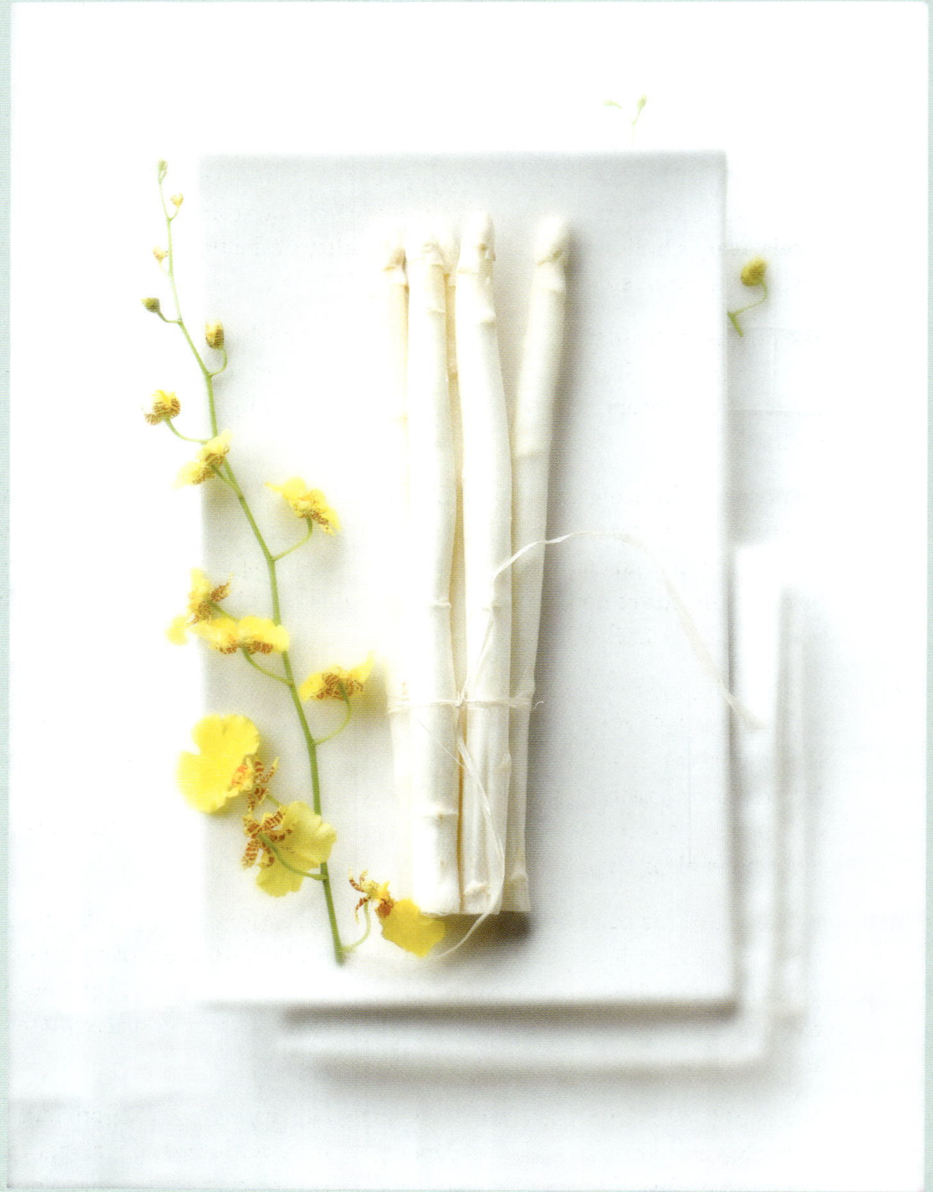

FIGURE 1.3 Asparagus lit to reduce dimensionality.

ISO 50, 1/60 sec., f/8.5, 100mm lens

creating diffused light. The quality of the light from these two sources is vastly different.

It's important to understand that the distance between the light and the subject is a factor in determining whether a light is a point source light or diffused light. The sun is a very large light source, but because of its distance from the earth it becomes relatively small and is therefore a point source light. Moving a diffused light source away from the subject makes it smaller in relation to the subject, and if it is moved far enough away from the subject, even a large diffused light can become a point source light. For instance, taking a large softbox and moving it across the studio from your subject makes it relatively smaller, and therefore the quality of the light will change from diffused to point source.

The photographs to the right were taken using both point source and diffused lighting, with the lights in the same position relative to the subject. Notice the differences between these two types of light sources (**FIGURES 1.4** and **1.5**).

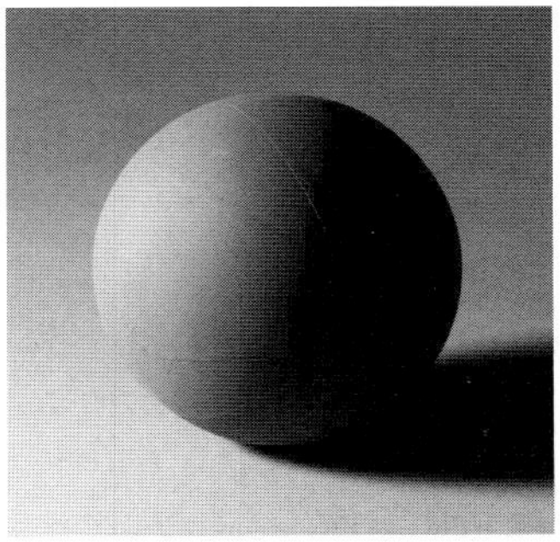

FIGURE 1.4 Point source lighting

Point source lighting creates intense specular highlights and strong, contrasty shadows. Specular highlights are small pinpoints of light that reflect off of reflective surfaces; think of the sun reflecting off of a bright chrome car bumper. There are no specular highlights on the ball shown above because it was painted with flat paint.

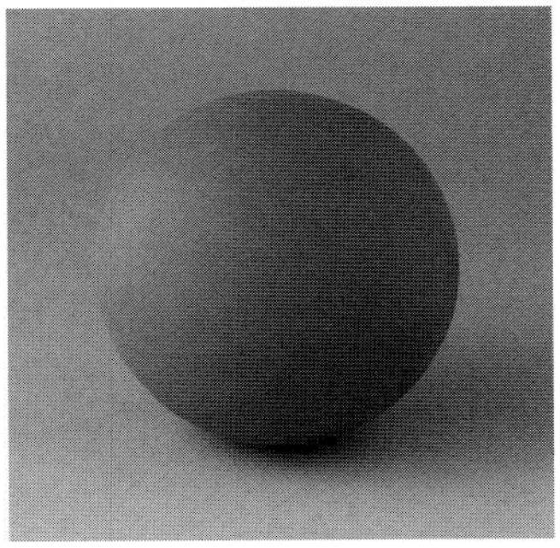

FIGURE 1.5 Diffused lighting

Diffused lighting spreads specular highlights out, creating softer, broader highlights. Diffused lighting also creates softer-edged shadows—both cast shadows as well as the shadows on the objects themselves. Specular lighting will have a faster transition between highlights and shadows, whereas diffused light will have more gradual transitions between the two. This is clearly visible in Figures 1.4 and 1.5.

In the studio we can create both point source and diffused light. Section 3 of this book will go into greater detail regarding various kinds of equipment you can use within the studio environment. But for now, we'll introduce you to some basic lighting equipment so that you can better understand the differences between point source and diffused light.

You could go to almost any hardware store and purchase a clip-on aluminum light that can serve as a point source light. You could also build a very simple device to diffuse the light. You can create the diffusion device, also known as a scrim, by buying PVC pipe cut to the desired lengths and PVC elbows, and then attaching these to one another to form a square or rectangle the size you want. You can then cover this frame with a semi-translucent material like a shower curtain or vellum paper. (We show examples of all of this in Chapter 3.) Make sure to keep the light far enough from the scrim that you don't risk lighting the material on fire. (I'm sure you're saying, "Duh, how stupid do you think we are?" Let's just say, "Better safe than sorry." After many years of teaching, although we have not seen actual flames, we have smelled a lot of smoke and molten plastic.)

The more of the scrim you cover with light and the closer the scrim is to your subject, the more diffused the light will become. The closer you bring the light to the scrim material, the further the scrim is from your subject, or both, the less diffused the light will be.

In order for a cube to look like a cube, you must light it so that you can discern three distinct planes, with each plane having a different tonal value. So how much different do the tonal values need to be? Sorry, there is no definitive answer to that. Sometimes you may want the values to be very similar and at other times you may want to have significant differences. *It all depends on your specific intent.*

Lighting Ratios

The differences in tonal values are often referred to as lighting ratios. If one plane is twice as bright as another plane, there is a 2:1 lighting ratio. Another way of looking at this is that one plane is receiving one stop more light than the other side; metering the two sides would show this difference. In **FIGURE 1.6**, the left side is one stop brighter than the top, which is one stop brighter than the right side. This means that the left side and top have a 2:1 ratio, the top and right side have a 2:1 ratio, and the two sides have a 3:1 ratio. Lighting this way gives each plane a distinct tone, and these three different values are what give the object its shape and dimension.

Moving the light higher would brighten the top plane. Adding a fill card to bounce light into the dark side would lighten that plane, thereby reducing the contrast between the planes. Removing the diffusion material and using a point source light increases the contrast and produces a 4:1 ratio between the two sides.

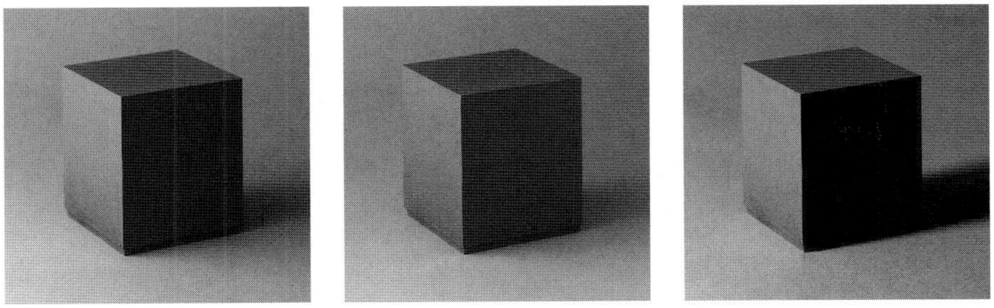

a) b) c)

FIGURE 1.6 **a)** A cube with diffused light, no fill; **b)** cube with diffused light and fill; **c)** cube with point source, no fill.

When we were first learning to shoot, photography lighting ratios were all the rage. We still hear photographers go on and on about how a particular portrait they took has a perfect 2:1 ratio, claiming that all portraits should have that ratio. But in reality, perfect for what? Back when everyone shot film and couldn't view images before taking the actual exposures, it was necessary to meter the shadows and highlights to achieve the desired results. Today, metering your highlights and shadows so that you understand the basic principles of shadows and highlights and how much range there can be before you start to lose detail in shadows and highlights is a good practice. However, with the advent of digital, it's far more important to analyze each image individually, not based on formulaic lighting ratios. Instead, you decide if your lighting achieves what you intended it to do. You can now look at the back of your camera or a computer monitor and see what your lighting looks like.

Reading Your LCD vs. Reality

A word of caution about judging your images by the LCD on the back of your camera—images often look very different once they are enlarged on a computer screen or printed. Sometimes the ambient lighting conditions under which you view the LCD can affect the way images appear. Bright sunlight can make viewing them difficult and can affect both perceived exposure and contrast. I can't tell you the number of times that I thought I had a winner by looking at the back of my DSLR, only to be disappointed when I viewed the image on a calibrated monitor. Images tend to look more contrasty on an LCD than they actually are. It's a learning process, and you will start to compensate for these differences as you light various subjects. A secret here is to learn to use your histogram, which we will address in a future chapter.

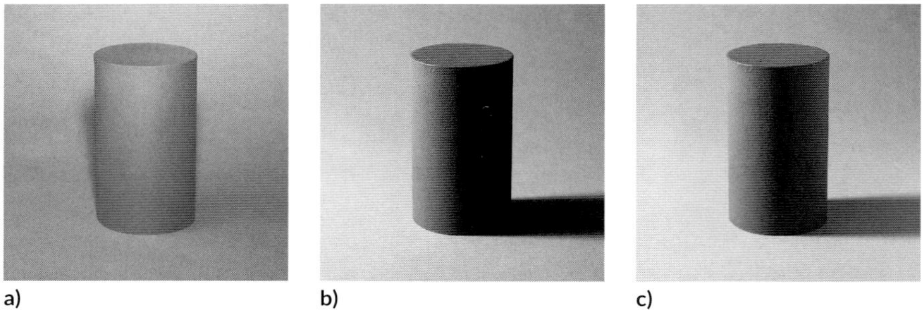

FIGURE 1.7 **a)** Cylinder with light from camera axis; **b)** cylinder with light from 90 degrees off camera axis; **c)** cylinder with light from 90 degrees off camera axis with fill card.

The final shape we will examine is the cylinder. It can be a combination of both a sphere and a cube. Like the sphere, a cylinder has a curved surface, and if you can see its top, it has a flat plane similar to a cube. In FIGURE 1.7, you will see a cylinder shot with the light on the camera axis, a light moved perpendicular to the camera axis, and that same light, but with a fill card, coming from the right side. In all three cases a point source light was used.

It may seem tedious, but spending a significant amount of time practicing lighting these three shapes will go a long way toward ensuring that you fully understand the way light plays off of the various surfaces and planes. Think of it as analogous to learning the scales when you first learn to play a musical instrument. Everyone wants to pick up a guitar and start playing like Eric Clapton or John Mayer, but you have to practice the basics first in order to refine your skills. If you can learn to light spheres, cubes, and cylinders as desired, you can light almost anything. Almost all subjects will be made up of balls, cubes, cylinders, or some combination of these shapes.

This photograph of a red apple (FIGURE 1.8), taken by professional photographer Howard Sokol, is an example of how refining a simple technique can lead to beautiful and dramatic results. This image was taken using a single diffused light source. In this case strobe light and a softbox were used, but you could achieve similar results using your tungsten clip-on light and a homemade diffuser.

The apple is a simple sphere, and moving the light source to the left and above the camera axis creates a highlight side and a shadow side. The highlights and shadows are what give the apple dimension. Notice how there is a brighter area within the overall highlight created by the actual light source reflected in the skin of the apple. This brighter highlight helps to

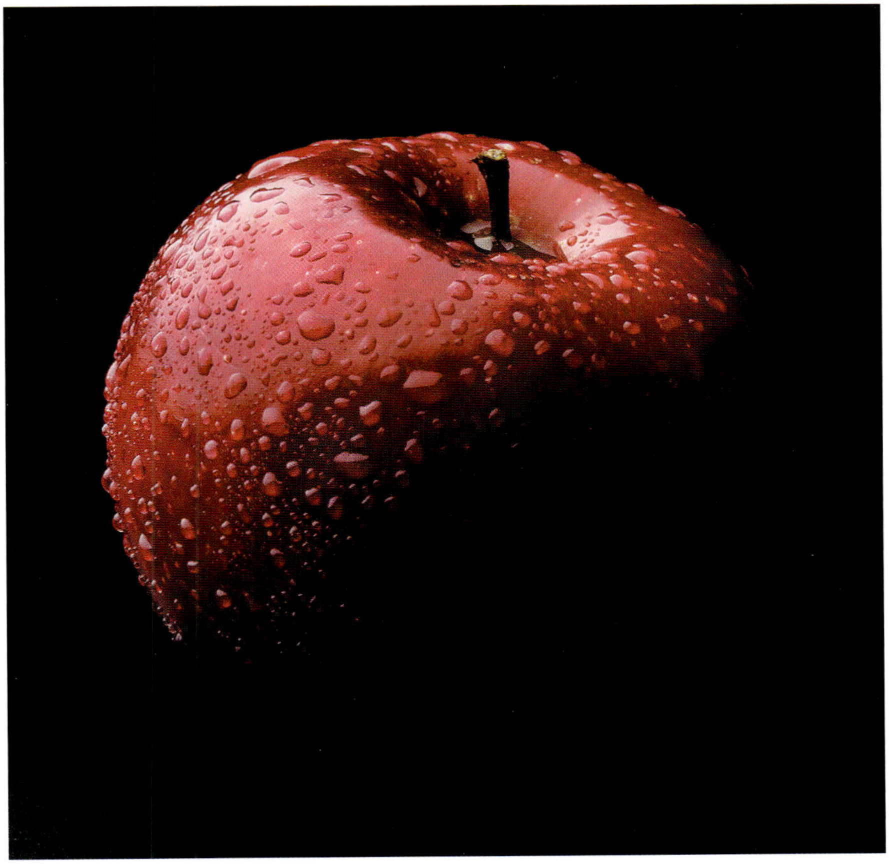

FIGURE 1.8 Apple photographed by Howard Sokol using single light to show dimension.

ISO 100, 1/125 sec., f/32, 210mm lens

further accentuate the sense of dimension. From the edge of this highlight, the light gradates from highlight to shadow until the light disappears into a completely black shadow. No fill light was used to separate the shadow side of the apple from the background. Separation will be discussed in a following section.

This shot of a baby (**FIGURE 1.9**) is another example of a sphere being lit with a single diffused light source. The same principles that applied to the apple are seen in this image. The light source was moved closer to the camera axis so that less shadow was produced and the gradation between highlight and shadow is more gradual and subtle. This works well to create both a sense of volume and softness in the baby's skin that is completely appropriate for

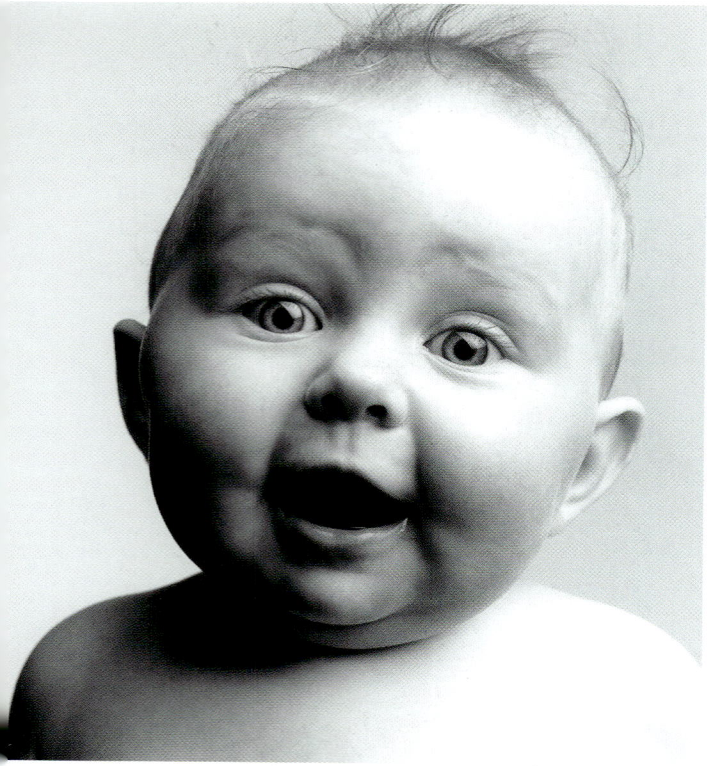

FIGURE 1.9 This image of a baby, also by Sokol, shows how diffused light can bring powerful dimension to a human subject.

ISO 100, 1/125 sec., f/22, 150mm lens

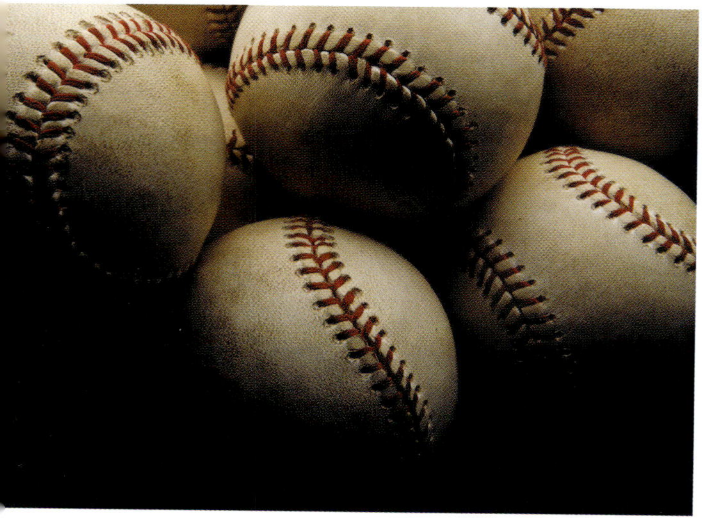

the subject. The word *appropriate* will appear many times in this book, as it refers directly to the idea that you should use the lighting that best meets your intention.

In this image (**FIGURE 1.10**), we see multiple spheres all lit with a single diffused light source and no fill.

FIGURE 1.11 uses a very dark shadow side on the box to emphasize the dimension of the box, which is simply a cube without a top.

The image seen in **FIGURE 1.12** is a great example of how a single diffused light source can be used to create dimension when lighting a cylindrical object. In this case, the wad of money goes from having a highlight side to a shadow side very quickly because of the way some of the bills stick out above the bills below them. You can see the soft gradation more in the rubber band. It's worth noting the subtle things Howard Sokol did in the shot to help create greater interest. The twist in the rubber band and the slight curl in the $100 bill are little touches that make a big difference in the shot.

In **FIGURES 1.13** and **1.14** we have two additional shots of rolled-up money, but the lighting and overall treatment of the subject matter are completely different.

Being able to light various subjects so that they appear to have volume, and therefore dimension, will be vitally important in creating three-dimensional worlds within the two-dimensional confines of the printed page or computer screen. By moving your lighting away from the camera axis,

FIGURE 1.10 Baseballs by Howard Sokol lit with a single diffused light source to create deep shadows that enhance dimension.

ISO 100, 1/125 sec., f/22, 210mm lens

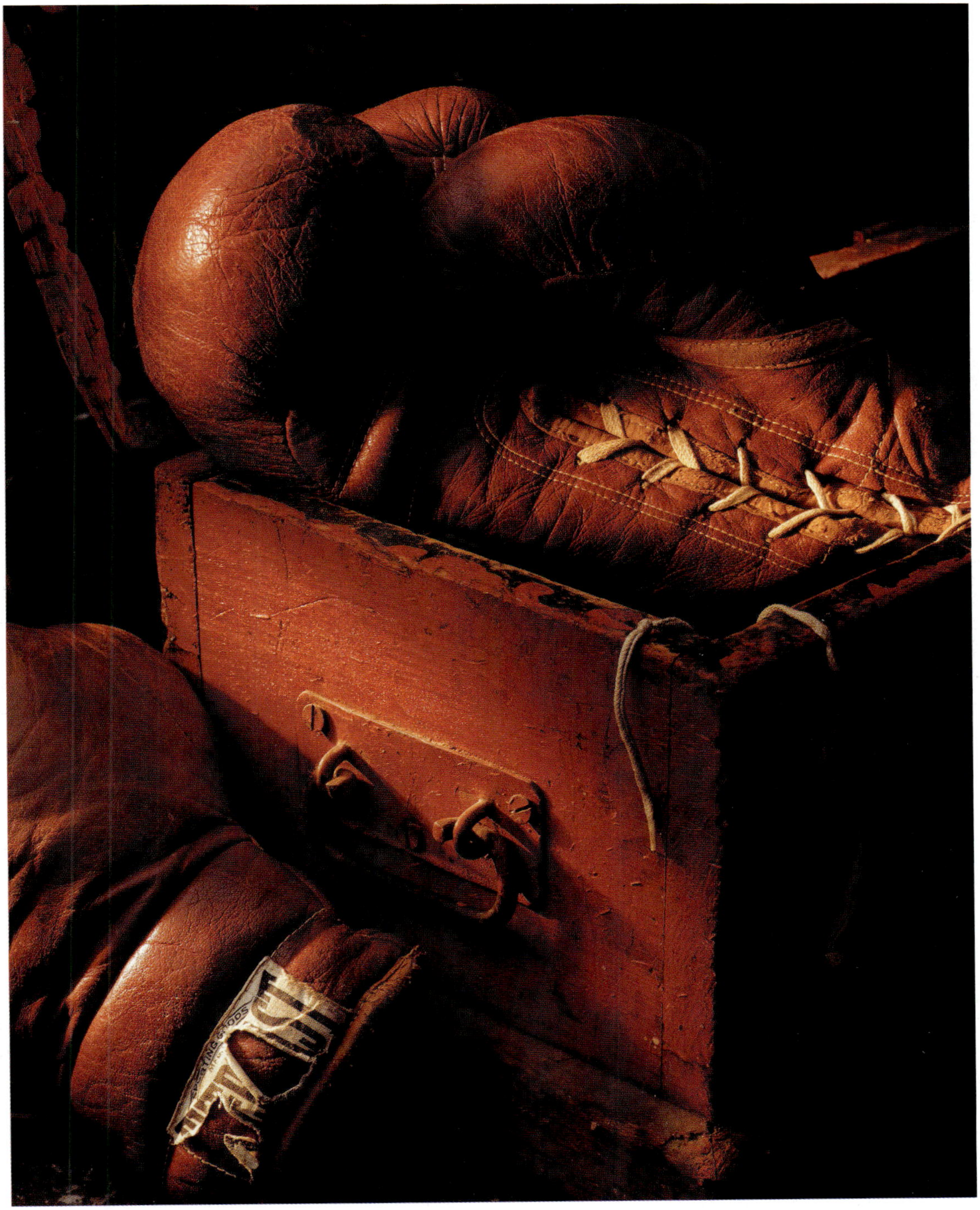

FIGURE 1.11 A cube photographed with a point source light.

ISO 100, 30 sec., f/22 1/3, 210mm lens

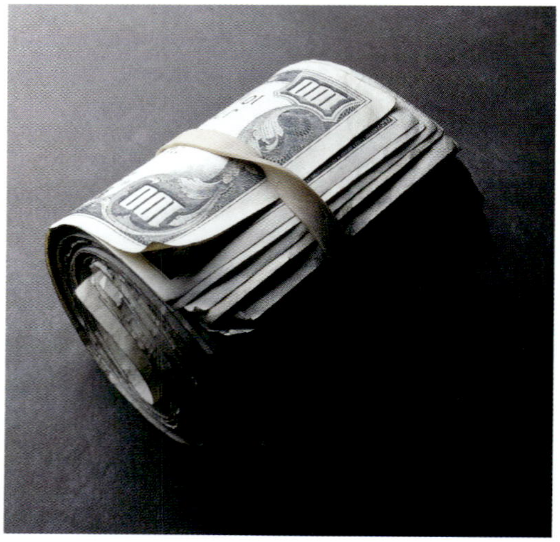

FIGURE 1.12 A cylinder shot with diffused light by Howard Sokol.

ISO 100, 1/125 sec., f/32, 90mm lens

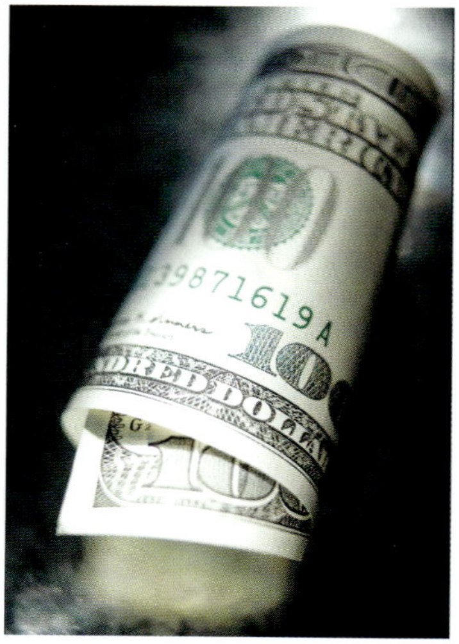

FIGURE 1.13 Example of a cylindrical money shot with a single point source light.

ISO 100, 1/125 sec., f/5.6, 90mm lens

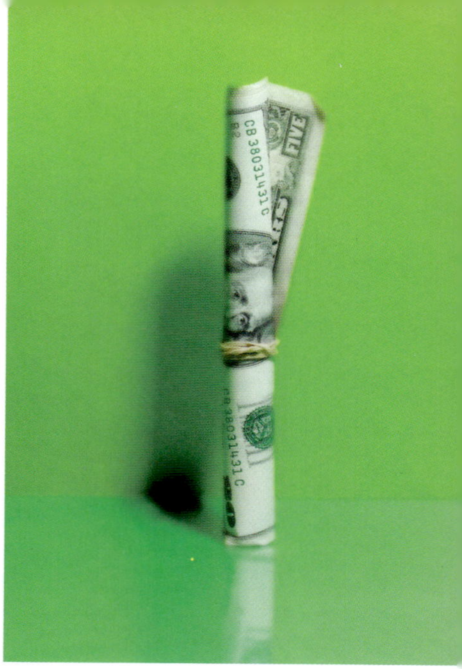

FIGURE 1.14 Another cylindrical money shot with a single light source.

ISO 50, 1/60 sec., f/22, 150mm lens

you can create highlights and shadows that will produce this dimensionality. Fully understanding these principles will come only with practice and experimentation. Once you can consistently light different forms and subjects with the type of dimension you desire, you will be ready to light objects to enhance texture so that they have separation from each other and separation from the backgrounds on which they are placed.

Texture

Have you ever looked at an image and just known what the subject felt like? If so, the lighting revealed the subject's texture. It's unfortunate that we cannot touch an image and feel the subject's texture, because touch is one of our most important senses; it allows us to know whether something is smooth, rough, sharp, dull, or even slimy. As photographers, we must always consider what we are photographing and imagine how the audience will react to an image. Since touch is not an option, we must help the audience see the texture. It's not enough to know that broken glass is sharp; the viewer must feel it with his or her eyes. Given that, it's easy to understand how knowing one's subject is important: Imagine trying to verbally explain the texture of a cantaloupe to someone without ever having held one. Odds are you would get it wrong. Knowing how the texture feels allows the photographer to devise a lighting plan to convey that in pictures (**FIGURE 1.15**).

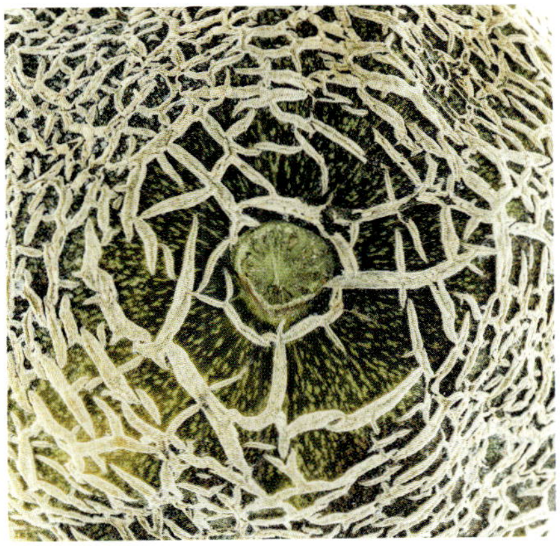

FIGURE 1.15 Macro image of a canteloupe, showing texture.

ISO 50, 1/60 sec., f/5.6, 100mm lens

Creating Texture

The question is, how do we see texture? We can't actually see it, but we can see its effects, which can be enhanced with lighting. Whether your subject is a piece of notepaper or brick wall, it has peaks and valleys, high points and low points. As light moves across the subject, it creates highlights on the peaks and shadows in the valleys. It is this combination that reveals texture. A bright highlight and a short, dark shadow will reveal a texture with sharp edges, but not much depth between the high and low point; however, if a similar image has a bright highlight and a long shadow, then it's easy to imagine the distance between the peak and valley is greater. Hence, the length of the shadow helps define the inherent texture (FIGURE 1.16).

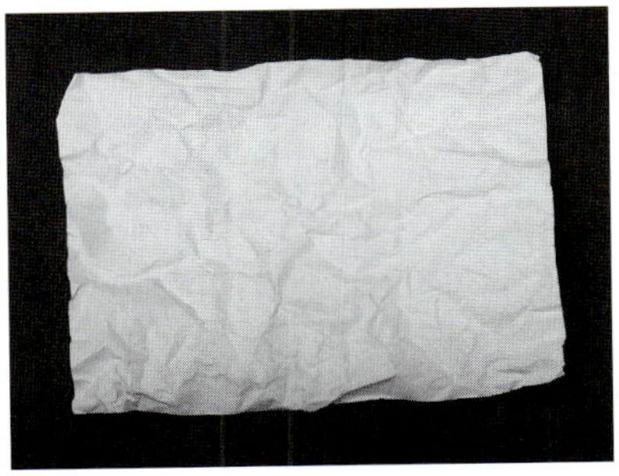

a)

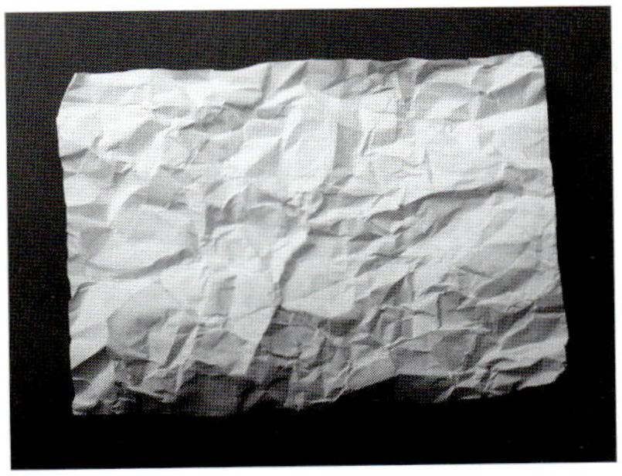

b)

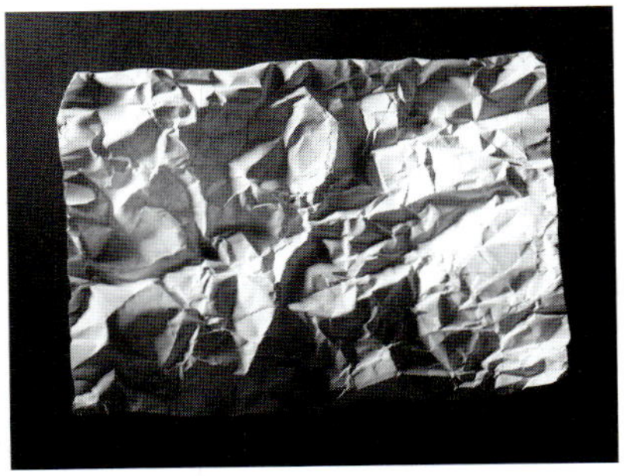

c)

FIGURE 1.16 **a)** Crumpled paper shot with a diffused light source placed directly above the subject (camera axis); **b)** shot with diffused light source brought lower and to the side of the subject (off camera axis); **c)** shot with point source light brought lower and to the side of the subject (off camera axis).

It's almost hard to believe that these three images show the exact same piece of notepaper. Two variables have not changed, the camera and the subject, which leaves us only with the lighting. The first two images used the same light source; however, the third used a different source. For Figure 1.16a, a large soft light (softbox) was placed on a similar axis to the camera and directed toward the paper. That doesn't allow many wrinkles to show, because there isn't much in the way of highlights and shadows. Figure 1.16b uses the same softbox, but now moved lower toward the set and angled to allow the light to rake across the paper. Here, we begin to see highlights and shadows form. In the third image, the softbox was replaced with a smaller, harder source (reflector with grid), in roughly the same location as with the second image. The texture really stands out as the light creates bright highlights and deep shadows.

There are three main components when revealing or suppressing texture: the camera, the subject, and the lighting. To be precise, it is the relationship between how the light falls on the subject when viewed from the angle of the camera. We already know that the highlights and shadows create the sense of texture, but that doesn't really matter unless the camera can see both the highlight and shadow side (**FIGURE 1.17**).

FIGURE 1.17 **a)** Here the texture is concealed, and here **b)** it's revealed.

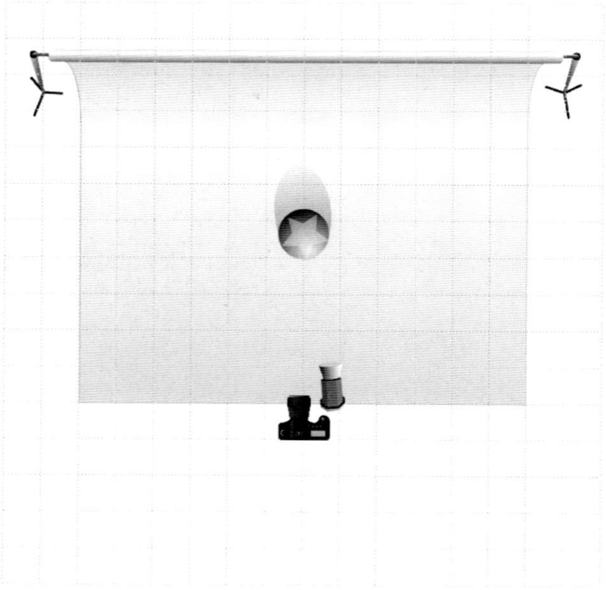

a)

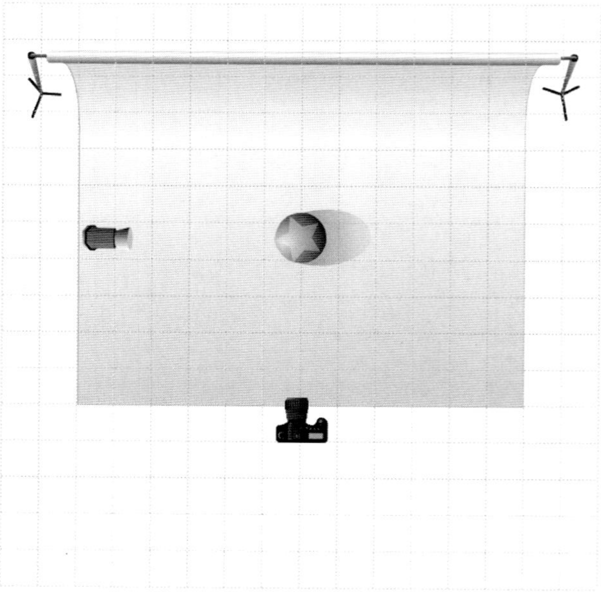

b)

Insight

Brad: Was this a job or personal shot?

Joe: I had done a fair amount of work for a small advertising agency in Colorado, and one day they called me asking whether I had ever photographed an airplane. Photographers hate to admit we can't handle a project, but I didn't have anything in my portfolio that would pass as an airplane. It was somewhat of a joke when I mentioned that I was a master with paper airplanes; in reality I meant that I could fly them, not photograph them. After the agency and the client batted the idea around, they decided I should actually photograph paper airplanes (FIGURE 1.18). I know that opting not to use real airplanes was a budgetary issue, but I like to think they went with paper airplanes because of my photographic skills.

The image needed to be more than just a white paper airplane on gray paper; I wanted the plane and the background to show the smooth texture of the paper while highlighting the texture of the surface. The lighting was very simple. I used a single light that was aimed to skim across the surface. I'm pleased to say that my concept flew; the client was happy.

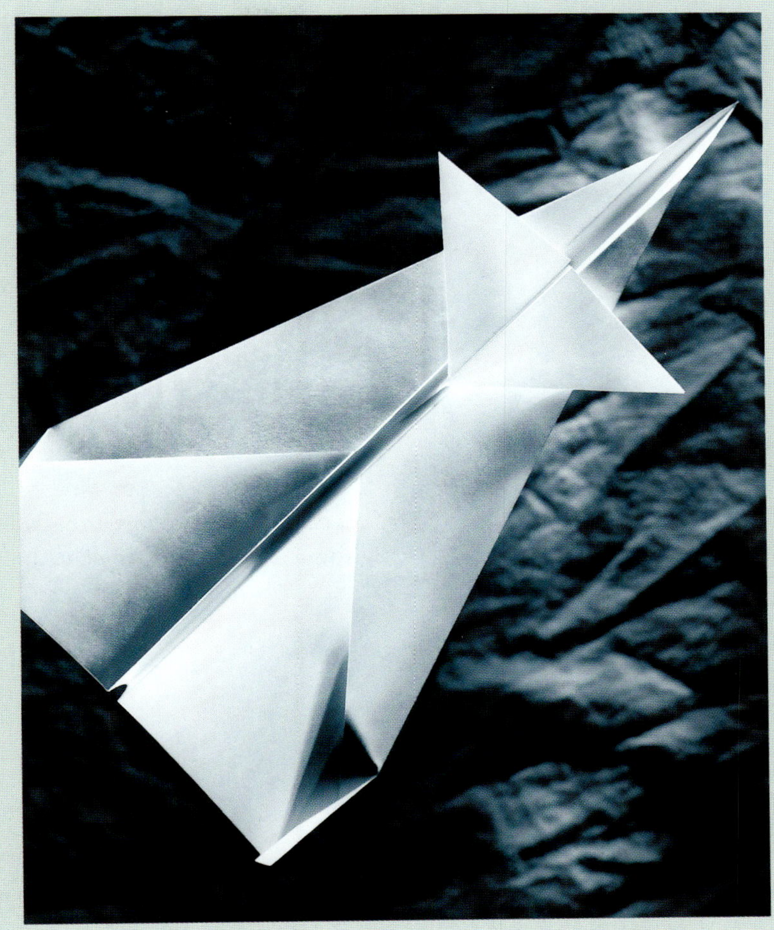

FIGURE 1.18 The paper airplane was shot with a single point source light.

ISO 100, 1/125 sec., f/4.5, 150mm lens

tip It's important to always judge your lighting from the same axis as the camera. Viewing the subject from a higher or lower vantage point, or even a slight movement side to side, doesn't allow you to see what the camera will capture. This is why photographers tend to place their head in front of the camera when setting up lighting. It might look funny, but it's necessary.

In Figure 1.18b, the light is raking across the subject, creating unique highlight and shadow sides visible from the camera. Having the light at a 90-degree axis from the camera is rather severe and may or may not fit the subject. At this angle, the shadow is long, which tells us that much texture will be revealed. Moving the light toward the camera doesn't change the length of the shadow but does change how much of it is visible to the camera, and thus how much texture is shown.

There is nothing technically wrong with the first baseball image (FIGURE 1.19A); it's exposed well and in focus. Unfortunately, the lighting doesn't help tell the story of what the baseball has endured. The lighting on the second image is also in focus and properly exposed, but now we see the informative scrapes, scars, and tears of years of use. The same light is used for both images, but for the first, the light is on the axis of the camera, and the shadow falls behind the ball, outside the view of the camera. Moving the light to the left side of the ball creates a visible shadow, revealing the texture. Some may argue that the shadow is a little dark, so the third image is identical to the second, except that a white card has been placed on the right side, kicking a little light back into the image and reducing the shadow and texture. This is simply a matter of preference. Both authors prefer the darker shadow.

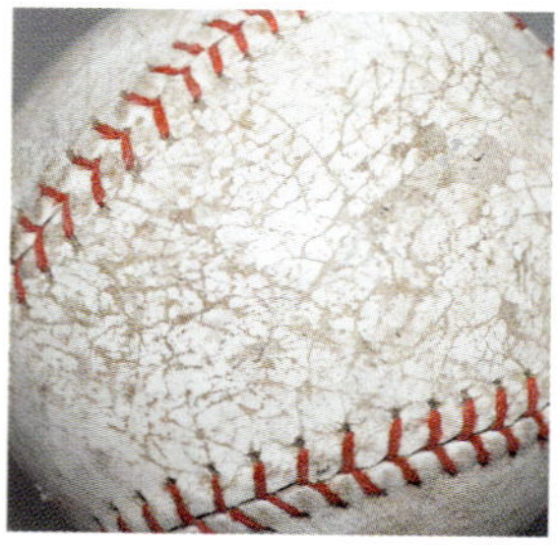

a)

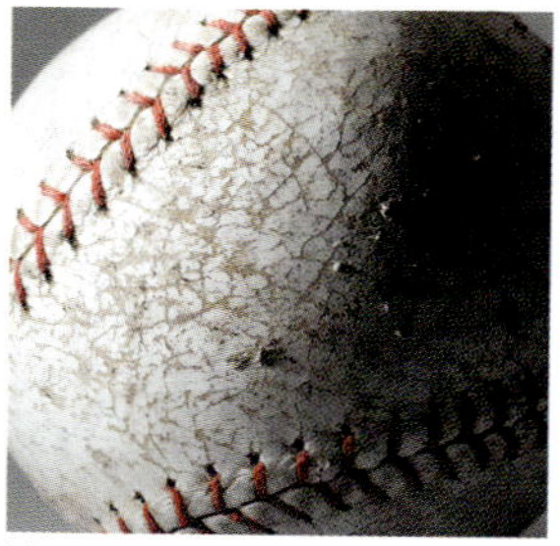

b)

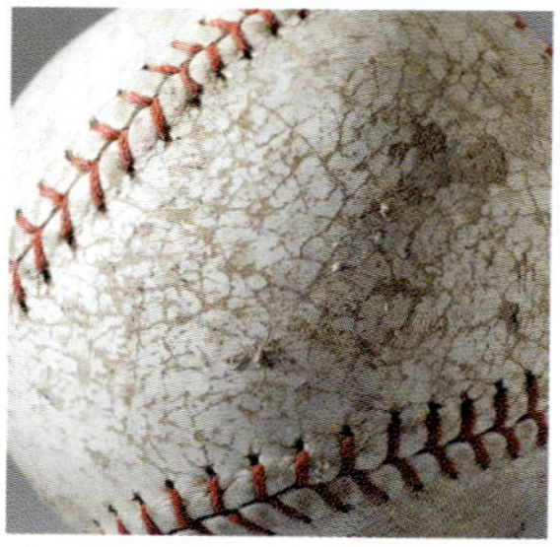

c)

FIGURE 1.19 **a)** A baseball shot with point source light from the camera axis; **b)** shot with point source light 90 degrees from the camera axis; **c)** shot with point source light 90 degrees from the camera axis with a fill card.

Remember, the authors aren't fans of following rules rigidly, which means that you'll encounter situations when your goal is not to enhance but rather to minimize texture. Fortunately, the same principles apply, just in reverse. If light raking across a subject creates visible highlights and shadows, and thus texture, then light falling on the subject from the same axis of the camera will hide the shadow and minimize the texture (FIGURE 1.20).

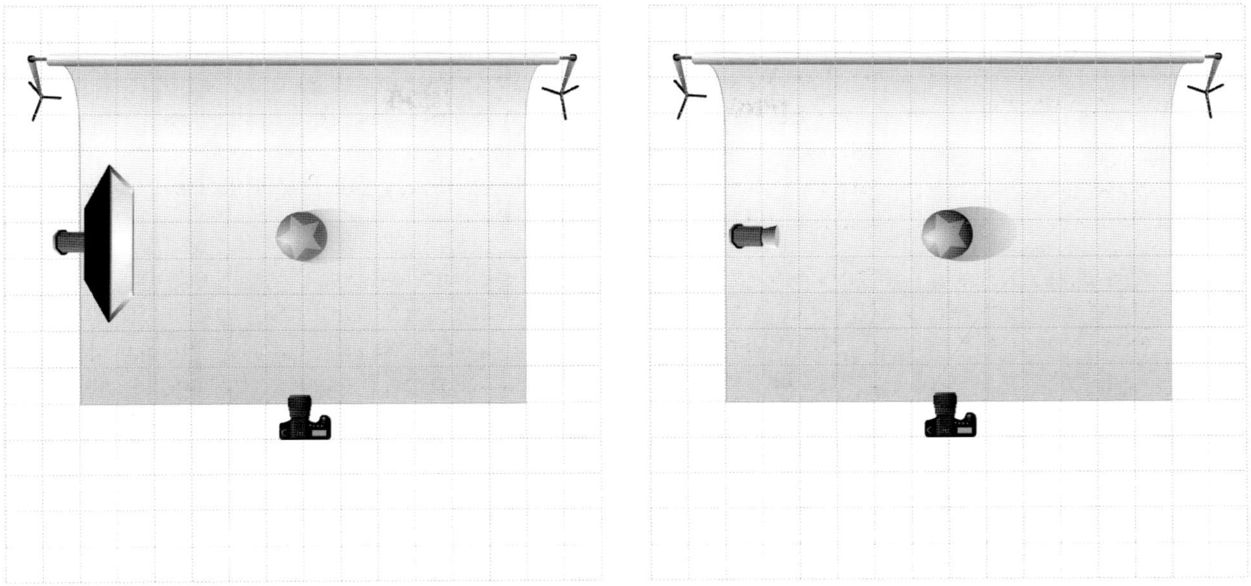

a) b)

FIGURE 1.20 **a)** Soft texture created with diffused light, and **b)** hard texture created with point source light.

Controlling Texture

Subjects vary, and so must a photographer's ability to control texture. Not only does the direction of light matter, but also the quality of light. In the soft texture example, the hard light has been swapped for a softer source, which produces a softer shadow. Although the position of the light has not changed, the revealed texture has been minimized. There is always a balance between dimension and texture when you're photographing people; luckily, the quality of light can be changed while still maintaining dimension.

Food for thought: When photographing your grandmother, which would she rather have you use, a soft or hard light source? Remember, you want to stay in her good graces.

One of the great things about studio photography is the photographer's ability to control light. Whereas shooting with natural light requires the photographer to wait for just the right moment, the studio photographer can envision the desired result, and then devise a lighting plan to match.

Experience will narrow down some options, but the process doesn't change. Here are some steps to keep in mind:

- Really look at your subject and consider what importance texture has for that particular subject.
- How much texture should be shown? Should it be enhanced or minimized?
- Experiment with different options. Begin with a single light source and slowly move it around the subject to see how the texture changes. Don't forget to keep your eyes on the same axis as the camera.
- Experiment some more: Once you like the direction of light and shadow, try a different source, maybe a harder or softer option.

The last two steps are what will help you understand the effect that lighting has on your subject. That, in turn, will help the viewer need only his eyes, not his fingers, to know what the subject feels like.

Separation

It's common in photography for a scene to have a foreground, middle ground, and background, and somewhere in there is the subject. All components are important, but one element must stand out: the subject, or in studio lingo, the hero. *Hero* is a great term because it places the connotation of importance on the one thing (or person) the audience should see first. In theatrical plays it's common to see one actor in the spotlight, while a supporting cast is in the background. Here, placement is important, but so is the lighting. Spotlighting the main actor while the supporting cast is washed with a softer quality of light creates separation. Photography requires the same consideration; lighting techniques need to separate the subject from the foreground, middle ground, and background. In the simplest terms, lighting and separation can be employed to make the subject "pop" in the image and act as the hero. This requires that we control the light on the subject and the other elements in the frame separately.

Separation is often subtle. In the flower image, the subject, aka the flower (**FIGURE 1.21**), is lit in a way that allows the texture of the dried petals and stem to appear coarse; you can visually feel the ridges. The background, however, has a much softer feel, and that's what allows the flower to stand out.

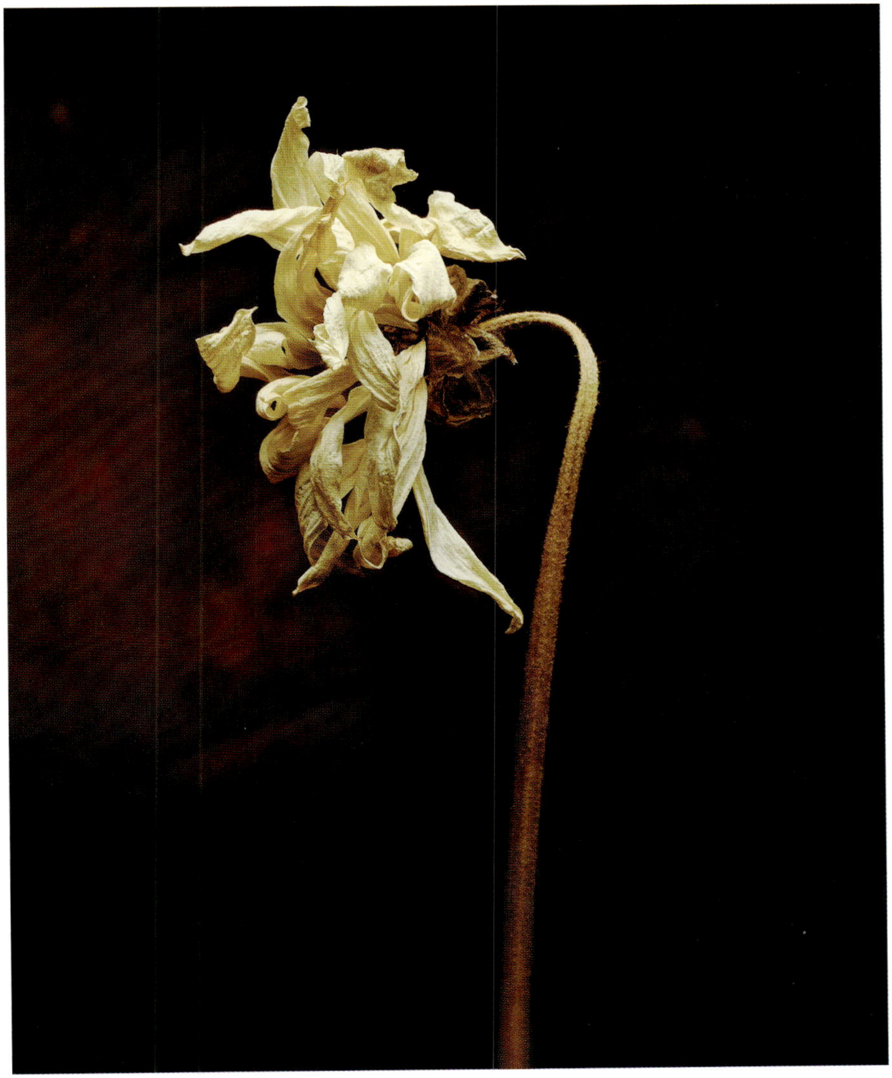

FIGURE 1.21 The dried flower is separated from the background.

ISO 100, 1/125 sec., f/8, 150mm lens

Two lights were used in this image, one for the flower and another for the background. It's important to control each light and not allow one to affect the other.

The next step to make the hero stand out in the scene is separation (**FIGURE 1.22**).

The images in Figure 1.22 take what was discussed in previous sections about how to use one light and add a second light to aid in separating the objects from the background. We would call the first image "flat;" no contrast, little

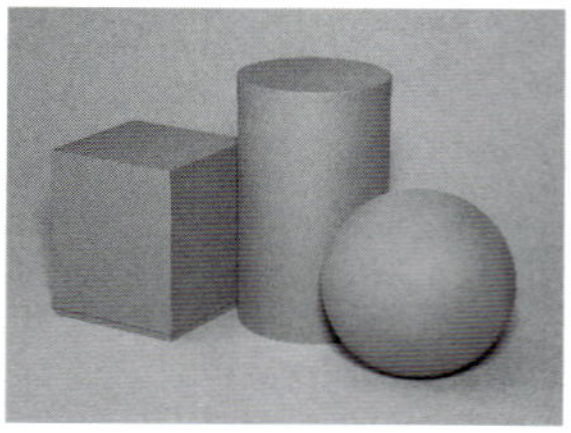

a)

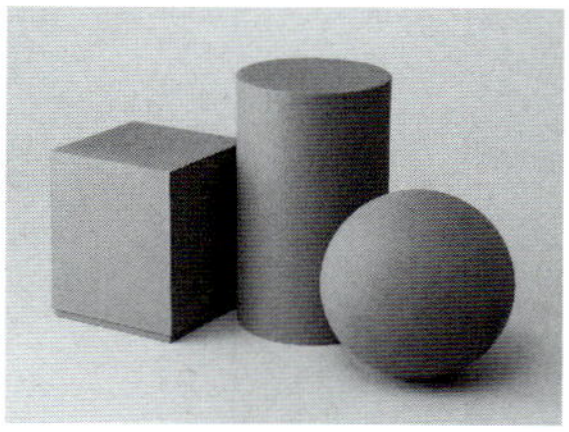

b)

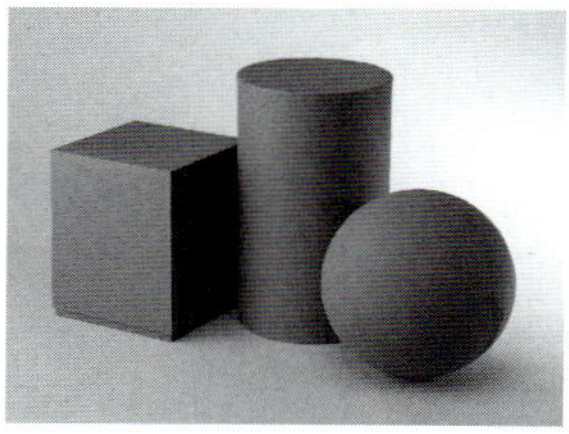

c)

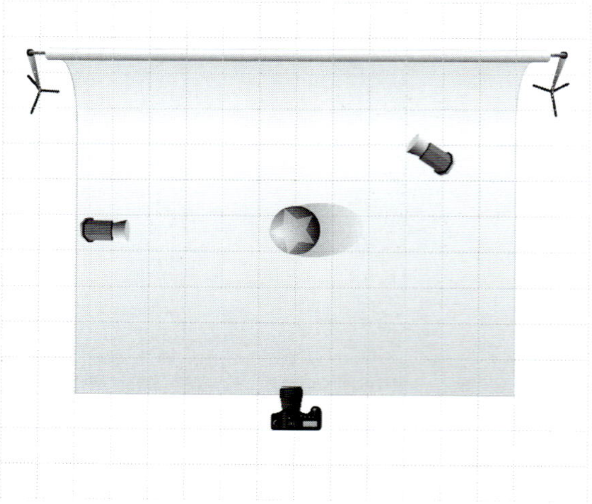

d)

FIGURE 1.22 **a)** A cube, cylinder, and ball photographed with light on the camera axis; **b)** cube, cylinder, and ball photographed with light off axis; **c)** background light added to increase separation; **d)** diagram showing background light added to increase separation.

tip The ball cube and cylinder used in Figure 1.22a, measuring 4 to 5 inches across, were purchased at a local hobby store for about $15 total. They were then painted with a flat gray spray paint. Make sure the objects are not much smaller than this, as that would make lighting them more difficult. Use sturdy, opaque objects and flat paint so that they're not too reflective. Wood or cardboard objects work well; foam objects aren't suitable, as the paint often reacts poorly with the foam.

dimension, little texture, and little separation. It is lit with a single light that is on axis with the camera. By moving the light out to the side, the second image shows dimension and separation between each object; however, the subject still blends into the background. The use of an additional light for the background creates the desired separation (Figure 1.22d). The image of the flower and the final cube-cylinder-ball photograph employ similar lighting techniques.

Throughout this book we suggest experimenting, and say that lighting is a process, and creating separation is no different. There are some basics to consider to get started. It sounds obvious, but the key is to create lighting that makes the subject stand out from its surroundings. The best place to begin is with the hero; light for dimension, drama and texture, and then consider how the surroundings should be addressed.

The following will provide a few common scenarios (FIGURE 1.23). These ideas can be used alone or in conjunction; if one alone creates a little separation, then maybe two will create even more. Either way, remember this is just a starting point for your own experiments.

Light on Dark

Light on dark is probably the most common method for creating separation between the hero and the background. The idea is to use contrast to create

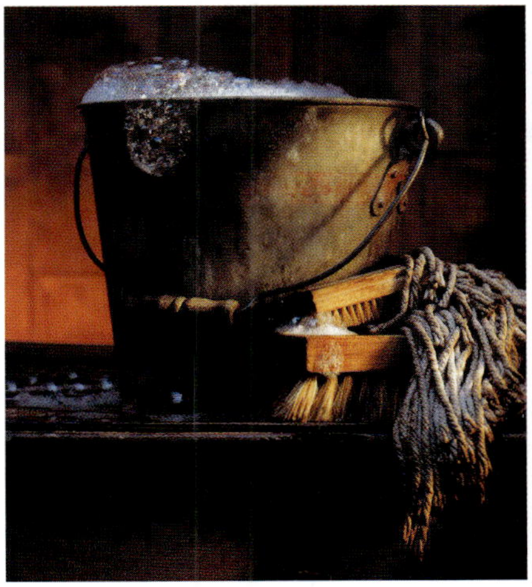

a)

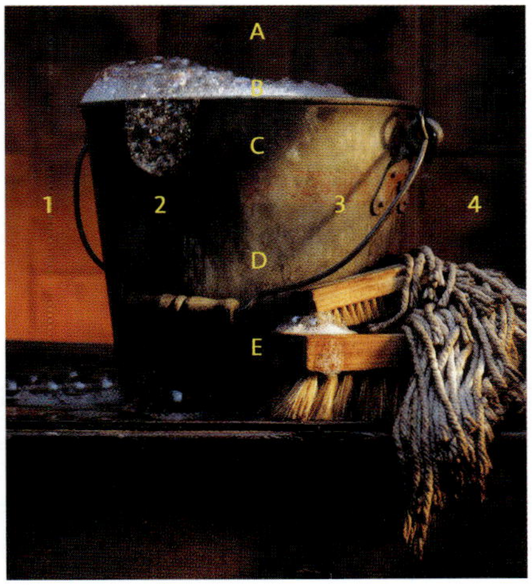

b)

FIGURE 1.23 **a)** Light on dark; **b)** light on dark schematic.

ISO 100, 30 sec., f/11, 150mm lens

the separation as the viewer "reads" across an image. It's common for people to read left to right and top to bottom. Adding numbers to the second soapy bucket image helps define this point.

1 = light, 2 = dark, 3 = light, 4 = dark

A = dark, B = light, C = dark, D = light, E = dark

What's great about this image is that the photographer went beyond simply creating a single element of contrast between the background and subject, instead creating multiple points of contrast. Sections 1 and 3 are both light and 2 and 4 are dark. This allows the dark portion of the bucket to separate from the light area of the background and the light portion of the bucket to separate from the dark area of the background. The bucket has dimension, texture, and pops out from the background. Pretty cool.

Warm vs. Cool

A similar technique is the warm versus cool method. Here, warm tones, such as yellow, contrast with cool tones, such as blue (FIGURE 1.24). Combining both methods will produce even greater results.

It's exciting to see images where texture, dimension, separation, and drama are all employed; these tend to be the images we remember.

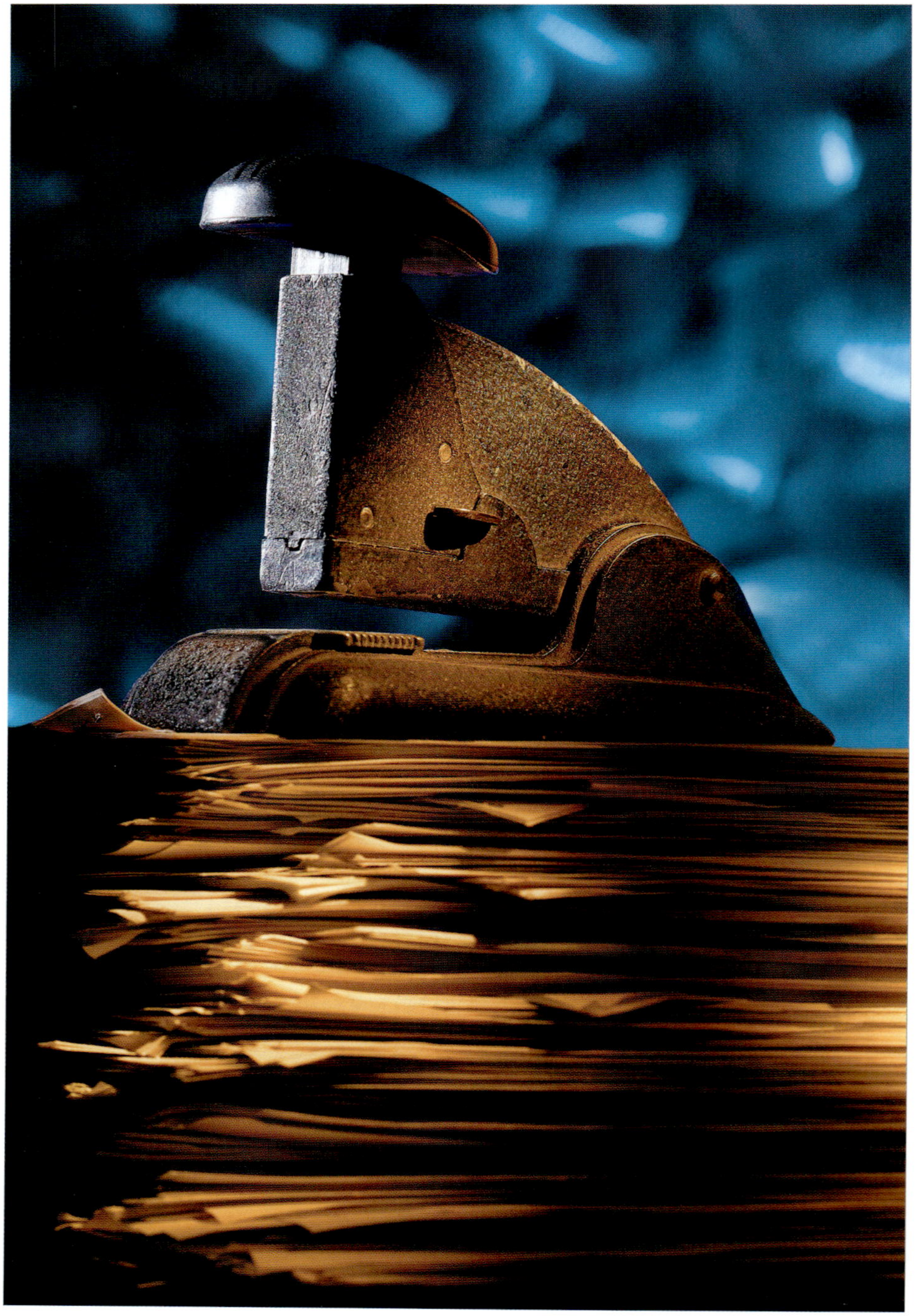

FIGURE 1.24 Here, separation is created using color.

ISO 100, 1/125 sec., f/11, 210mm lens

Backlighting/Rim Lighting

Having contrasting colors or tones is not always an option. What do you do when the tones or colors of the subject and background are similar? This is where rim lighting, often called backlighting, works well. Rim lighting involves a light shone on the backside of the subject, creating a white outline, or rim light. In the portrait of the three brothers (**FIGURE 1.25**), all are wearing dark suits and appear against a dark background. To complicate the issue, one brother has black hair. As you can see, there is a slight white halo outlining the subjects, separating them from the black background. This effect was achieved by using two lights located near the background and placed on each side of the set; the lights were then aimed to the backside of the subjects.

Controlling separation brings your photography to an entirely new level. It's wonderful to be able to light a single subject to have dimension and texture, but separation can really make the subject pop from its surroundings.

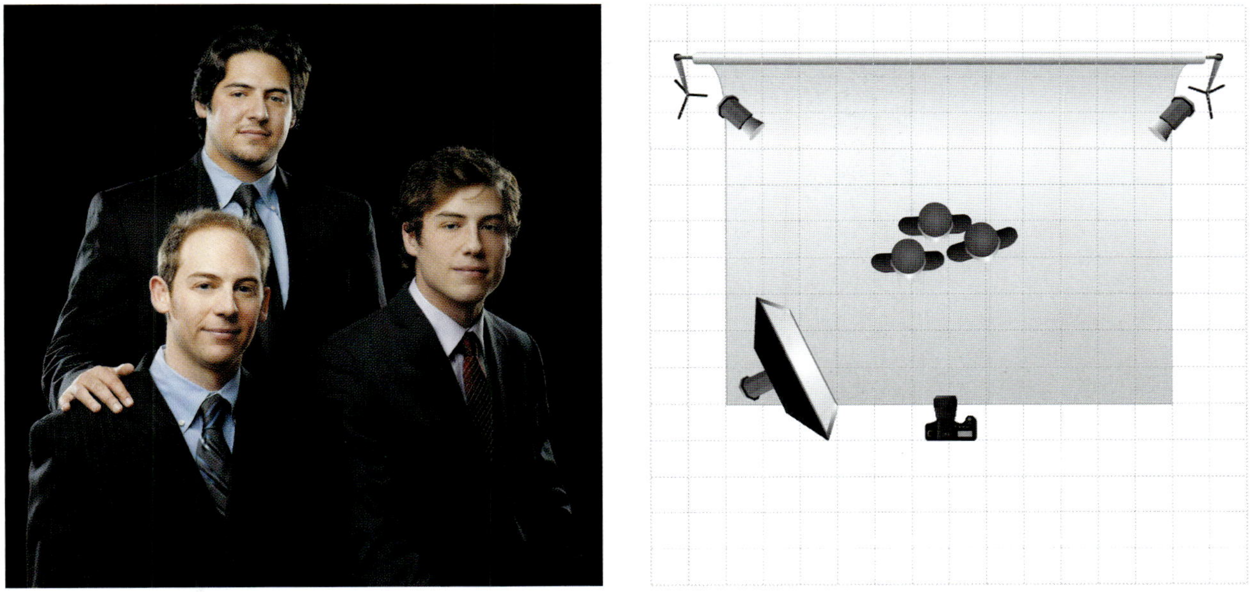

a) b)

FIGURE 1.25 **a)** A family portrait using rim lighting; **b)** diagram of rim lighting.

ISO 50, 1/125 sec., f/16, 150mm lens

Drama

Lighting to create dimension, separation, and texture is relatively straightforward. Lighting to achieve drama within a photograph is a more complicated idea. What is meant by drama? Perhaps the easiest way to describe it is that dramatic lighting provides the "wow" factor. This is true of all lighting: natural light, natural combined with supplemental lighting, and studio lighting. Think of the times you have been captivated by natural light, whether it was a sunrise or sunset, light streaks breaking through clouds, or a simple leaf with the sun behind it defining every vein. The light made you stop, observe, and gaze in wonder. It reached you on an emotional level. Great photographers understand how to tap into the emotional power of light.

The goal of all photographers is to reach viewers on an emotional level. You want your images to move people. It doesn't matter what kind of photography you are creating; whether it is powerful documentary work, beautiful consumer or editorial portraiture, or compelling advertising images, your ultimate goal is to make the viewer feel something. Lighting is one of the most powerful and effective tools you have at your disposal to do this. When we discuss dramatic lighting we are talking about this emotional content, and therefore dramatic lighting and emotional lighting are interchangeable.

It is easy to see dark, moody lighting as dramatic (FIGURE 1.26).

It is important to remember that bright high-key scenes can be dramatic, as can shots with soft, even lighting. Examine the following images and decide if you think they use dramatic lighting to reach you on an emotional level (FIGURE 1.27).

The shot of the tie and grass does not employ lighting that adds much emotional content to the image. The lighting is clean and crisp, making it easy to read all the detail in the image. It's important to understand what the photographer's intent was when creating the image in order to decide whether or not it was successful. The shot of the tie was produced for an environmentally friendly dry-cleaning company. It was part of a campaign that used the grass as a metaphor for a safe environment and then employed a wide variety of clothing and accessories to illustrate the broad scope of items the company was able to clean.

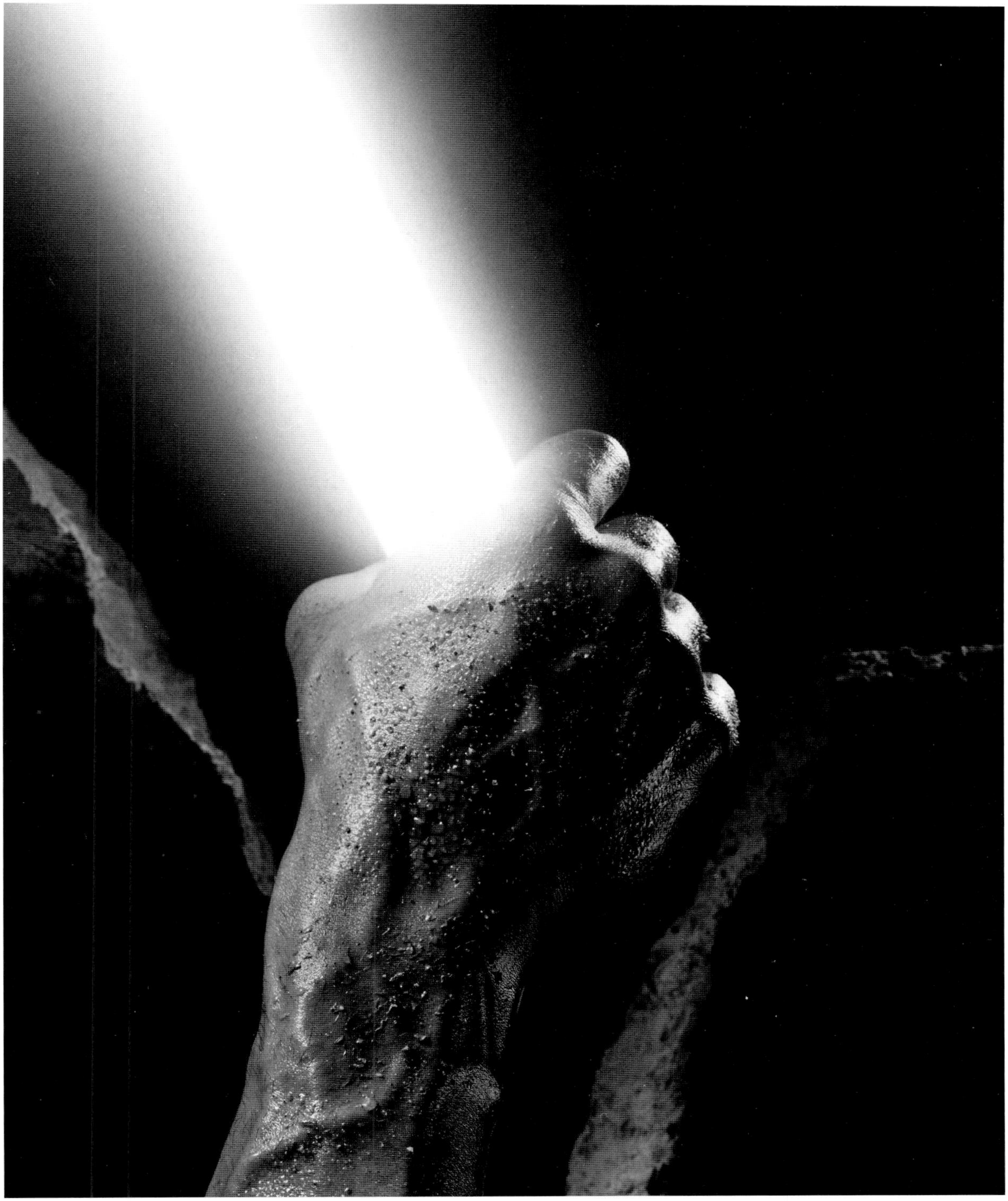

FIGURE 1.26 Dramatic lighting makes this hand much more than a hand.

ISO 100, 1 sec., f/8, 210mm lens

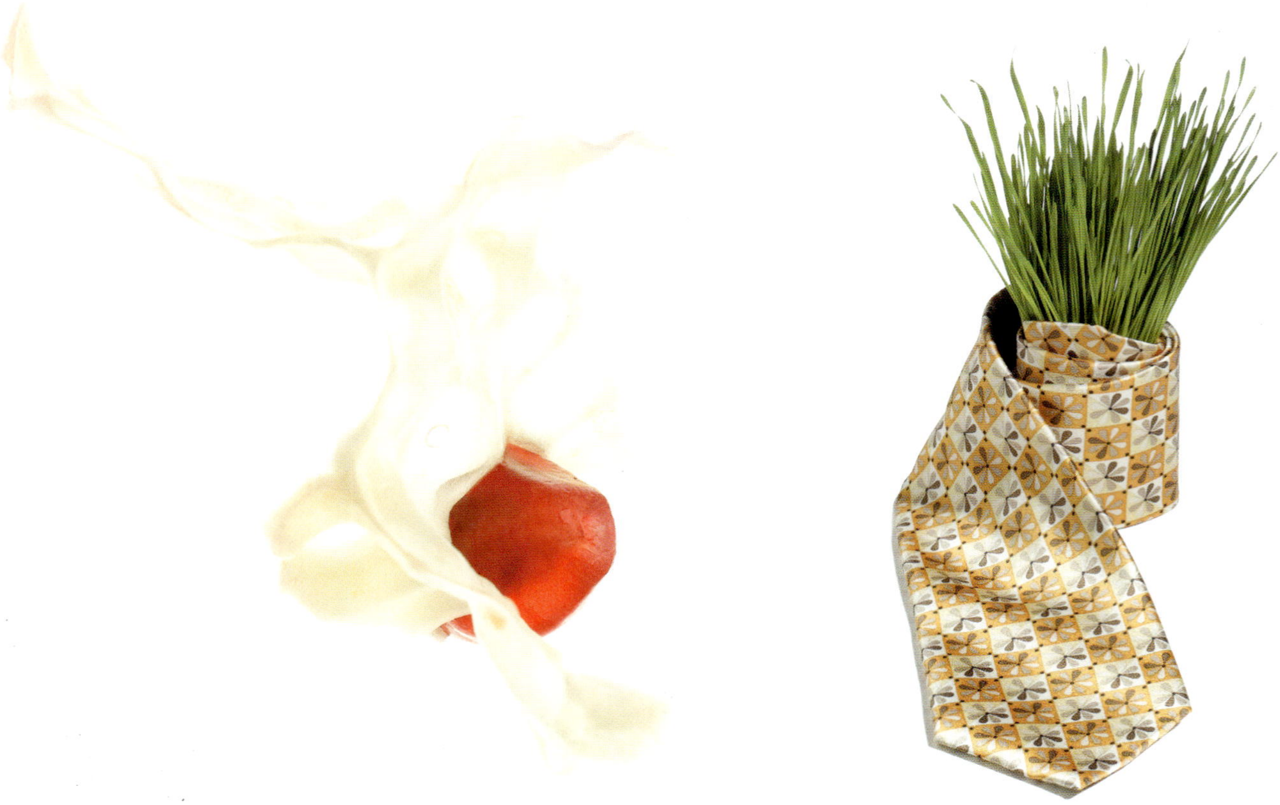

a) ISO 50, 1/60 sec., f/11 2/3, 100mm lens

b) ISO 100, 1/60 sec., f/22, 150mm lens

FIGURE 1.27 **a)** The pomegranate seed with membrane is lit dramatically; **b)** the tie with grass isn't.

The other shot, of a single pomegranate seed and some of the surrounding membrane, was lit exclusively from below. The concept behind the shot is more ambiguous than that of the tie image, and the lighting helps to create a sense of mystery. A photographer we featured previously, Howard Sokol, often uses dark shadows to create mystery within his images. In the case of the pomegranate seed, the white space and the diaphanous membrane surrounding the bright red seed also create a sense of mystery. Sokol's apple shot and the pomegranate image both use deeply saturated red fruit as their main subject, but their approaches on how to cloak that fruit in mystery are completely different.

Emotional impact does not mean that the lighting brings you to tears, hysterical laughter, or the verge of a nervous breakdown. It just needs to make you feel something. That something could be a subtle sense of wonder or unease. A great example of the emotional impact that lighting can have is found in classic horror movies. Often the monsters in those movies are lit from below so that the shadows run up their faces and bodies; this helps to make the audience feel uneasy. The reason for this is simple; the sun, our most familiar source of light, is always either above us or horizontal to us, but never below us. A subject lit from below looks unnatural and therefore makes us feel uncomfortable.

Let's look at some other ways to add drama to your images. As was mentioned earlier, all of your decisions emanate from having a clear understanding of what it is you're trying to say about your subject. You need to know how you want viewers to respond to your image and then make the appropriate lighting decisions to help facilitate that response. The following images serve as a simple example of lighting that went from less to more dramatic. All were photographed using strobe lighting equipment but could have just as easily been shot with continuous light sources.

CRITIQUING PHOTOGRAPHS

When you look at images and decide that you like or don't like them, you need to ask why you arrived at that decision—what about the image is working or not working? Did the artist make successful decisions about lighting, composition, location, propping, casting, backgrounds, and wardrobe? What was the artist's intent, and was she successful in conveying this intent? If you don't agree with some of the decisions or you think that they could have been made and executed more successfully, that doesn't mean that the photograph is bad. It may mean that you have different tastes from those of the artist. Recognize those differences, but don't simply dismiss other people's work out of hand.

The photographs used for the Chapter 7 comparison (Figure 7.9) are a prime example of differences in interpretation. The same subject matter was used, but Joe and I approached it very differently. Some of you may like one image while others may prefer the other. That doesn't mean that one is inherently better than the other, although I'm pretty sure that my image is better than Joe's.

—BRAD BARTHOLOMEW

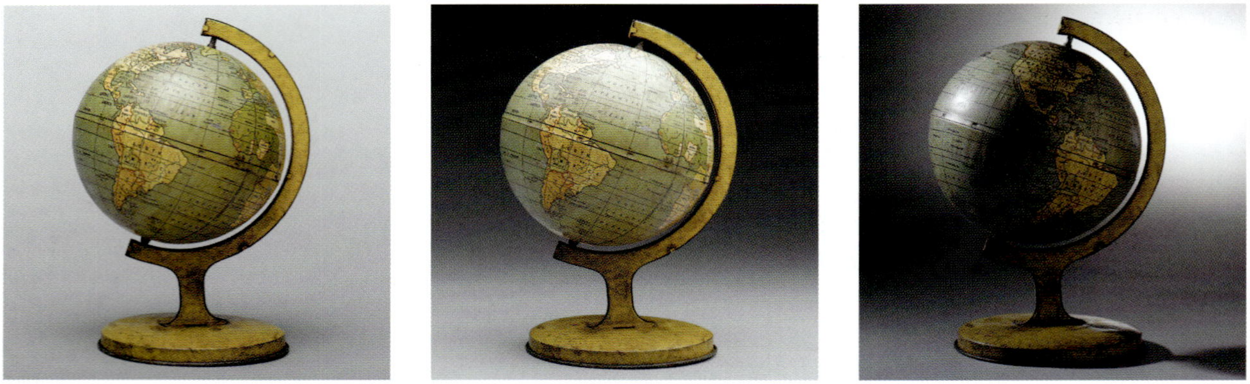

a) b) c)

FIGURE 1.28 **a)** Lighting showing minimal drama; **b)** lighting with increased drama; **c)** lighting with further enhanced drama.

FIGURE 1.28A was photographed using a single source diffused light. The light was placed above the camera slightly above the camera axis. The lighting is relatively flat, and you can see detail throughout the subject. It is safe to say that there is very little drama in the way that this image has been lit.

In this next image, FIGURE 1.28B, the diffused light source has been moved off the camera axis so that it is directly above the globe, tilting slightly forward, away from the background, thereby taking light off the background. This does two things—it creates more of a highlight side on the top of the globe and a shadow side on the bottom of the globe, and it creates a gradation on the background going from dark on the top to lighter on the bottom. The gradation on the background does much to increase the drama in the image, as does the change in the light on the subject itself. This change in light also creates greater separation of the object from the background.

The final version of this image, FIGURE 1.28C, has arguably the most dramatic light. In this particular image two spotlights were used. The light on the subject was moved perpendicular to and slightly above the camera axis; the second spotlight was directly on the background. The second light enabled us to maintain separation between the globe and the background without having to place another light directly onto the globe. Finally, a fill card was used to bounce light back into the front right side of the globe.

So which image is better? We prefer the final image because we tend to like that darker, more dramatic lighting scheme. But to know which image is better we need to know how the images are going to be used and what the photographer's ultimate intent is. For instance, if the images are part of a catalog in which being able to see all the detail in the globe is ultimately the most important thing, then the first image is the best. If the photographer wants to be able to use the image to show off the globe but feels like there needs to be a greater sense of depth within the overall shot, then the second is the best. If the photographer wants a bold image to be used on the cover of the catalog, where he can sacrifice detail in order to get people to stop and pay attention to the image, then the third image is best. Again, it is of overriding importance that you thoroughly analyze your subject and then make conscious decisions about how lighting will enhance those decisions.

The images in FIGURE 1.29, on the next two pages, are examples of how dramatic light can play a major role in portraying relatively ordinary subject matter.

(It is worth noting that decisions beyond lighting were also made in each of these images to try to make them more dramatic. For instance, the shot of the cardboard tubes was made with a wide-angle lens to help force the perspective. All four images use color to help enhance the subject matter and increase the drama, and the shot of the mushrooms uses a unique point of view to help create an interesting composition.)

Creating dramatically lit images can be an elusive endeavor. Our best advice is to analyze your subject matter, choose the type of light you want to use for your main light source, and then move this light around your subject until it gives you the effect you are looking for. Understand that often your initial choice may not be the best one; you need to keep an open mind and be willing to experiment using different types of light. Once you have established your main light you can add additional lights to the background and subject to further enhance the hero and your concept. Adding light to certain areas of the image as well as limiting or subtracting light from other areas is what helps to create a dramatic photograph.

Lighting successfully is a building process. Constructing anything requires that you have a good grasp of what it is you're trying to build and what you want that object to represent, an ability to previsualize what the final result will look like, and a willingness to make changes through addition and subtraction to your initial plan. Chapter 2 will go into greater detail regarding the building process of lighting a successful photograph.

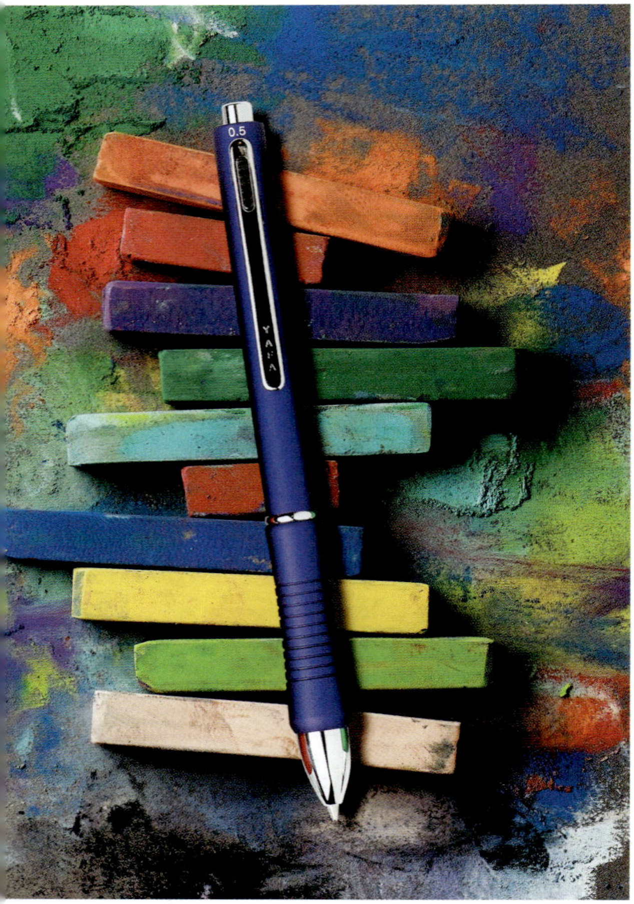

a) ISO 100, 1/125 sec., f/22, 150mm lens

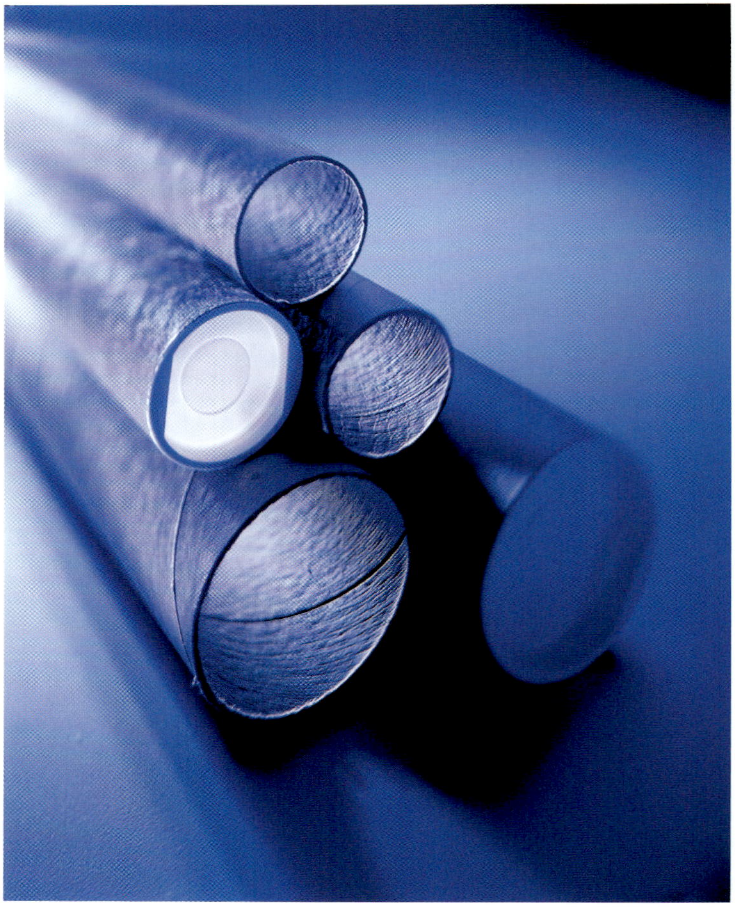

b) ISO 100, 1/60 sec., f/22, 50mm lens

FIGURE 1.29 In these shots of **a)** chalk and a pen, **b)** packing tubes, **c)** mushrooms, and **d)** a messy desk, ordinary items take on some drama.

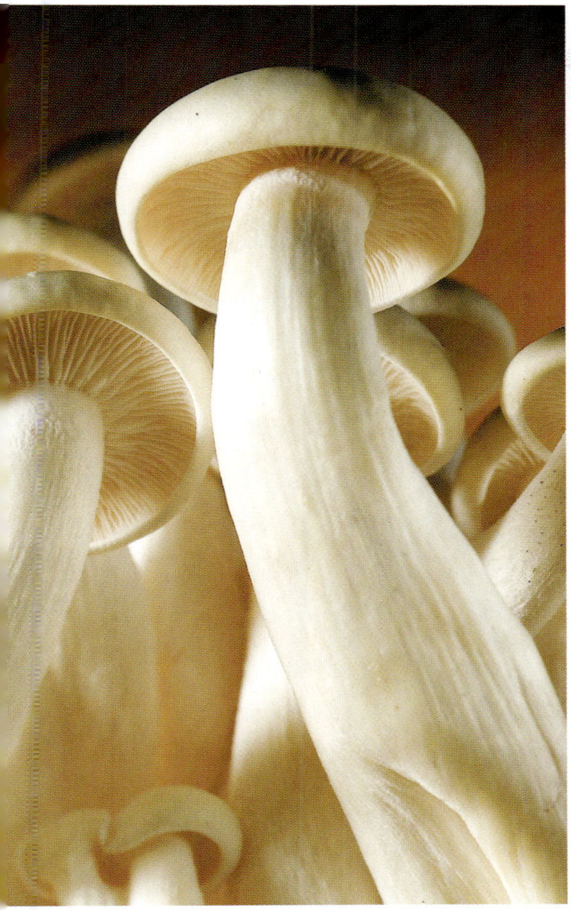

c) ISO 100, 1/125 sec., f/11, 100mm lens

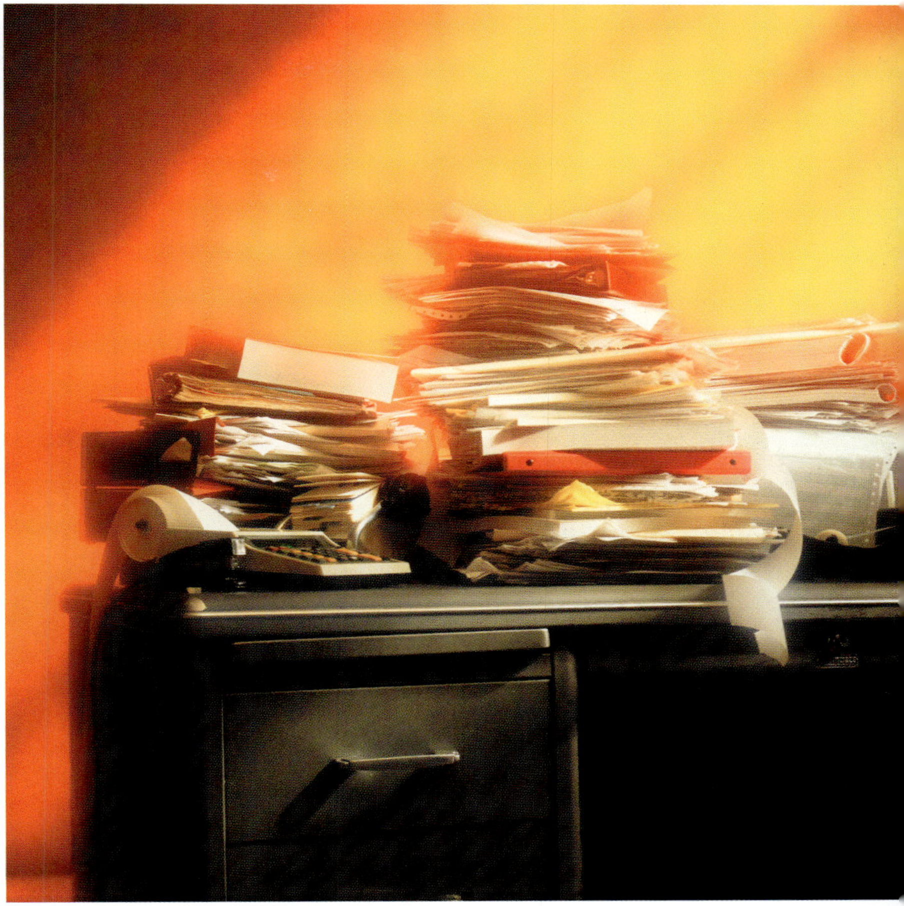

d) ISO 100, 125 sec., f/16, 210mm lens

interview

HOWARD SOKOL

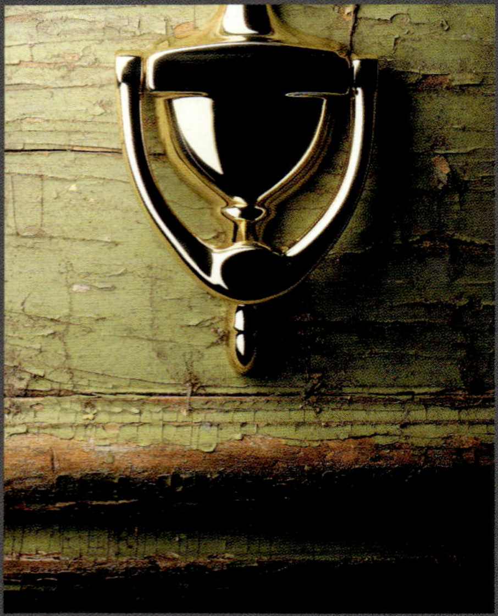

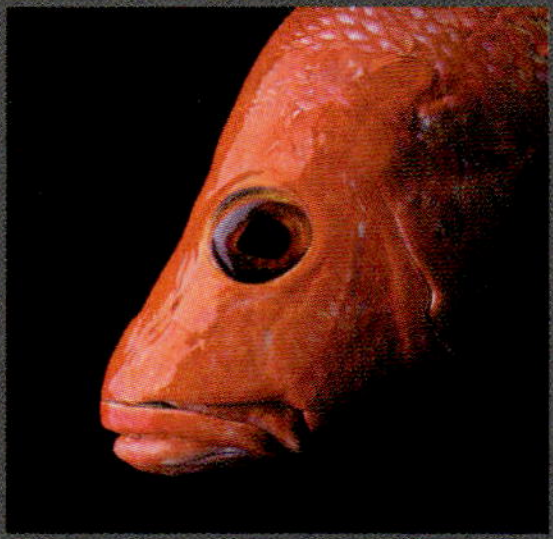

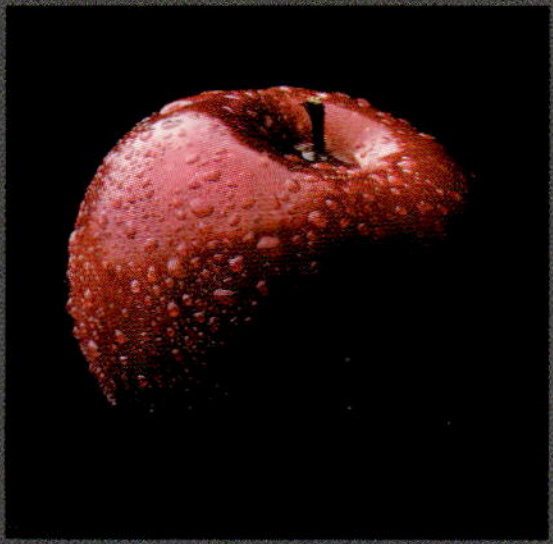

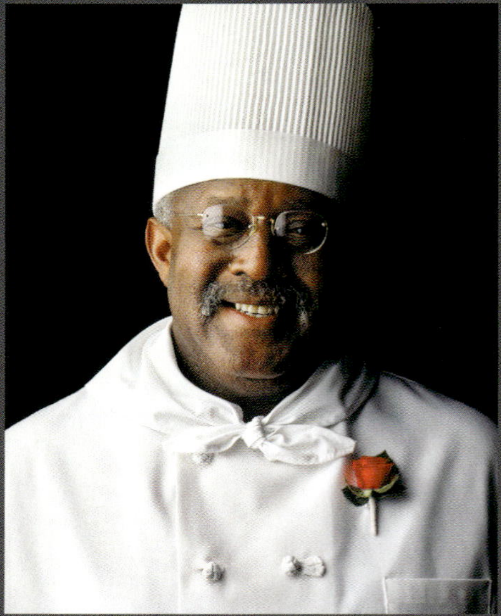

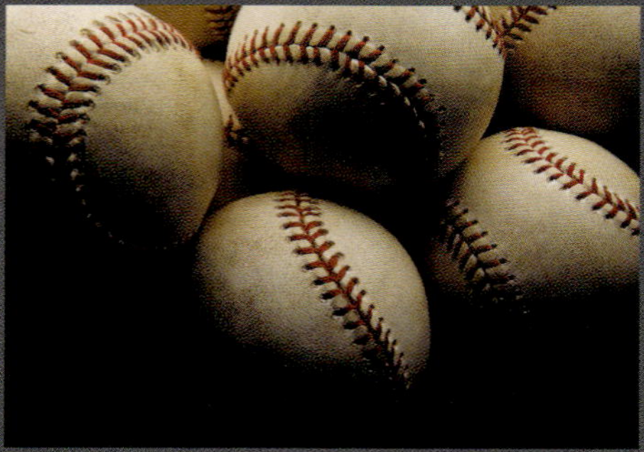

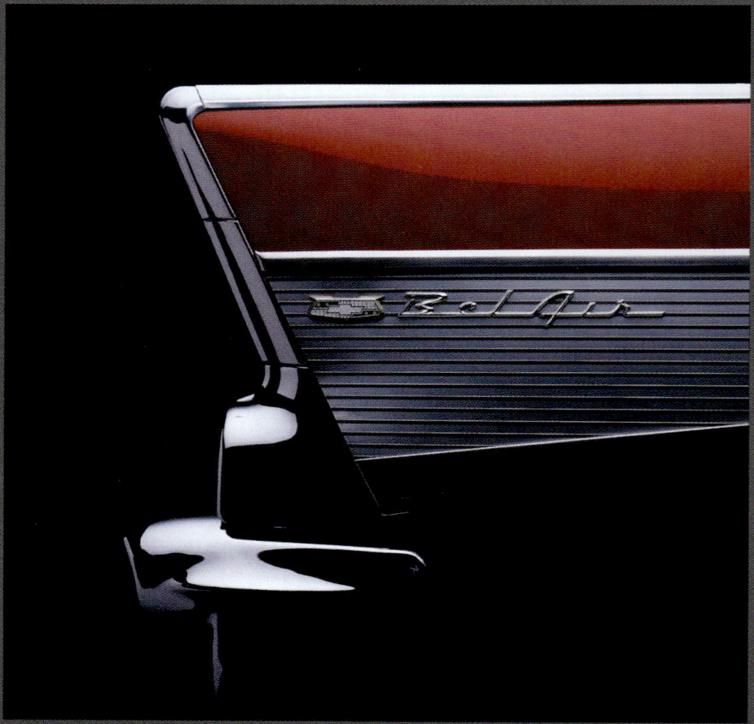

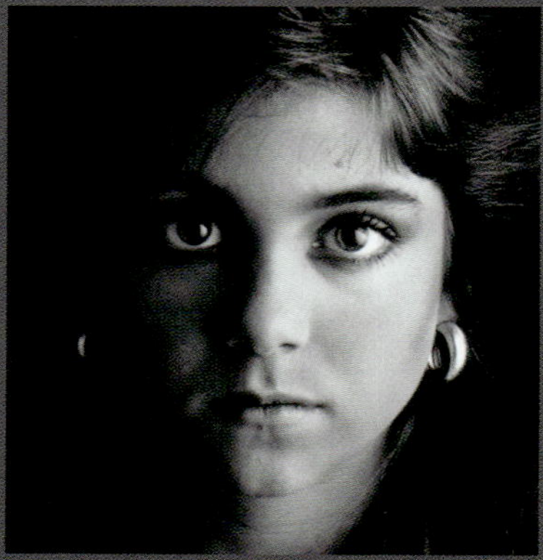

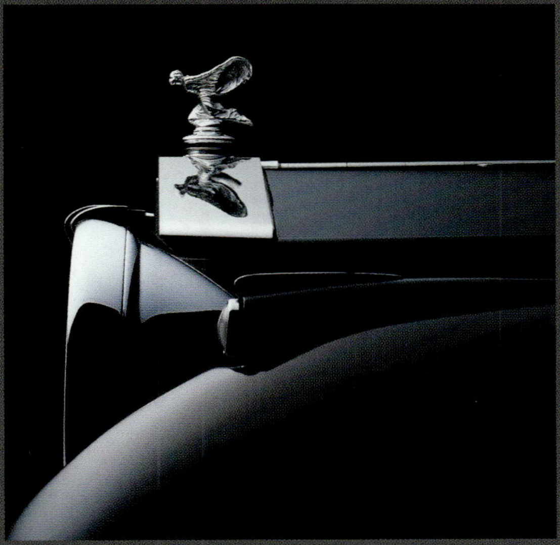

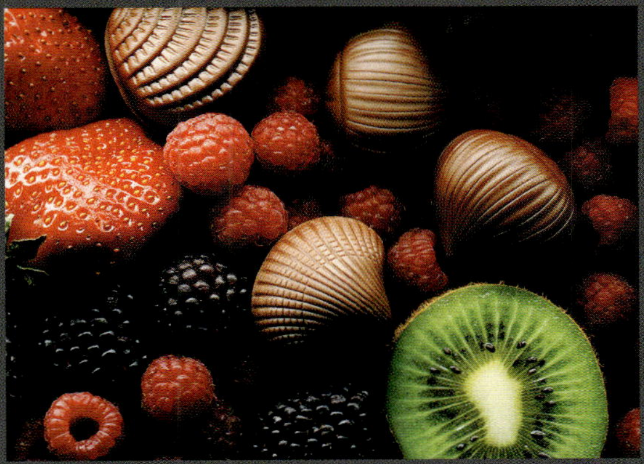

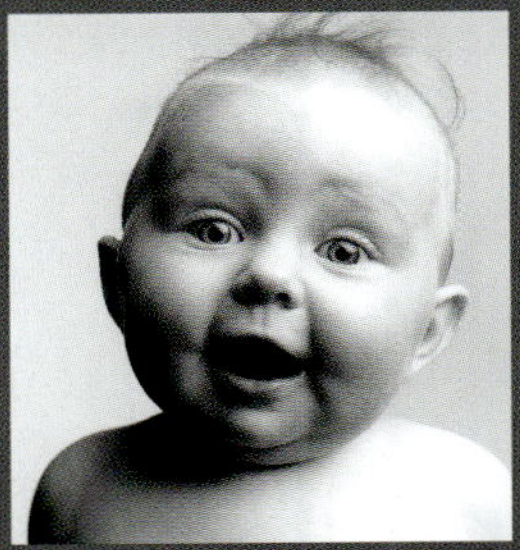

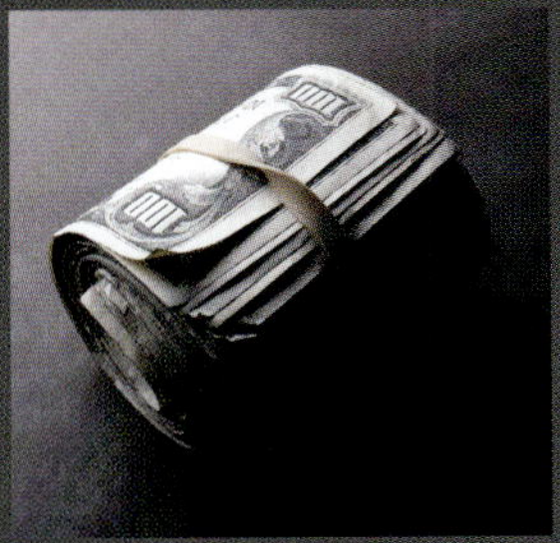

All images © Howard Sokol

How long have you been a professional photographer?

In 1973 my wife and I moved from California to Denver, Colorado. I had just finished getting my BFA in photography from the Art Center College of Design, and we felt like Denver would be a good place to start our lives together. I got a job as an associate working for an established photographer. It was a great way to get started in that I could get my own jobs and shoot within his studio and at the same time assist him on his commercial work. In this way I could earn money helping him, while paying him a percentage of the photo fees I received on my jobs to offset any rent. In addition to this I also assisted other photographers. So I would say 1973 was the beginning of my professional photography career.

How did you get started?

I was not one of those kids who started running around at an early age with a camera around my neck. I did not become interested in photography until I joined the Army and became an Army photographer in Vietnam and Germany.

Do you have formal training or education?

Yes, I do. I was wounded in Vietnam, and while I was recovering someone from the VA said that they would pay for my education once I recovered. Like a lot of soldiers, I enjoyed getting mail. I would send for various catalogs just so that I could receive an occasional piece of mail. While I was recovering I remembered that I had gotten a catalog from the Art Center College of Design, and I thought wouldn't it be wonderful to go to school there and continue my education in photography? Then I looked at the cost and put that idea on the back burner until a representative from the VA said that they would pay for my continuing education. In the end the VA didn't pay, but by that time I was already committed and excited to pursue my education. I attended the Art

Center for almost three years, going straight through, and receiving my BFA in photography.

You have a very distinctive lighting style. How would you describe it, and how did you arrive at it?

I use a single source light. It's a softbox that I use to try to create the kind of light you would see on an overcast day. When I started using that style of light, there really weren't manufactured softboxes available, so we created our own using pieces of foam core that we would put strobe heads inside of and then use translucent material to diffuse the light.

Let's look at your shot of the apple (Figure 1.8)—describe how your lighting accomplishes dimension, separation, drama, and texture. Why did you choose not to fill the shadow side of the apple?

With the shot of the apple I wasn't all that concerned about separation. The highlights on the water droplets create texture on the apple. My main concern was to create a dramatic image with a great deal of dimension. To do this I used a softbox that I was able to move around the apple using just the corner of the box, so that I was able to control the amount of wraparound fill light that I got. I did not fill the shadows at all, and to be honest, I often don't care about shadow detail. I want to see detail in the highlights, but by allowing the shadows to go to total darkness it creates a sense of mystery that's appealing to me. I feel the image is more interesting because you don't see detail in the shadows. In this way, the apple appears to emerge from the black background.

Do you remember what this image was used for?

It was part of a series of images that were used by a color separation house in Denver. We photographed different pieces of fruit in a similar manner to the apple; we were interested in creating rich saturated color and volume in the objects.

Was the client pleased with the final result?

Absolutely. I usually find that if I'm happy with the image, the client is happy as well.

You appear to employ a similar lighting style to both people and product. Is that correct? Why?

Yes, I do use a similar style in both. You can see that lighting style in much of my work. It's why art directors and clients come to me. They know what to expect. I'm interested in creating similar emotional results in whatever subjects I am photographing.

How often do you deviate from your primary lighting style?

When I'm forced to. Seriously, I'll use different lighting styles if the art director really needs something different. As I mentioned before, I'm generally getting hired to shoot using my particular style, though.

Is it important to be able to light using many styles of light, or do you think it's better to stick with one main style and refine it and adapt it to different subjects?

Some people love the challenge of constantly solving new problems and reinventing the wheel. I choose to concentrate on one main style of lighting, and each subject I photograph requires something slightly different, so I am constantly refining and adapting that basic style to a variety of different subjects.

Do you have a favorite of the images selected for this book? If so, why?

I would probably choose something like the apple or a similar simple subject. I like to try to create images that resemble what could be if the viewer happened to walk by and saw a lovely scene in real life.

Do you have any advice for photographers just starting out?

If you have a passion for photography, whatever kind of photography that might be, pick where you want to live and compete within that market. You don't have to live somewhere just because the market is bigger or you think there will be less competition or more work in that market. I believe you can compete on a global level and live anywhere.

Another thing I would suggest is to light your subjects initially the way you think they should be lit. Then move around the subject and see the way the light plays off the subject from different angles. Maybe there is something more dramatic or more beautiful than your initial setup. ■

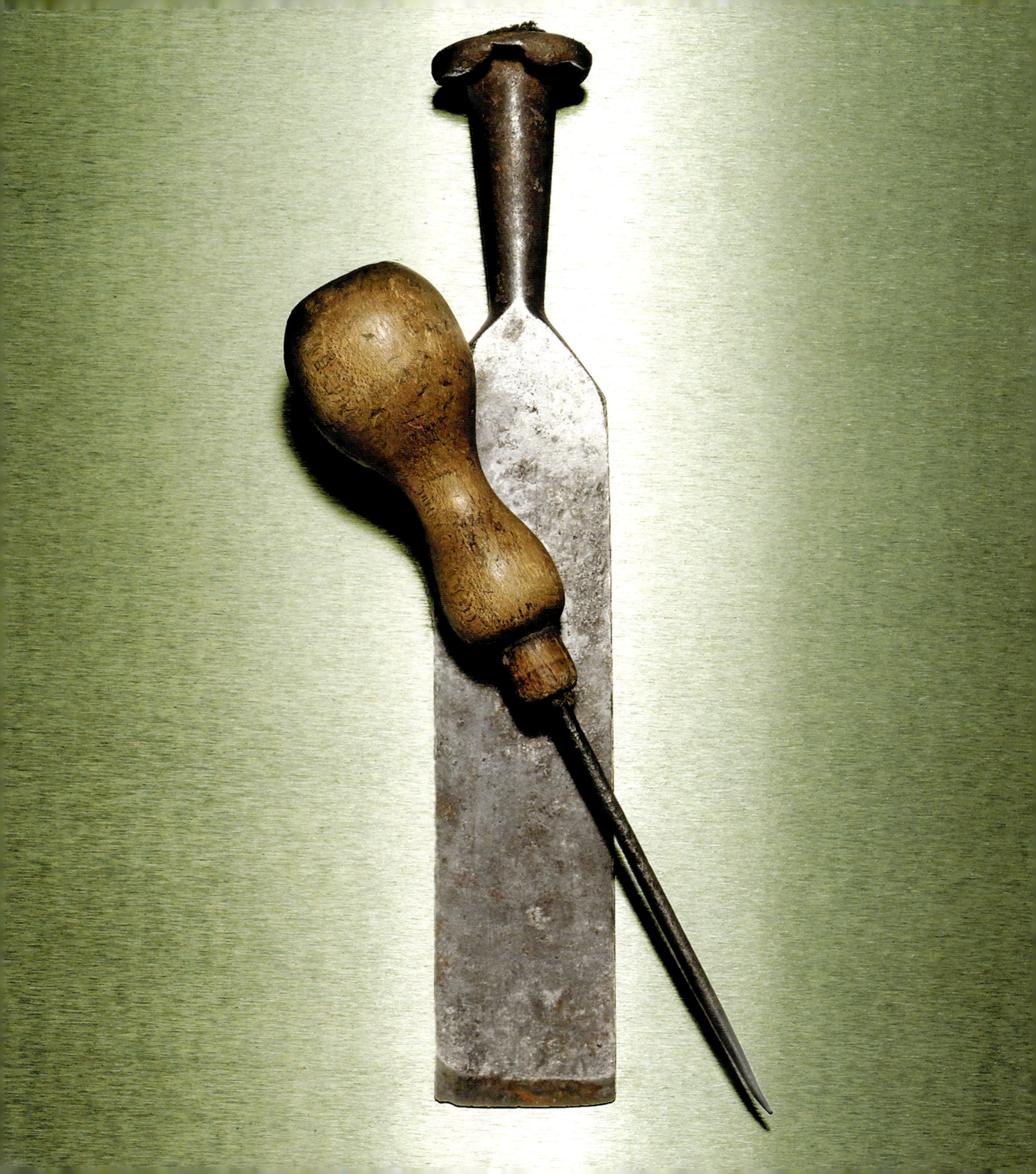

chapter two

THE BUILDING PROCESS

We believe that creating compelling images is a building process. For each successful image, you have to make a series of decisions and then implement them. When constructing a home, an architect must create a set of drawings; then the builder has to acquire materials and assemble them correctly in order for the structure to come to life. You've all been in cookie-cutter neighborhoods where every home looks almost exactly the same. Each one has the same foundation, with minor variations to the finish work, layout, and color. It usually looks like little thought went into creating unique living spaces geared to the individual needs of the people who live in the homes.

ISO 50, 1/125 sec., f/11, 150mm lens

Opening Image: Photographic Equipment

Camera: Sinar 4 × 5 view camera with Leaf Aptus-II digital back

Lens: Schneider 150mm

Lighting: Profoto Acute2 2400 generator and two strobe heads

Light modifiers: One head used a medium softbox; the other head had a 20-degree grid

The softbox, placed over the set, washed the entire set with green light. The grid light was set to a more powerful setting, thereby overpowering the green light and creating bright highlights on the metal and lighting the chisel and awl with neutral light.

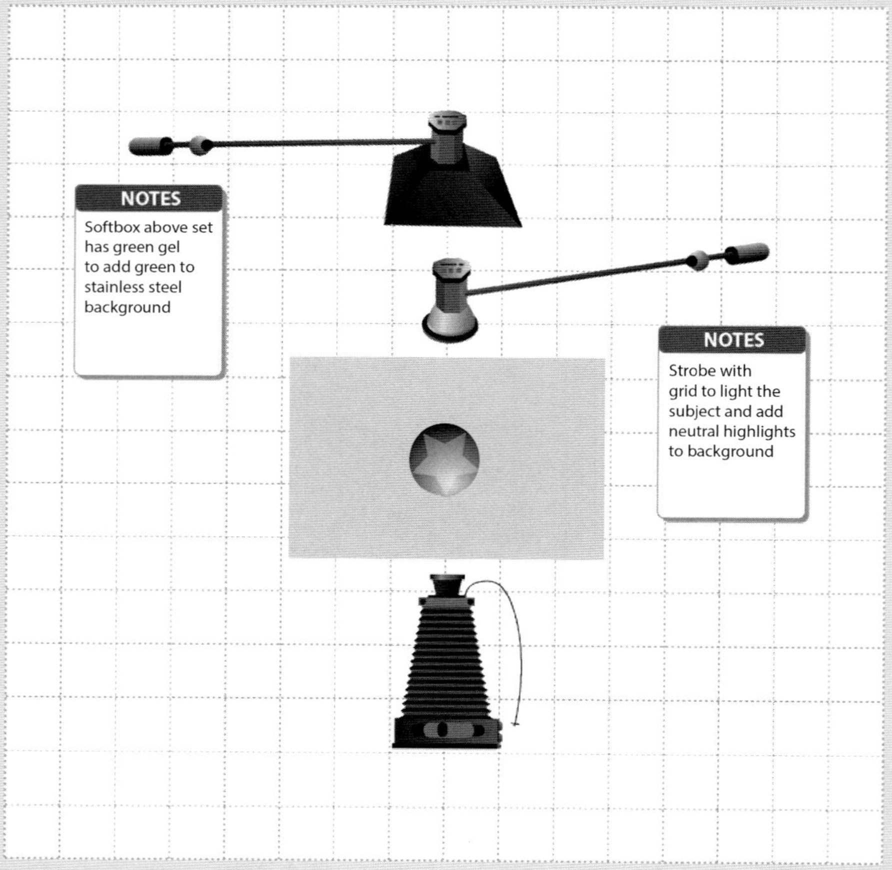

To create a unique and interesting neighborhood, each home needs to have its own set of characteristics while still maintaining the integrity of the overall neighborhood. Creating your portfolio of photographic images will be no different. You'll build each unique image based on careful consideration of the subject and precisely what you want to say about it. You'll previsualize the final results and then build a lighting scheme, by adding and subtracting light, until you achieve the desired results (**FIGURE 2.1**).

Sounds easy, right? Well, if it were easy, anyone could do it. This chapter will examine ways to effectively build images that strongly communicate your vision and intent.

FIGURE 2.1 Although it's a rather simple image, much thought went into the decisions made before producing this shot. It was built with the goal of conveying the feeling of morning light coming through the window at breakfast.

ISO 50, 1/60 sec., f/8, 100mm lens

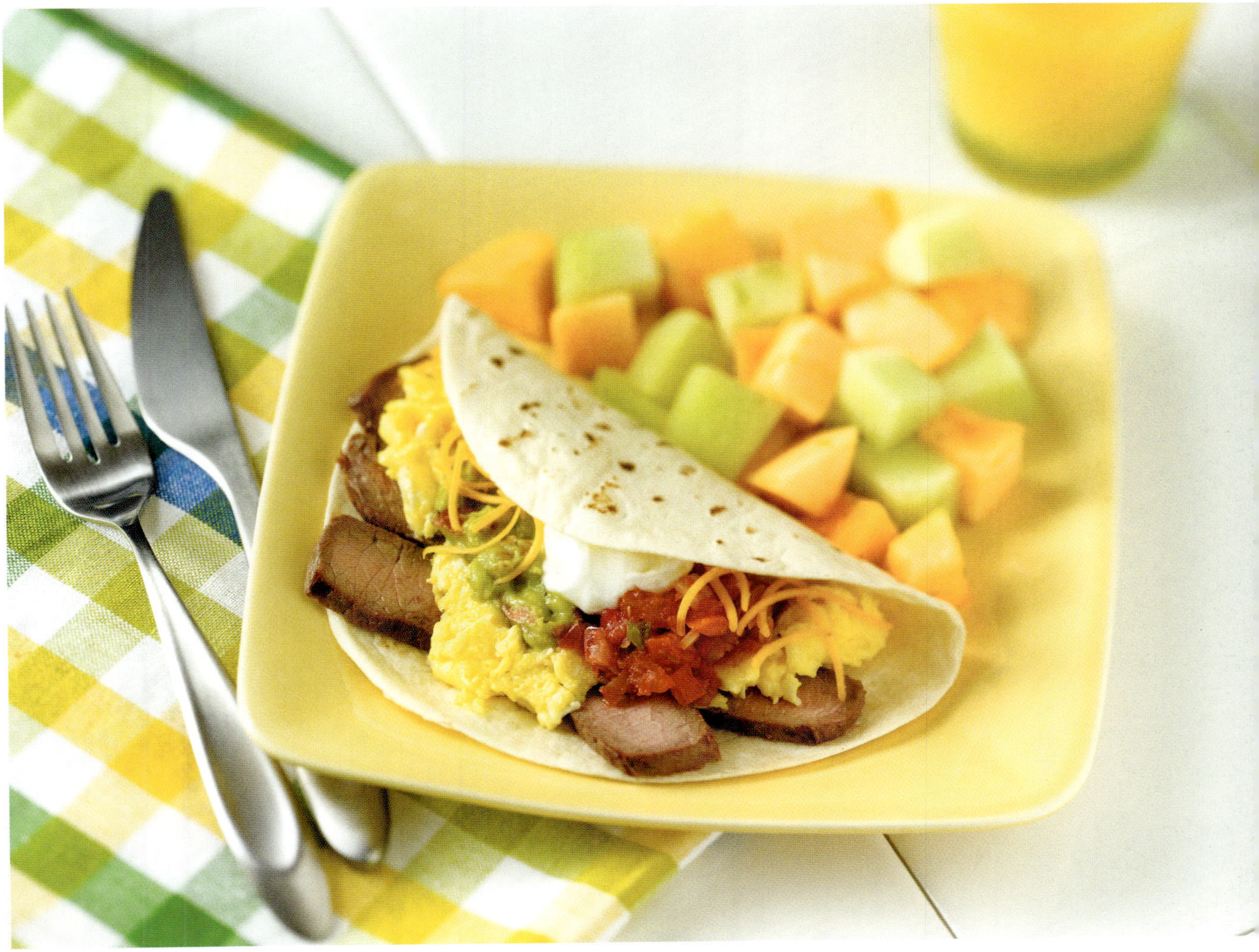

Understand Your Subject

"Any fool can know. The point is to understand."

—Albert Einstein

It's not enough to know what you want to photograph; rather, you must truly understand what it is you're planning to shoot.

It can be difficult coming up with a list of potential photographic subjects. We have all struggled trying to pin down what we want to shoot for class assignments or for our portfolios. The truth is, that's really the easy part. The hard part is fully understanding each particular object. The more you understand your subject, the easier it will be to create an image that accentuates its unique attributes.

This process often requires research and insight into what makes the object unique. This research can be relatively straightforward but sometimes requires more time and in-depth study. A good place to start is to ask some basic questions. The answers will help guide you to make decisions about the best way to photograph your subjects.

On the surface, some of these questions may seem sort of silly. Do we really need to ask what it is and what it does? The short answer is yes. Starting with the most basic questions is a good way to establish a foundation of information upon which you can build smart, captivating images. Let's apply some of

Important Questions About Your Subject

- What is it?
- What does it do?
- What is important about it?
- What are some of its key features?
- What are some of its physical properties (is it rough, smooth, heavy, light)?
- Is it inherently beautiful?
- What makes it different from similar subjects?

these questions to a fairly simple image. The following photo (**FIGURE 2.2**) will show us how asking such questions can be helpful in constructing a shot.

What are they? Automotive transmission gears.

What do they do? They're able to engage and disengage from one another. When engaged, one gear can drive the other gear. If they are different sizes, they will rotate at differing speeds.

What is important about them? They're instrumental in keeping machinery, in this case an automobile, running smoothly and efficiently. They are machined to precise specifications.

What are some key features? The teeth are at an angle. They are made from very durable materials.

What are their physical properties? They are large, heavy, somewhat reflective, smooth overall, but with some texture in carved surfaces. They are strong, solid, simple, and silver in color.

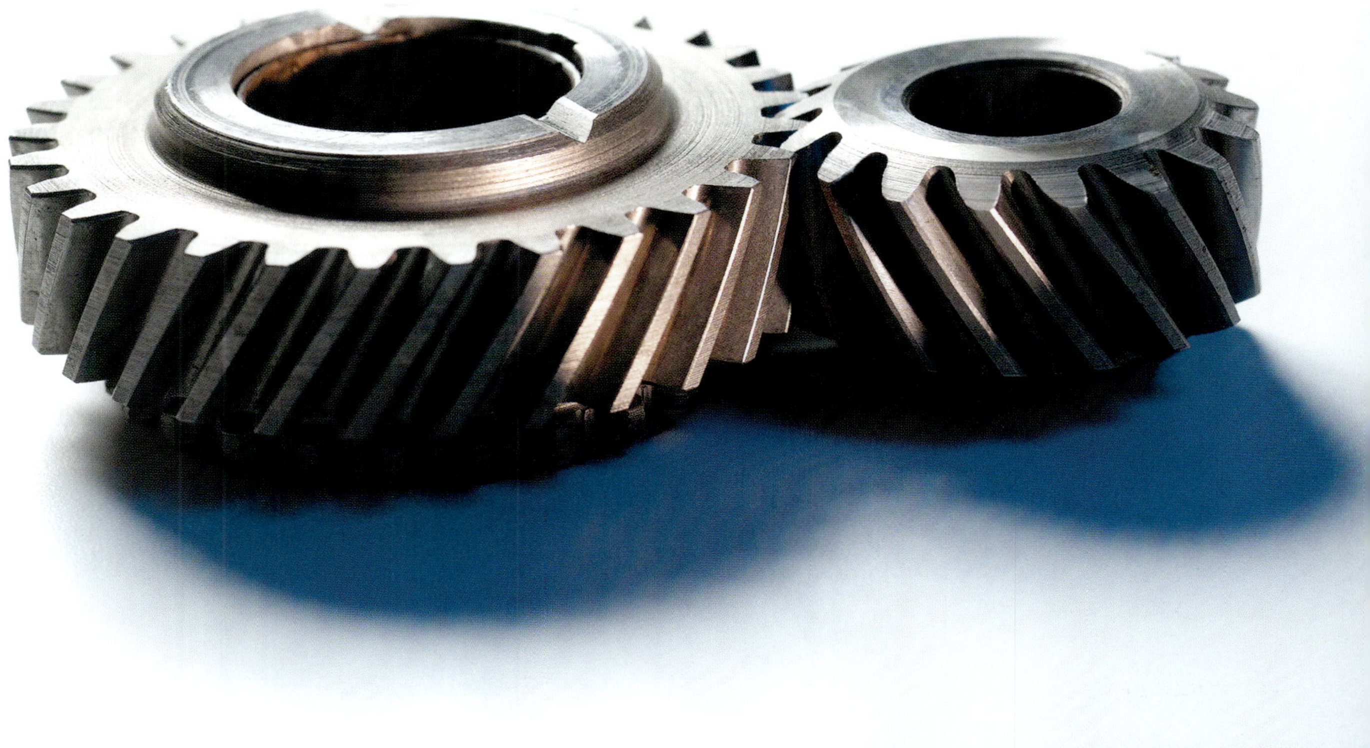

FIGURE 2.2 Transmission gears photographed using a softbox, a tungsten light, and a blue reflector.

ISO 50, 1/60 sec., f/5.6, 210mm lens

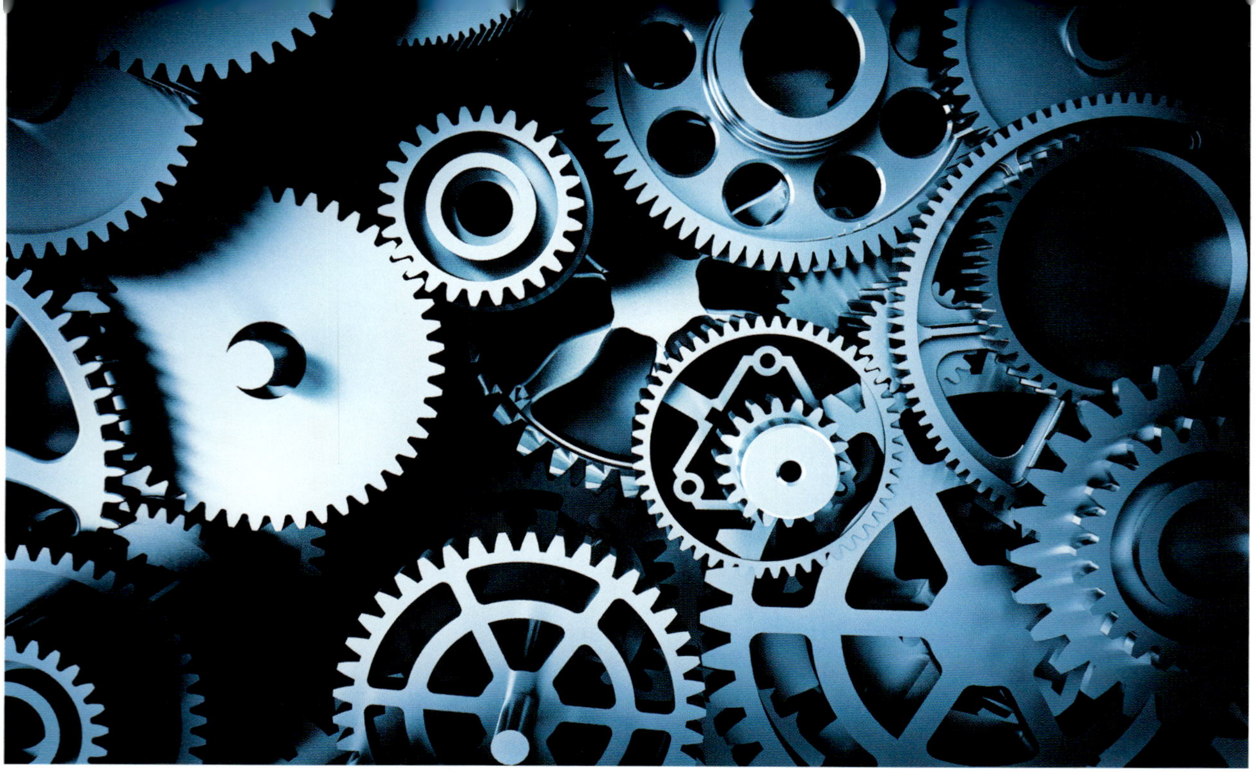

FIGURE 2.3 Image of clock gears.

ISO 100, 1/125 sec., f/22, 90mm lens

Are they inherently beautiful? Not particularly, unless you are a total motor head.

What makes them different from similar objects? Their size, their weight, the depth of the teeth, their width, their color, and their strength.

Now let's compare these gears with the gears found in a different image (**FIGURE 2.3**). We don't need to answer all of those questions for this shot to get a good idea of some of the similarities and differences.

What are they? They're the gears found in a clock or watch.

What do they do? They rotate, meshed to one another, in order to drive the hands of a clock or watch.

What are their physical properties? They're small, delicate, lightweight, and thin, and together they are complicated and precise.

Are they inherently beautiful? Yes.

What makes them different from similar objects? Their size, their weight, the depth of the teeth, their width, their color, and their strength.

So you've analyzed the subjects, answered some basic questions, and reached some simple conclusions about the purpose, structure, and qualities of each of them. Now what are you to do with all of this information?

What Are You Trying to Say?

What you do with the information you've gathered is what this book is all about. It's the essence of what will make you a better photographer and set you apart from your competition. Thoughtful analysis of your subject matter is at the very heart of creating terrific photographs. Every time you take a photograph, you should be asking yourself, "What am I trying to say about my subject?" It doesn't matter if you're photographing a rock star, a car battery, a new hotel, or a mountain vista; what is the message you're trying to convey? You use the answers to construct an image that reinforces the underlying message or concept.

In the previous section, we discussed the process of looking at what you're photographing and then analyzing its various characteristics. You have the concept first, and then you need to find objects that will help to illustrate the concept. Using the two images from above, let's explore this idea in greater depth.

The first image, Figure 2.2, was shot for a real estate developer in Colorado. The art director at the advertising agency suggested using gears to get an idea across—the concept that multiple parts of the company work in sync with one another. It was left to us to find the appropriate gears. We knew that we wanted to create an image that would be simple in composition and easy to read. Two or three gears would do the trick.

By asking ourselves the simple questions listed previously, it became clear that one set of gears was more appropriate for this project than other sets. The gears we chose convey strength and integration, symbolizing the meshing of various parts of the company. Shining a small warm colored light where the gears meet helped to accentuate both the size and strength of the gears as well as the way they work together. That light draws the viewer's eye to the part of the shot that directly relates to what the photographer is trying to say about the subject.

Visual Metaphors

A visual metaphor is when one thing is used to represent something else. For instance, the two gears were used to represent the strength and synchronicity of the real estate company. A bald eagle (**FIGURE 2.4**) might be used to represent patriotism or the United States itself. A sleeping baby could be used to suggest innocence (**FIGURE 2.5**). Visual metaphors are incredibly powerful tools you can employ to create unusual and imaginative concepts.

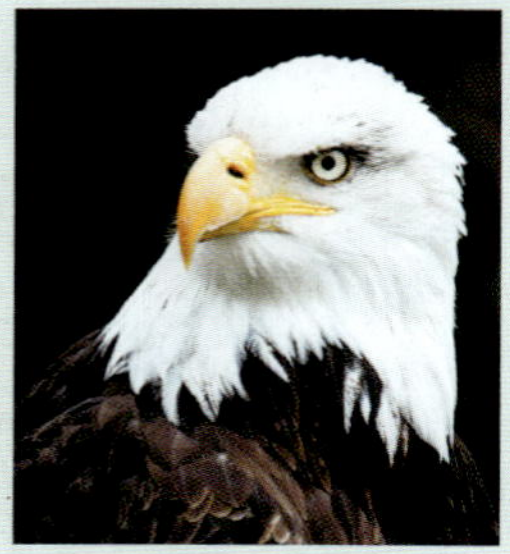

FIGURE 2.4 This image could be used as a visual metaphor for strength or patriotism.

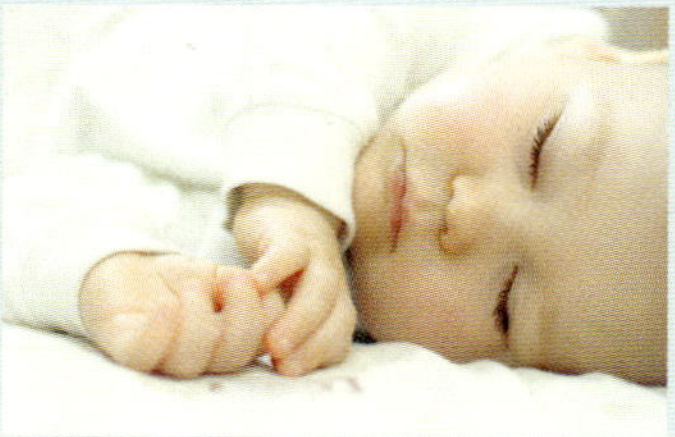

FIGURE 2.5 Babies can symbolize things like innocence, peace, or tranquility.

The gears in Figure 2.3 are intricate, and while they certainly convey the theme of many parts working together, they're too small and delicate to illustrate the strength and solidity that we were looking for. Nonetheless, all the different sizes and shapes add interest and help create a beautiful image. This might be an appropriate photograph for certain situations when you are trying to illustrate complexity or cooperation.

Before we move on, let's examine one more image and how understanding the subject and what you're trying to say about it helps to guide decisions made in the photographic process.

This relatively simple-looking image (**FIGURE 2.6**) is in fact one of the most difficult photographs I've ever taken (Brad speaking here). Most of the objects in the shot were already sitting around the studio; the old wooden table, the mop, and the brushes, as well as the backdrop, were things I

FIGURE 2.6 The lighting scheme for this image was developed after careful analysis of the subjects being photographed (opposite).

ISO 100, 30 sec, f/11, 150mm lens

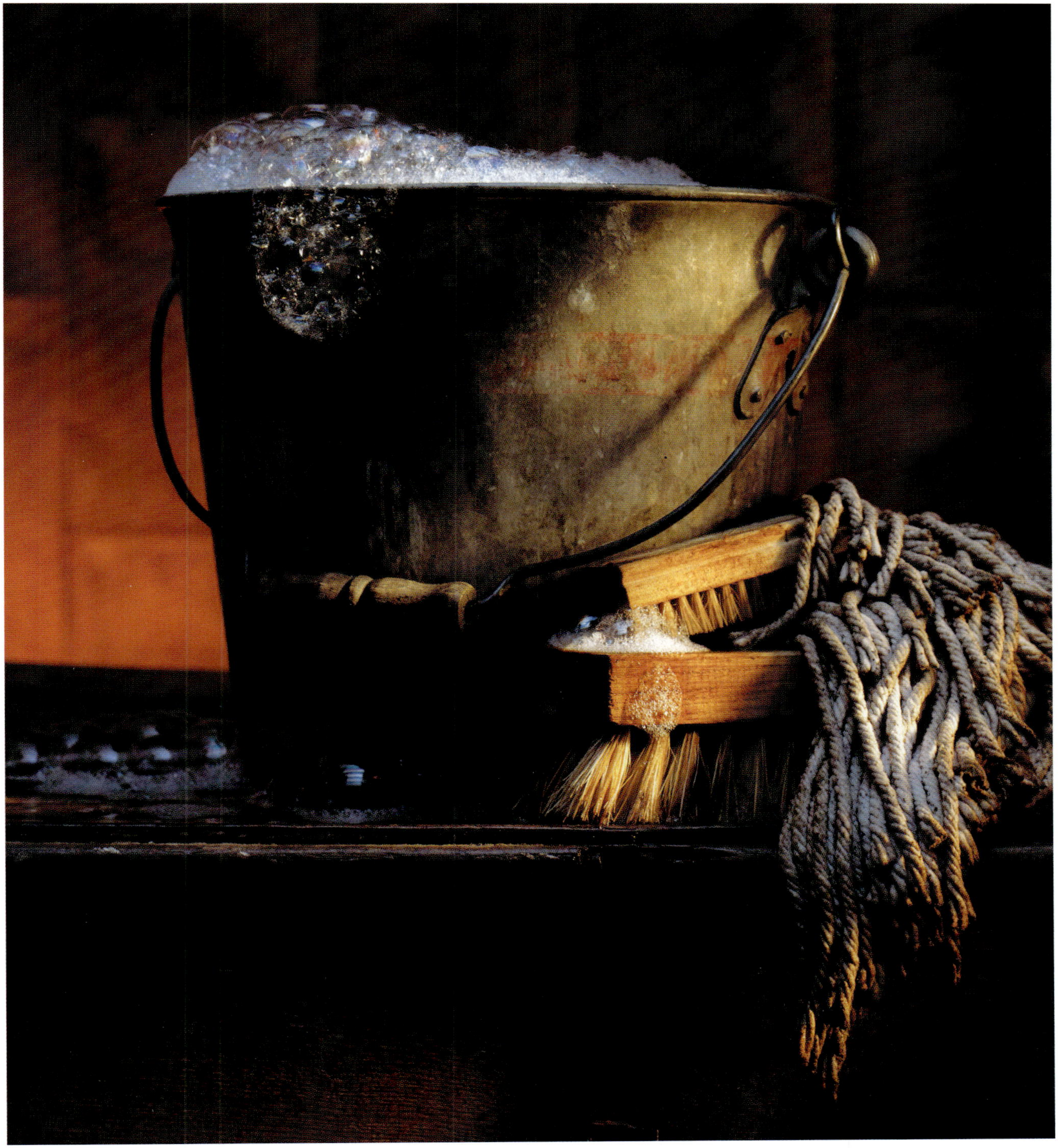

Traditional Composition

In traditional Dutch-master still life painting, you'll often see this type of composition used. It starts with a strong horizontal line (the table's edge), and objects rise above this horizontal line (the bucket) and break below the line (the mop), causing tension between the rising and falling objects. FIGURE 2.7 is another example of this type of composition, using more traditional subject matter.

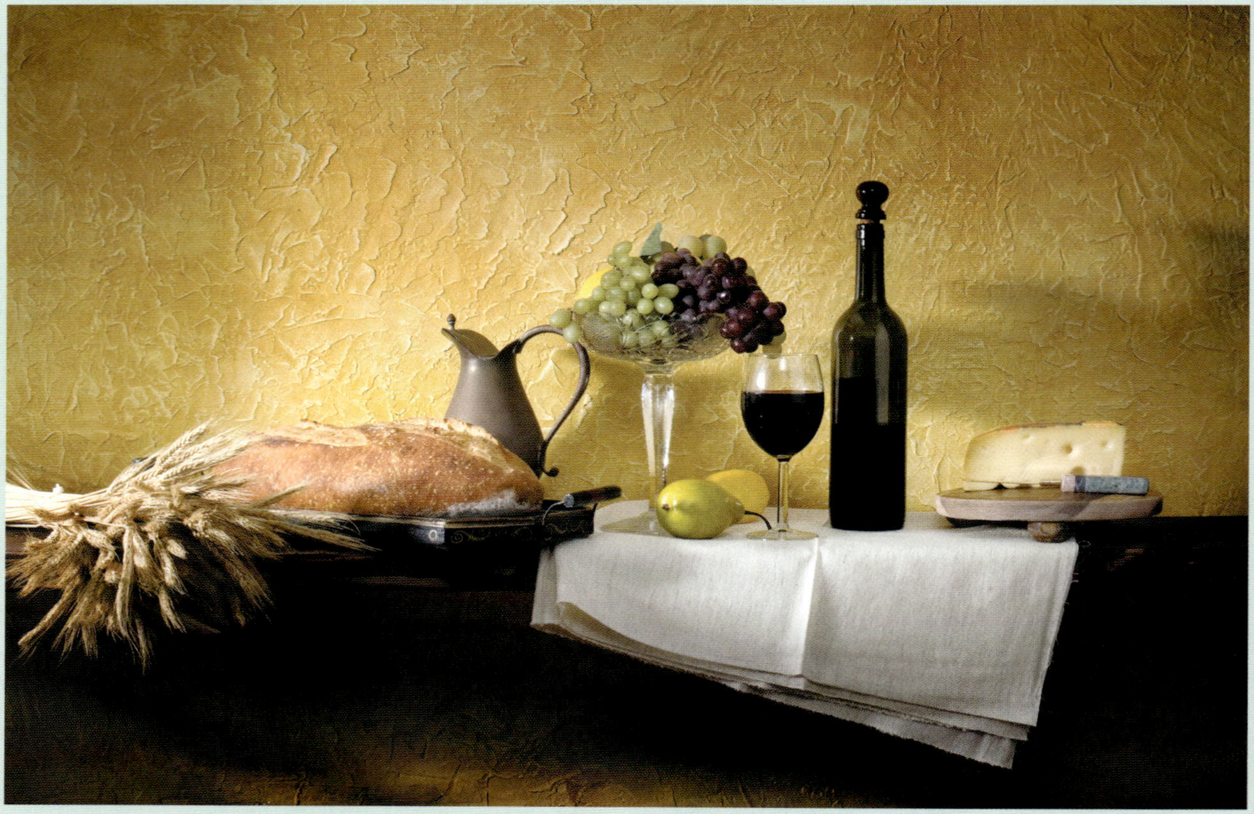

FIGURE 2.7 This type of composition can help organize subject matter while still creating drama and tension within the shot.

already had. I knew I wanted an old bucket to be the hero of the shot, so I prowled antique stores until I was able to locate this one. I loved the wooden handle, and the red stripe was a bonus.

The analysis of the subject was relatively simple and straightforward; everything in the shot was old and had a fair amount of texture. The objects are used to clean and yet they themselves were dirty. The texture in all the objects was the overriding thing that I wanted to accentuate. The wooden handle on the bucket makes this bucket different from others and was something important that I wanted to feature. I also wanted the image to have a timeless quality, and therefore I alluded to the composition of Dutch-master painting.

Once I analyzed the subjects and determined what I wanted to say about them, the lighting became clear. Three types of light were used in this image. A strobe was bounced off the ceiling to provide a little fill to some of the shadows. A fixed tungsten light with a warming gel was placed behind the table and pointed onto the background. The main light was a flashlight, which I used to create the highlights on the bucket, the bucket handle, the brushes and mop, and the front of the table (Figure 2.6). I did this using a technique called light painting, which will be discussed in the next chapter.

For now what's important to understand is that I employed lighting to realize the goals set out in the original analysis of the subjects. Raking a point source light across the subject matter enabled me to bring out the maximum amount of texture in the bucket, mop, and brushes. It also allowed me to put a bright highlight on the wooden handle, which helped separate it from the dark bucket behind it, thereby making it one of the more important parts of the shot. A similar thing happened with the bottom of the mop, where those highlights separated from the dark part of the table, accentuating their fall below the horizontal line. The lighting was not arbitrary. It was predicated on the answers to the basic questions presented at the beginning of this chapter, the initial step in the image-building process.

Next we'll look at additional ways to help you previsualize what you want your final images to look like and then more nuts-and-bolts techniques to help you realize these goals.

Previsualize

"The ability to anticipate a finished image before making the exposure."
—Ansel Adams

It's common to hear studio photographers say that the act of shooting a job is easy; it's everything else that takes work. Many steps lead up to a photo shoot, and one of the more important ones is previsualization.

You've already read about the importance of knowing your subject and defining what you are trying to say, but now we need to go a step further and previsualize the results. Previsualizing is seeing how something will look before you ever begin setting it up. The movie industry uses previsualization in the form of storyboarding; long before a studio incurs the cost of shooting, it lays out exactly how each scene will look. It's common for commercial photographers to work from art director layouts, which are a form of previsualization.

What do you do when a client comes to you and says that you're being hired to photograph a rolled-up $100 bill on a textured surface, captured from above, and using a shallow depth of field to accent the denomination? The two images in **FIGURE 2.8** both seem to satisfy the client's request, but they are significantly different. You need to ask yourself more questions. Does the client prefer a warm-toned image or one with a cooler color palette?

STRESS AND PREVISUALIZATION

As a commercial photographer, I never work without previsualizing the desired result. My preference is to have a layout with as many details as possible. Photography can be a stressful business, and knowing the client's wishes and—better yet—knowing that I can produce the desired results makes all shoots seem much easier.

I remember setting up a photo shoot for a national restaurant chain earlier in my career; I was thinking that I had the mood and lighting dialed in when the creative director walked over and asked when I would start working on the lighting. I about fell over. I muttered something about addressing the composition first, and then immediately started asking questions about the look they were after. Lesson learned. I hadn't previsualized what the client wanted.

—JOE LAVINE

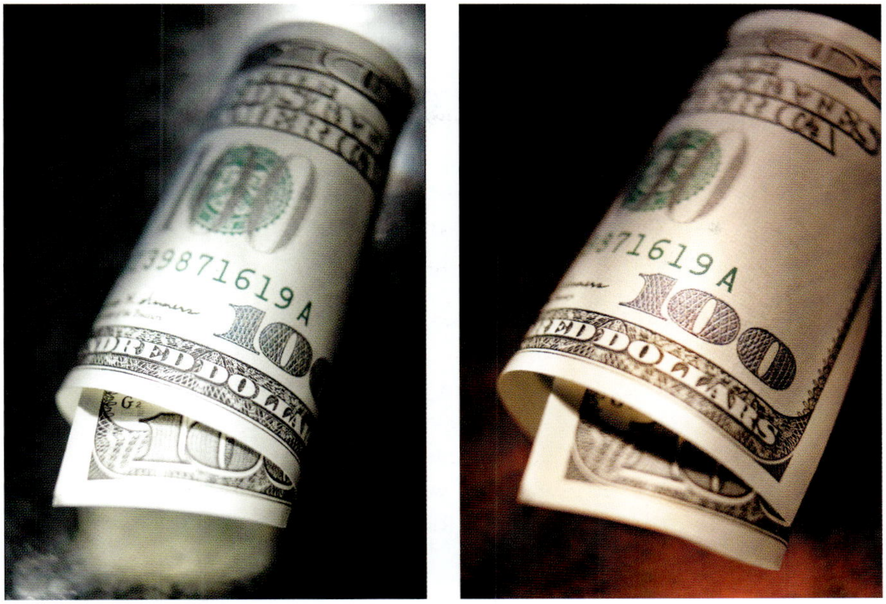

a) b)

FIGURE 2.8 **a)** A $100 bill photographed on cool metal surface with neutral lighting; **b)** same bill captured on rusty metal surface with warm lighting.

ISO 100, 1/125 sec., f/4, 90mm lens

What do you see when you close your eyes and envision your image? Previsualization doesn't have to entail an elaborate sketch or drawing; it can be a combination of a mental image and a few written notes. Let's take a look at a handful of items to consider. Please note that this is just a starting point; every project will have its own parameters.

- **Overall mood:** All images have a mood. Photographers often don't realize it, but they can project their current mood onto an image. In most cases the image needs to be telling a story, and it's often not the same story as what you're personally feeling at the time. For example, do you want the image to say happy, sad, angry, or something else? Considering the mood will help you figure out how to address the subject.
- **Theme:** Although themes are often associated with a series of images, a single image should also have a theme. A simple way to think of themes is to ask yourself, what is the central topic or concept?
- **The look:** Ask yourself, what is the overall look? Should the image have a rustic, western feel, or are you aiming for a modern, high-tech feel? Previsualizing the answer will help you prepare for the photo shoot.

BEING OPEN TO A DIFFERENT VISION

Previsualization is essential, but the following example also shows the need to keep an open mind. I had always wanted to shoot the concept of pressure using pipes that are about to burst as the metaphor. I set up a bunch of old pipes and gauges under the skylight of my studio so that I had a soft, even quality of light. I added a little warmth in post-production, but the image you see was pretty much straight out of the camera (**FIGURE 2.9A**). I was thrilled. It was just what I had always envisioned. I brought the image home only to have my young daughter look at it and say "Really, Dad, warm light is so 1995." I reworked the image in Photoshop, changing the color to a cool cyan/blue (**FIGURE 2.9B**). The change in color created a much more appropriate mood and really enhanced the image. I added the steam to finish off the concept (**FIGURE 2.9C**).

Listening to a different opinion helped to enhance my initial vision. In the end my daughter was right. (I hate it when she's right.)

—BRAD BARTHOLOMEW

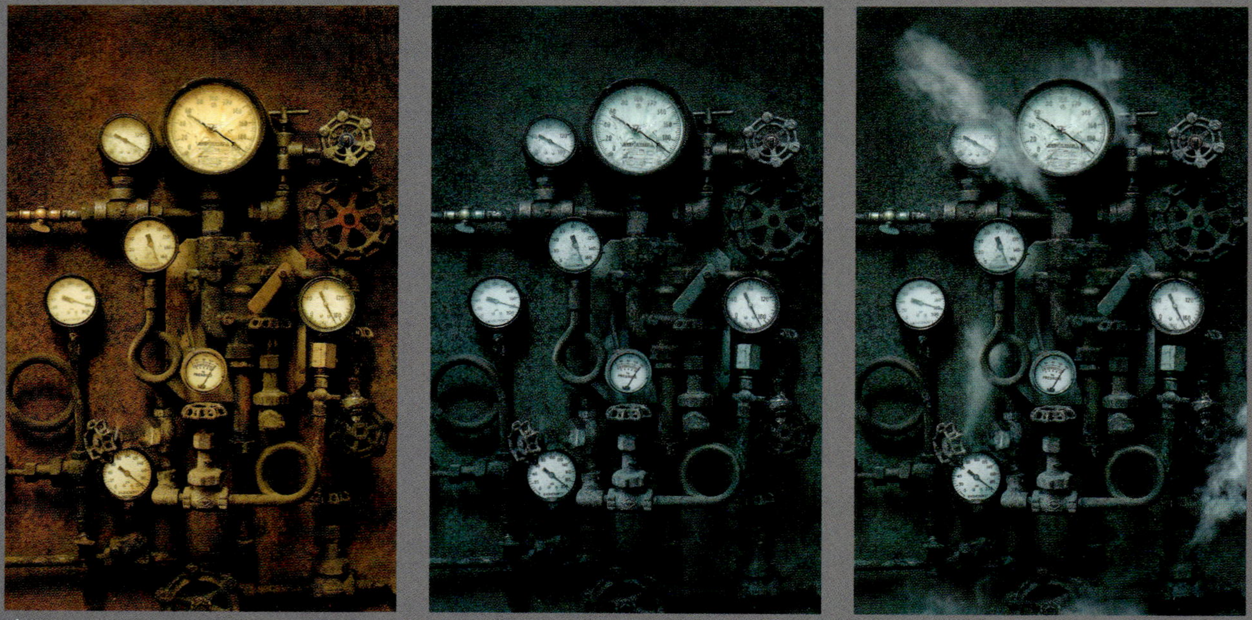

a) b) c)

FIGURE 2.9 a and **b)** How a simple change in the overall color cast of an image can radically change its mood; **c)** adding one more element, steam, completes the concept of pressure.

ISO 50, 1/4 sec., f/16, 150mm lens

- **Props:** These can be great, and they're often a necessary element in the visual story you are creating. You need to visualize how props will interact with the subject. If you use them, they should support, not overpower.
- **Set construction:** Never leave this to the last minute or to chance. Imagine what would happen if the director of a theatrical play didn't previsualize how the set enhanced the mood of the scene or interacted with the performers; the disconnect would certainly detract from the show. Again, the set doesn't have to be a major production. Sometimes a simple surface can make a big difference.
- **Lighting:** Lighting is the single element that connects all the former factors together. We're not only talking about direction and quality but also about how the light from one object affects the rest.

It's interesting to compare two similar but different images. The honey photos in FIGURE 2.10 are almost identical; they have the same subject, similar camera angles, and similar lighting, and both were photographed on a wood surface. However, the wood surface is rather different.

You can previsualize the lighting, honey, bowl, honey stick, and even a wood surface, but it's important to go beyond just any wood surface; you need to visualize which wood surface. It's not that one image is good and the other bad; they are simply different. The question is, which one were you expecting?

Visualizing Light

It can take some practice to previsualize light and how it interacts with all the elements in an image.

Try this simple exercise: On a bright, sunny day, sit down in a city environment and look at the light. Really look. See how the light from the sky falls onto one object and then reflects onto another. See how the shadow cast from one item connects with something else. Taking the time to see light when you are not the one creating it makes it easier to visualize what will happen when you light a set.

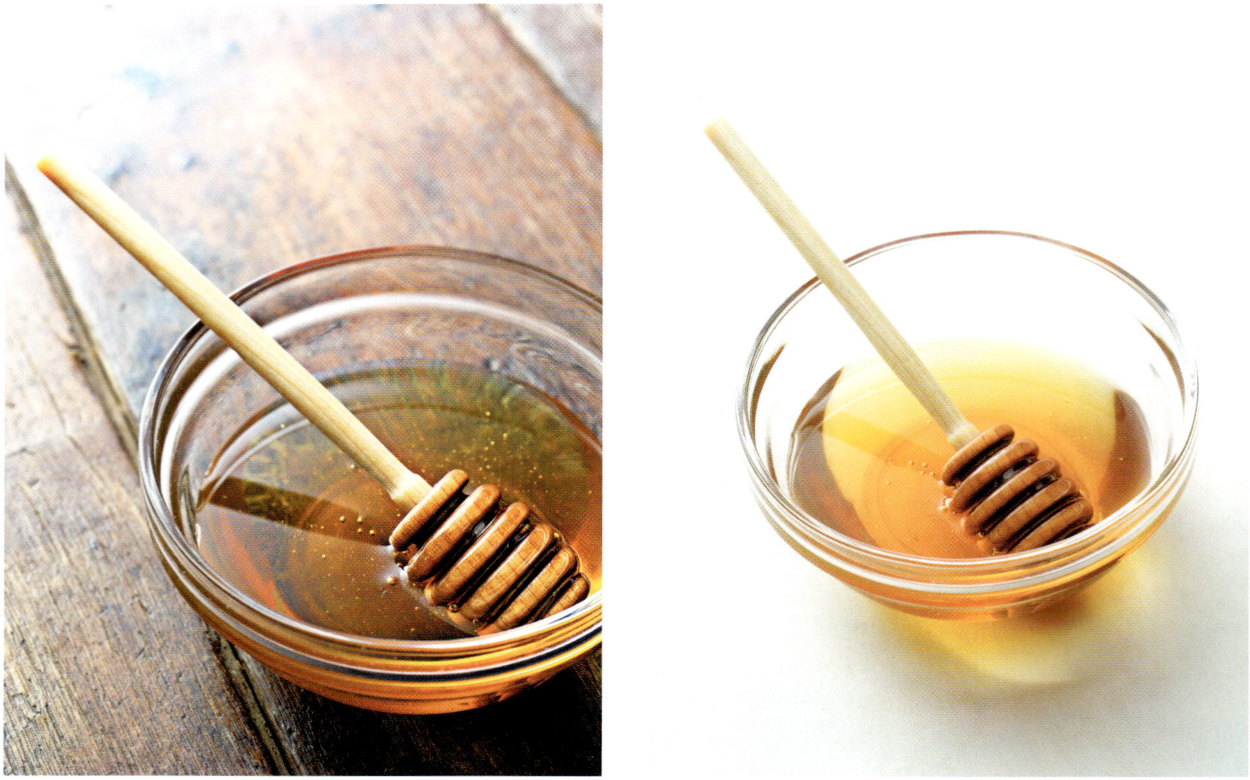

a) b)

FIGURE 2.10 **a)** Here, the rich, rustic wood creates an inviting cabin feel. The surface becomes part of the subject. **b)** The lighter wood surface provides a cleaner, almost clinical feel. The subject is clearly the honey bowl.

ISO 100, 1/125 sec., f/8, 150mm lens

Addition and Subtraction

We often think of lighting as the act of adding something to create an image. When the sun rises, it adds light to a scene, allowing the photographer to capture an image. In the studio, a photographer adds lights to illuminate the subject. Professional photographers do more than merely add light; they must control it. This means that there are times when they add light to an image and other times when they subtract it.

My general philosophy about lighting is to start with one light and get it to do exactly what you want it to do. Only then should you even consider adding another piece of lighting equipment. Here's the issue: When working with one light you can see exactly what that light is doing, but when you add a second light you see the combination of both lights. That's fine if everything looks great, but if it doesn't, which light is the problem?

So, I begin with one light, adjust its position, change its modifiers, and alter its output until it's right. At this point I determine whether I need to add a second light. Sometimes I decide one light is enough, and I may be able to use other options to add or subtract light. Whenever possible, it's easier to work with just one light source. One light also tends to look natural because we are accustomed to one light source in nature, the sun.

This chapter is called "The Building Process," and every process requires a plan. So, where to start?

Addition

The concept behind addition is at times we need to build upon a single light source to enhance, define, and elevate the subject. This is achieved by studying the subject and analyzing its key features and then adding the necessary light to achieve the lighting goals.

Key/Main Light

The terms *key* and *main* are often used interchangeably; both refer to the primary light source. You always begin with the key light. This light will determine the main highlight and directions of the shadows. Because it sets the overall mood and direction of an image, it's important to take the necessary time when determining this light. It's not that you can't come back and change the key light, but all the subsequent steps in the process will also need to be adjusted.

These images of the camera still life (**FIGURE 2.11**) show how slight variations in the key light can affect an image's starting point. The same light, modifier, and output were used for each; the only change was its position. The first image reveals good texture, but the overall image has too much contrast. The next image lowers the contrast but doesn't have the same overall pop and texture as the first one. The third brings back the texture detail and gives us a good starting point. The image still needs some work, but again, this is a building process.

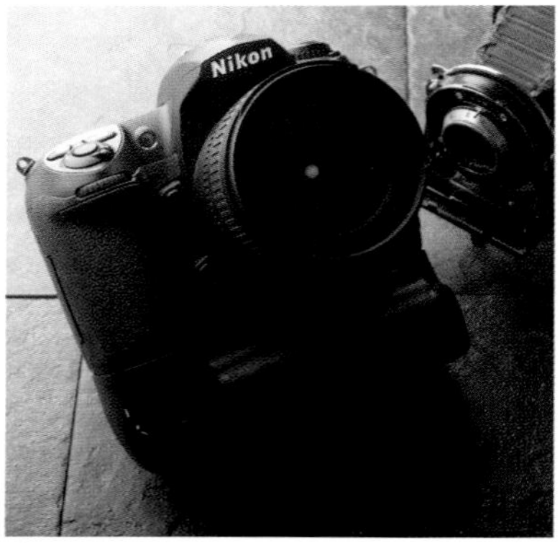

a)

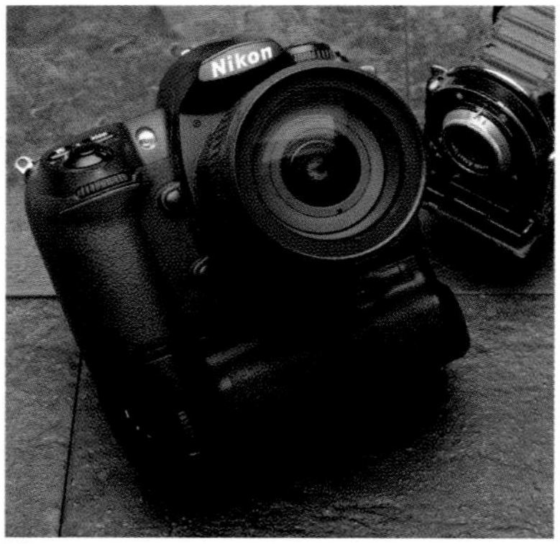

b)

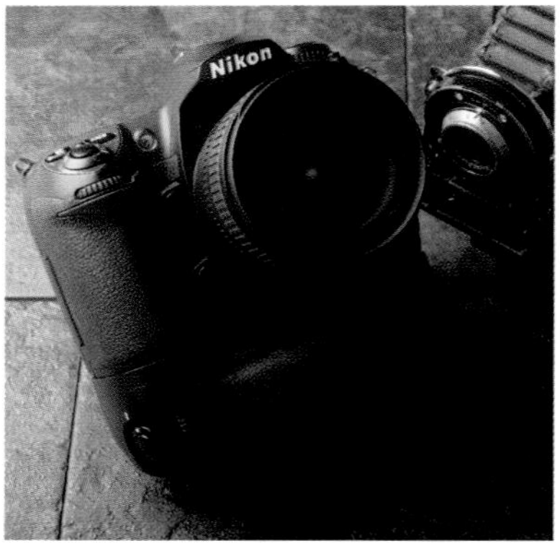

c)

FIGURE 2.11 a) The key light is low in the upper left quadrant and is slightly above the set. **b)** Here, the key light is almost directly above the subject. **c)** The final image splits the difference between the first two.

ISO 50, 1/60 sec., f/13, 80mm lens

Angle of Incidence Equals Angle of Reflection

Setting up mirrors and cards is just like making a bank shot in pool; the angle at which the ball hits the bank is the same angle at which the ball comes off the wall. Light works the same way. The card must be angled to catch the key light and then bounce light back onto the subject.

I am sure that many of you remember being outside and using a small mirror or watch to catch the sun and reflect it into a sibling's eye; that is angle of incidence equaling the angle of reflection (**FIGURE 2.12**).

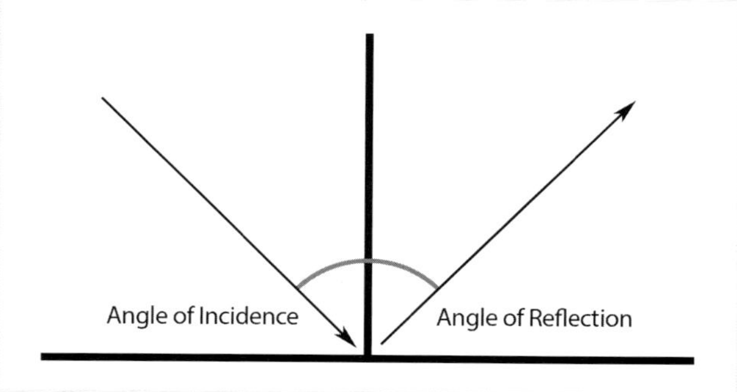

FIGURE 2.12 Angle of incidence equals angle of reflection is one of the key principles for controlling light.

Cards and Mirrors

Where do we go from here? Although the texture looks good on the camera, the shadows are dark, and we can't see all the detail. As someone who always starts with one light, I want to see whether white cards, mirrors, or both are the right tools to complete the image.

Cards and mirrors serve a similar purpose in that they both reflect light from the key light onto the subject, thus working as part of the *addition* process. They are both simple ways to add light into an image without worrying about another light, power settings, modifiers, and so on.

A white card has been added to the lower right side of the set just outside the view of the camera. You can see how the bottom and right side of the camera get a little brighter and more detail starts to appear (**FIGURE 2.13A**). Thinking that the image still could use a bit more depth, I decided to see whether adding a mirror would help. The mirror added a little ray of light from the upper right corner (**FIGURE 2.13B**).

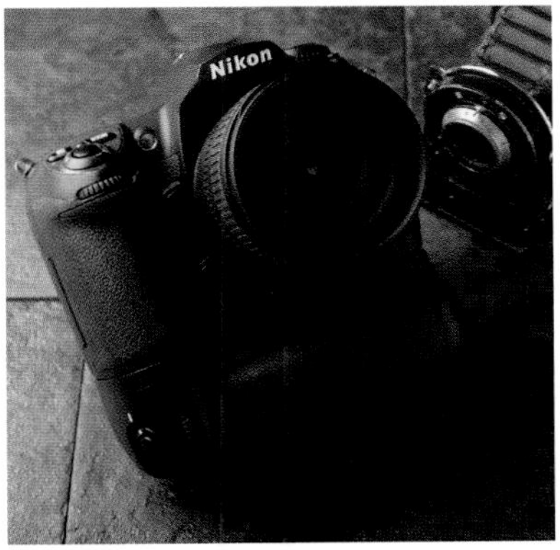

a)

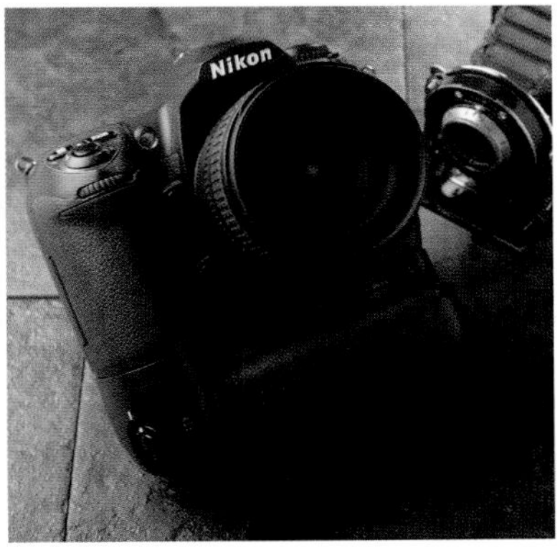

b)

FIGURE 2.13 **a)** Key light plus white card; **b)** key light plus white card and mirror.

ISO 50, 1/60 sec., f/13, 80mm lens

Fill Light

A fill light is exactly what it sounds like; it's a second light that's added to fill the shadows. The idea is to use the fill light to add a subtle amount of light to the darker values of the image without drawing attention to itself. Generally, a modifier is added to the light to create a soft, almost shadowless quality of light. In the final camera still life image (**FIGURE 2.14**), a fill light was placed directly above the set. You can see that the highlight values haven't been altered, but now the shadow detail is visible. **FIGURE 2.15** is an image of the actual lighting setup.

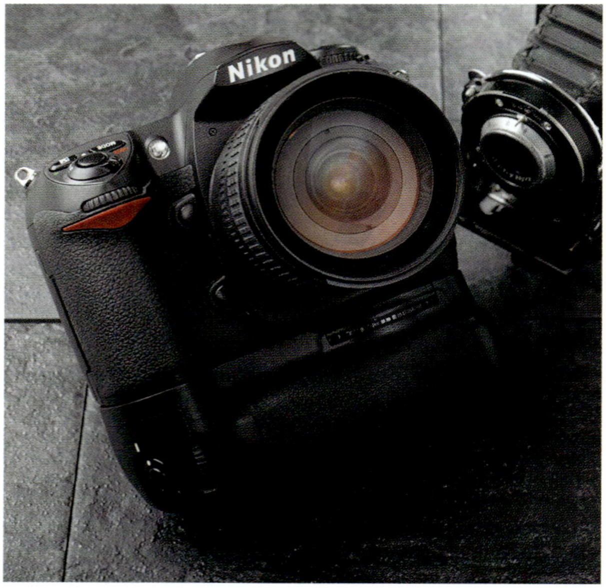

FIGURE 2.14 Camera still life lit with key light, fill light, mirror, and white card.

ISO 50, 1/60 sec., f/13, 80mm lens

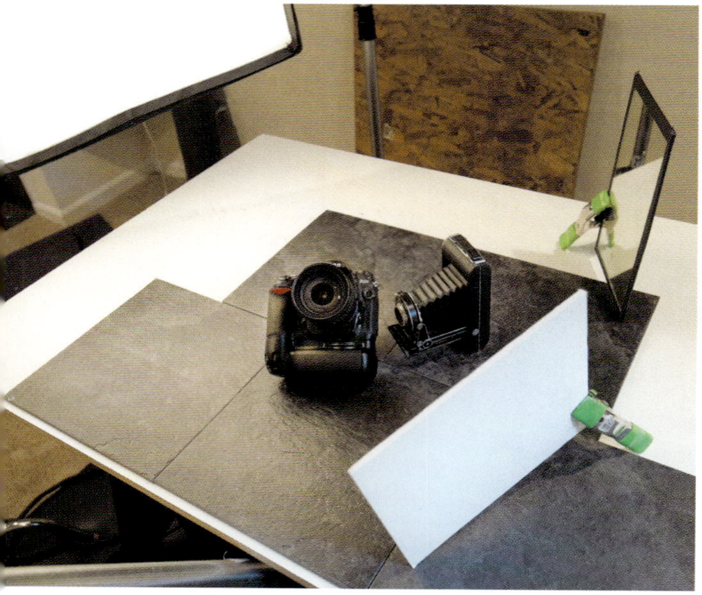

FIGURE 2.15 In this image, notice the use of white bounce board and mirror to direct light onto the subject.

Subtraction

Subtraction is a key lighting skill that really gives a photographer control over his or her images. One may ask, why is subtraction needed if a person has different light modifiers and lighting tools to carefully place light? The reason is that it's common to run into subjects with a mix of bright and dark areas or surfaces that both absorb or reflect light. It's all about control.

The concept behind subtraction is to carefully reduce the amount of light falling on part of the subject without affecting other areas. You can use subtraction to control a large or small portion of an image; it all depends on the subject matter.

Beverages are one of my favorite subjects, and living in Colorado, I've gained much experience photographing beers. Fun subject, but the white head on a beer creates a challenging lighting scenario (FIGURE 2.16). As you can see, the tops of the beers have little detail.

Gobo and Flag

The terms *gobo* and *flag* are often used interchangeably. Gobo stands for go-between, meaning you place something that goes between the light and the subject. *Flag* is often used as a verb to describe an action, such as, "I need to flag the light." Despite the different phrasing, they both refer to subtracting some of the light falling on the subject. When used as a noun, flag is synonymous with gobo.

Pretty much any item can be used as a gobo, but the more common ones include black matte or gator boards and diffusion material. Dots and fingers are commercial gobos that are made of different mesh material to allow a controlled amount of light to pass through. You can purchase a variety of sizes and a variety of levels of diffusion.

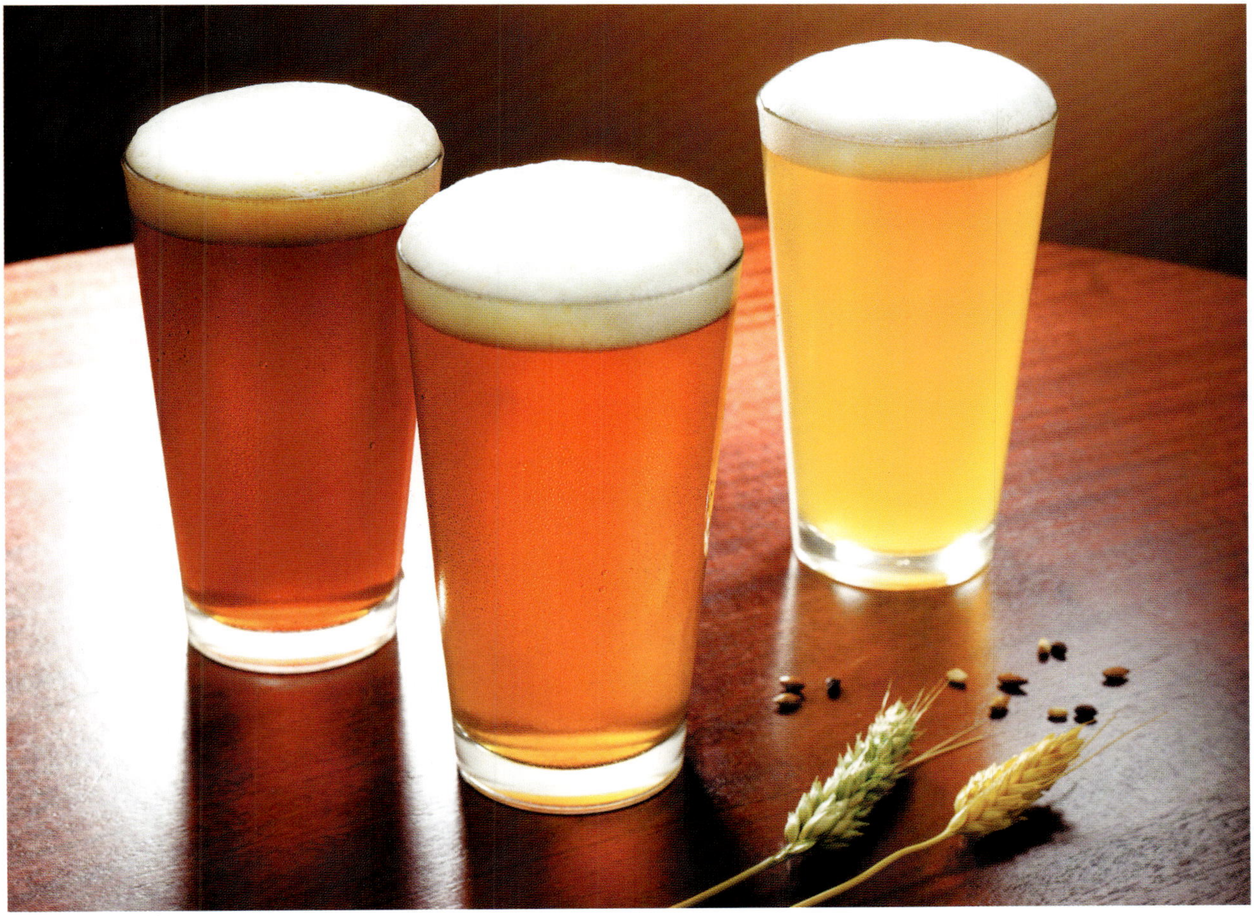

FIGURE 2.16 Without added controls, the tops of the beers have lost detail.

ISO 50, 1/60 sec., f/16, 100mm lens

More Subtraction

Brad: Have you found that your students do not subtract light from parts of images as often as they should?

Joe: My experience has been that too much time is spent learning to add fill light to images and not enough time is given to subtracting light from areas of a shot. Educators, myself included, are always harping on shadow detail and the need to fill shadows with light. There is a place for that, to be sure, but I encourage students to subtract light as well. Take light off the background to increase dimension and drama within your shots. Reduce highlights with flags to make sure you're maintaining highlight detail.

The second beer image (**FIGURE 2.17**) is the same setup, but now, a small gobo has been placed between the light and each of the heads of beer. Notice how this slight subtraction of light allows the detail to show. The lighting diagram (**FIGURE 2.18**) shows the position of the gobos.

Creating a beautiful photographic image is not like building a model airplane from a kit. There is no concrete set of instructions to guide you. You may have a layout to steer you in the right direction, but many of the decisions you make will be the result of educated choices.

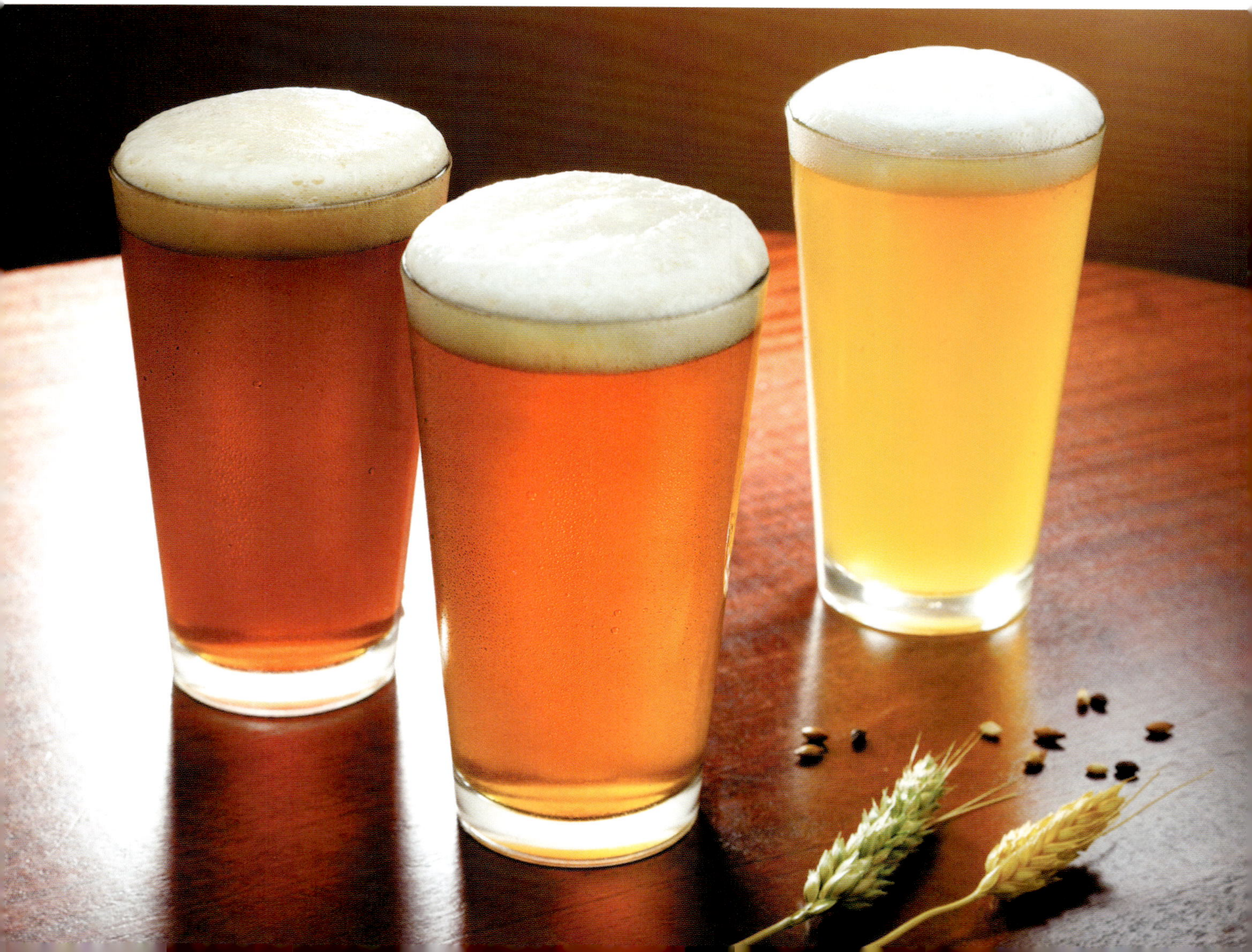

FIGURE 2.17 The use of gobos in this image brought back the desired detail in the heads of the beer.

ISO 50, 1/60 sec., f/16, 100mm lens

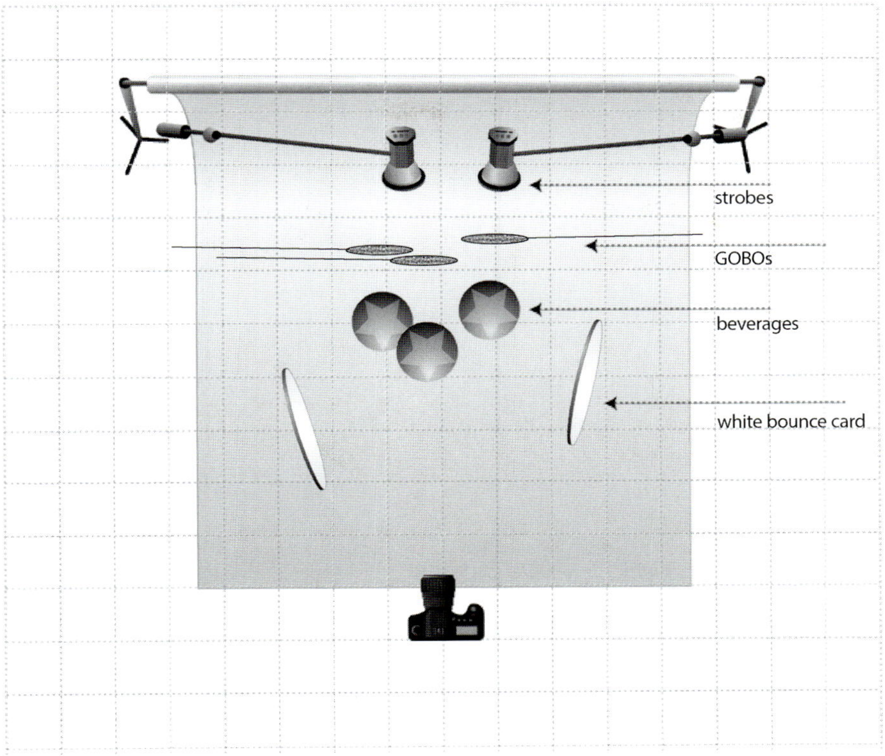

FIGURE 2.18 The angle of incidence equaling the angle of reflection means that the gobo needs to be slightly behind, not directly above, the beer.

As discussed, fully understanding your subject and knowing what you want to say about it are the first steps to constructing a successful image. Asking the right basic questions will help you assess the look and feel an image should have before you actually take the photograph. Once you know the direction you want, you can add and subtract light until you build the final result you envisioned. Great images integrate light into the composition.

Comparison

Throughout the book we'll be presenting a comparison of images taken by the authors. Sometimes we'll use the exact same subject, and others we'll use a similar subject, such as for this chapter. The only parameter here was that we both had to photograph an apple or apples in the studio. Clearly, we took a different approach, but that is the beauty of photography (FIGURE 2.19).

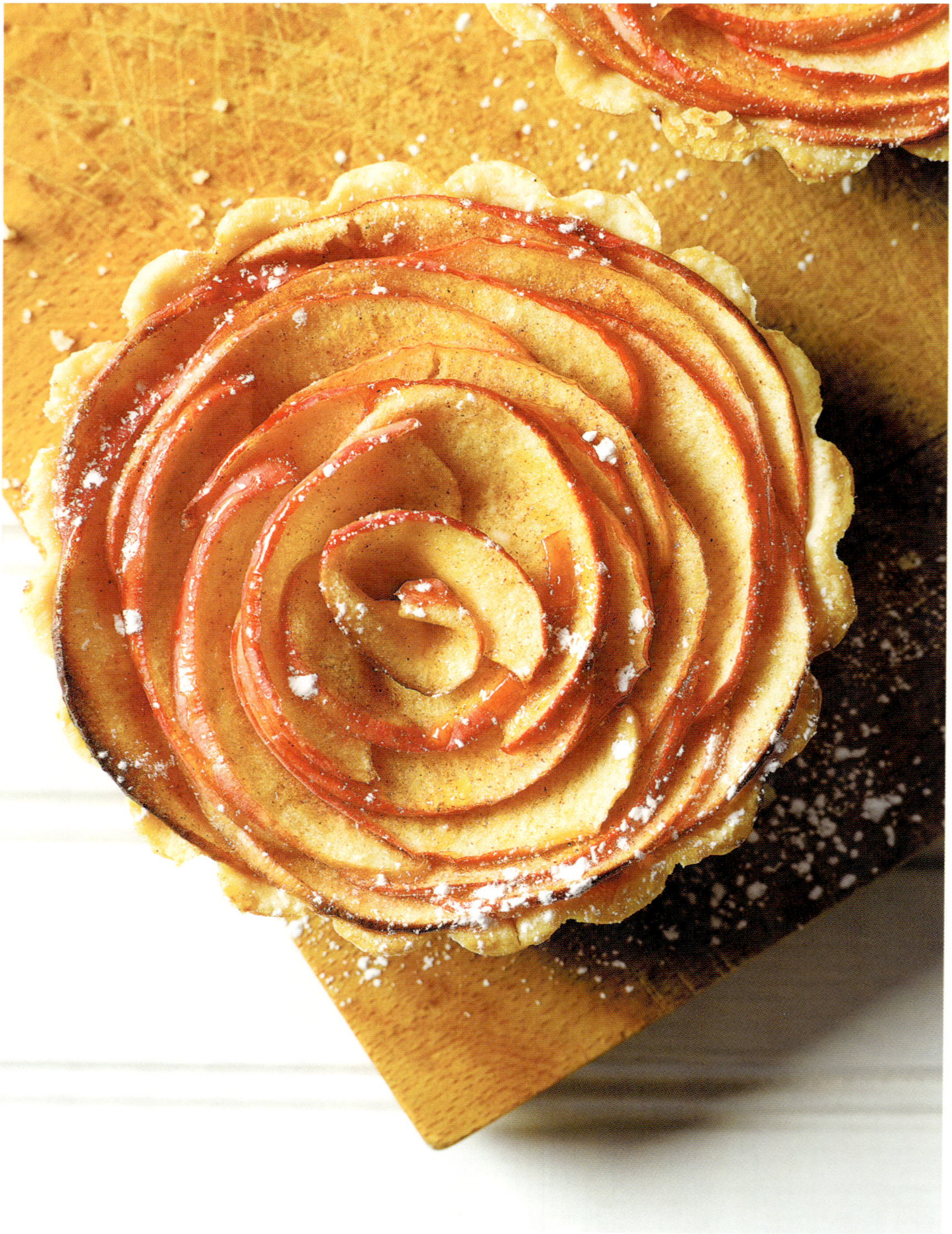

a)

ISO 50, 1/60 sec., f/8.5 , 150mm lens

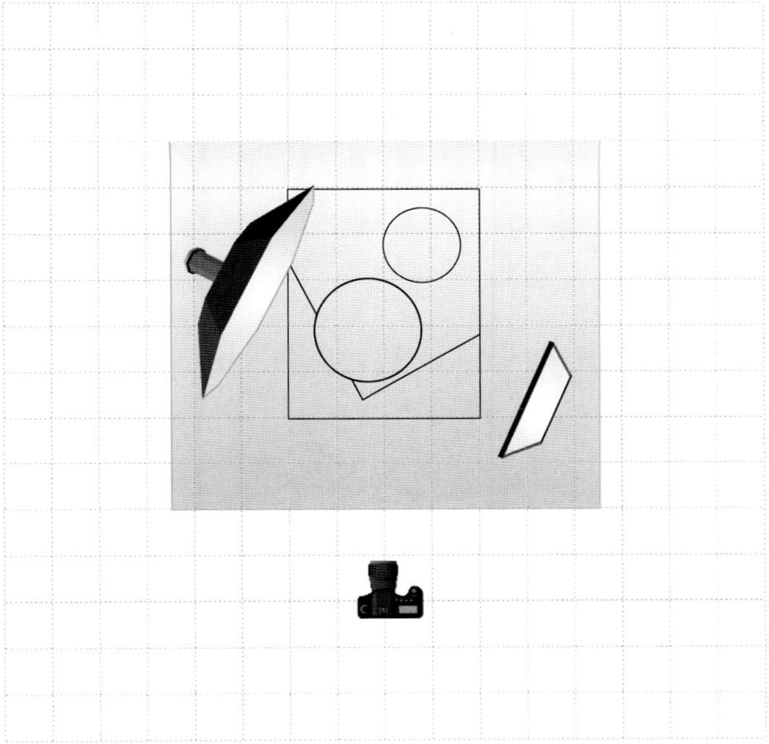

b)

FIGURE 2.19 **a)** Apple tart: The original concept for this image was based on a low camera angle showing coffee and a window in the background, but after trying a handful of versions, we decided the top-down look worked best. **b)** The small octagon-shaped softbox allowed just the right amount of wraparound light.

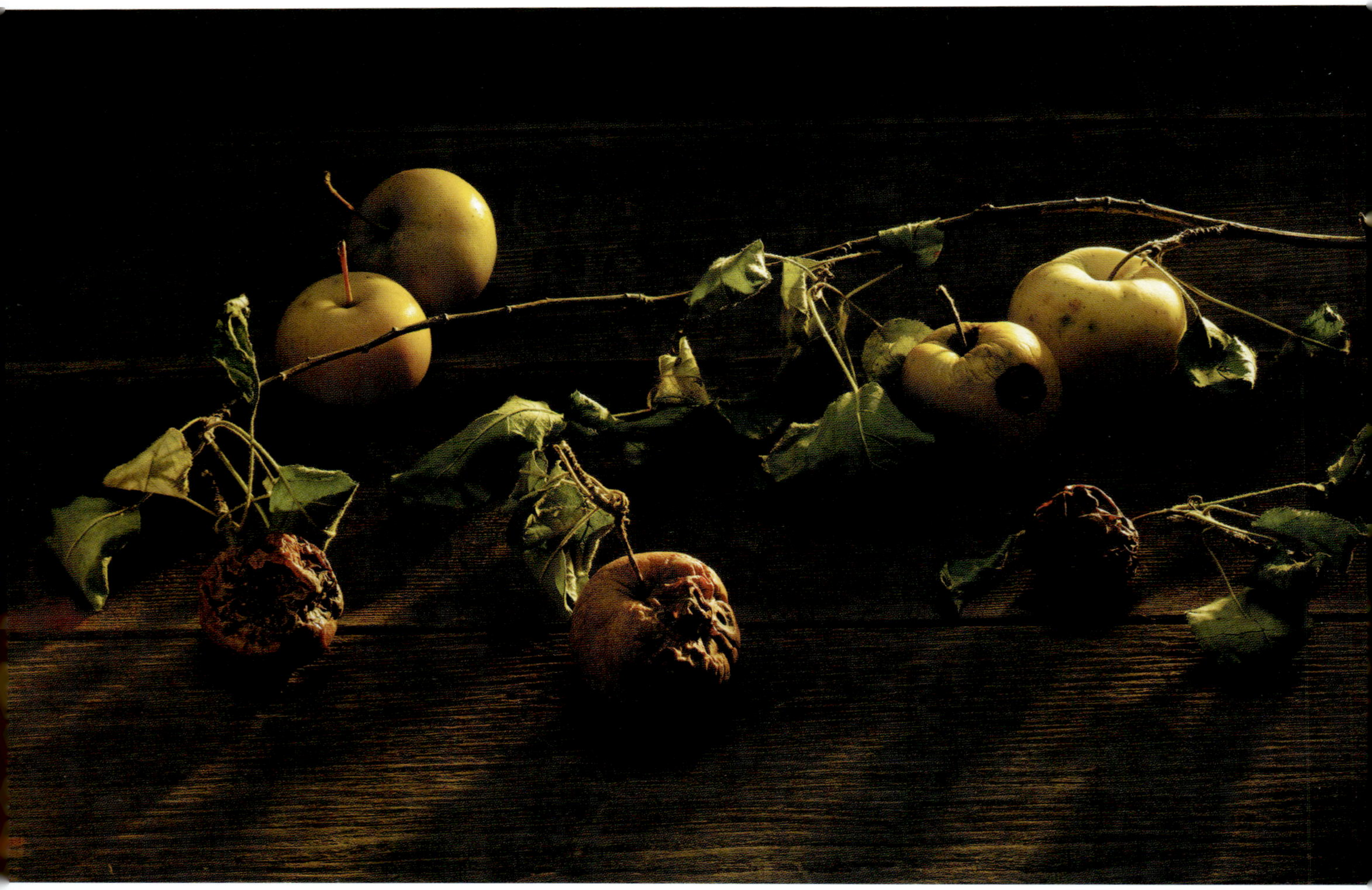

c)

ISO 100, 20 sec., f/4.5, 150mm lens

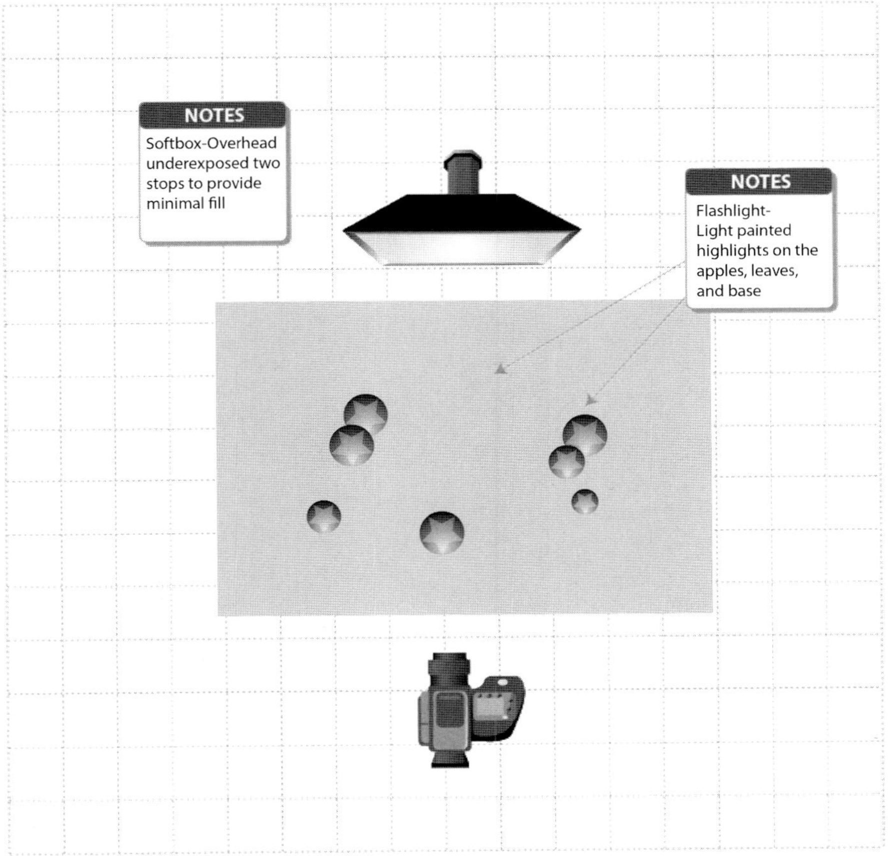

d)

FIGURE 2.19 **c)** Sometimes ideas just come to you, which was the case when we were doing a little prewinter backyard cleanup. **d)** The strobe in the softbox was triggered first, and then with the room totally dark, we used a flashlight to add the direction of light.

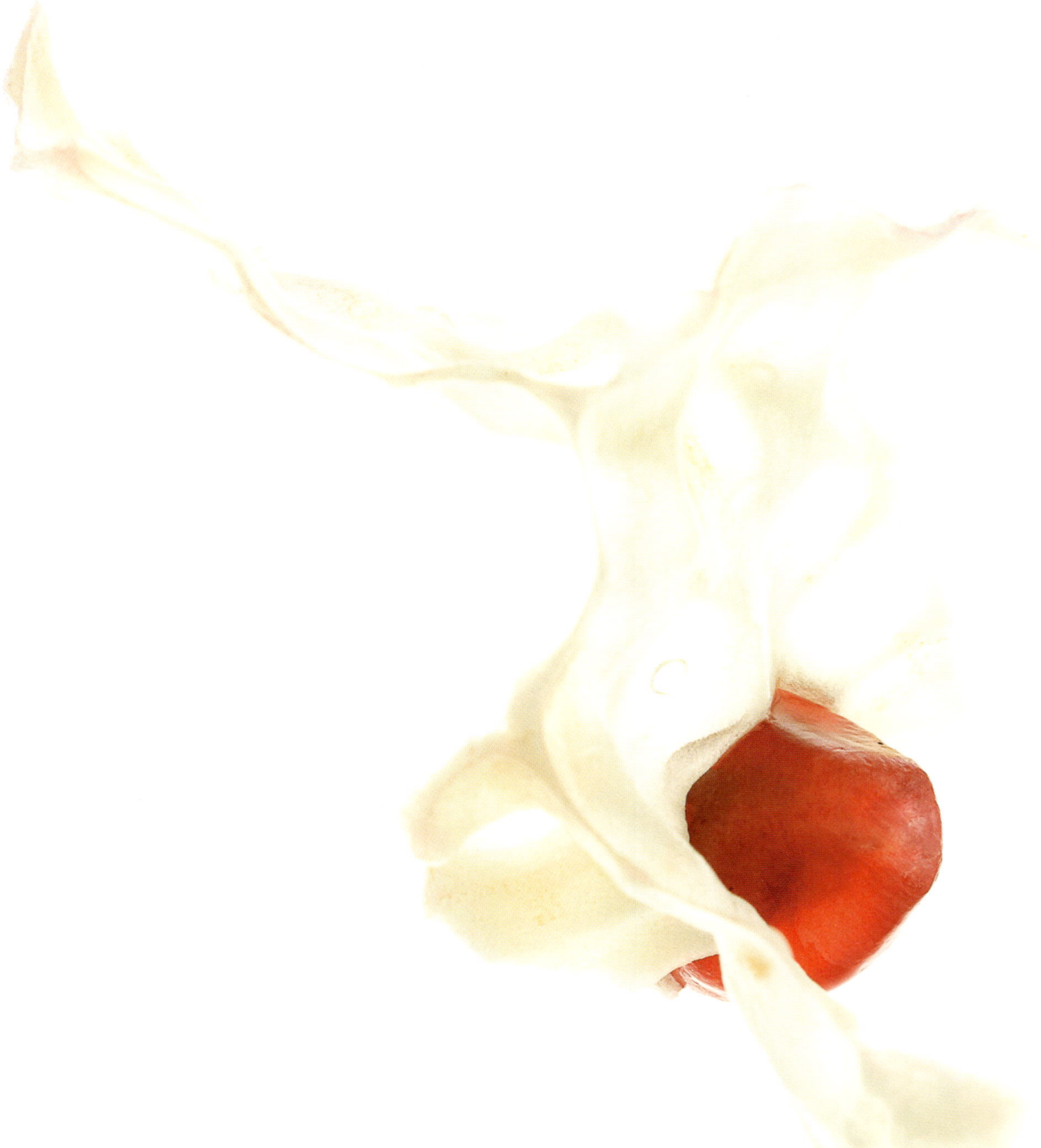

chapter three

LIGHTING AS PART OF COMPOSITION

Proper lighting is more than achieving the right exposure. Exposure is easy; today's modern cameras and meters make getting a good exposure almost a foregone conclusion, and when in doubt, you always have the image histogram to confirm whether the exposure is correct. We all know people who claim to be accomplished photographers because their family vacation pictures look good on social media sites or because they captured a pretty sunset while visiting the islands. The lighting might be exposed properly, but what did they do?

ISO 50, 1/60 sec., f/16, 100mm lens

Opening Image: Photographic Equipment

Camera: Sinar 4 × 5 view camera with Leaf Valeo 22 Digital Back

Lens: Nikkor 100mm

Lighting: Profoto Acute2

Light modifiers: Small softbox and custom-built glass set

Simple but effective: One hundred percent of the light for the image on the previous page is coming from below the set and shining through the subject.

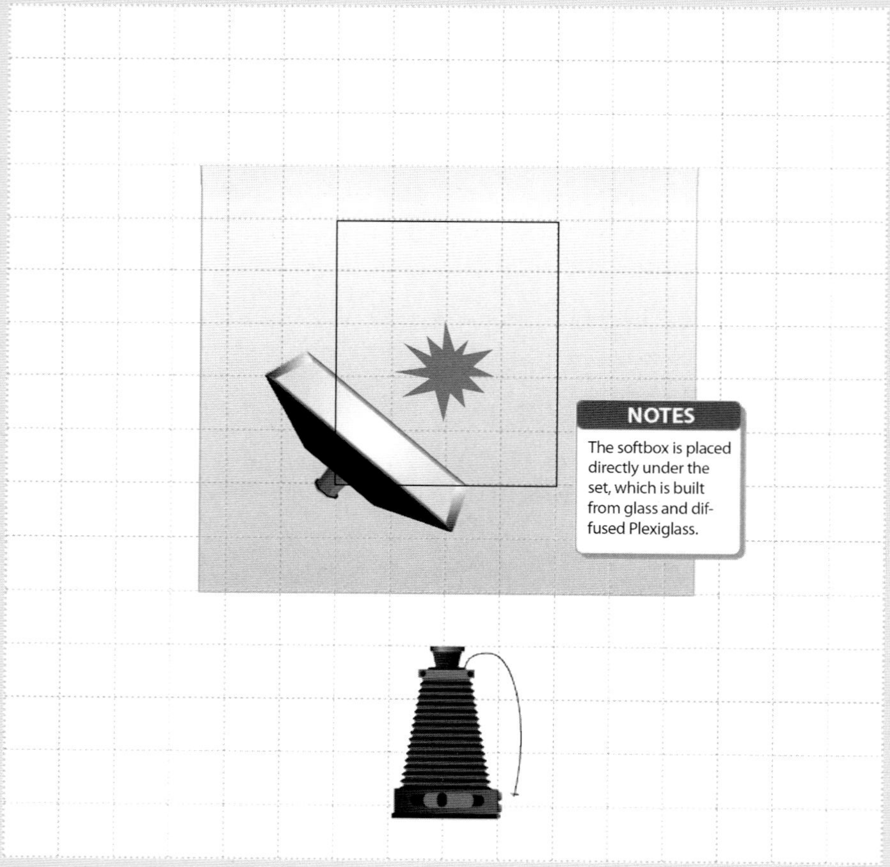

Creating a magnificent image requires the artist to have control over all of his or her tools. Think about Claude Monet's *Water Lilies*, Vincent Van Gogh's *Starry Night*, and Rembrandt's portraits, and consider how your eyes move through the images. It's not merely the subject matter that brings the painting to life but the artist's control over his medium. Just as a painter controls paint and brush, a photographer must control the placement of light.

Lighting helps tell the story. You can have the greatest subject and the best arrangement, but it's the light that brings life to an image. We refer to this as "lighting as part of composition." Your eyes travel through an image with good composition; your gaze lands where the photographer intended and then moves along almost as if you are following a path with arrows. The lighting becomes an element in the image, not merely the means to proper exposure.

Direct the Viewer's Eye

It may sound odd, but a good studio photographer needs to be a puppet master and control the viewer—or at least the viewer's eyes. It's the job of the professional photographer to guide the viewer through an image.

The idea is to give the image a key element that catches the viewer's attention, and then use a supporting cast to move and hold his or her attention in the image. It's important to ask yourself why you find an image interesting. Even the most intriguing subject will warrant only a passing glance unless there is something to hold interest. Light plays a big role in how an image is experienced. Again, we are going beyond proper exposure; we want to see how light becomes part of the composition.

The following still life images of the three wineglasses and cork (FIGURE 3.1A and B) are identical, except for the lighting. The exposure is spot-on in the first image. If we were merely lighting for exposure this would be great; however, a professional photograph requires more; it demands that the subject, exposure, and lighting work together to create the overall composition. The second image has more character. Again, the subjects and camera have not changed, but the lighting has been altered to add greater depth—some would say more soul. No longer does the still life comprise only the glasses and cork but also rose highlights cast by the wine and directional shadows that move your eyes across the scene.

FIGURE 3.1 **a)** The softbox is placed directly above the subject; **b)** the subject is lit with a 10-degree grid, which creates a spotlight effect.

ISO 100, 1/125 sec., f/11, 100mm macro lens

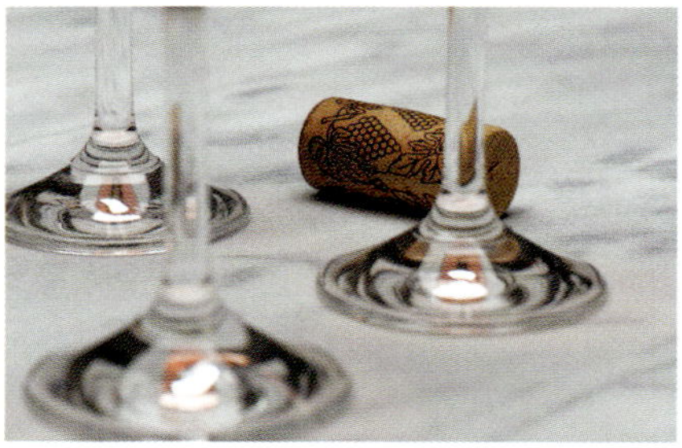

a)

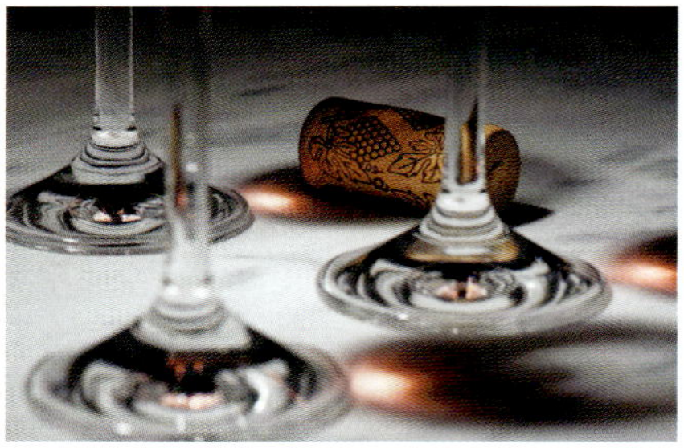

b)

Jan Oswald, Artist with Light

Parts of this section will take a slightly different approach than usual, analyzing the images of the well-known photographer Jan Oswald.

A comfortable use of lighting often mimics how books are read, from left to right. Simply put, it's natural for us to move our vision across a page, and thus across an image. *Zen Tulips* (FIGURE 3.2) is a comfortable image; it's easy on the eyes. There is no incredibly creative or dramatic lighting, but the direction of light begins on the left and then gently moves across the image. The flow travels from the blue vase, along the green stems, and finally comes to rest on the red tulips. The composition and lighting work together.

The lighting in *Single Calla on Painted Background* (FIGURE 3.3) follows a similar path as with *Zen Tulips*, but here we have an image with a completely

TWENTY-PLUS YEARS IN THE MAKING

I feel extremely fortunate to be able to share Jan Oswald's images for this part of the book. As a very young photographer, I moved to Colorado to enjoy the outdoor lifestyle and to pursue my studio photography career. As luck would have it, Jan was one of the first photographers that I called, and one of the first who gave me a shot at working as a photography assistant. Jan taught me a ton about studio lighting, food photography, and how to be a professional photographer. Twenty-plus years later, she still introduces me as her old assistant and tells everyone that she taught me everything that I know. She is probably right.

—JOE LAVINE

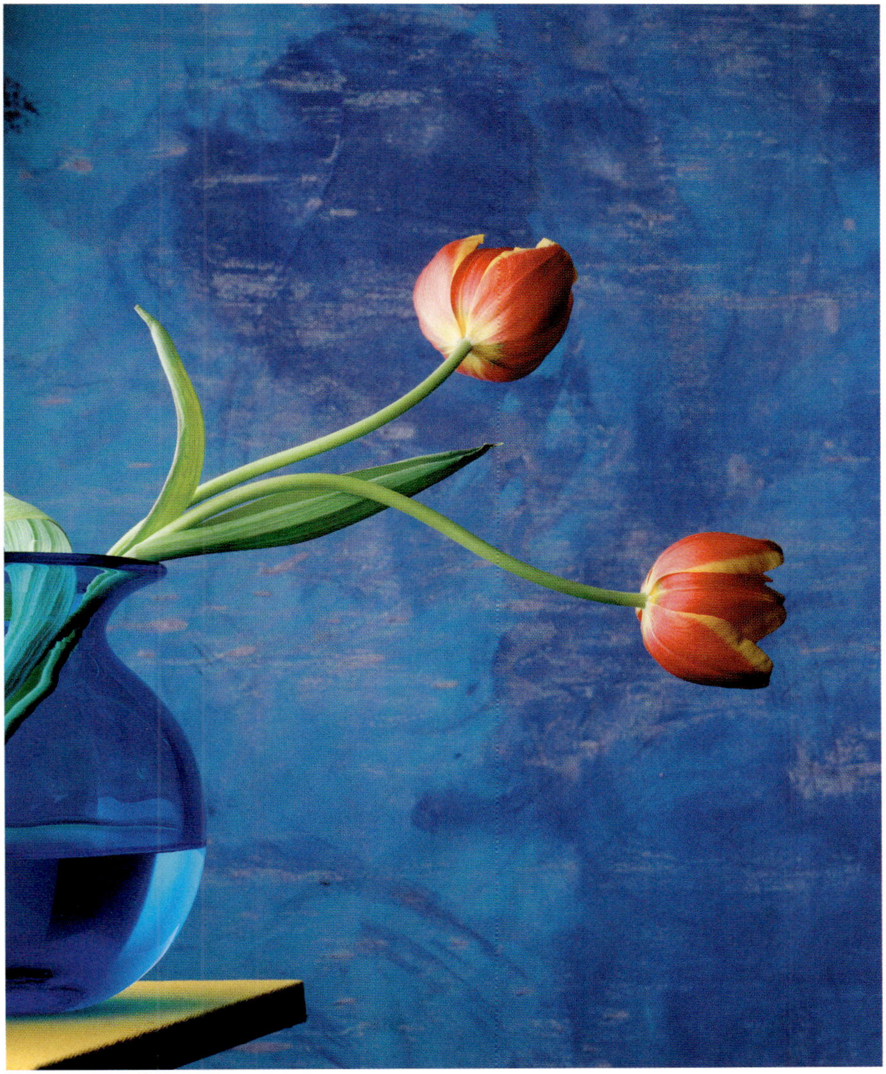

FIGURE 3.2 *Zen Tulips*, by Jan Oswald

ISO 64, 1/250 sec., f/32, 150mm lens

different energy. Where the previous image was comfortable, now we have drama. Interestingly, the subjects of the two images are soft, sensual flowers, but it's the photographic treatment that is different. Again, the lighting works with the image and not against it. The background of the image, and the curve of the calla lily, convey motion, almost as if the wind is blowing from left to right. Notice the highlight side and shadow side. The left

FIGURE 3.3 *Single Calla on Painted Background*, by Jan Oswald

ISO 64, 1/250 sec., f/32, 150mm lens

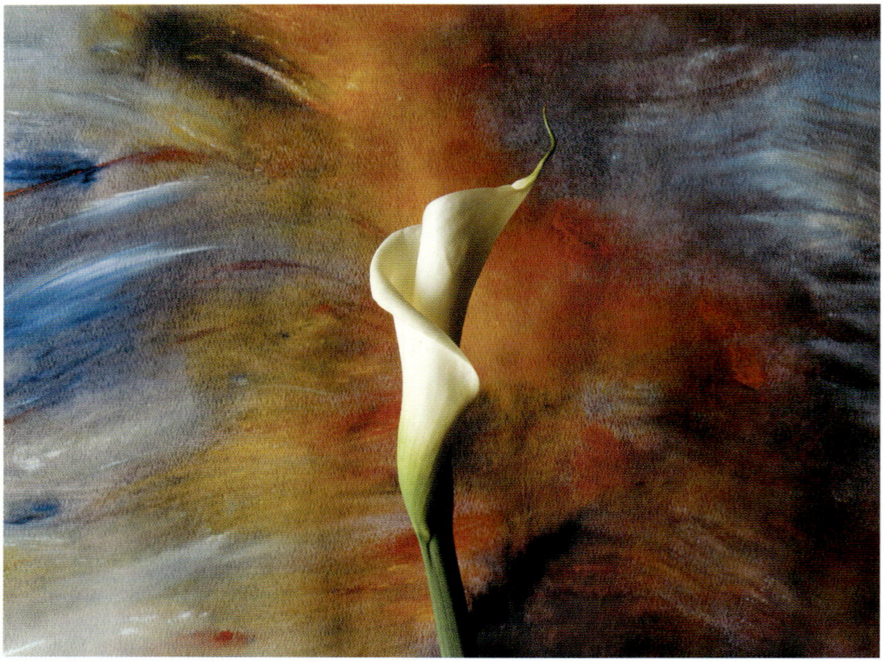

FIGURE 3.4 *Melon on Blue Plate*, by Jan Oswald

ISO 64, 1/250 sec., f/32, 150mm lens

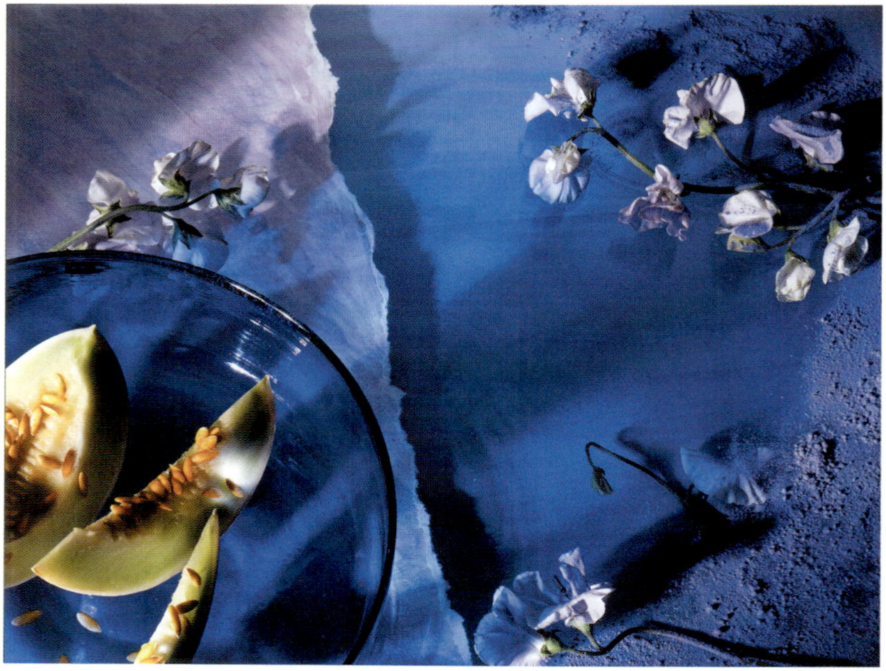

highlight side mirrors the bright area of the background, while the shadow portion tucks behind, mimicking the far right. Everything about the image—subject, background, and lighting—contributes to the composition of the final image.

When is it OK to break the rules? Lighting aside, *Melon on Blue Plate* (**FIGURE 3.4**) breaks a handful of basic design rules. First, there is a dividing line that splits the image in two, and then the flowers on the right compete for attention with the melon on the left. So, why does the image work? It's the lighting—the lighting connects the two sides. You could say that it creates a bridge spanning the dividing line. The highlights on the melon and flowers are the two brightest areas of the image, telling the viewer of their importance. The connection is solidified by the shadow cast by the melons and ends directly in front of the flowers, leading the viewer across the scene.

There is little doubt in *Watching* (**FIGURE 3.5**) about where Jan wanted the visual focus to be. Unlike the previous examples, *Watching* provides us with a bulls-eye of light. It's not a spot of light only in the center but rather a pool of light directed from the left that enhances the subject. Whereas the leaves are lit to show texture, the same lighting focuses our gaze on the only part of the image without texture. Other photographic elements that enhance the image are the warm-versus-cool color palette and the geometrical circular pattern.

The common thread so far has been that the lighting is part of the composition and not merely a tool for exposure.

In a departure from floral images, Jan Oswald's *Still Life with Broken Glass* (**FIGURE 3.6**), from her *Dutch Masters* series, closely resembles the lighting characteristics of the great master painters. The subject is no single object, but rather all the elements as a whole.

Unless done carefully, this approach makes it easy to end up with an image that has no focal point and thus is easy to dismiss. *Still Life with Broken Glass* uses carefully controlled highlights to direct the viewer's attention around the image; we move from element to element, never losing attention.

FIGURE 3.5 *Watching*, by Jan Oswald (following page)

ISO 64, 20 sec., f/32, 150mm lens

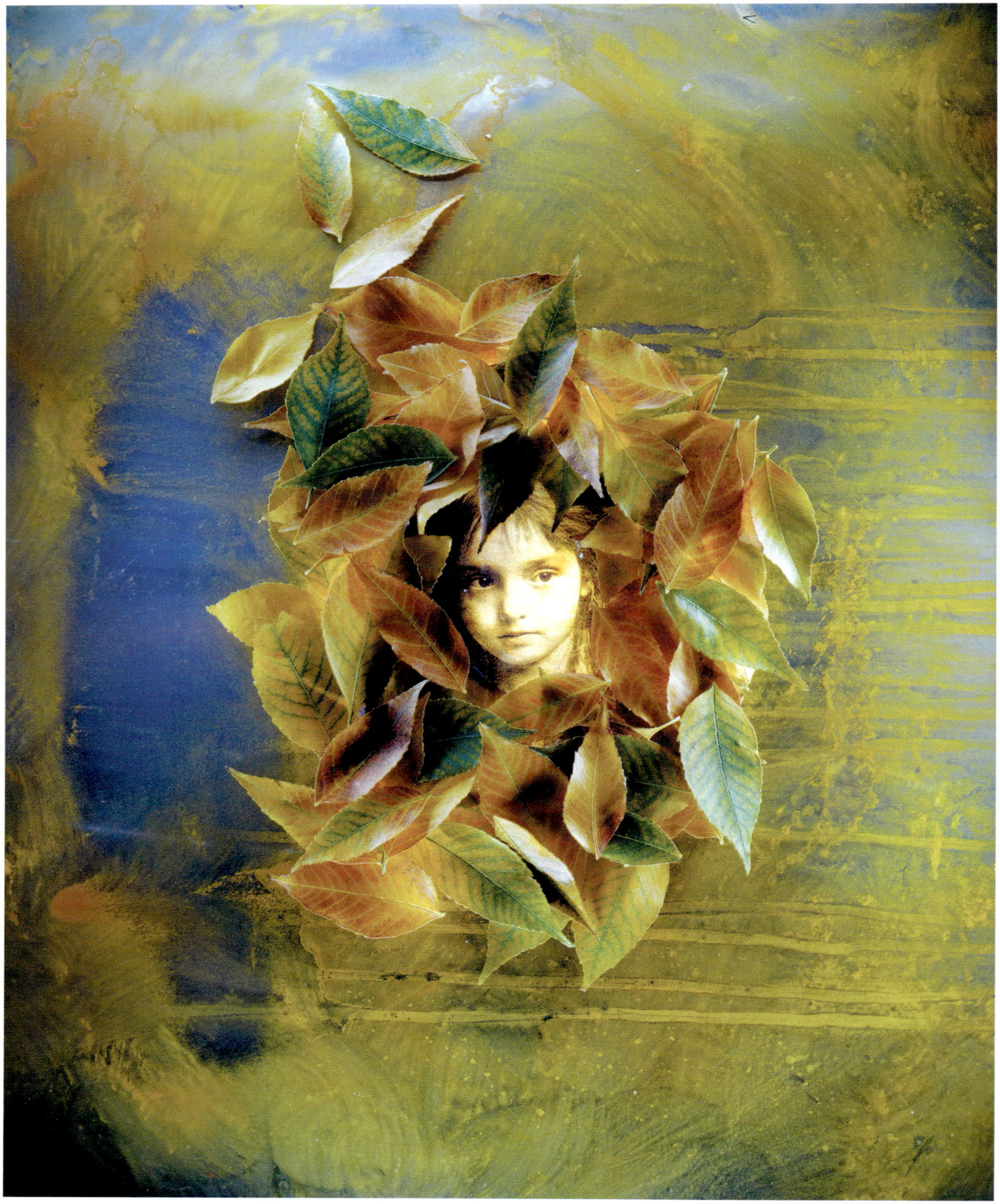

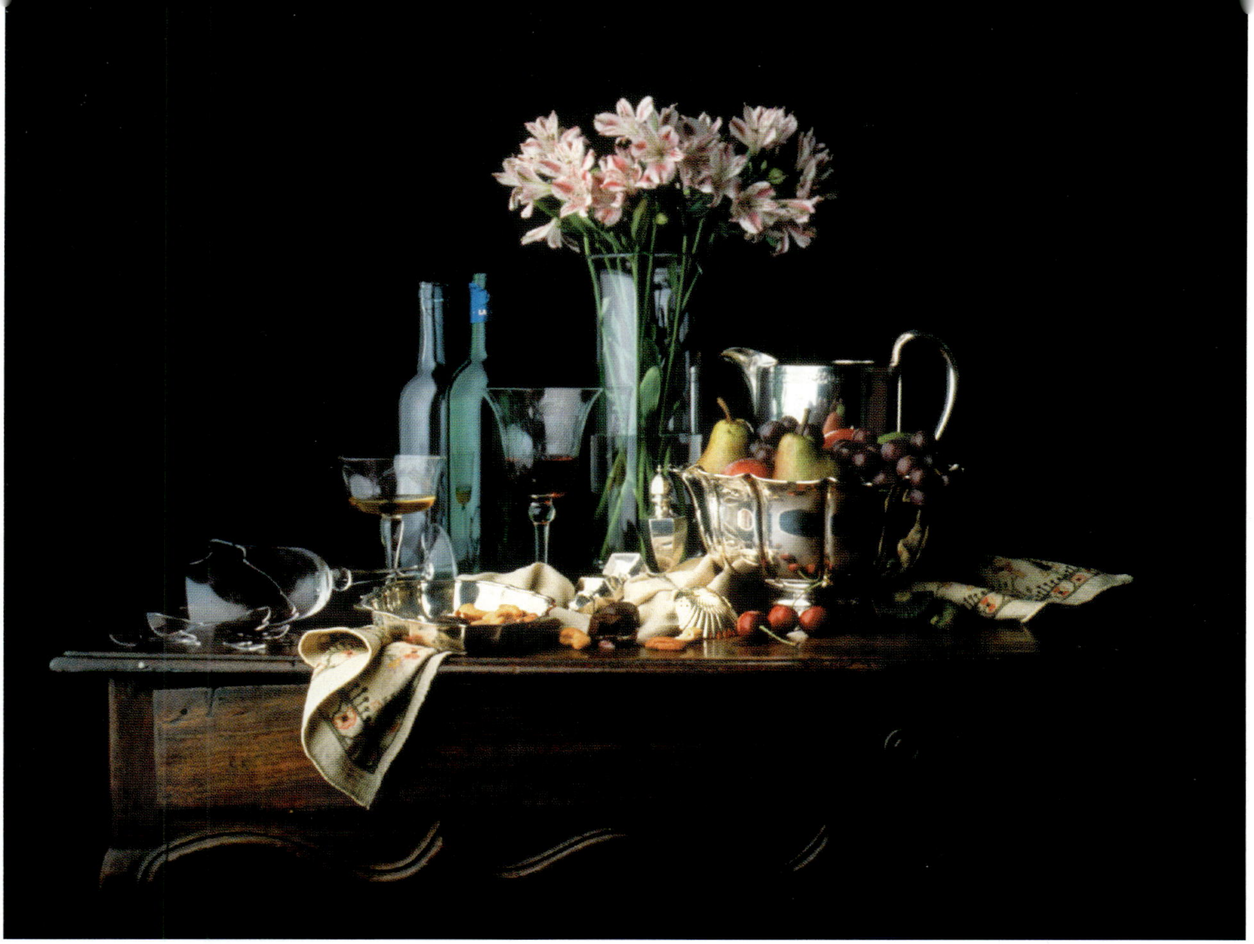

FIGURE 3.6 *Still Life with Broken Glass*, by Jan Oswald

ISO 64, 1/250 sec., f/22, 310mm lens

BLURRING VISION

It can often be difficult to understand why we are drawn to certain areas of an image and not others. A simple trick that I learned years ago when viewing images on a monitor or book is to sit back a few feet and blur your vision slightly. Because you can no longer distinguish objects, your mind will focus on elements with the greatest contrast, whether that is based on light versus dark or on colors. These are the areas that you tend to be drawn to.

Try this technique with *Still Life with Broken Glass*. When I do it, I am quickly drawn to the highlights on each element.

—JOE LAVINE

Subject Hierarchy

Along with directing the viewer's eye, lighting also tells us what is important in an image, or its hierarchy. It's common to have multiple objects in a scene, but how does someone know what the main subject is? As photographers we have many tools at our disposal; we have composition, depth of field, and—sometimes overlooked—we have lighting to help control subject hierarchy. One of the more difficult tasks as a professional photographer is to guide the

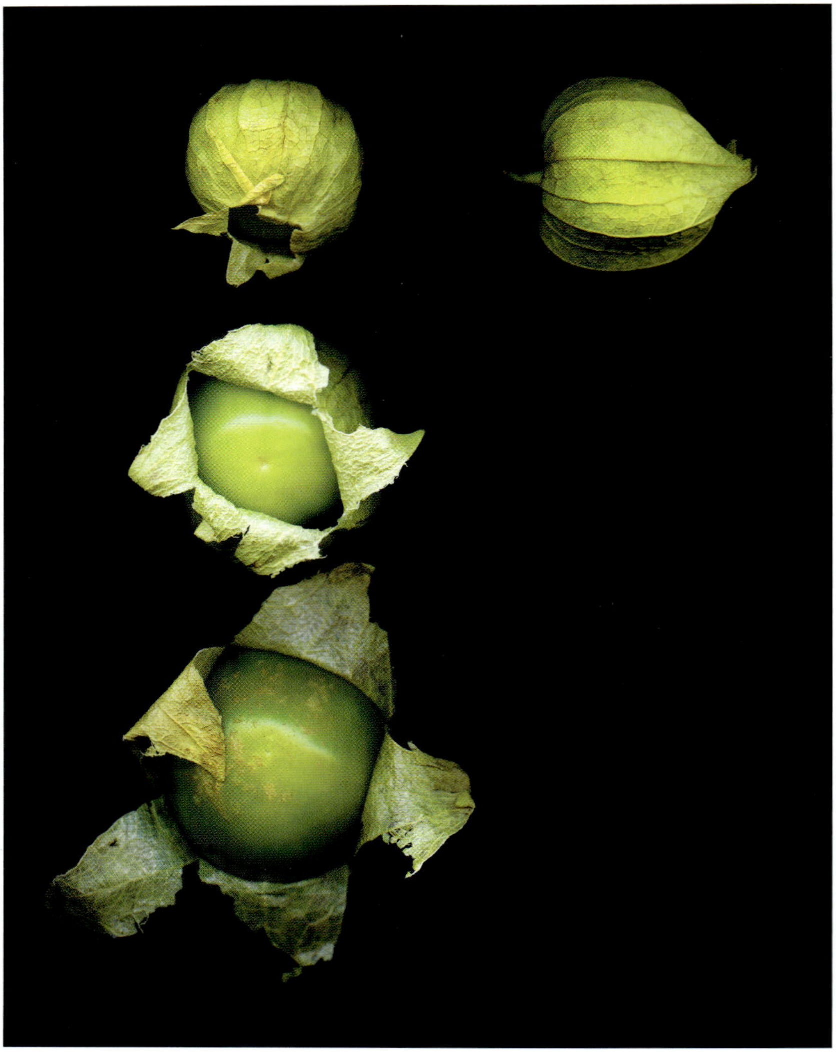

FIGURE 3.7 These tomatillos demonstrate how simple lighting variance directs viewers.

ISO 100, 1/125 sec., f/5.6, 100mm lens

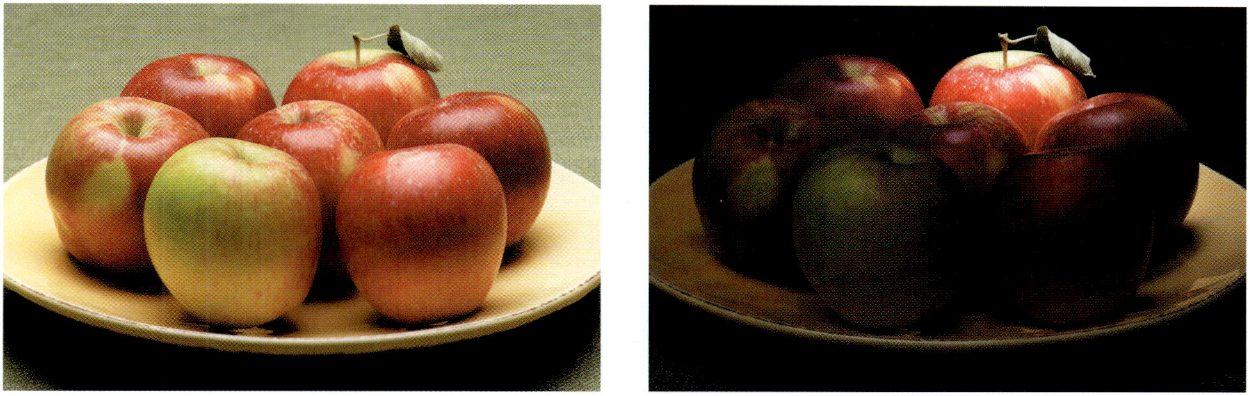

a) b)

FIGURE 3.8 **a)** A well-exposed still life of apples with no standout; **b)** spotlighting a single apple makes it the hero.

ISO 100, 1/125 sec., f/22, 100mm lens

viewer to where you, as the artist, want that person to look. It's important to use as many techniques as necessary to direct the viewer's gaze.

An easy way to think about this concept is to relate it to contrast control. If everything in an image is neutral gray, then nothing shows dominance. However, if one object is brighter, or sometimes darker, than the rest, it will stand out. The middle tomatillo (FIGURE 3.7) isn't the largest, but because it is slightly brighter it grabs the attention. It's not that one component is under- or overexposed, it's simply that one shows a slight variance from the others.

Similarly to the previous wineglass images (Figure 3.1), these two apple images (FIGURE 3.8A and B) demonstrate two lighting variations. The first image is properly exposed; however, it lacks a focus. Each apple is treated equally; there is no hero. A strobe and softbox are used to illuminate the entire scene equally. The second image takes a different approach in that one apple stands out from the rest. The lighting directs the viewer to exactly where the photographer intended; the back-right apple is the key subject. This time the same softbox is used to add a base exposure, which is roughly two stops underexposed, and then a second strobe with a grid is added to spotlight one apple and make it the hero.

The series below (FIGURES 3.9A–E) relies on multiple photographic techniques, but lighting adds much of the interest. There is nothing elaborate about the subject matter; it's simply a collection of fruits and vegetables. Each subject was analyzed to determine what was unique, and then controlled lighting highlighted those specific areas while allowing the other elements to recede.

Although these images were lit using strobes, the next section, *Light Painting*, addresses a specialized lighting technique that can produce similar results with greater control, enabling you to place light wherever you desire.

FIGURE 3.9 In this series—**a)** gourd; **b)** kiwi; **c)** mushroom; **d)** Pink Lady; **e)** star fruit—unique lighting is used to focus the viewer's attention.

ISO 50, 1/60 sec., f/4, 100mm lens

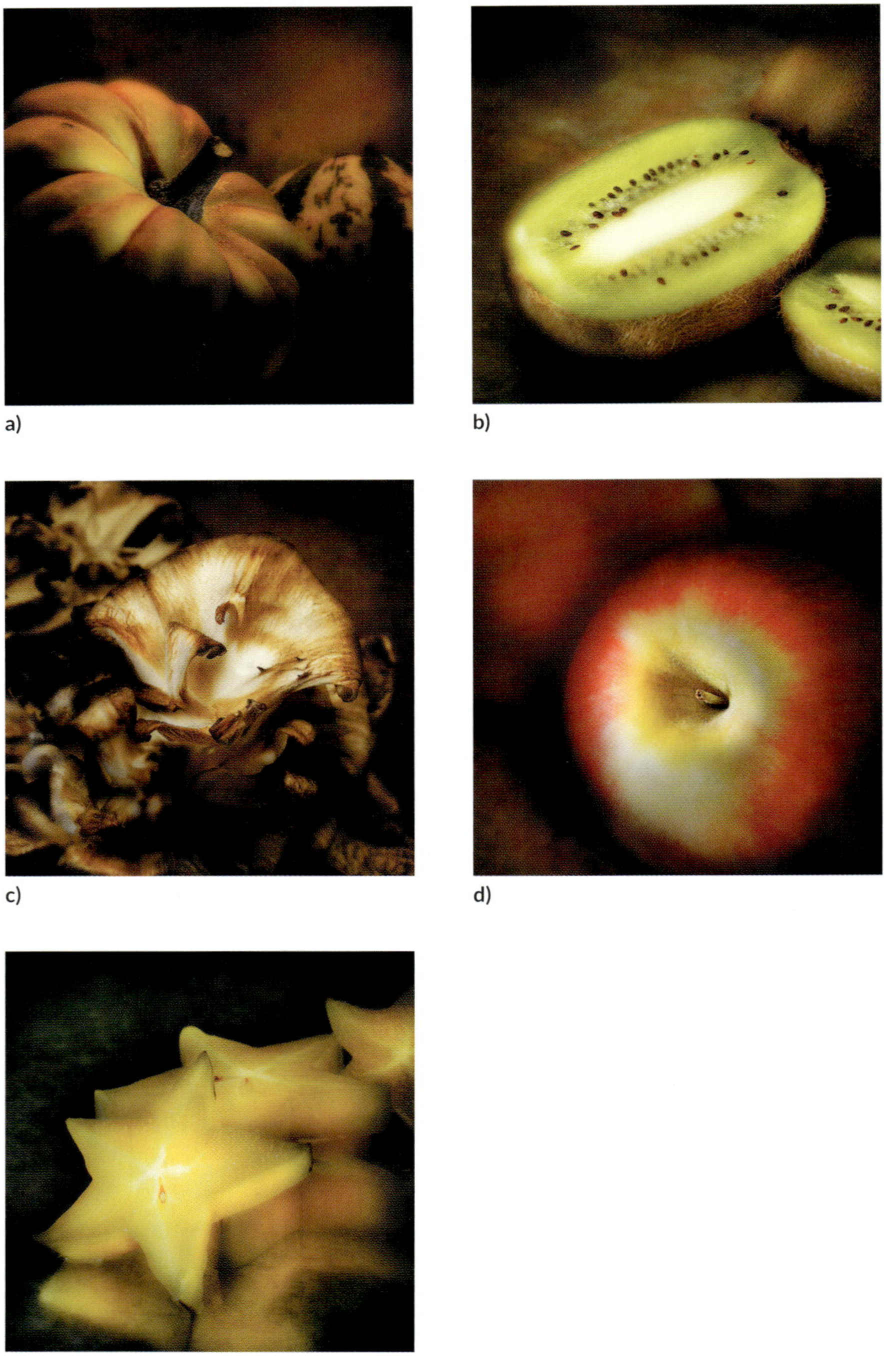

a) b) c) d) e)

Painting with Light

The previous sections discussed the importance of moving the viewer's eyes through the scene as you intended. Wouldn't it be great if there was a way to place light throughout the image with exact precision? Fortunately, there is a lighting technique that allows you to do just that. *Painting with light* or *light painting* allows you to place light exactly where you desire. As the name implies, you actually paint light onto specific areas of the photo while avoiding other areas.

Different Ways to Light Paint

The term *light painting* is used to refer to two distinct techniques of lighting. In one, the light source itself is directed throughout the scene, creating lines and swirls that move through the image. Think of when you have taken a sparkler or a stick with a red-hot ember and twirled it around in the dark, creating interesting patterns. Leaving the shutter open for a set amount of time allows the light to produce an exposure as it moves through the scene.

In the image below (**FIGURE 3.10**), a stick with a red-hot end was moved to create the two hearts. If you look closely you can see the face and hands of the person creating the hearts as well as the stick that serves as the light

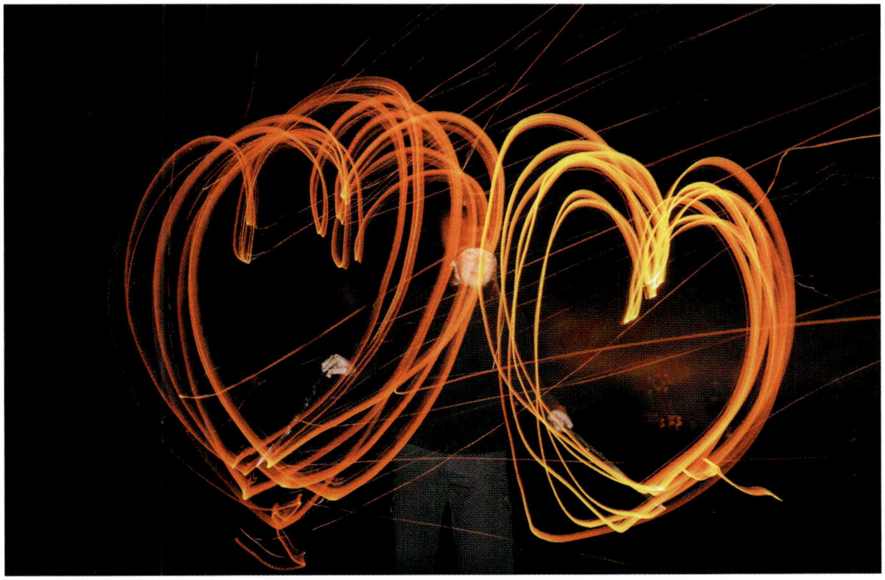

FIGURE 3.10 A light source moved through the scene in this image creates two hearts.

source. Anything that creates light can be used to produce these kinds of images. Adding colored gels over the light source can create different colored swirls in endless combinations. This can be fun, but it's not the technique we will be concentrating on.

The other way to light paint is to turn the light source onto the scene itself. Instead of pointing the light into the camera as seen in Figure 3.10, you make sure that the light itself isn't seen; rather, what you record is the light reflecting off the subjects in the image. The reflected light strikes the film or sensor, thereby recording an image.

This technique has been around for decades. It was used by architectural photographers who needed to light huge spaces but didn't have enough lighting to illuminate such large interiors. With the shutter open, they could use a single light and move it across the interior space, leaving the light longer in some areas than in others so that some elements would be brighter. In this way they were able to direct the viewer's eye to the parts of the room that were most important. We've had students who have used this technique to light up things as large as waterfalls, parts of forests, and huge arches in places like Moab and Arches National Monument (**FIGURE 3.11**).

The image Casey took is beautiful and dramatic and helps to illustrate the diversity and potential that painting with light has. Since this is a book about studio lighting, though, we will concentrate on how this technique can be used in a studio environment.

LIGHTING AND COMPOSITION

I have found that whenever I create a photograph, I'm bouncing back and forth between the composition and the way I light that composition. I'll usually start with the basic layout and a general overall lighting scheme. I'll decide to feature certain items in the shot and make others less prominent. The more important items generally receive more light, and the less important ones receive less light. I go back and forth several times during this process, adding and subtracting light while I move the subject matter within the scene to create the best composition possible.

—BRAD BARTHOLOMEW

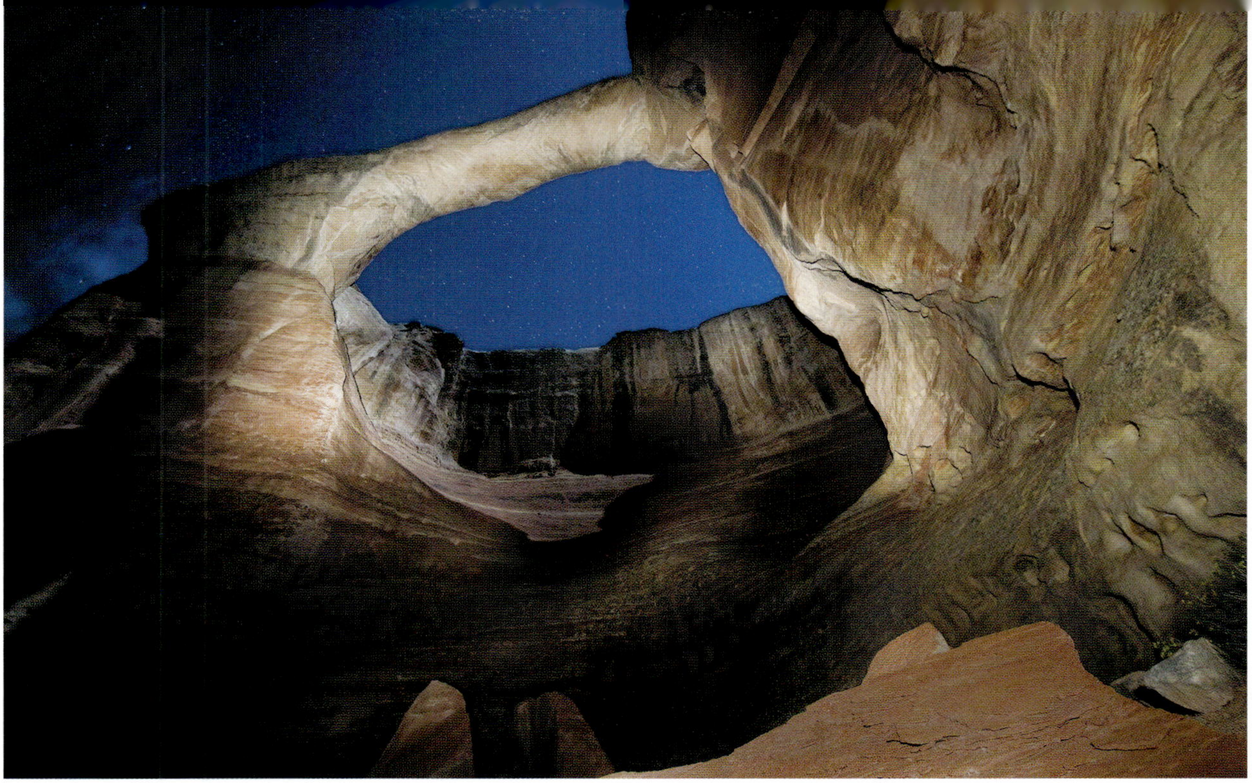

FIGURE 3.11 A light-painting image taken by Casey Bieker of an arch at Arches National Monument.

ISO 100, 30 sec., f/11, 100mm lens

Light Painting in the Studio

In the late 1980s and into the 1990s, a photographer named Aaron Jones helped to popularize light painting by inventing a piece of equipment called the Hosemaster. It used fiber optics and various attachments to produce different qualities of light. It also included a device that could be placed in front of the lens to employ different diffusion filters during exposure, so that parts of the image would be rendered sharp while other parts would be diffused.

His images were stunningly beautiful and had a mysterious painterly quality to them. For a long time no one knew how he created them, but eventually as word got out he started marketing the Hosemaster and graciously taught other photographers how to use it. The Hosemaster was relatively expensive, so many photographers used flashlights to try to achieve similar results. You couldn't get some of the nuanced quality of lighting with the flashlight, but the results could still be interesting and effective.

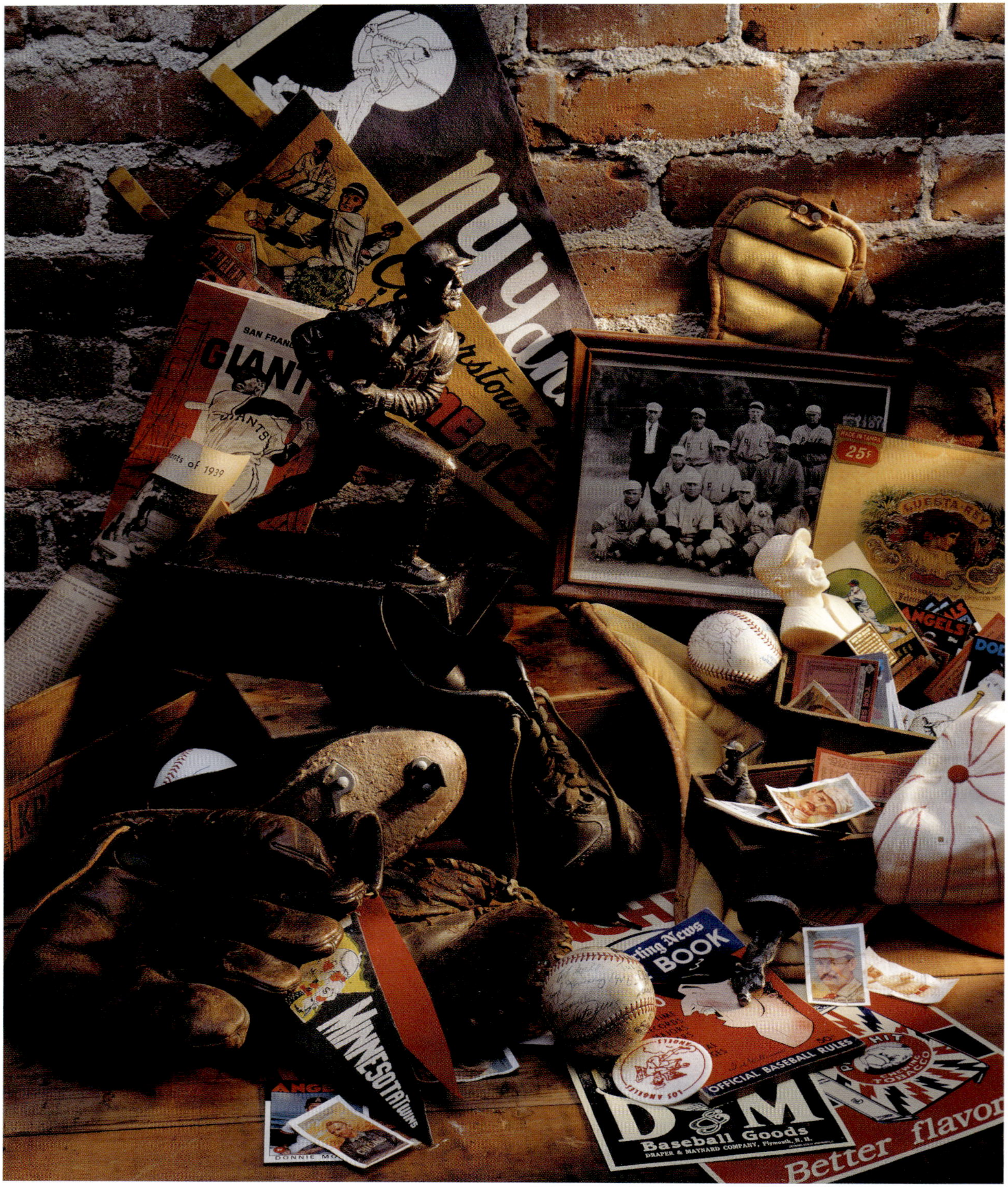
GIANTS
MADE IN TAMPA
25¢
ANGELS
BOOK
OFFICIAL BASEBALL RULES
MINNESOTA TWINS
Baseball Goods
DRAPER & MAYNARD COMPANY, Plymouth, N.H.
Better flavor

What is so exciting about this technique is that it really allows you to make lighting a central part of the composition. We'll review the basic technique, which allows you to be extremely precise with where you choose to put your light (**FIGURE 3.12**).

FIGURE 3.12 A fairly complicated composition simplified by painting highlights onto specific areas of the image (opposite).

ISO 100, 30 sec., f/11, 210mm lens

The Process

Light painting begins much the way any other lighting technique does. First, you set up your shot while deciding what's going to be most important in the image and what you're trying to say about it. Although there are many ways to go about light painting, the following is a good general way to start.

If you're going for a dramatic image with significant contrast between highlights and shadows, you want to set up your overall fill light along the camera axis so that all the shadows will receive some amount of fill. Meter that light, and then, depending on how dark you want your shadows to go, underexpose the light by between one and three stops (**FIGURES 3.13A–D**). This is just your base exposure; you'll be adding highlights to the image by painting them on using a flashlight.

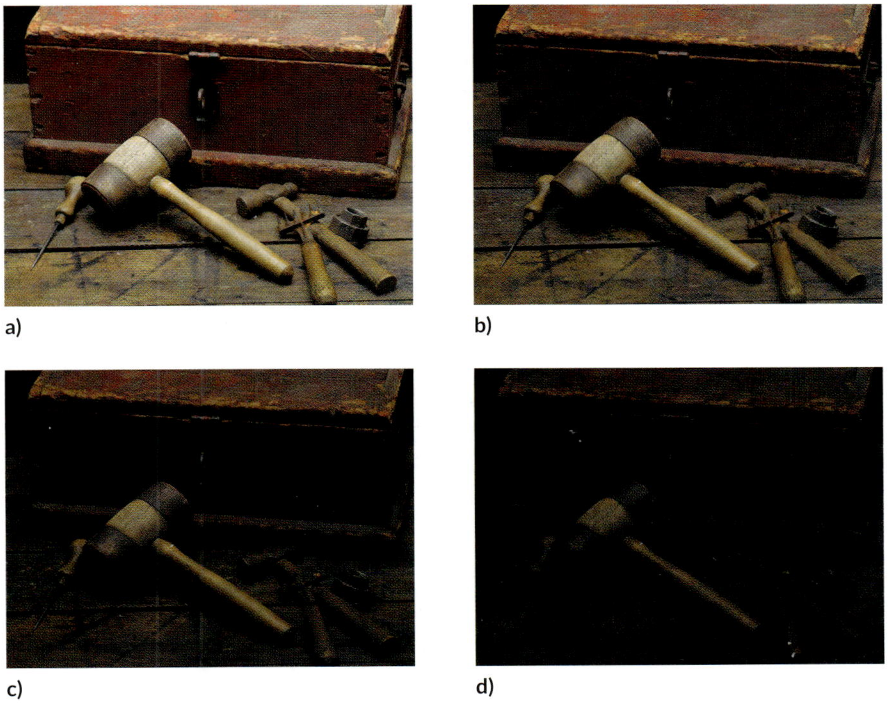

FIGURE 3.13 **a)** Image exposed per meter reading at f/8; **b)** one stop underexposed at f/11; **c)** two stops underexposed at f/16; **d)** three stops underexposed at f/22.

ISO 50, 1/125 sec., f/8, f/11, f/16, f/22, 150mm lens

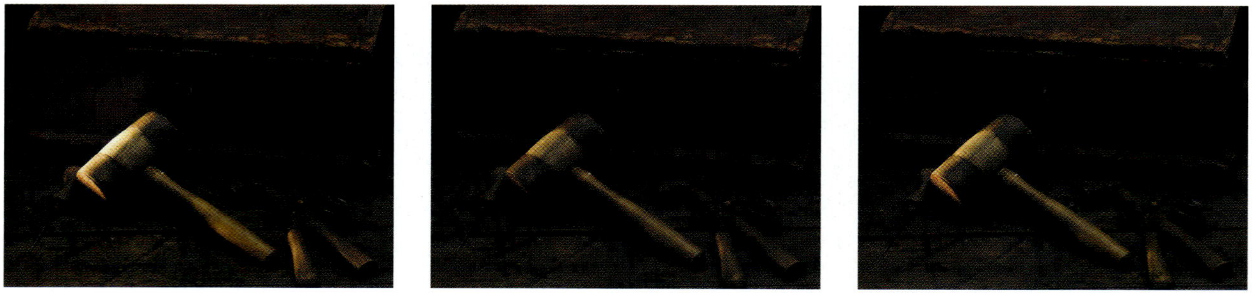

a) b) c)

FIGURE 3.14 **a)** Too much light was painted onto the hammer; **b)** too little light was added to the hammer; **c)** the correct amount of light was added to the hammer.

ISO 50, 20 sec., f/11, 150mm lens

Goldilocks

The image captions for Figure 3.14 should sound somewhat familiar; a little too bright, a little too dark, just right. One of the wonderful, but also frustrating, things about light painting is that no two images will ever be exactly the same. It's virtually impossible to repeat the movements for exactly the same amount of time from image to image. What's lost in consistency is often made up for with serendipitous accidents that result in even better images.

Now comes the fun part! You get to choose what you want to highlight within the image, both literally and figuratively. The hammer is the main subject, so most of the highlights will be concentrated on it. Texture will be added to the background, and other highlights will be added to some of the secondary props. The lighting used will make it clear what is most important and where we want the viewers to look.

In the last chapter we talked about lighting being a building process, and that's especially true when you light paint. Start by adding light to the hero, analyze the results, and then make the necessary adjustments. Once you're satisfied, you can move on to lighting other parts of the image (FIGURES 3.14A–C).

The final image (FIGURE 3.15) was created by underexposing a strobe softbox by two stops. The shutter can be set on T or B to keep it open during the entire exposure. Once the shutter was open, we popped the strobe to give the base fill exposure. Then we used the flashlight to add the necessary highlights. The flashlight was at a fairly low angle, to bring out as much texture in the objects as possible. With the shutter open, the flashlight was in constant motion, literally painting highlights onto those areas of the shot that we were trying to call attention to. It's important to not leave the flashlight stationary for too long, as this will create obvious hotspots.

We used a cone made of matte black Cinefoil to limit the size of the light and to help ensure that it didn't shine directly into the lens (FIGURE 3.16).

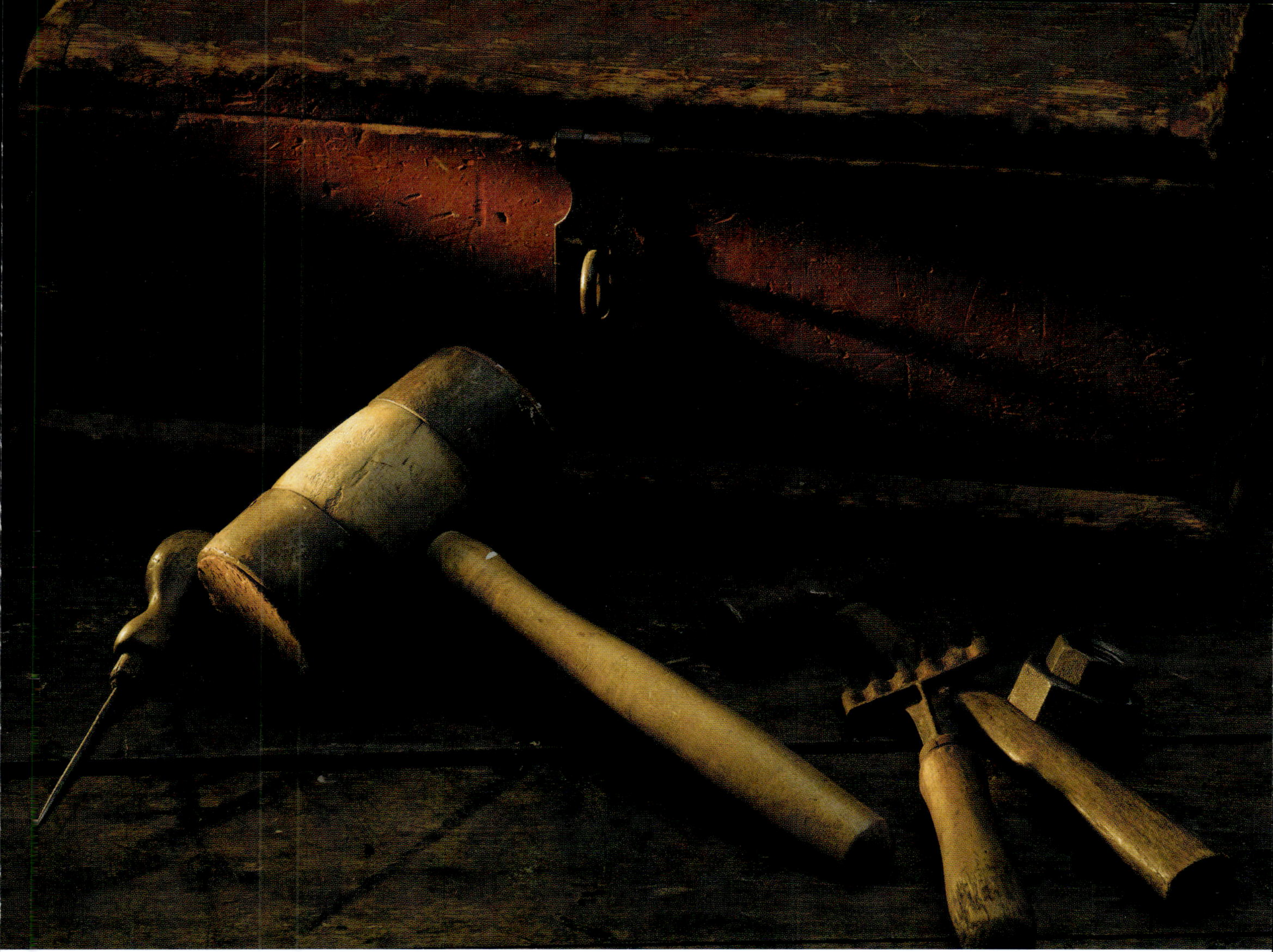

FIGURE 3.15 This image has the right amount of light on the hammer, and light has been added to the background and props for additional interest.

ISO 50, 30 sec., f/11, 150mm lens

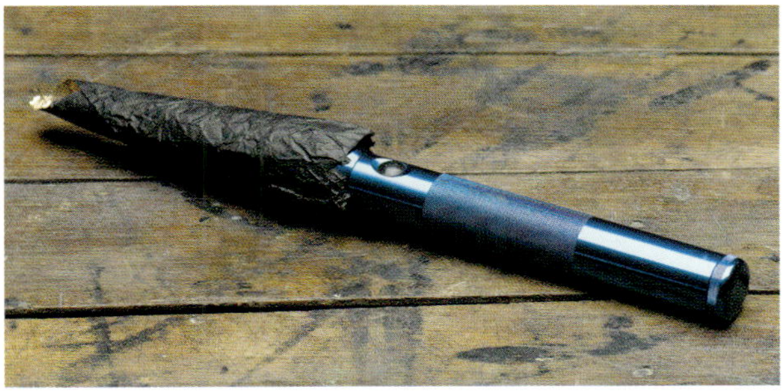

FIGURE 3.16 This is the flashlight and cone setup used to create Figure 3.15.

High-Key Shots

The majority of the examples shown have involved pretty dramatic contrast between highlights and shadows. This technique can also be used in high-key shots, where the overall shot is bright but you still want to add some additional highlights to certain areas of the image. It can also be used to add fill to limited areas of an image when using any other kind of fill may be inappropriate because it fills all of the shadows (**FIGURE 3.17**).

Light Painting and Color Temperature

If you're using both a strobe and a flashlight, you'll be dealing with light sources that have different color temperatures. In most of the preceding examples, the camera's white balance was set to daylight so that it would match the strobes. The light from the flashlight was warm because it's a tungsten light source. This lighting mimics end-of-day sunlight, when the shadows are either a little cool or neutral, whereas the highlights from the sun have warmth. You can always filter the lights so that they match one another if you want an overall neutral color cast.

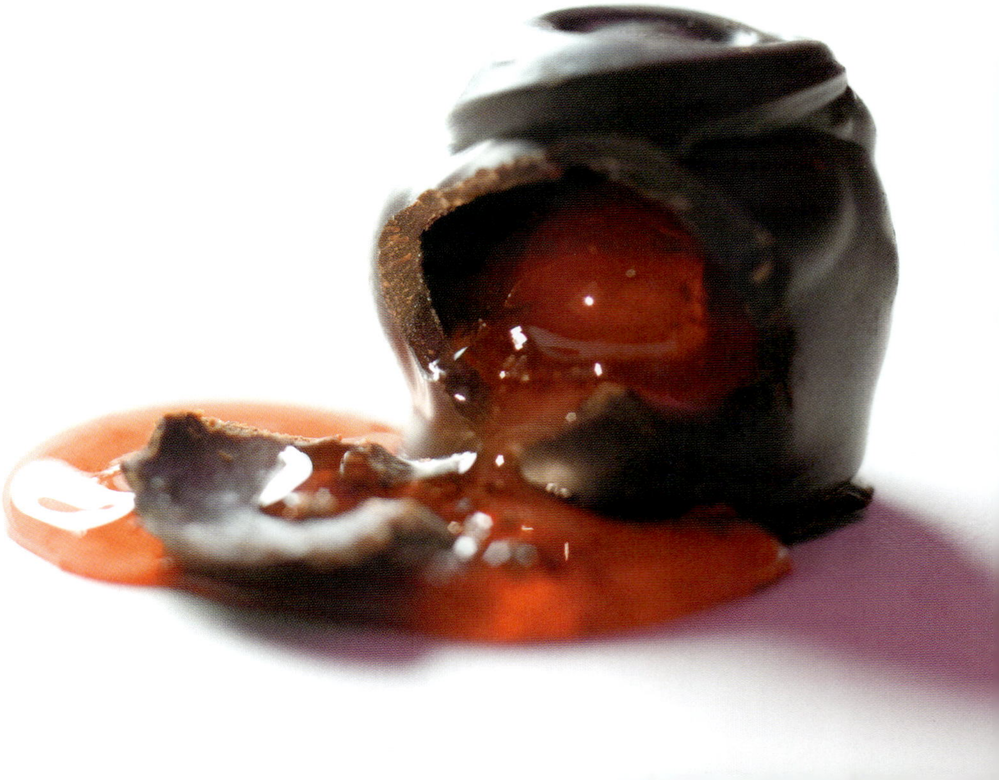

FIGURE 3.17 A flashlight was used to fill the inside of the cherry and add some specular highlights. The flashlight had a blue gel over it to make it daylight balanced. The red in the shadow was created by using a red fill card to bounce light back into the shadows.

ISO 50, 15 sec., f/5.6, 210mm lens

Exposure

It's impossible to tell you how long each exposure will be. The length of exposure is determined by many factors, including the power of the flashlight, the distance the light is from the subject matter, the amount of area you want to paint with light, and the f-stop you're using. Clearly, the more you stop down the lens, the longer the exposure will be.

Depending on the camera you're using, you may need to be concerned about digital noise appearing, especially in the shadow areas of your image, if you're using long exposures.

This may not be your number one way of lighting, but it's a great way to become more aware of subject hierarchy and ways you can use light to direct the viewer's eye throughout an entire image. All of this will require a certain amount of trial and error and experimentation. Play around with it—the practice will make you better.

Chasing Styles

Joe: Light painting was all the rage for a while, and then new techniques became popular. How do you feel about the need to stay current versus chasing every new lighting style that comes along?

Brad: I think it's important for everyone who's starting out to experiment with a number of different styles until they find a look that resonates with them. It may be a combination of a styles and techniques that they make their own. It will be necessary to adapt and evolve your look over time, but I don't recommend putting every new style into your portfolio. It's important to be true to yourself and the way you see the world, while still being open to new techniques.

JAN OSWALD

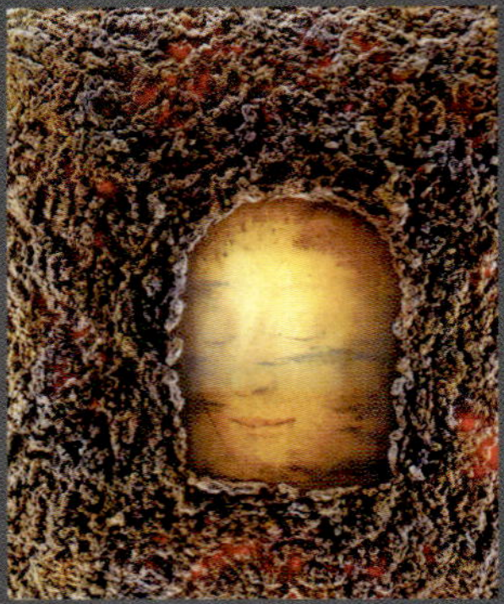

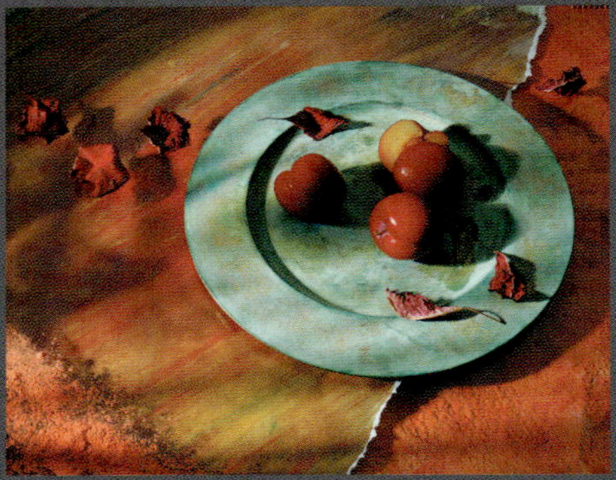

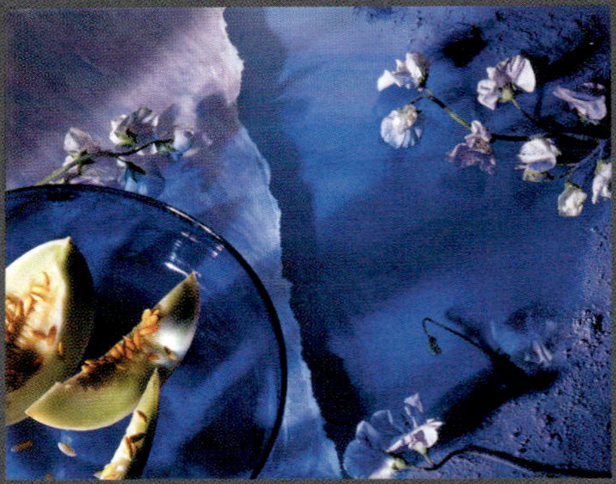

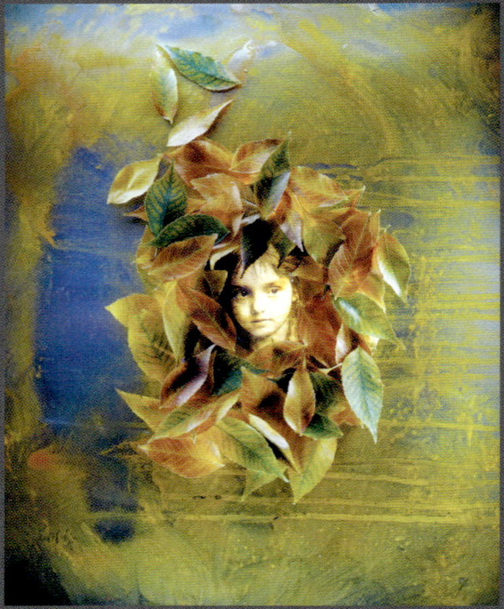

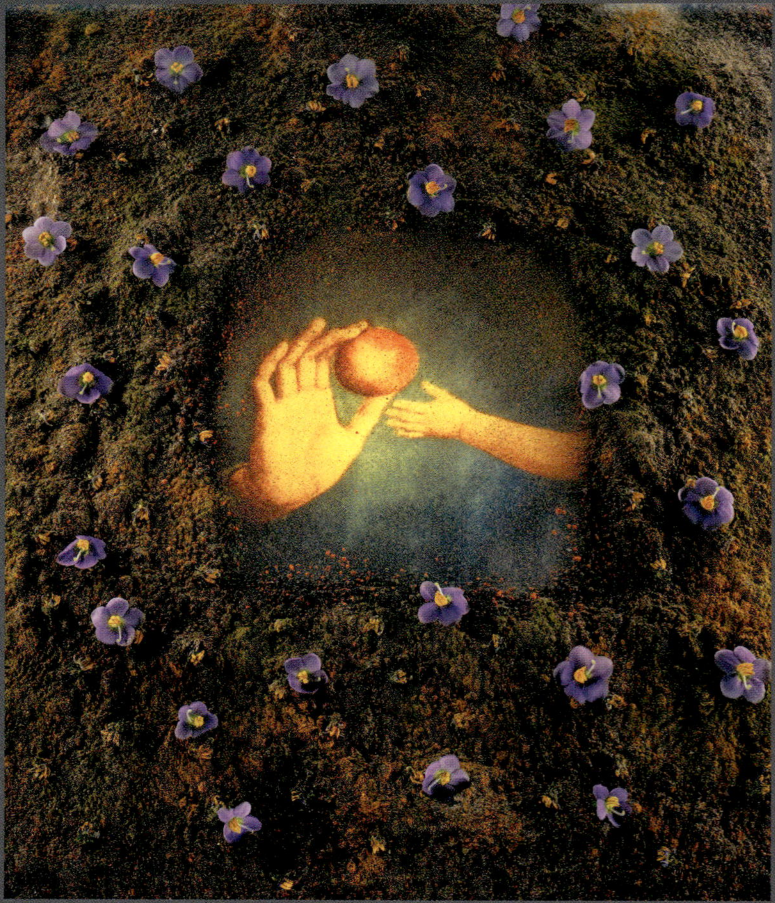

All images © Jan Oswald

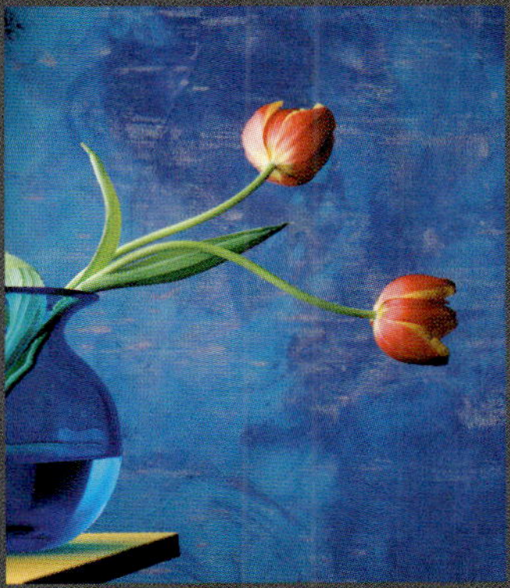
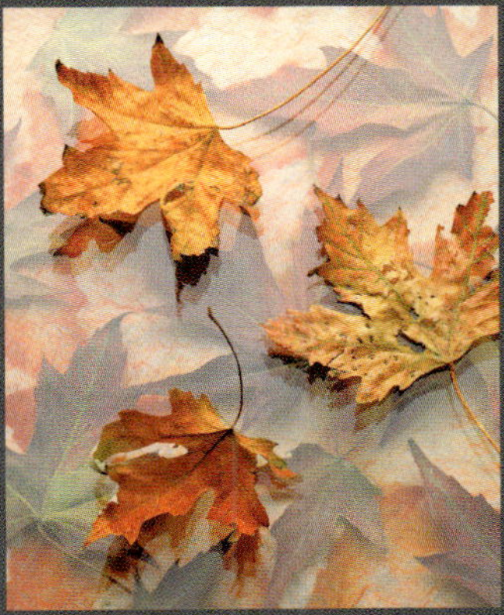
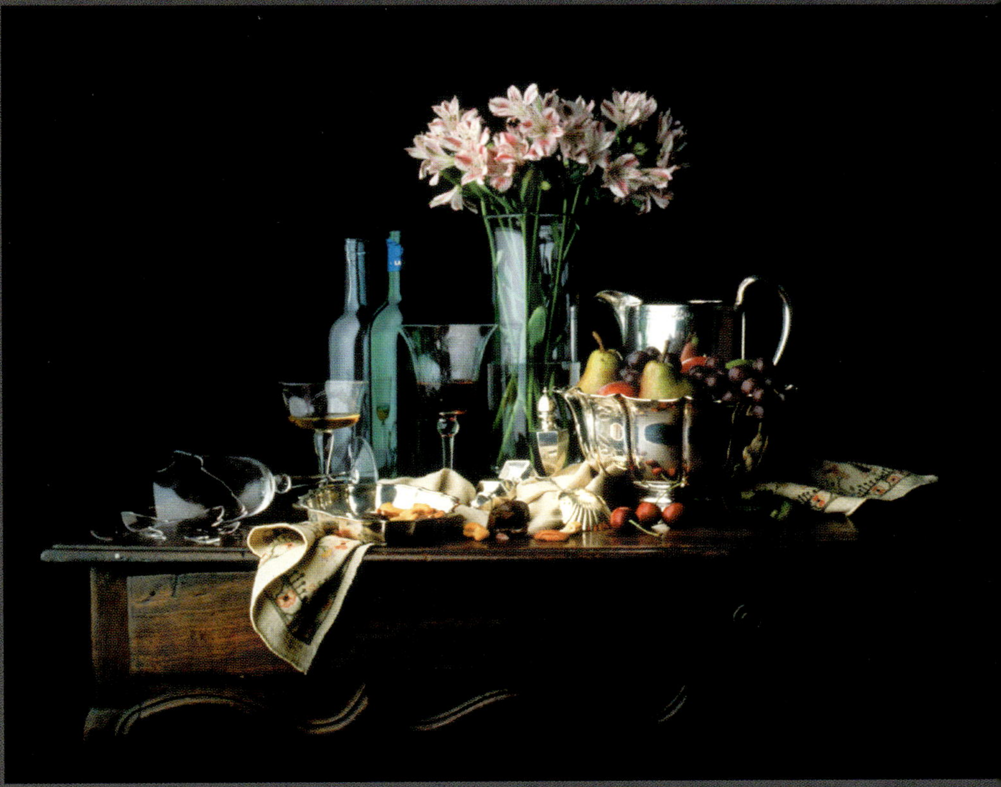
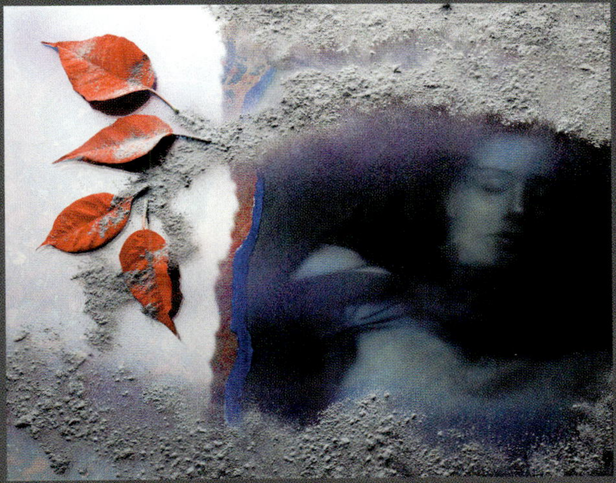
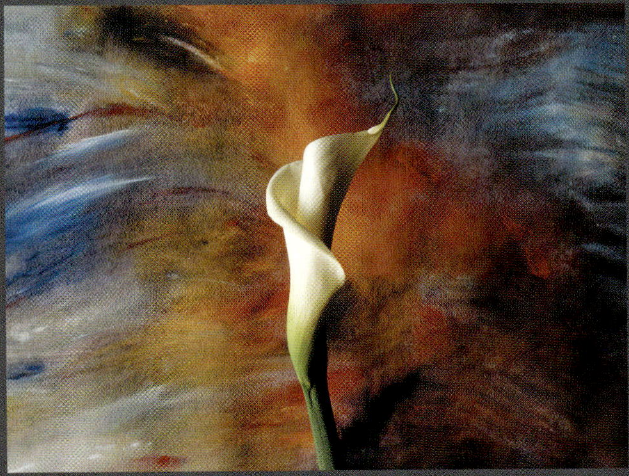

How long have you been a professional photographer?

Since I graduated from school in 1973, it's the only profession I've had.

How did you get started, and why photography?

My uncle took family photos, and as a child I loved watching him take the portraits and then develop them in his darkroom at my grandmother's house.

I got my first camera at age ten. I loved being able to stand back and observe and then record my observations on film.

Do you have formal training or education?

Brooks Institute, where I had an exceptional teacher and mentor, Phil Cohen.

Your images seem to bridge a gap between fine art and commercial advertising. Many photographers talk about doing that; however, most are unable to do so. How were you able to achieve this?

I had a very strong background in art history—my mother took us to museums from a young age. And I wanted to be an artist and even had a museum show while still in school. So it has always been fine art that inspired me. I do a lot of experimental work when not doing commercial work, and that has always guided my approach to commercial jobs.

How would you describe your lighting style?

Based on an understanding of natural light as point (the sun) and broad (the shade) sourced. It has to be natural to gain the viewers' acceptance so they accept the image as a real possibility. Then I like to add luminous aspects for interest.

At what stage of your creative process do you consider lighting?

From the initial stage. I previsualize my final image and work backward to achieve the desired lighting effect I've conceived.

Let's look at your image titled* Melon on Blue Plate*—describe how your lighting acts as part of the image composition.

Highlight and shadow are always part of any composition in photography, as they become part of the abstract tonal range of the image as much as any other element or object in the design. In this image I had become interested in very low early-morning light situations where the sun streaks across objects and creates a lot of contrast. And in this case it holds the image elements together.

What is the first element you wish the viewer to see?

The highlight on the melon slice.

Zen Tulips *and* Melon on Blue Plate *use two very different lighting styles. How did you determine the best style for each image?*

When I did *Zen Tulips*, I was inspired by flowers in a vase on my dining room table. They had bent and turned in an evocative manner toward the large glass expanse in the back of my house. I gathered them up and took them to the studio, where I had painted a blue background, and lit them with my broad 6-foot bank light. I aimed them to flow from left to right to enhance that "yearning" effect. I wanted a broad window lighting effect, as that's what I had observed in my house.

In the *Melon* image I had been observing the light from the sun as it just crept in that same glass expanse and skimmed across the floor. And I was doing a series of simple food items on plates on backgrounds I had painted. *Plums on Copper Plate* is also in that series. In this case it was a monochromatic palette, and the strong light was needed to give it some contrast and visual interest.

Over the decades my style has evolved. I began experimenting by imitating the style of others. First it was the Dutch still life compositions. The Dutch masters used window light for their paintings, and I wanted to explore that style. It is exemplified in my image *Still Life with Broken Glass*.

I admired the purity of the lighting style of Irving Penn, and his work had a strong influence, as seen in *Single Calla* and *Zen Tulips*.

Later I started using the early-morning strong cross-lighting I had observed on my dining room floor. This is seen in *Melon on Blue Plate* and *Plums on Copper Plate*.

Next I combined those elements with luminous lighting elements, as seen in *Watching*.

How do you determine what lights and modifiers you'll use? Do you have any favorites? If so, what are they and why?

I've always used a limited number of lights. The large bank light duplicates the clear sky or foggy day that is so desirable for outdoor photography. When it's placed very close to an object, the light actually wraps around the object.

I use a couple of spotlights, one larger and one with a more focused spot. And I use a light painting tool with a very intense beam in some cases.

Most of the time I have a fill card or mirror or even a small light box of some sort to slightly fill the shadows.

Do you have a favorite of the images selected for this book?

My favorite of these images is *Watching*. Conceptually, to me, it embodies my approach to lighting and composition. I observe, take it all in, then apply it outward to create the final image. ■

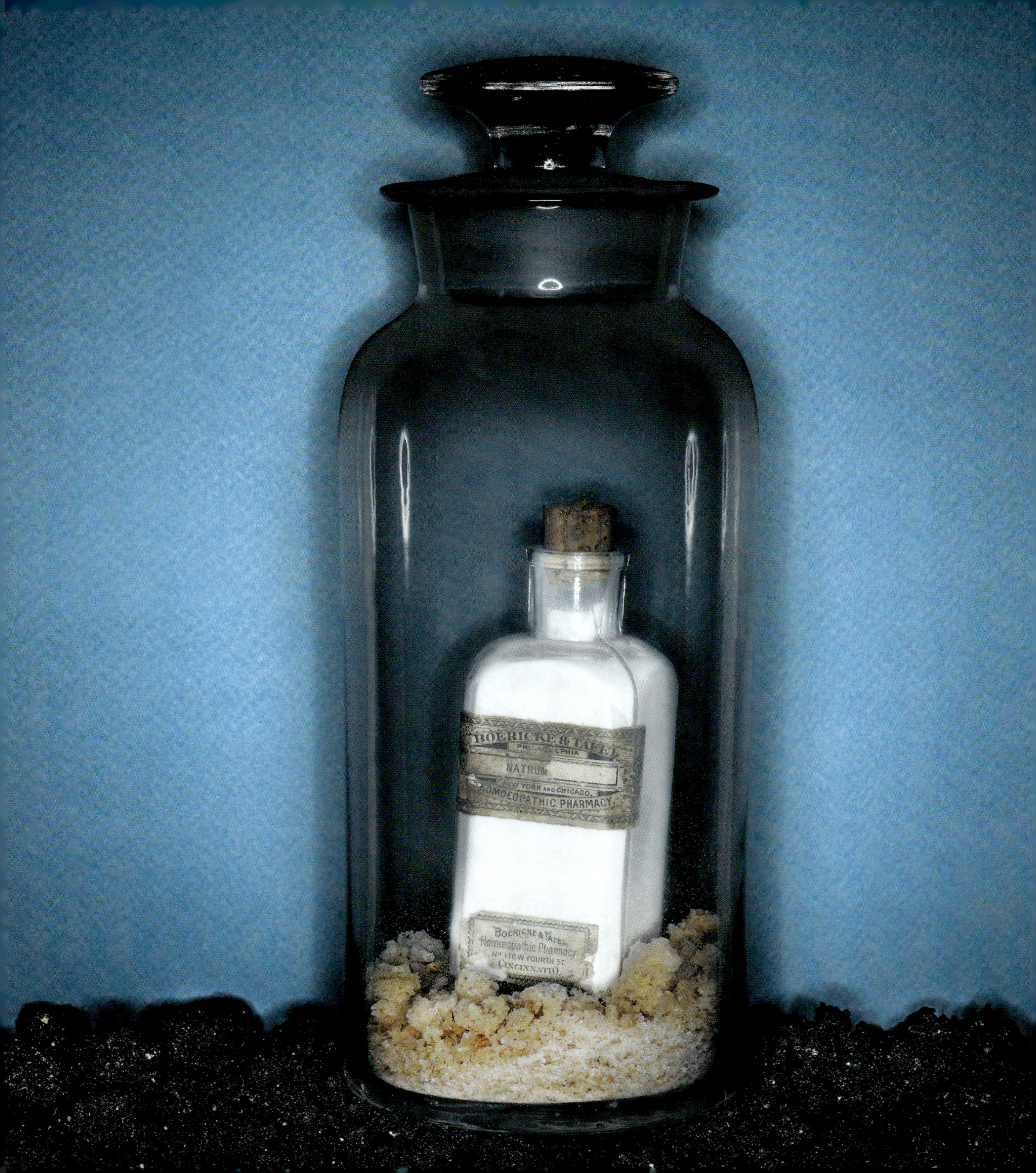
BOERICKE & TAFEL
NATRUM
NEW YORK AND CHICAGO.
HOMOEOPATHIC PHARMACY.
BOERICKE & TAFEL
Homœopathic Pharmacy
Nº 170 W FOURTH ST
CINCINNATI O.

chapter four

EXPERIMENTATION

It's impossible to get better at something without practice. The more you practice, the better you get, until at some point what was difficult becomes second nature. This is certainly true with photography in general and specifically with lighting. It's rewarding to see your skills improve to the point where you're comfortable with the tools and techniques you have available. What once took a tremendous amount of time and effort now can be done quickly and easily.

On the surface this sounds great, but there's a danger that this new level of comfort can begin to stifle creativity. For this reason, it's essential that you constantly experiment and push to create new ways of seeing and lighting familiar subjects. It's important not to settle for old results but to realize there're always a myriad of solutions available. By experimenting and trying new things, you'll help both your creativity and your business grow.

ISO 50, 1/125 sec., f/22, 210mm lens

Opening Image: Photographic Equipment

Camera: Sinar 4 × 5 view camera with Leaf Aptus-II digital back

Lens: Nikkor 100mm

Lighting: Profoto Acute2 generator with Profoto Ringflash

This simple lighting scheme for the image on the previous page includes one ring flash and nothing else. Light throws a distinctive shadow that surrounds the subject.

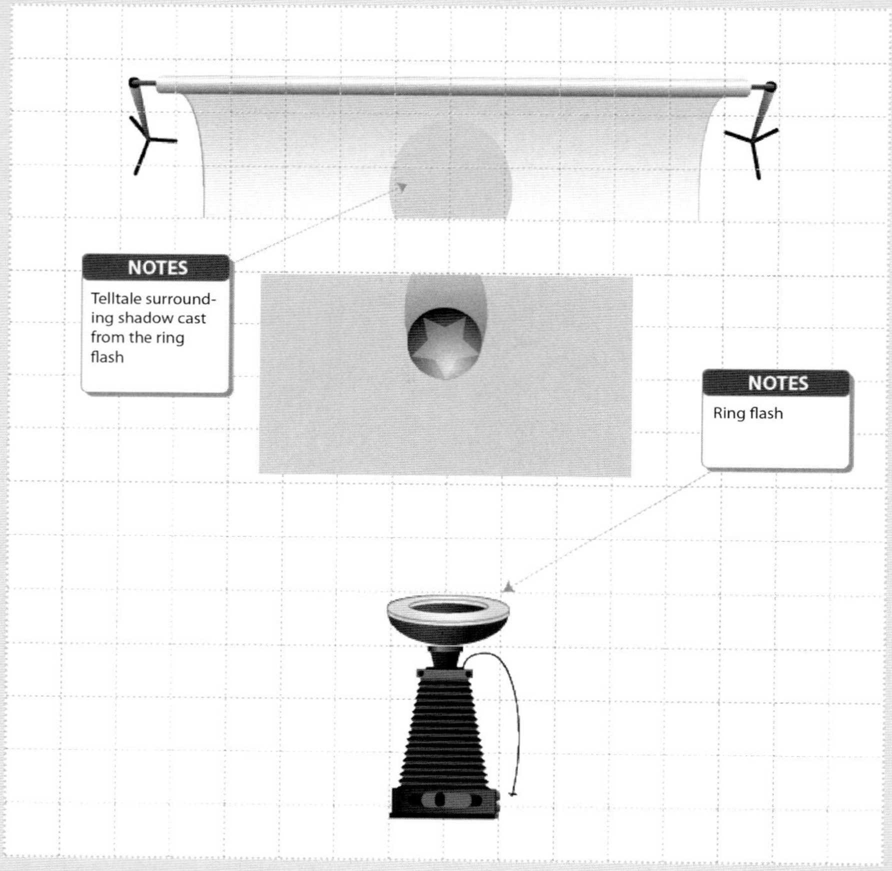

Don't Settle

The two most dangerous words you can think or say are "good enough." Let's say you've been working on an image for a while, things are starting to come together, and overall the image looks pretty good. The concept is solid, the composition is working, the exposure is good, and the overall lighting is working well. Seems like time to move on to the next shot or call it a day. Wrong! "Pretty good," "good," "working well"—are those the kind of words you want associated with your work?

It's easy to get to a point where things are good enough. Once you have improved your lighting skills, you'll be able to set up your lighting quickly to give you satisfactory results. The more you work on similar subject matter, the more you'll know the way light plays off of certain surfaces; it becomes easy to use tried-and-true methods. The issue then becomes, when is good enough not good enough? When do the images need to be great?

The easy answer is that your images should always be great, but the truth is, that's not always practical. In the commercial world, if you're photographing a catalog and you need to complete 50 shots a day, it's highly unlikely that all 50 shots are going to be truly great. You may only have time to produce good, strong, competent images.

A Tough Balancing Act

It can often be difficult to find the right balance between quality and quantity. Obviously the clients are going to want to get the most bang for their buck, and this can mean as many shots as possible within a limited budget. You're going to want to create the most beautiful images you can, but your finest work may not always be doable given time and budgetary constraints.

What is key is to have an honest discussion with your client about what the trade-offs will be between shooting things fast and shooting them right. For certain projects the clients may not need fabulous lighting for all the images. They may need a gorgeous cover shot for their catalog, but the interior product shots require only simple lighting to properly render their wares.

TRY SOMETHING NEW

The image at the beginning of this chapter is another example of how pushing yourself can greatly improve your work. The main subject in this image is the big glass bottle. Ordinarily a broad light source such as a scrim or a softbox would be the logical choice because of the reflective nature of the subject. I started with a softbox, which gave me a long vertical highlight running down the left side of the bottle, but I found that this distracted from the smaller bottle. It also created light that was more traditional than I wanted for this particular shot, so I borrowed a ring flash from a friend. A ring flash is a crisp, hard light source that produces a telltale shadow surrounding the subject (**FIGURE 4.1**). Using this device gave me what I desired, something that looked a little more contemporary and edgy.

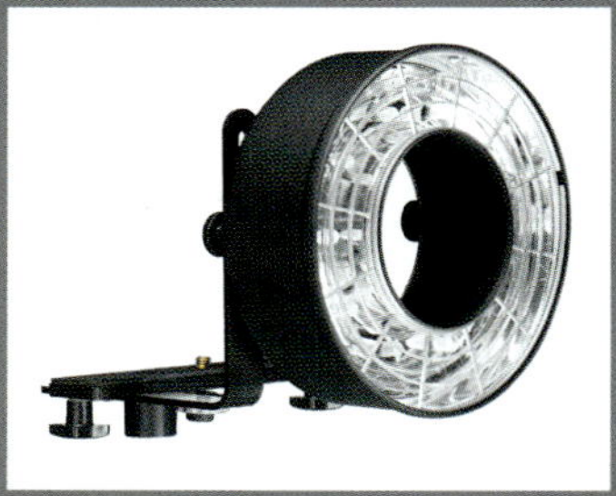

FIGURE 4.1 The design of the ring flash can give you a dramatic shadow around your subject.

—BRAD BARTHOLOMEW

However, in many cases, you want to work on an image, trying a variety of lighting solutions, until you know the final result is the best it can be. Be sure to move the light around the set looking at what happens to the various objects and surfaces as you make these changes. Just because a particular light modifier worked in the past doesn't mean it will be the best solution for similar situations. Be willing to swap out modifiers, observing the unique characteristics that each one adds to the scene.

A couple of the images in the last chapter are good examples of this (Figure 3.1 and Figure 3.15). The initial shots of the wineglasses and cork and the hammer started out as pretty decent images. Additional experimentation using a variety of light sources and modifiers helped to create even stronger ones. It would've been easy to settle for those initial images, but in the end the extra effort paid off.

Experimenting with different light sources enhanced the overall concept of the shot. As a bonus, the ring light added some creepy specular highlights to the bottle, which suited the client in this case.

Let's take some time to examine another example. The shot below (**FIGURE 4.2A**) was taken using a large softbox placed above and slightly behind the set. The light illuminates much of the set but still creates some edge light to provide dimension and separation.

This is the kind of shot that you don't want to settle for. The exposure is fine and the image is OK, but we don't want to settle for just OK. Here's where experimenting and adding and subtracting light becomes important. Using additional edge lights will add more dimension and sparkle to the image. Taking light away from part of the background helps to give the image depth (**FIGURE 4.3**).

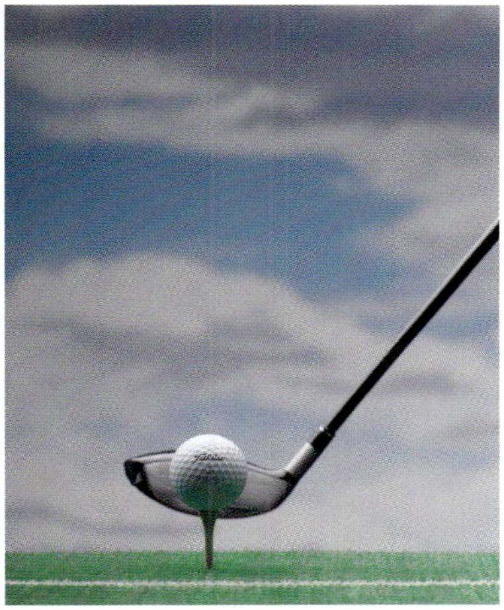

a)

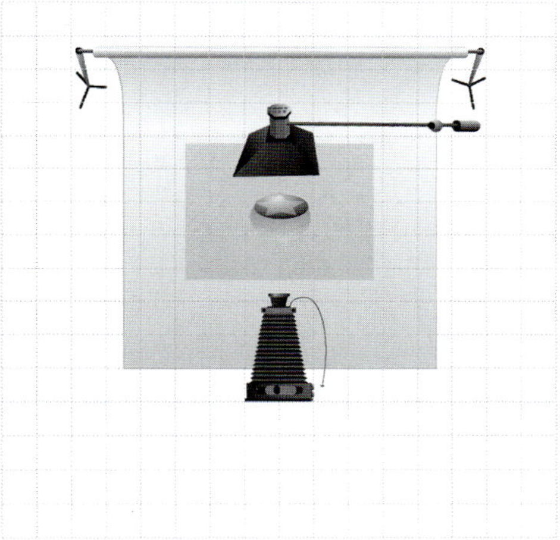

b)

FIGURE 4.2 **a)** The softbox is placed above and slightly behind the subject. This light provides overall illumination and is a good starting place, but the setup needs some work. **b)** A single softbox provides overall light that needs refinement.

ISO 50, 1/125 sec., f/11, 150mm lens

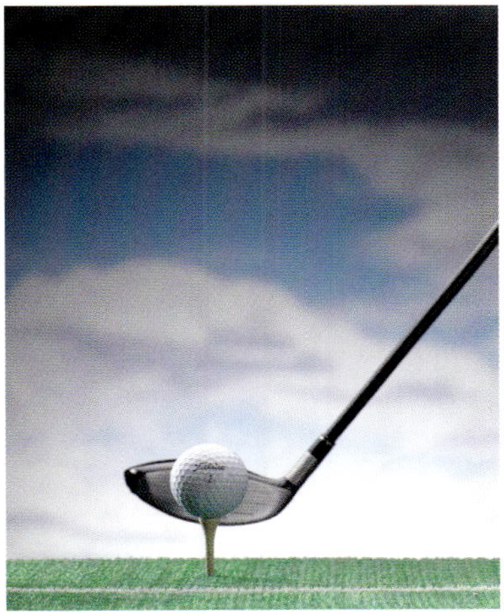

a)

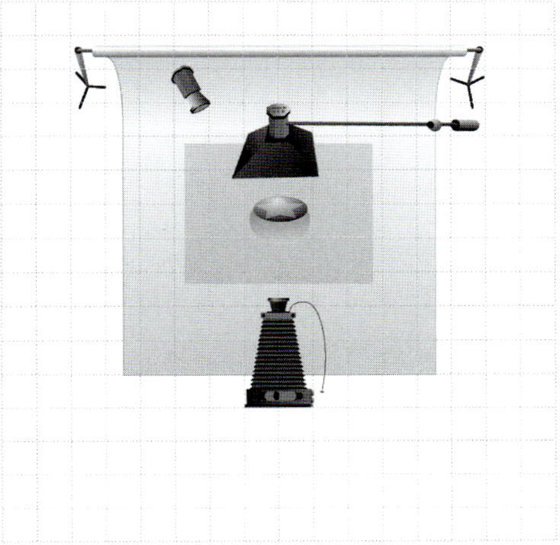

b)

FIGURE 4.3 **a)** A grid spot was used to add an edge light, and a light was added to gradate the background; **b)** the diagram shows the placement of the edge light.

ISO 50, 1/125 sec. ,f/11, 150mm lens

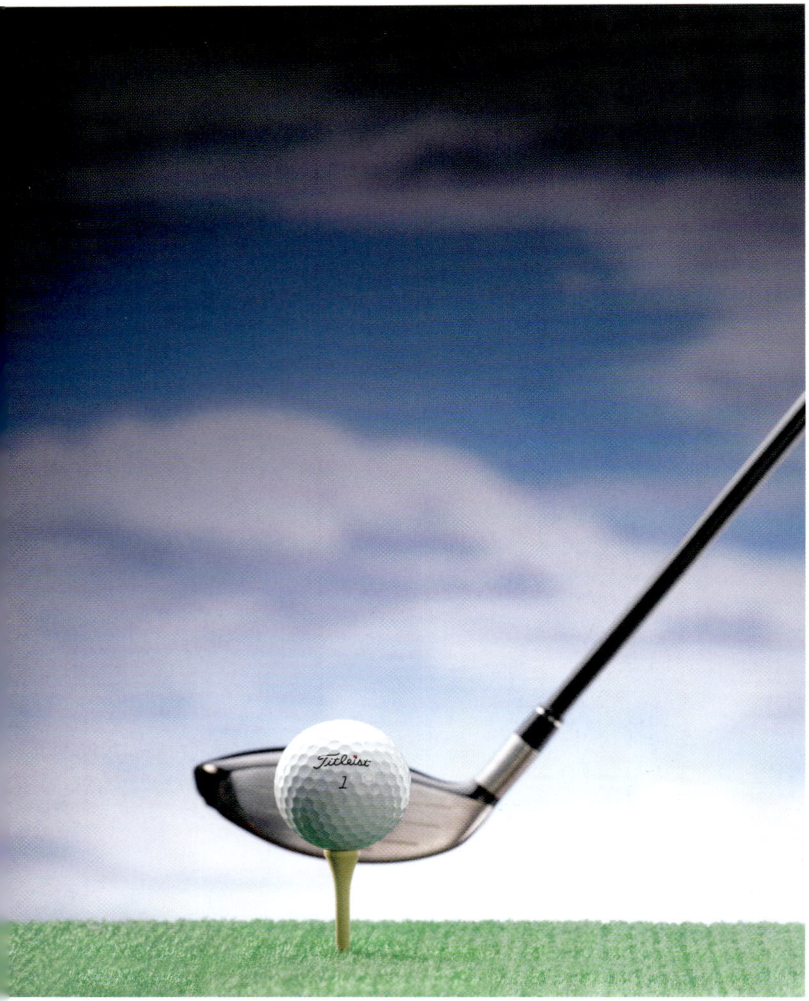

a)

FIGURE 4.4 **a)** The final image after modifications to lighting. We're happy with this one. **b)** The addition of the reflector added the necessary highlights.

ISO 50, 1/125 sec., f/11, 150mm lens

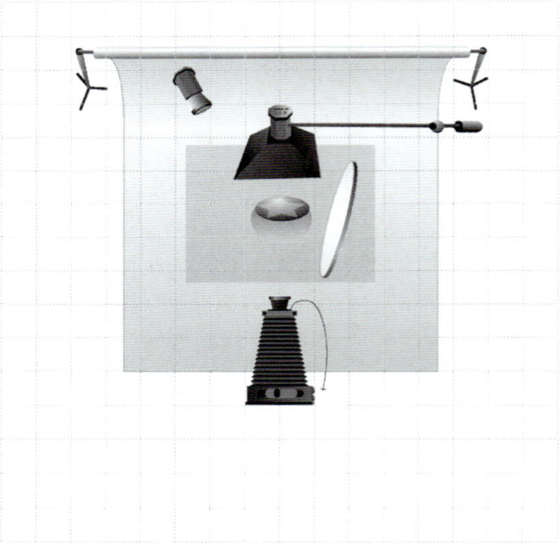

b)

This new image is better, but it still needs more life. We used a few mirrors for additional edge lights and to fill certain areas, and we retouched out the white line on the grass (FIGURE 4.4).

A willingness to experiment with various types of light will quickly help you understand what does and doesn't work in a variety of situations. Not settling for what you've done before will add to your arsenal, enabling you to solve increasingly difficult lighting problems. Every subject is different—which means there are no one-size-fits-all solutions.

No Pat Answers

Early on in the book, we said that this wasn't going to be a cookbook type of lighting book, where recipes (or lighting diagrams) are provided for the reader to follow. Plenty of those are available, but the underlying problem is that they tell you one answer, and in photography, there are no pat answers. Yes, lighting principles and design rules exist, but they are merely a starting point.

What's the problem with pat answers? Let's address three big reasons: photographer, client, and subject. Don't be surprised if the same couple of words keep popping up in the answers.

Photographer: What's the Vision?

No two photographers are alike; each is unique. Every photographer brings her unique vision, style, expertise, and life experiences to a project. In photography schools, assignments are given and demonstrated by an instructor, and miraculously, the students' work often looks similar to the instructor's. This is because the students are giving the instructor what they think the teacher wants to see. This is great for learning basic principles, but for a student's work to stand out, he must incorporate his personality into his images.

Photographers should celebrate their differences. When starting a project, think about what you, the photographer, bring to the process. Is it technical expertise, creative vision, or life experience? Or is it something else we haven't even thought of yet?

A Piece of Yourself

Joe: Can you think of a specific shot you have done where you relied on a personal experience?

Brad: A couple of years ago I did a personal shot for my portfolio. It involved a couple of kids out in a field catching butterflies, with a huge jar of pond water holding a couple of frogs. I spent my entire childhood doing just that. It was so easy for me to put this shot together in terms of props, wardrobe, and so on, because I had lived it.

Client: What's the Goal?

It's been said that photography would be a great business if it didn't require clients. But photographers can't survive without clients unless they're independently wealthy. Just as photographers have distinctive styles, so do clients. A successful photographer-client relationship is not too different from a successful marriage; it entails some give and take, and the two parties must mostly be compatible. Photographers who rely on pat answers generally have a limited client base. Although it's necessary for a photographer to have a style, he must also be able to adapt his style to meet a client's demands.

Subject: How to Showcase It Best?

As if the individuality of the photographer and the client weren't enough, there is also the subject. It's easy to say that no two subjects are the same. Some differences might include color, texture, shape, size, and surface (reflective versus matte). Some situations call out for a different approach to lighting, but what happens when the subjects are similar?

Imagine the scenario of two beer client projects. Although the bottles are similar, neither client wants their beer bottle to look like the next company's. The look and the resulting image must be distinctive and striking. The two bottle images in FIGURE 4.5 are of similar subjects but required two unique lighting solutions. The first image is a clean subject on a white background. The idea is to let the bottle stand out on its own; it's the hero. The second image has less to do with the bottle and more to do with conveying an overall mood.

Two Photographers: Brad and Joe

Throughout this book, we've included multiple images taken separately by us, Brad Bartholomew and Joe Lavine. We'd be curious to see if you, the readers, could pick up on our style differences. We have shared studio space for many years, sometimes shared clients, worked on joint projects, and taught the same classes, but we're still two unique photographers. One is more controlling, focusing on the small details and mapping out an image, while the other often lets the image emerge through the process. Both of us begin with a similar building process, but we frequently (or maybe usually) arrive at two different destinations. Can you spot the different styles?

CHAMELEON

I've often joked that to be successful as a commercial photographer, one must be part chameleon and be able to blend into multiple situations. The majority of my work comes through advertising agencies, design firms, and in-house marketing departments at large corporations. This means that I deal with many very different people. The ages of my clients range from mid-20s to early 60s, and somehow, I must be able to tweak my lighting in a way that remains still true to my style, but also fits the client's vision.

One of my favorite things about being a professional photographer is that I get to meet such different people and experience their work worlds. How many professions are there in which a person can work with clients ranging from owners of mom-and-pop startups to executives at Fortune 500 companies and even representatives of foreign governments?

—JOE LAVINE

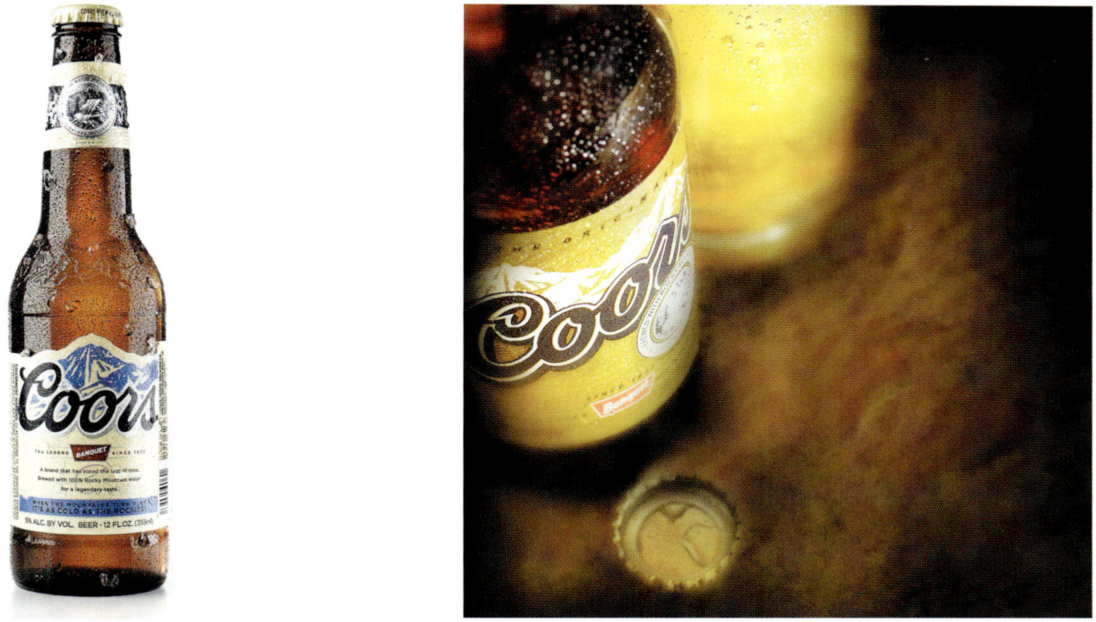

a) ISO 100, 1/60 sec., f/11, 100mm lens

b) ISO 50, 1/60 sec., f/4.5, 90mm lens

FIGURE 4.5 **a)** A clean product image in which the bottle is the hero; **b)** although the bottle is important, the overall mood is the main focus.

Two Lighting Scenarios

The image in Figure 4.5a required a three-light setup; one light was used to create the clean white background, and another was directed into the back of the bottle, giving it the inside glow. The third came from the bottle's front-left side, lighting the label and creating the long highlight. I added a little spritz of water to the bottle to give it the just-pulled-from-the-ice-chest look.

A key lighting difference between Figure 4.5a and 4.5b is that in Figure 4.5a, the idea was to separate the bottle from the background, but in 4.5b, we wanted to connect the bottle to the background, which happened to be an old piece of rusty metal. The main light came from the left side of the image and was used to equally graze across the label, cap, and surface. A second light was used to light the beer from the back of the glass. A slight blur was added in post-production to enhance the mood of the image.

There are simply too many factors involved in photography to rely on formulaic approaches. Being a little unsure and a little nervous going into a photography project is actually a good thing. It means that you're not relying on a standard solution and are open to trying more than one way to solve a problem or achieve a goal.

More Than One Solution

Building on the idea that there are no pat answers, it's easy to see why there is always more than one solution to a photographic problem. Often, discovering the most appropriate one requires a bit of experimentation.

Every once in a while a subject will present itself that leaves a photographer scratching his head asking how he should approach a project. The watch image (FIGURE 4.6) was just one of those times.

Let's take a moment to address why this task presented concerns. The client's concept was to photograph the watch, which has a camera lens's diaphragm look to its face, on a metal surface with photographic elements such as film-processing reels and processed film. Sounds easy enough, except the watch is a combination of shiny metal and glass and needed to be captured on a bright metal surface. Oh yes, and the shot needed to have a contemporary style, not something one would find in a department store catalog.

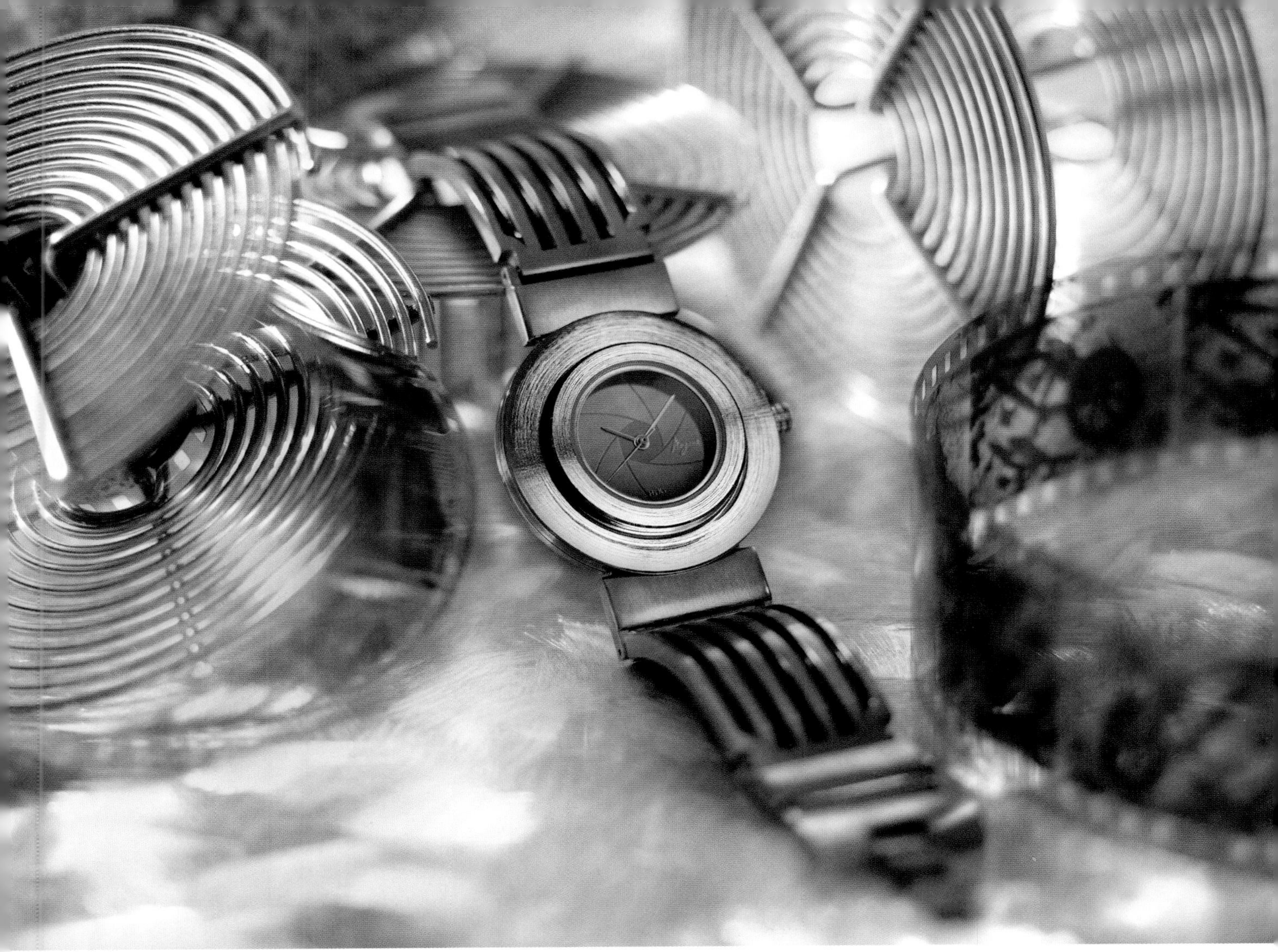

FIGURE 4.6 Despite the competing elements, this watch needed to look craveworthy, exciting, and modern. We think our final select does the job.

ISO 50, 1/60 sec., f/4.5, 150mm lens with extension tube

Equipment Used for the Watch Image

Camera: Mamiya 645 with Leaf Aptus-II 7 digital back

Lens: Mamiya 150mm with extension tube

Lighting: Profoto D1 monoblock

Light modifiers: zoom reflector with 5-degree grid or XS softbox (depending on image)

Part of the reason this concept was difficult to execute was the need to maintain detail in the product so it didn't get lost in its complex background. This required that the metal surrounding the face of the watch appear shiny but still maintain its dark ridges; not an easy task.

Once the props, composition, and camera angle were determined, it was time to experiment with the lighting. In all, over 40 images were captured, testing different light modifiers, angles, and exposures. A review of the images showed some interesting results; while many images were pretty good and met the client's parameters, none of them were exactly what the photographer had envisioned. As addressed previously, "good enough" just wasn't acceptable.

Many of the images had some redeeming qualities. Let's take a moment to analyze the pros and cons of five of them (FIGURES 4.7–4.11).

The big question: What were we going to do now? We had some interesting images, but none of them was what would be called finished. One option was to reshoot the watch using a single light source, and then add a handful of mirrors, cards, and gobos to control how much light fell on each area of the scene. Another option, and the one used to create Figure 4.6, was to treat the previous images as a list of ingredients from which we could develop a recipe.

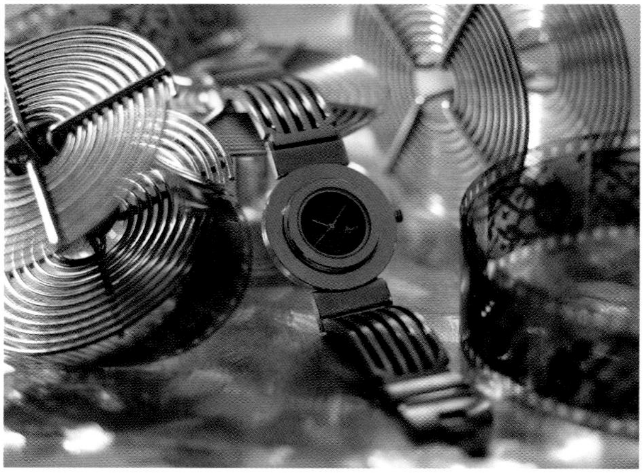

FIGURE 4.7 This is a decent image overall. Other than a few specular highlights, the shadows look relatively good and have detail. The issue is that the image lacks "pop"; it's kind of boring.

ISO 50, 1/60 sec., f/4.5, 150mm lens with extension tube

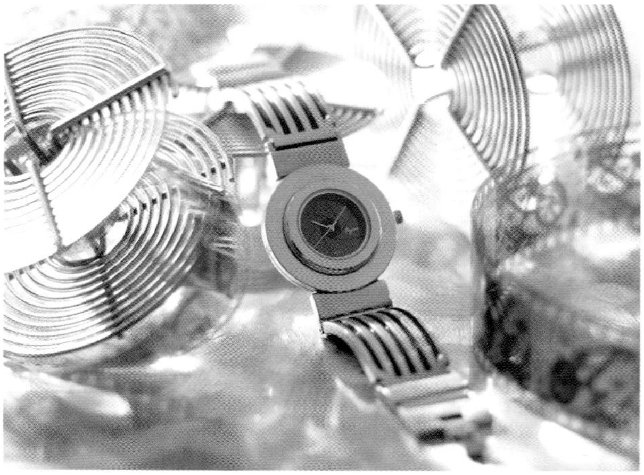

FIGURE 4.8 Sometimes it's hard to describe in photographic terms why something is the best fit, but the upper right spool here just feels right. It's bright, airy, and could stand on its own.

ISO 50, 1/60 sec., f/4.5, 150mm lens with extension tube

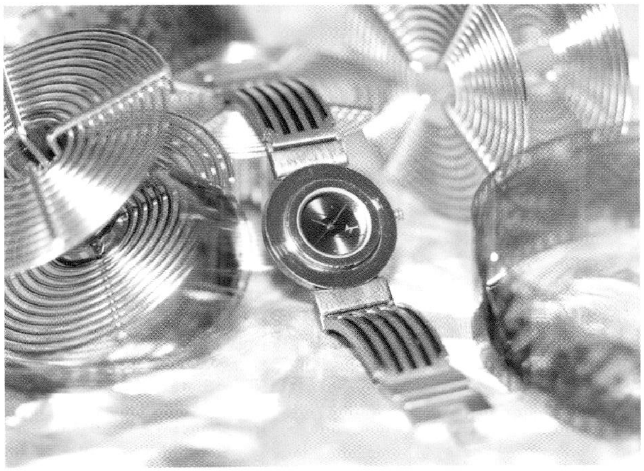

FIGURE 4.9 Although the image is overexposed, the mood of the scene begins to show the desired energy. The top portion is too bright, but the lower part of the frame demonstrates good detail.

ISO 50, 1/60 sec., f/4.5, 150mm lens with extension tube

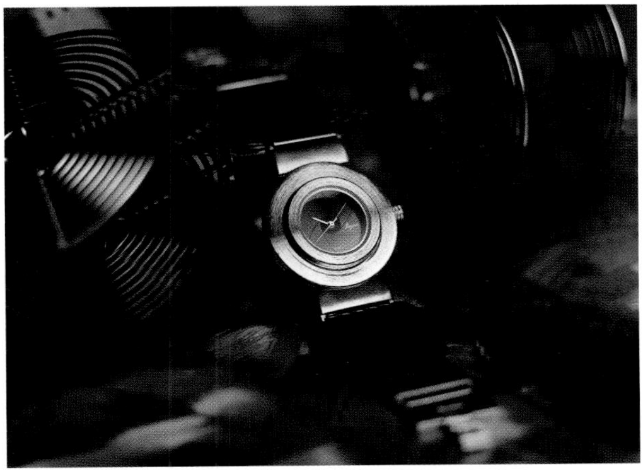

FIGURE 4.10 Out of the nonfinal group, this is the one that maintains the necessary detail, but the remainder of the image is underexposed.

ISO 50, 1/60 sec., f/4.5, 150mm lens with extension tube

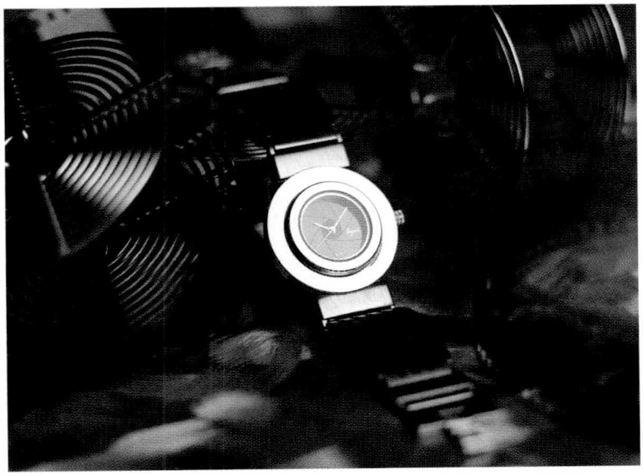

FIGURE 4.11 The last image of the group is all about the face of the watch. The face looks good, but as in Figure 4.10, the rest of the image is underexposed.

ISO 50, 1/60 sec., f/4.5, 150mm lens with extension tube

Now the task focused less on shooting and more on determining how to use our ingredients.

We carried out the following steps in Adobe Photoshop (FIGURE 4.12).

1. Combine all five images into a single Photoshop document. Adobe Bridge has a great feature that makes this step simple. From Adobe Bridge, choose Tools > Photoshop > Load Files into Photoshop Layers. It's important to confirm that all layers are lined up.
2. Rename each layer with a descriptive term that easily identifies what it will be used for. This step makes it much easier to get going again after you've stepped away from the file for a while.
3. Apply Hide All layer masks to all layers except for the bottom layer.

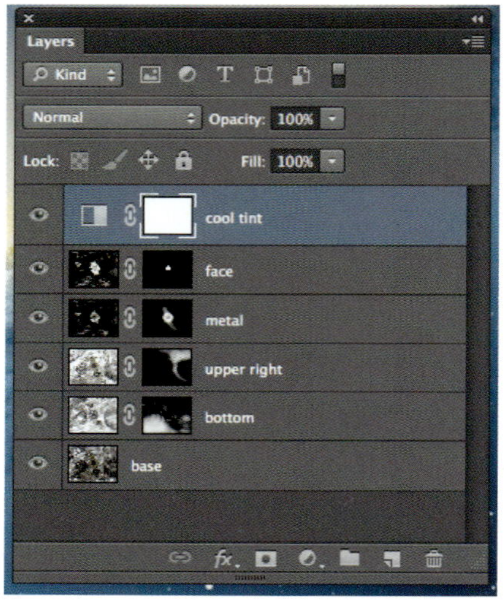

FIGURE 4.12 Here, we choose a cool tint as the last step.

4. Using Photoshop's Airbrush tool, paint with different levels of white to reveal the areas that you deem right for the image.
5. The final step in creating Figure 4.6 was to add a Black & White adjustment layer that used a slight cool tint. Shiny metal and cool tints often work well together.

Our watch project was a good reminder that there's never only one solution and one right way to do things. The final watch image (Figure 4.6) ended up being the sum of multiple parts. Our original plan didn't start out that way, but through experimentation and keeping an open mind, we found the best solution: the one that pleased both photographer and client.

Constantly Grow

We tell all our graduating students, "Look at your portfolios; that's the worst they should ever look." On the surface that doesn't sound particularly inspirational, but think about it for a minute. What it means is that you'll continually become a better photographer. You and your work will improve over time.

Of course this can only occur if you're always willing to experiment. In order to grow as an artist you must leave your comfort zone and try new lighting techniques. This means you'll fail at times, and most of us don't enjoy failure. Learn to see failure as a teaching tool. An unwillingness to experiment and fail will lead to stale, predictable, and outdated work. You shouldn't chase every new fad, but you do want to evolve and grow throughout your career.

Let's look at a really simple example of how trying something new can help make a shot better. The images below were taken for a local Colorado client. The final shot was part of a series of images of single subjects shot on white backgrounds. The first image (**FIGURE 4.13**) was taken using a medium softbox above and slightly to the left of the purse. This is pretty straightforward product lighting. It gives the purse some dimension, and the drop shadow keeps it grounded to the background.

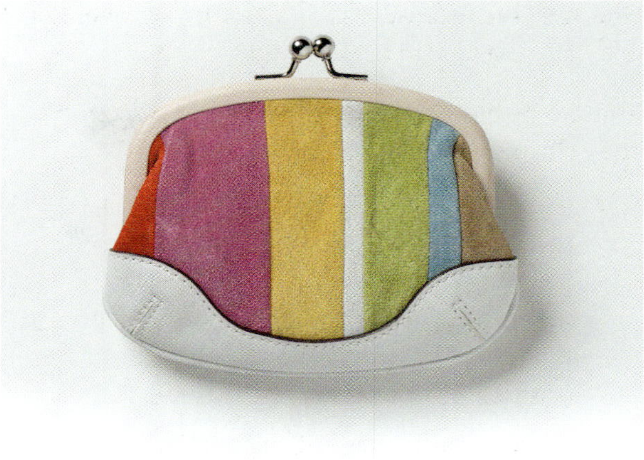

FIGURE 4.13 The initial lighting scheme didn't work as well as necessary.

ISO 50, 1/125 sec., f/11, 150mm lens

The problem is it's also a bit boring. The image had to stay simple. We couldn't add any props, and the overall background needed to stay white. The only choice we had was to do something different with the lighting.

For quite a while we were stymied. Adding other lights would also add unwanted shadows, and the light on the purse itself was fine. It created texture in the leather and the right amount of dimension. What we wanted was more vibrant color in the shot, but the background had to stay white.

The only thing left was the drop shadow itself. By covering a white foam core fill card with a magenta gel, we were able to reflect a light with a pinkish colorcast into the shadows. For the most part this light bouncing off the pink fill card did not affect the color of the rest of scene because the main light was strong enough to overpower the fill (**FIGURE 4.14**).

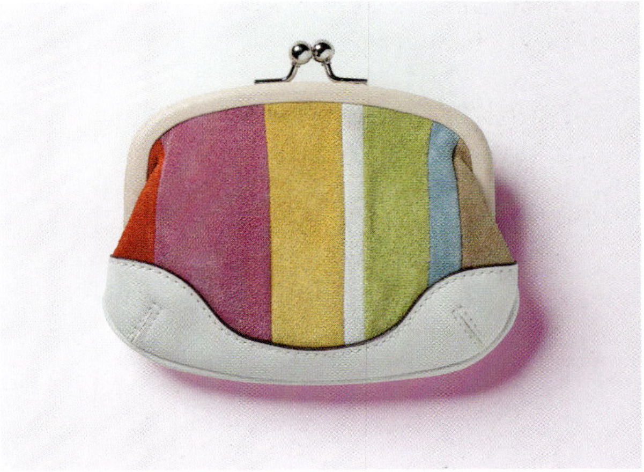

FIGURE 4.14 To add interest, a colored bounce board was added to bring color into the shadow.

ISO 50, 1/125 sec., f/11, 150mm lens

This new version was better but the entire background turned a little pink due to the fill light. The last remaining step was to combine the two images into a single Photoshop document with the pink version on top. By adding a layer mask to this layer and then using the brush tool, we were able to reveal the white background in the bottom layer. In this way, the clean white background accentuates the pink in the shadows (**FIGURE 4.15**).

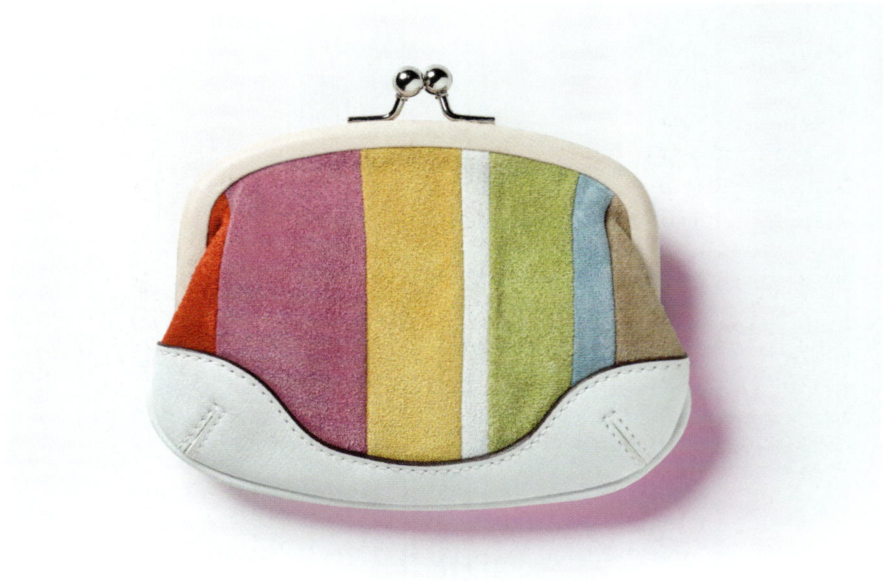

FIGURE 4.15 Figures 4.13 and 4.14 were combined in Photoshop to create a stronger overall effect.

ISO 50, 1/125 sec., f/11, 150mm lens

Developing a Personal Style

The ultimate goal of all this experimentation is to develop your personal style. This style won't be completely reliant on the way you light, but your lighting will be a major factor in the look of your images. Earlier in this chapter we mentioned the differences between our own photographic styles. Although we're cowriting this book, we have different personalities and different interests, and we bring all of this with us to everything we shoot. Our basic philosophy of lighting is much the same, but the way we approach individual situations can be very different. We could imitate one another's lighting style, but in the end that's all it would be, a mere imitation.

Most clients will hire you for your unique voice, for the way you see the world. We'll discuss developing a personal style in greater detail in Section Three, but for now it's important to realize that development begins with a very simple thing—your willingness to push beyond the solutions you've already tried, experiment with different types of lighting, and never settle for an image until you've exhausted many different options.

Using Gels to Add to Realism

You can create realistic "outdoor scenes" shot in the studio by adding a slight blue gel to your fill light. By doing so you will give your shadows a blue cast, which is what happens outdoors (**FIGURE 4.16A** and **B**). The blue of the sky fills in the shadows with a bluish colorcast. Look at the shadows in a snowy area on a day with a blue sky to see this effect.

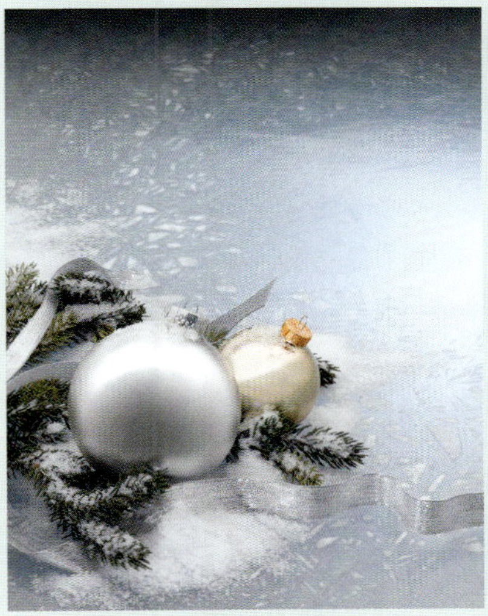

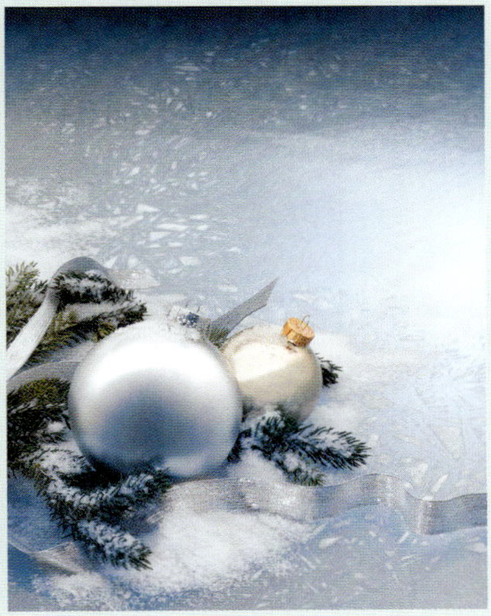

FIGURE 4.16 **a)** This scene was lit with a neutral fill light; **b)** a blue gel was added to the fill light to give a more realistic look for a cold winter day.

ISO 100, 1/60 sec., f/11, 150mm lens

Comparison

Photographing watches tends to present a handful of challenges. For this chapter's comparison, we each photographed the watch of our choice, but one was to be rugged looking and the other was to have a modern, high-key feel. Interestingly, both final images were created by combining multiple images.

Close examination of the watch faces reveals two important observations. First, **FIGURE 4.17A** has a camera lens design, which is supported by the film and film reels for props, and **FIGURE 4.17B** uses rocks to back up the Fossil name. In addition, both watches are set to roughly the same time. This placement of the hands is common because it allows easy reading of the product name and looks like a smiley face.

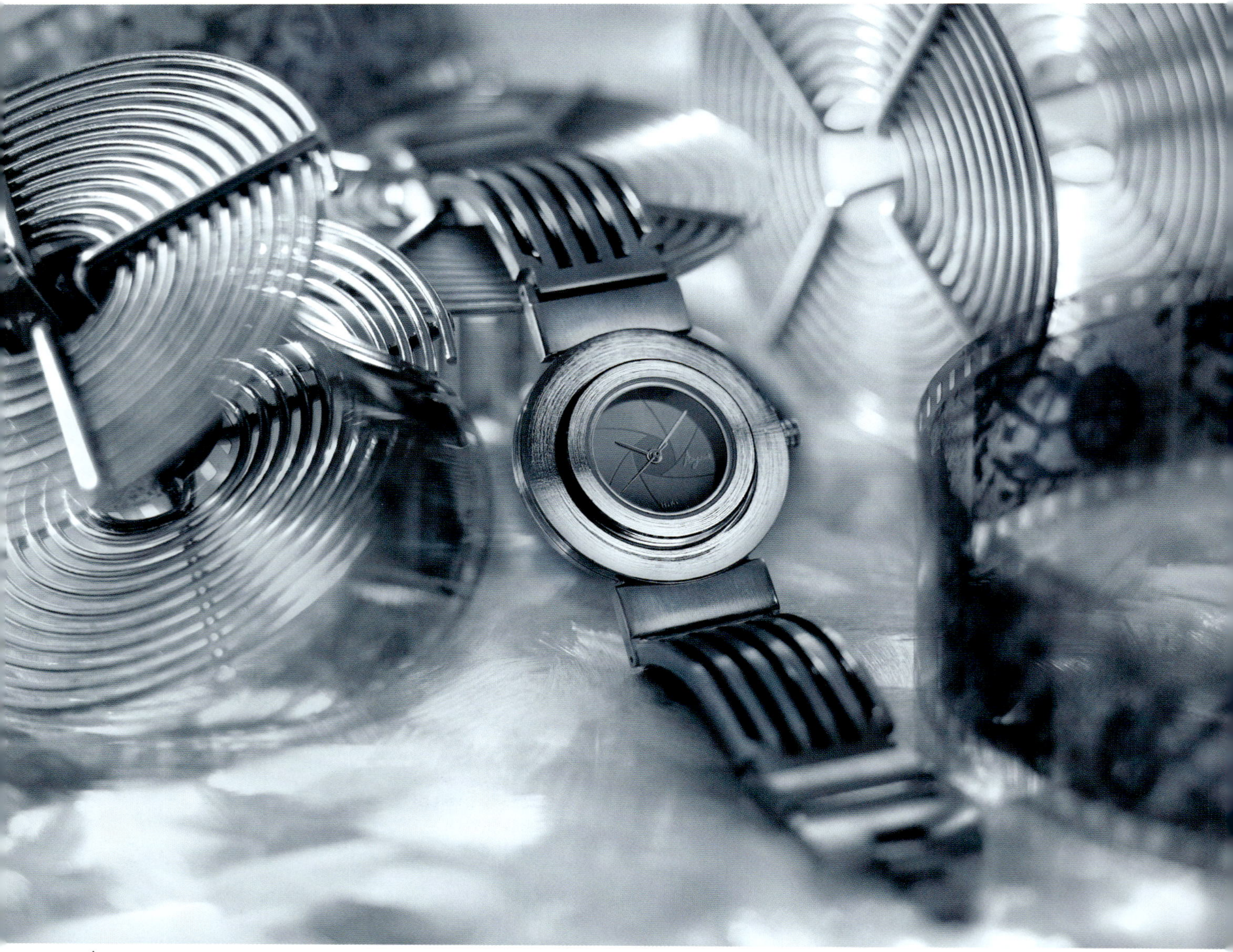

a)

ISO 50, 1/60 sec., f/8.5 , 150mm lens with extension tube

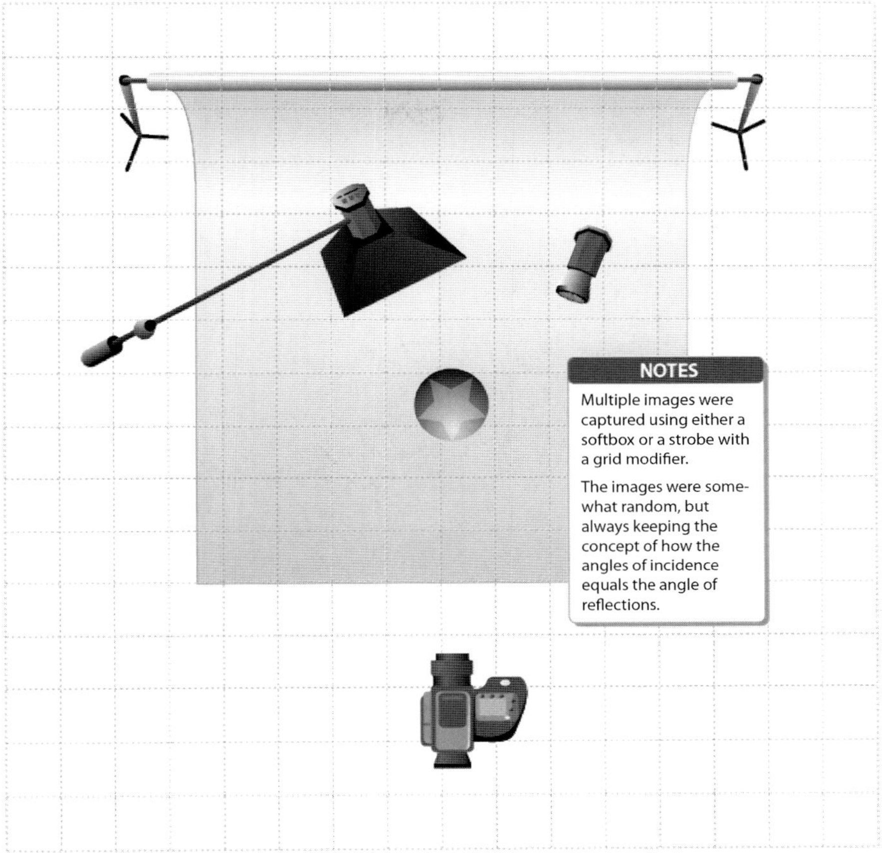

b)

FIGURE 4.17 **a)** A more high-tech approach was employed for this watch. **b)** Multiple images were captured using a single light source that was moved to various positions. **c)** A more rustic look was used to enhance the features of this watch (next page). **d)** This image was created using multiple images in which the light source was stationary but mirrors were moved to add highlights (next page).

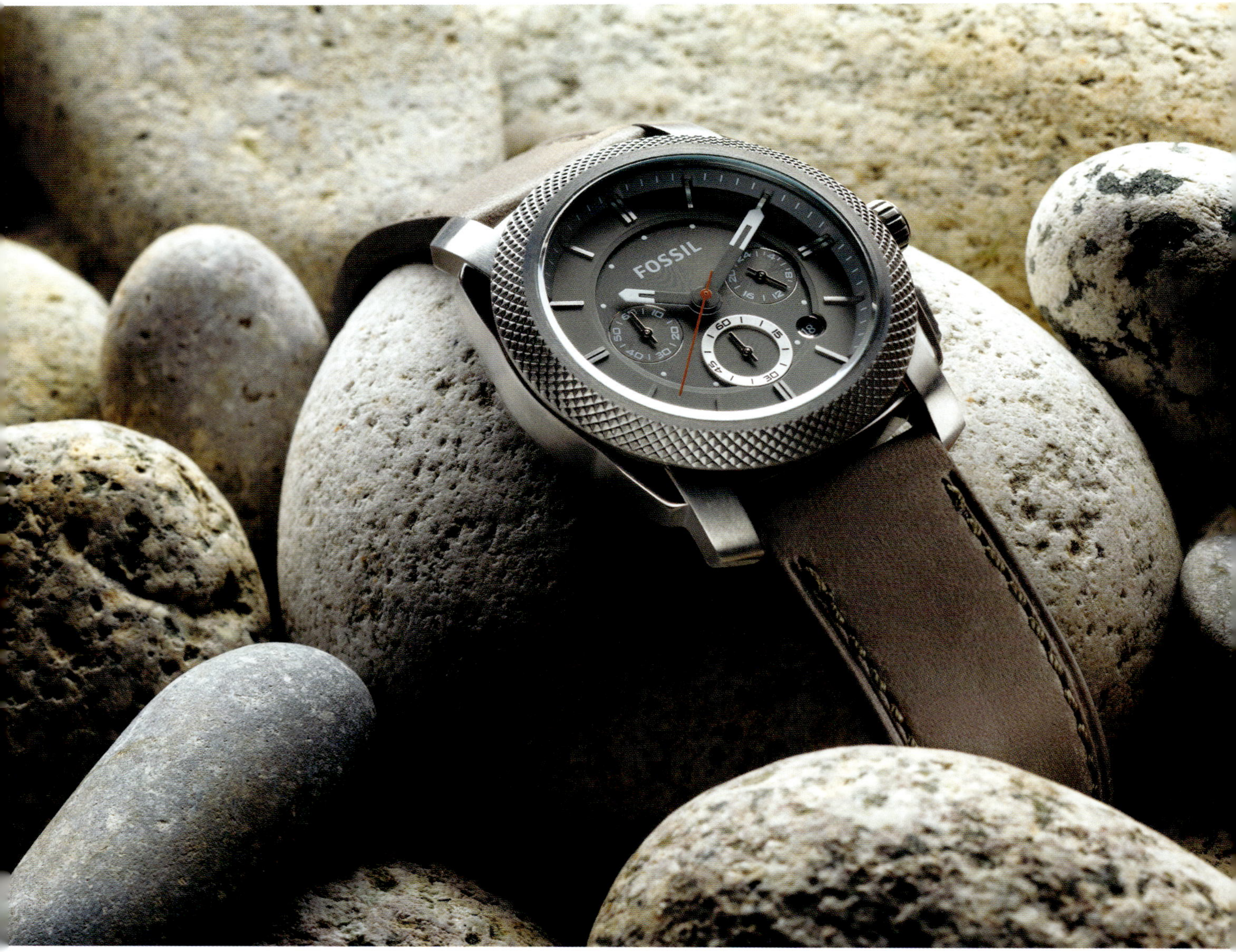

c)

ISO 50, 1/60 sec., f/16, 100mm lens

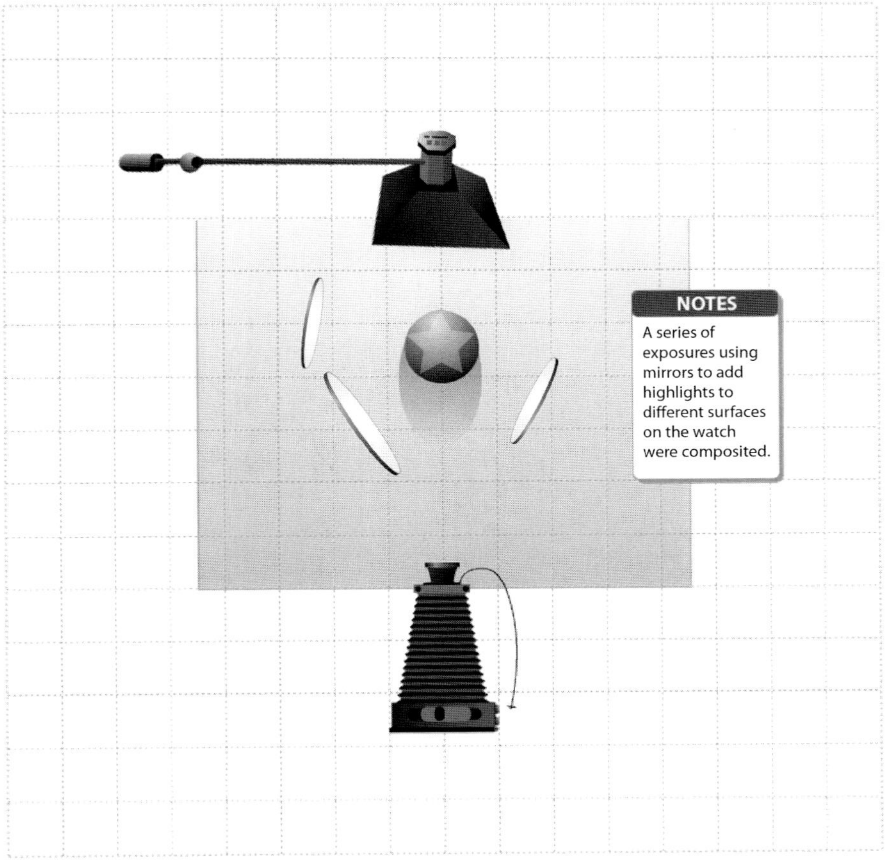
NOTES
A series of exposures using mirrors to add highlights to different surfaces on the watch were composited.

d)

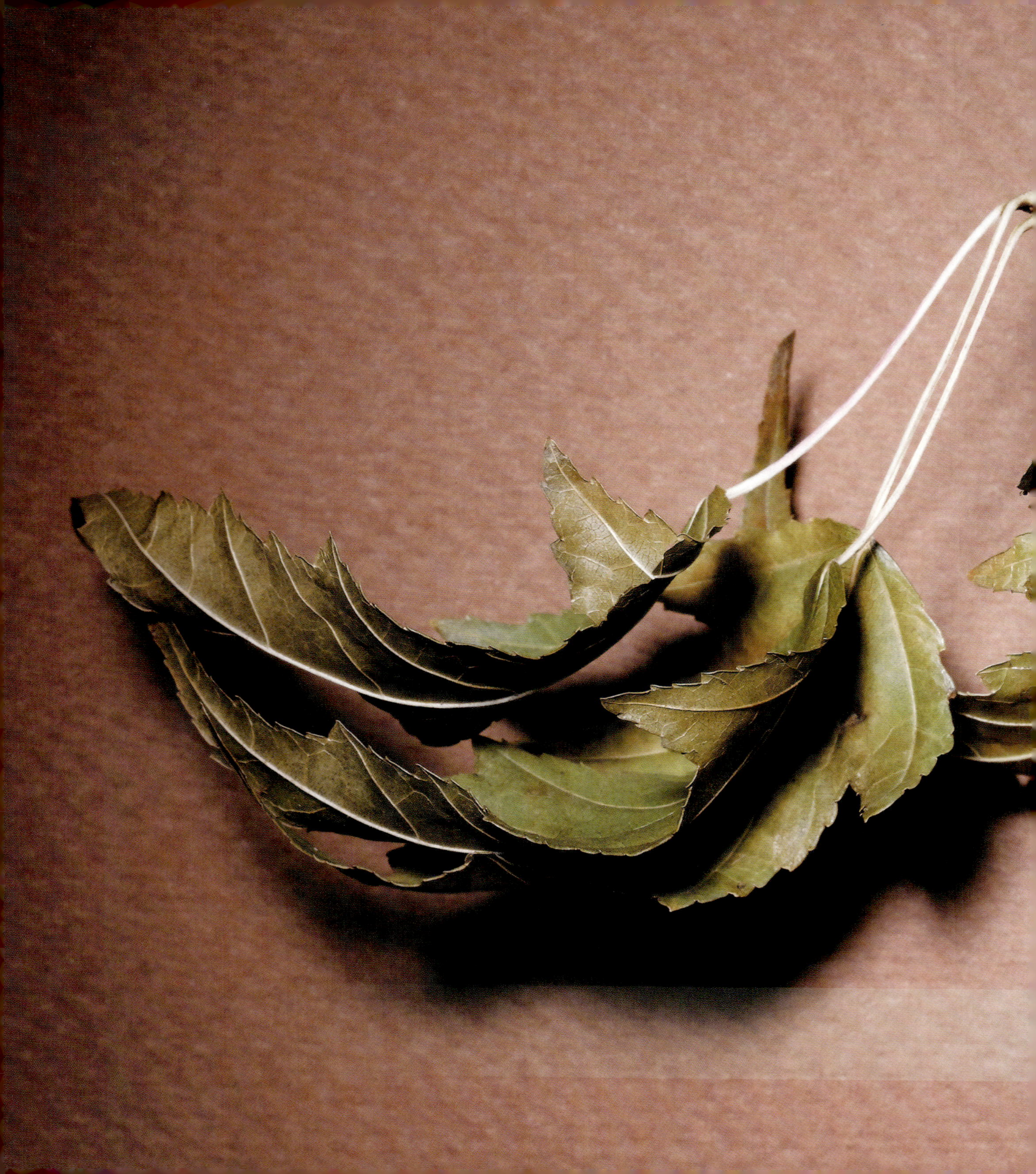

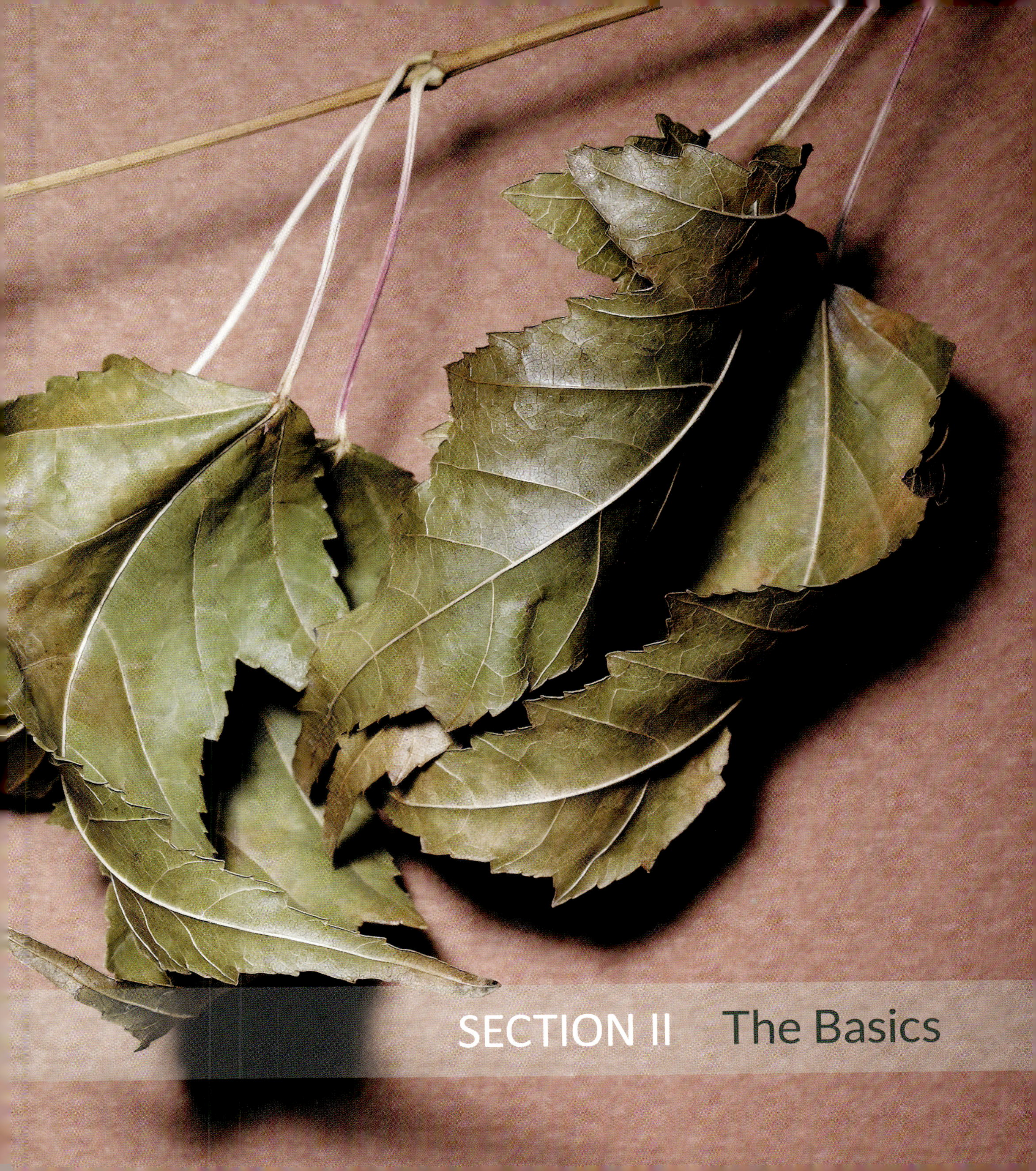

SECTION II The Basics

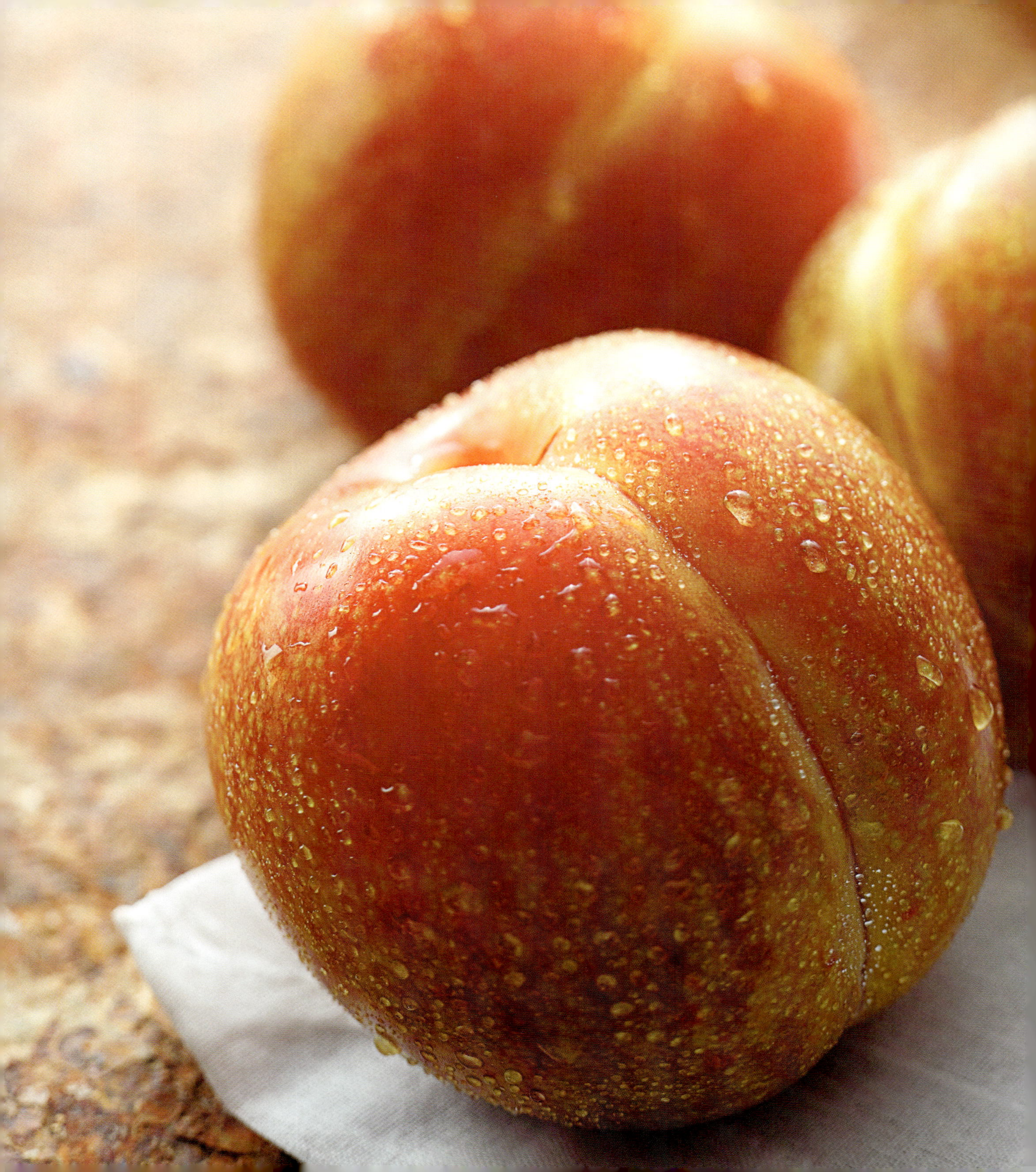

chapter five

LIGHTING EQUIPMENT

Just like any good craftsman, a photographer requires some basic knowledge and tools. It doesn't get more basic than a camera, lighting, and how a photographer uses those tools to create an image. A professional photographer doesn't want just any image; a pro wants a well-crafted and technically accurate image, and that is where metering and its visual cousin, the histogram, come in.

With the enormous amount of purchasing options and quickly changing technologies, it's impossible to address the function of every light and every camera on the market. Fortunately, there is much common ground. This section will take a look at lighting equipment, especially the differences between strobe and continuous light sources, DSLR cameras, metering, and how to read a histogram.

ISO 50, 1/60 sec., f/8, 100mm lens

Opening Image: Photographic Equipment

Camera: Sinar 4 × 5 view camera with Leaf Aptus-II digital back

Lens: Schneider 100mm

Lighting: Profoto Acute2 2400 generator and two strobe heads

Light modifiers: Small white card

Using multiple strobes behind a large scrim is an inexpensive method for creating a big, controllable light source for the fruit image on the previous page. Here, two different power settings were used to control the brightness and the foreground.

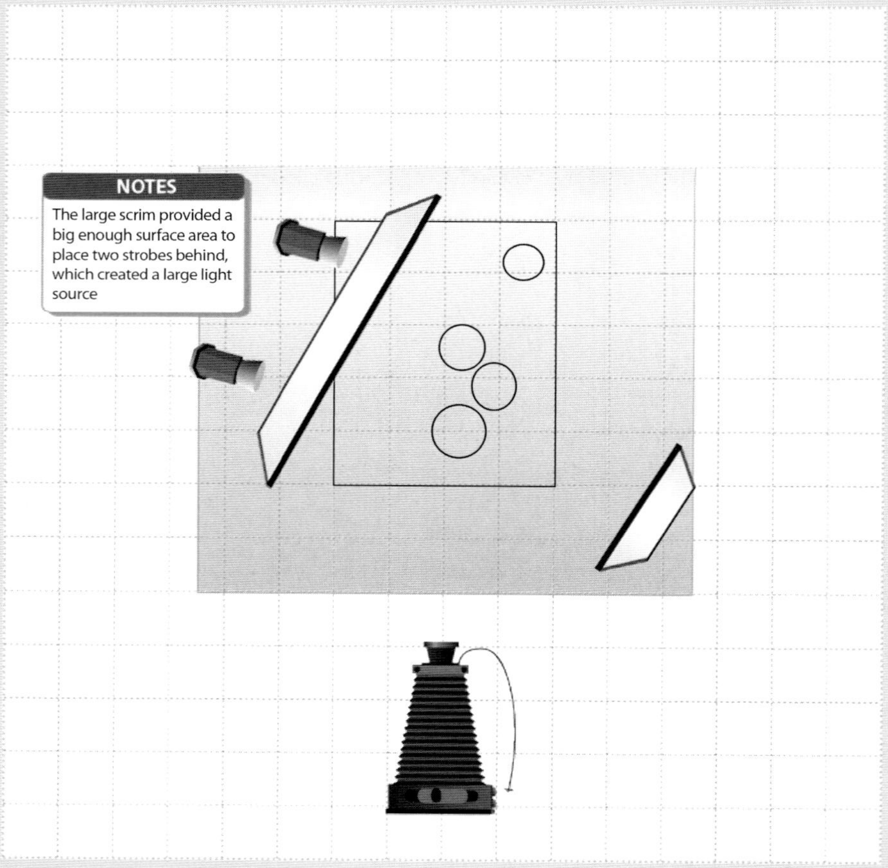

Whereas the nature and wildlife photographer use the power of the sun, the studio photographer relies on the power of artificial lighting. For some, the notion of having to light something is scary, but in reality it isn't too difficult. Which is more difficult, moving the sun or a light in the studio?

Studio photographers love control. One of the greatest things about being a studio photographer is that you don't have to wait for the sun to rise or set or worry that the clouds will fill the sky moments before you click the shutter. You control the light.

Going into a camera store and telling a salesperson that you are there to purchase some lights will probably lead to an overload of information and give you that deer-in-the-headlights look. Imagine walking into a car dealership and saying you want to purchase a car without having thought about what you need to use it for and which key features you want. You have to do your research before test-driving and signing on the dotted line.

This chapter, "Lighting Equipment," is intended to give you the tools to understand your options. Remember, no one size fits all; consider your individual needs before you buy.

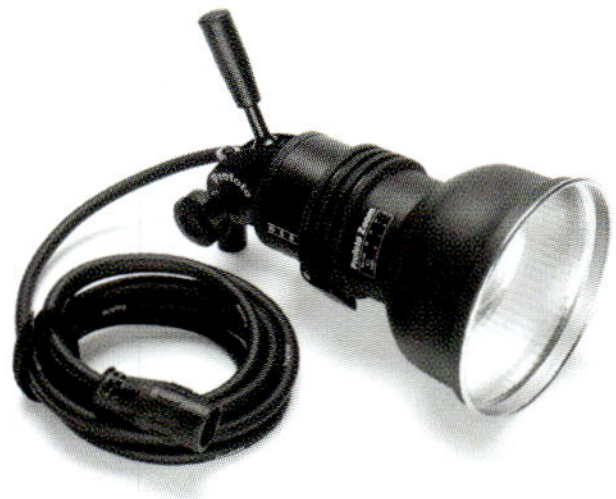

a)

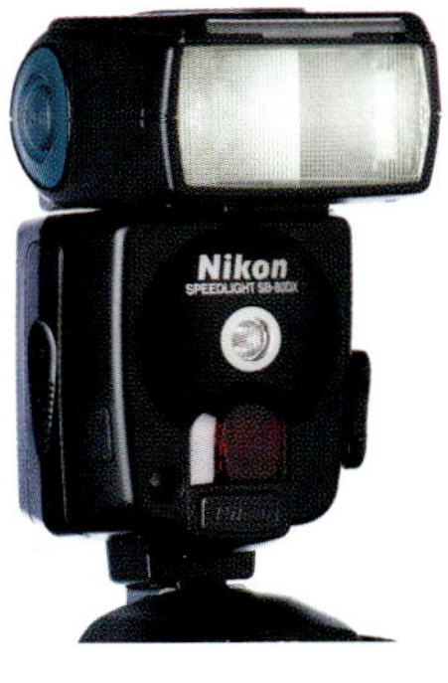

b)

FIGURE 5.1 **a)** An image of a strobe; **b)** a speedlight.

Strobe/Flash

Two main categories of lights fall under strobes and flashes, and these are speedlights and studio strobes. Most amateur photographers are pretty comfortable with speedlights. They can be considered the big brother to the camera's built-in pop-up flash. Speedlights have become more powerful and more technologically advanced in recent years. But just because amateurs are comfortable with these doesn't mean they're not professional tools. Because of their portability, they are a go-to light for photojournalists and editorial photographers, but because of their low cost, they are also a great way to begin a studio career. Their downside is they don't have the power to light a large set or the ability to alter the quality of light, and they lack a modeling lamp (FIGURE 5.1).

Although speedlights and strobes are somewhat different tools, they share an important function: Both produce a burst or flash of light. Whether you're shooting portraits of a newly engaged couple or the pop of a champagne cork, it's that instantaneous burst of light that allows you to freeze the action.

Modeling Lamps

Because strobes and flashes produce an instantaneous burst of light, it's difficult to judge how the quality of light will affect the subject. Modeling lamps are low-powered continuous lamps; in most cases, your studio strobes will come with a modeling lamp. The idea is that you use the modeling lamp to place your lights, previsualizing the lighting, and then use the strobes to capture the image. It's important to remember to take your meter readings with the strobes and not the modeling lamps (**FIGURE 5.2**).

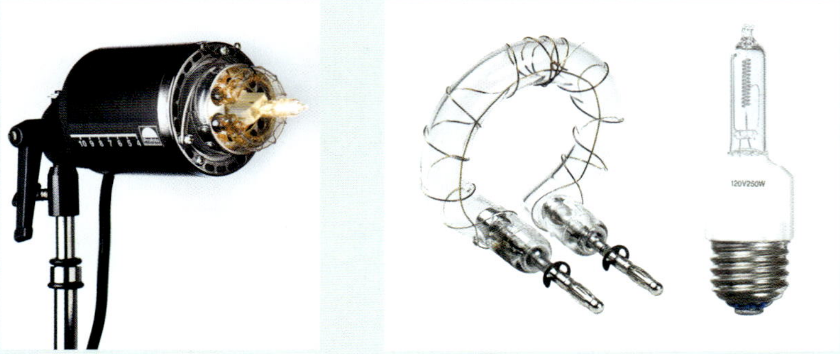

a) b)

FIGURE 5.2 **a)** The outer ring is the flash tube, and the inner bulb is the modeling lamp; **b)** detail of flash tube and modeling lamp.

Studios strobes generally have two main components, the generator (aka power pack), which stores the power in capacitors, and the strobe head (aka flash head). The generator, which is plugged into an electrical outlet, accumulates and stores power and, when the camera is triggered, sends the current to the strobe head to produce the flash of light. Studio strobes come in a vast array of power and output options. Although not as portable as speedlights, studio strobes offer much greater control (**FIGURE 5.3**).

Here are a few key benefits of studio strobes:

- Greater power
- Ability to plug multiple strobe heads into a single generator
- Accessories: The quality of light can be easily modified
- Modeling lamps

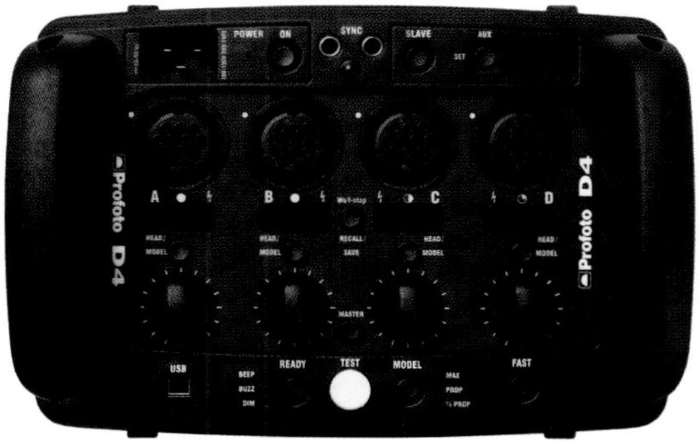

FIGURE 5.3 This generator has the capabilities to accept four separate strobe heads and have the power output controlled asymmetrically.

Benefits of speedlights:

- Portability
- In-camera metering: Most speedlights offer auto or TTL (through the lens)
- Cost (although the cost per watt second is higher)

Flash Duration

Not all strobes are created equal. It's easy to say that strobes fire in a fraction of a second, but there are times when you also want to consider how long the burst of light is visible. This is called flash duration. A couple of things can affect flash duration. The first is the manufacturer and model of the strobe; pricier models tend to have a quicker duration. Second, consider the power output. The duration can vary on a single generator depending on the desired output. As a general rule, the lower the power, the faster the duration.

Watt Seconds

The power output of studio strobes is commonly measured in watt seconds. The higher the number, the greater the power. Whereas speedlights might have an output of 75ws–150ws, it's not uncommon to see studio strobe generators rated to 4000ws. More is not always better: Portrait photographers tend to use a lower power, while still life photographers and those lighting larger sets prefer more power.

FIGURE 5.4 **a)** An image of long flash duration does not freeze milk droplets and there is motion; **b)** an image of short flash duration freezes each droplet in place.

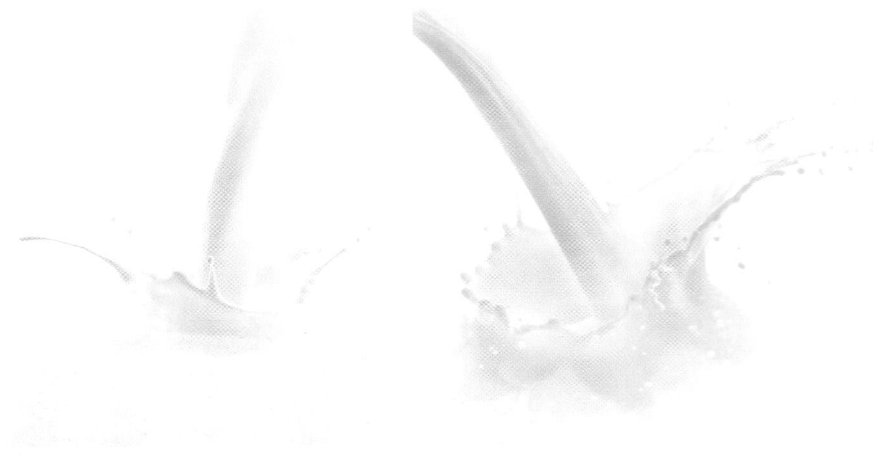

© Shutterstock

a) b)

© Shutterstock

Profoto is a well-known manufacturer of lighting equipment, and within its line of strobes and generators are options to fit many needs and budgets. As mentioned, the more expensive units tend to have a faster flash duration. One of Profoto's generators has a very quick flash duration of 1/12000 and another unit lists a range of 1/560 to 1/3200 depending on the power output (FIGURE 5.4).

Why would someone care about flash duration? For most applications, you won't, but for certain special shots it's necessary to think about it—an image that requires water being frozen in time, for example (FIGURE 5.5).

Strobes and Shutter Speeds

How many people have taken a photograph using their on-camera flash or speedlight and then noticed that parts of the resulting image are dark, as if the flash failed to light some of the image? Don't feel bad if you've done that; it's a common mistake, but there's an easy fix. The problem was that the shutter speed was too fast for the flash; the shutter had opened and already begun to close when the flash was fired. All DSLR cameras have a maximum flash sync, aka maximum shutter speed, when using a flash. You'll want to check the camera manual, because different models have different maximums. Most range from 1/60 to 1/250 shutter speed. You can always use a slower shutter speed but never faster.

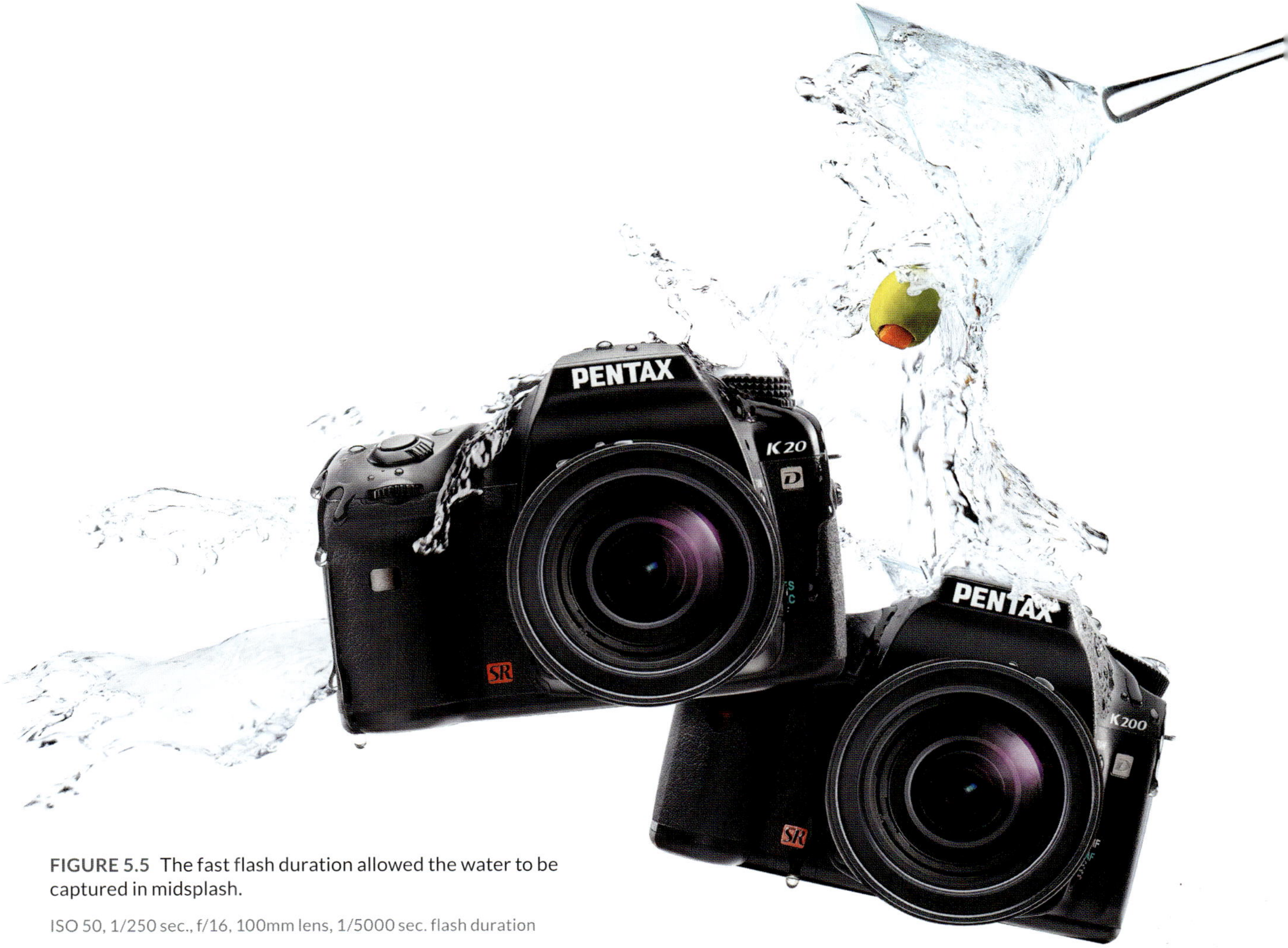

FIGURE 5.5 The fast flash duration allowed the water to be captured in midsplash.

ISO 50, 1/250 sec., f/16, 100mm lens, 1/5000 sec. flash duration

Temperature

When discussing temperature and studio light, we aren't talking about the heat generated but rather the temperature of the light, which is also called the color of the light.

In photography, the color temperature of light is measured by using the Kelvin (k) scale. The Kelvin scale is named after the British scientist William Kelvin. In an experiment, he discovered that when he heated a block of carbon, it changed color depending on its temperature.

Here are a handful of common sources of light and their approximate Kelvin values:

- Candle: 1900k
- Sunrise and sunset: 2500k
- Household incandescent bulb: 2800k
- Tungsten lamp: 3200–3400k
- Daylight (midday): 5500k
- Overcast day: 6500–7500k

As you can deduce from the examples, the lower the value, the warmer—or yellower—the color of the light. The key one to remember is daylight's value, 5500k.

Strobes and flashes have a color temperature of 5500k, the same as daylight. It's common to hear photographers refer to this as white light. For film photographers, this is crucial, because most film is rated for daylight lighting. It's also important for digital photographers, because the auto white balance setting on DSLR cameras is also based on 5500k.

The multitude of light choices and camera white balance options requires photographers to carefully select the appropriate settings. The following images (**FIGURE 5.6**) illustrate what happens when the correct and incorrect white balance are selected based on the light's color temperature.

Photography gets a little more tricky when you combine multiple light sources, but it really helps when the sources have the same color temperature, such as when you are shooting outdoors in daylight and adding strobes or speedlights.

Continuous

The second category of studio lighting is continuous lighting. Whereas strobes create an instantaneous flash of light, continuous lighting is similar to your household bulbs in that once on, they are ready to use. When shooting outdoors, we're all pretty aware of the largest continuous light source, the sun.

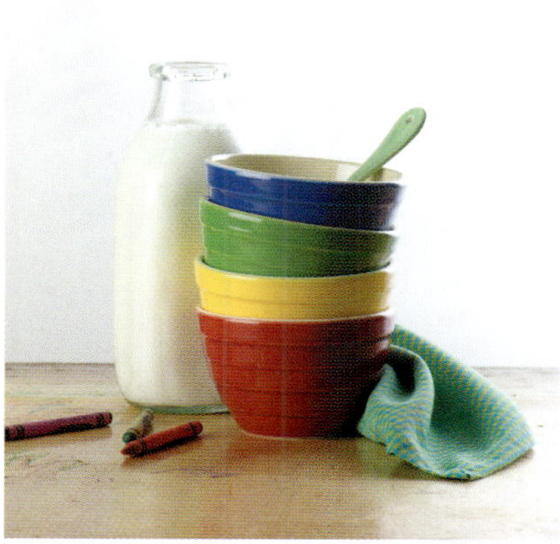

a) ISO 100, 1/125 sec., f/16 , 150mm lens

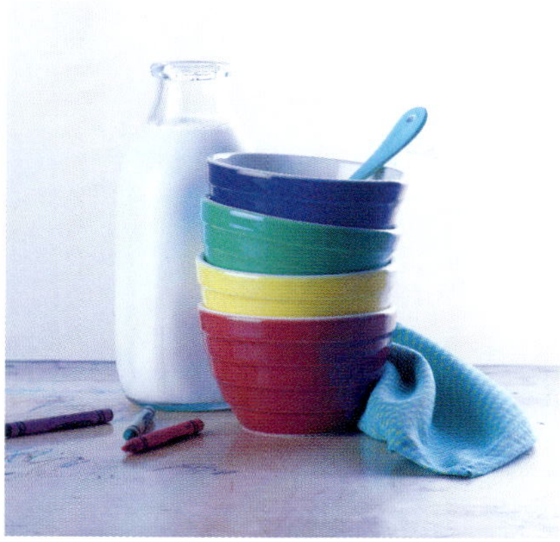

b) ISO 100, 1/125 sec., f/16 , 150mm lens

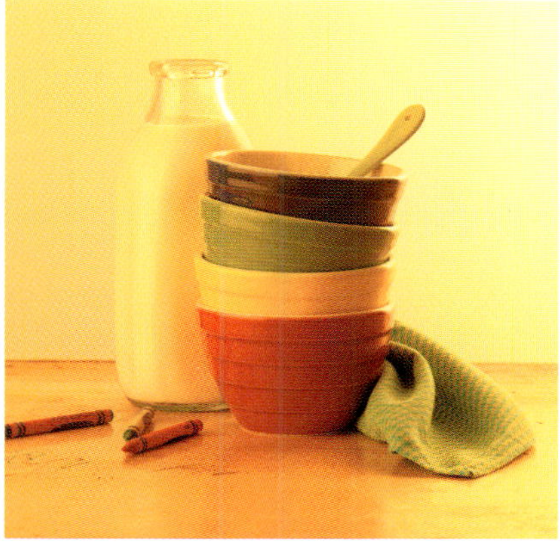

c) ISO 100, 1/4 sec., f/16 , 150mm lens

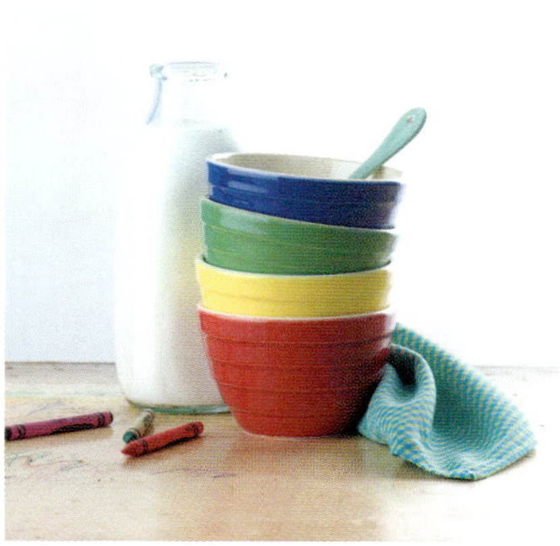

d) ISO 100, 1/4 sec., f/16 , 150mm lens

FIGURE 5.6 **a)** Here the light source (strobe) and the camera's white balance (daylight) match, which creates a pleasant image. **b)** We have the identical light source as the first, but now the camera's white balance is incorrectly set to Tungsten, creating a blue color cast. **c)** The light source has been changed to Tungsten; however, the camera's white balance is incorrectly set on Daylight, resulting in a very warm image. **d)** The final image uses tungsten as the source and tungsten as the white balance setting. Here, the temperatures match, producing a neutral image.

What are some of the key elements of continuous lighting?

The most obvious and most important is that the light is continuous; however, from there, many small nuances must be addressed.

- **Power:** Tungsten lights come in a wide range of power options; power is measured in watts. The higher the watts, the brighter the light.
- **Heat:** It's common to hear the term *hot lights* used to describe tungsten lights. Just as with your household bulbs, this continuous light source produces heat; a lot of heat. You wouldn't want to touch your 75-watt household bulb, so imagine what a 500-watt tungsten light would feel like. It's not just about touch; you need to be cautious with what materials are surrounding the lights.

- **Temperature:** Here, we are referring to the Kelvin scale and not heat. Tungsten lights are generally rated around 3200–3400k. When compared with daylight, this appears very warm. Film photographers would either need to purchase tungsten-rated film or use a color-correcting filter to cool the temperature if using daylight film. Digital shooting allows the white balance to be corrected in camera or in post-production.
- **WYSIWYG:** What you see is what you get. Unlike strobes, continuous lights do not require a secondary modeling lamp to see how the lighting will look when the image is captured. For many, this is the number-one benefit of working with tungsten lights compared with strobes. Because lighting is a building process, meaning you add one light and see what it does before adding another, working with continuous lighting really allows you to visualize your images.
- **Cost:** Surprisingly, the cost difference between watts and watt seconds isn't too great. This is primarily true when comparing basic strobe setups; when comparing strobe setups that have many technological options, the price discrepancy widens. A well-made tungsten light will consist of a good housing designed to dissipate heat, optional accessories, and an on/off switch (FIGURE 5.7).

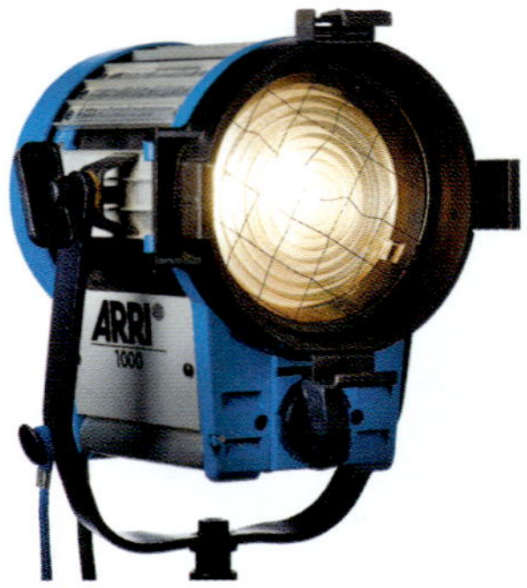

FIGURE 5.7 A tungsten light.

HEAT AND SUBJECT MATTER

Subject matter should be considered when making a choice on lighting equipment. In a handful of scenarios, the heat of tungsten lights would not be the appropriate choice. As a photographer, it's helpful to put yourself in the position of the subject. Would you want to have a hot light aimed at your face while someone is telling you to smile?

As a food photographer, I have seen the way light can wilt food. It's pretty easy to understand that ice cream and hot lights don't mix well. I used to have an ice-cream client, and not only was the heat of the lights a concern, but so was the temperature of the entire studio. We had a section designed as a freezer area where we could maintain a brisk temperature of 18 degrees.

—JOE LAVINE

Other Continuous Options

So far our discussion has focused on the most common studio continuous lights, tungstens, but other options are worth mentioning.

HMI (hydrargyrum medium-arc iodide): HMIs are commonly used in the motion picture industry and outdoors because they are daylight balanced (5500k). They cost significantly more than tungsten lights.

LED (light-emitting diode): Alone, a single LED is very small and doesn't produce much light. However, this technology allows many LEDs to be placed side by side, creating a larger, brighter source. Most LEDs are daylight balanced, but some models offer the option to adjust the color temperature without the use of gels.

Fluorescent: Long before CFL became common for household use, photographers used daylight-balanced fluorescent tubes for studio use. Key benefits include shallow depth of field and a softly diffused output that is flattering for skin.

Filtering

Photographic filtering is an easy way to alter the color temperature of a light, regardless of its design. Filtering simply involves placing colored material, called gel, between the light and the subject. Usually, the gel is placed on or near the light; however, when used with tungsten lamps it's important that the gel doesn't touch the bulb.

Photographic gels are generally made from either polycarbonate plastic or dyed polyester. Gels come in all different sizes, including long rolls, sheets, and even small precut options to fit over speedlights. It may be more economical to purchase larger gels and cut them down to fit your individual needs (FIGURE 5.8).

Although using gels seems as though you are adding something to control light, the process is actually one of subtraction. Gels work by subtracting wavelengths of light; a blue gel absorbs (subtracts) red and green wavelengths of light, allowing only the blue spectrum to pass. It's important to note that besides absorbing wavelengths of light, the amount of light is

FIGURE 5.8 A variety of gels.

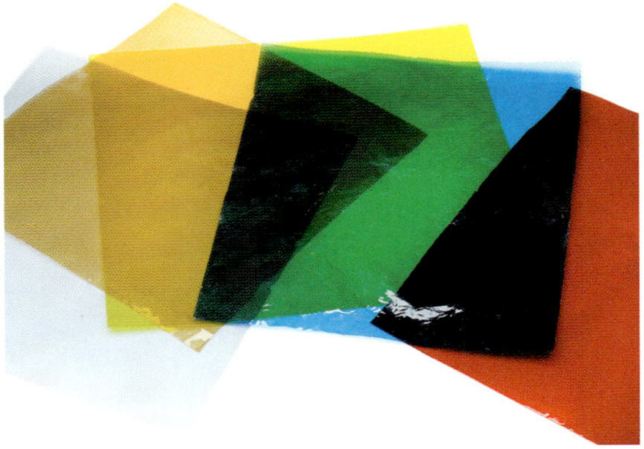

reduced depending on its color density. A deep blue gel will absorb more light than one that is light amber. Remember to meter or remeter after the gel has been put into place.

Filtering falls into two main categories, color correction and creative.

Color Correction

Color correction gels are designed to "correct" the color temperature of lights to match film or adjust the color to daylight. For example, if you are using tungsten lights with daylight film, then the color temperature of the light needs to be altered. This is also important when working with multiple light sources. Whether you're on location, where you can't always change the overall lighting, or in the studio, there are times when you'll be using mixed lighting, such as daylight and tungsten, or daylight and fluorescent, and even some occasions where you'll need to mix three or more. In these situations, the color of light needs to be corrected.

It just so happens that there are specific gels for the occasions when your light source does not match your film or white balance, or when using multiple types of lights that must be corrected to match.

CTO (color temperature orange): As the name implies, a CTO has an orange color, which when used on a strobe lowers the color temperature of the light. The technical use is to convert daylight to work with tungsten film. As with all gels, CTO comes in different levels.

Full CTO: Converts 5500k to 2900k

¾ CTO: Converts 5500k to 3200k

½ CTO: Converts 5500k to 3800k

¼ CTO: Converts 5500 to 4500k

CTB (color temperature blue): CTB gels have a blue appearance and raises the color temperature of the light. Their technical use is to place them over tungsten lights when daylight film or a daylight white balance is desired.

Full blue: 3200k to 5500k

½ blue: 3200k to 4100k

¼ blue: 3200k to 3500k

PlusGreen: PlusGreen is designed to match the color of fluorescent lights; not the daylight CFLs, but rather the common ones found in many large buildings such as corporate offices, hospitals, and schools. These gels work similarly to CTB and CTO gels in that they absorb specific wavelengths of light and allow others to pass, but since there are no fluorescent films, there is another step required. Step one requires the PlusGreen gel to be placed over the strobes, and then when shooting daylight film a magenta filter is placed over the lens, which absorbs the green color cast. When shooting digitally, the last step is replaced with setting the correct camera white balance.

Creative

When it comes to creative filtering, the sky's the limit. You have two options: Enhance what nature has already given us, or go against what is natural to define a new look.

Enhancing a natural look takes a subtle touch. A common technique is to add a CTO gel to a strobe to give the light a warm appearance, similar to morning light coming in a kitchen window (FIGURE 5.9).

In Figure 5.9, the extra warmth helps the viewer make an emotional connection between the image and the wonderful feeling of sitting down to breakfast.

The other direction is to go bold with gels and let it be obvious that the colors aren't natural (FIGURE 5.10).

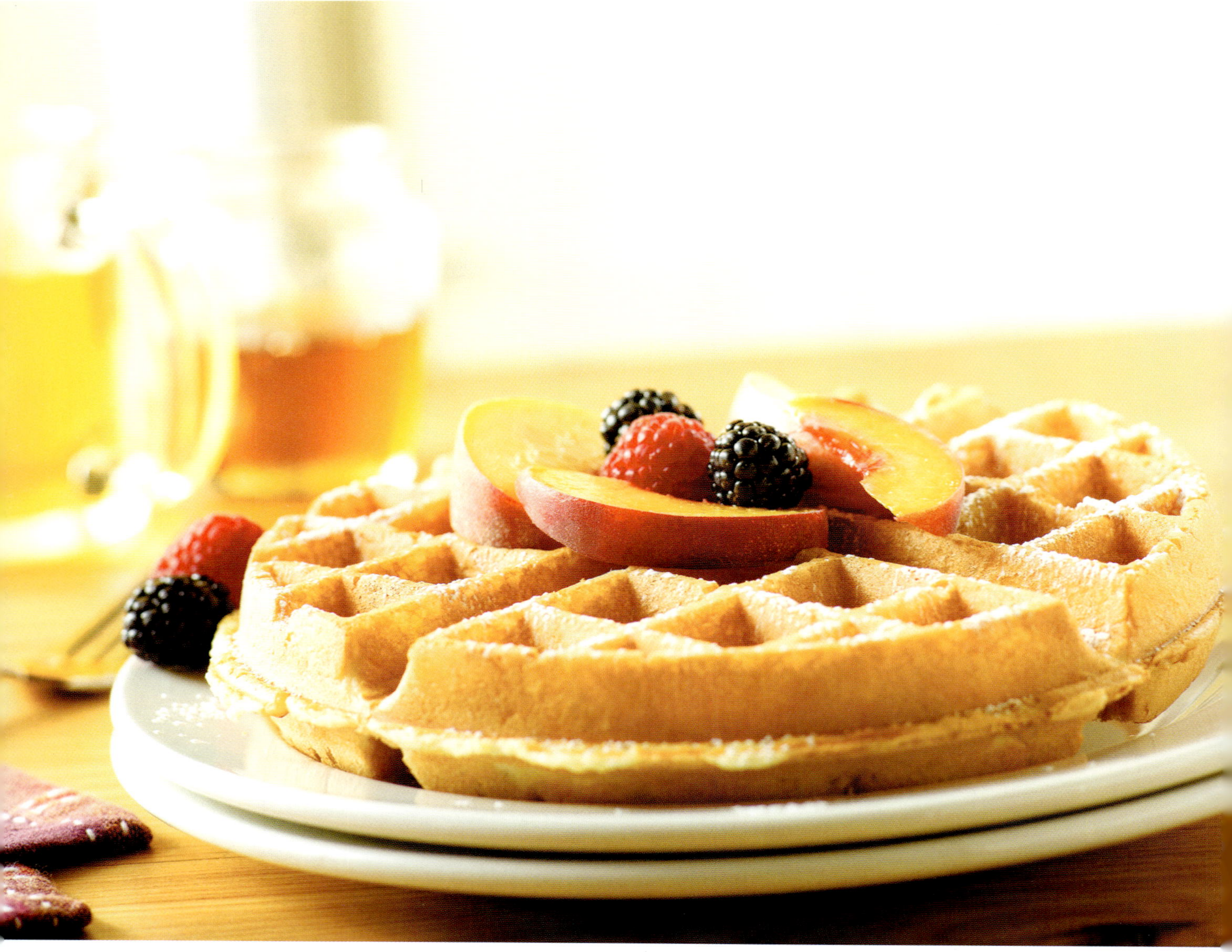

FIGURE 5.9 The waffle image above uses a simple two-light setup; however, the light coming from the back of the set was warmed by the addition of a ½ CTO.

ISO 50 , 1/60 sec., f/8, 100mm lens

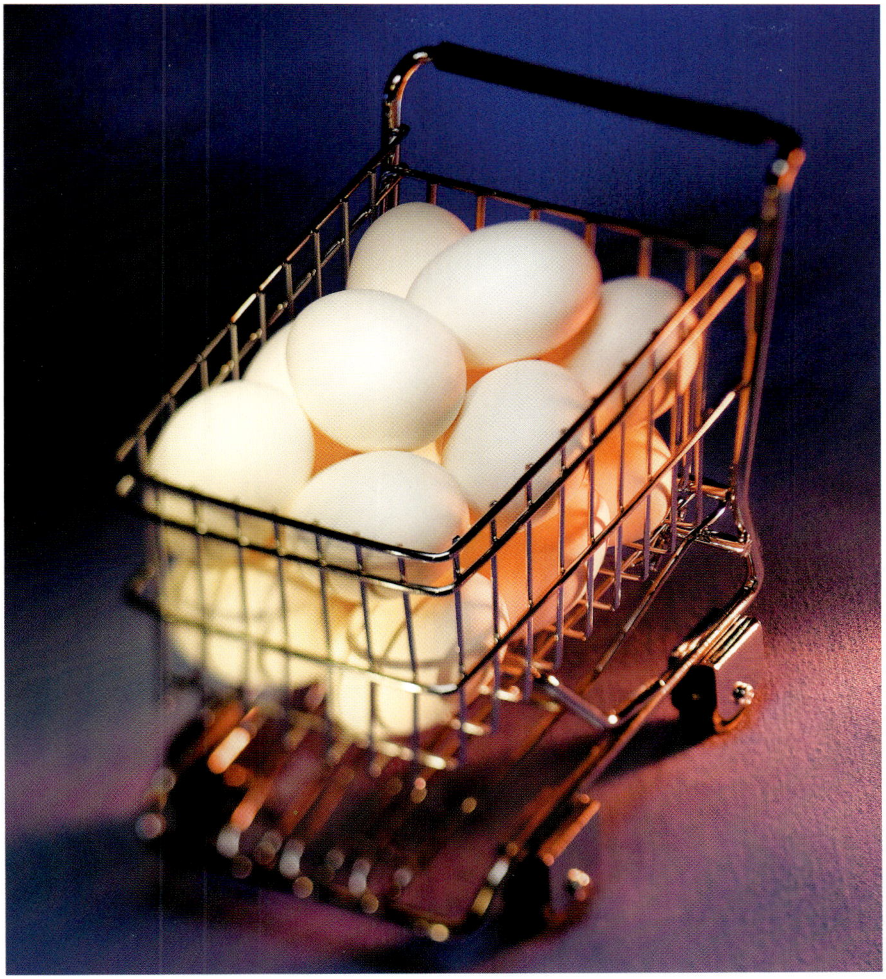

FIGURE 5.10 Gels used to create dramatic yet unnatural color.

ISO 100, 1/125 sec., f/22, 90mm lens

Accessories

Anything we use in conjunction with our lights can be considered an accessory. These range from items that are necessary, such as light stands, to those that add control, like barn doors, to some that simply make out lives easier. Photographers love their gadgets; the key is deciding which ones are must-haves and which aren't really necessary. Remember, what's vital for one photographer might not be required for another.

Grip (Gear)

In the movie and video industry, the term *grip* is used as a job description for someone responsible for rigging the equipment, which can be anything from lighting gear to camera supports. Photographers use the term as a catchall phrase to describe the support equipment.

- **Light stands:** Here is an item that you just can't have enough of. At times you'll want a small enough stand to have your light a foot off the floor; at other times the light needs to be 12 feet in the air. Consider the cost of your lighting gear before purchasing inexpensive light stands; make sure the stands are sturdy enough to hold your lights securely. Stands are an important investment that will last your entire career. Both authors own stands older than the average college student.
- **Booms:** Lighting booms are one of those pieces of equipment that you might not need all the time, but when you do, there is simply no substitute. Booms allow you to extend a light above and over a set; this is great whether you are working on a still life or are using a hair light during a portrait sitting. Two components generally make up a boom: a heavy-duty stand and an arm that extends horizontally over the floor.
- **Weights:** Whether you're using a light stand or boom, a lot of expensive weight is being supported by one end of a small piece of metal. To safeguard your investment, and anyone under the light, it is smart to counterbalance with a weight. Weights are usually heavy-duty bags filled with sand or shot, or are molded iron (counter balance) with a built-in clamp that allows easy attachment to a boom arm.

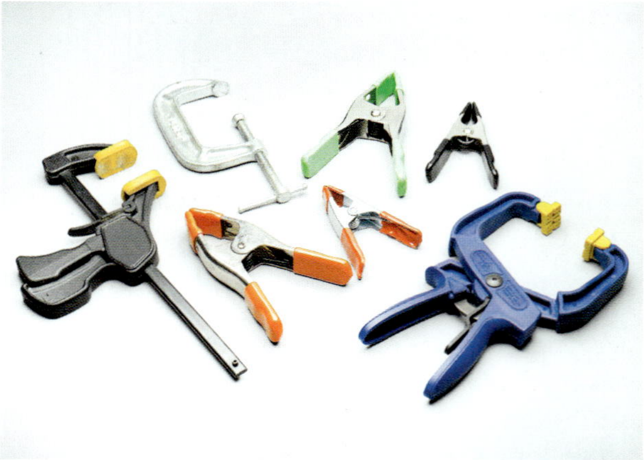

FIGURE 5.11 Assorted clamps.

- **Clamps:** There is no such thing as a studio photographer having too many clamps. A-clamps, sometimes called carpenter clamps, are items of choice for photographers; they are durable and easy to use. You'll use clamps for everything from holding up a background on a stand to organizing cords around a set. Most photographers use the 1- and 2-inch models, but it's good to have a few large 3-inch clamps on hand for the big jobs (FIGURE 5.11).

Light Modifiers

The term *light modifier* is another catchall phrase, used to describe any device that alters the quality or direction of light coming from the light source. This can mean a simple piece of matte board to block light, or an elaborate multipanel softbox to diffuse light; each is modifying the light before it reaches the subject. The correct purchase really depends on your individual style of photography.

The items below are in no way an extensive list but rather a sampling of options.

Barn doors: Barn doors attach directly to a light head and use four metal leaves to direct light. The quality of light is not altered, just where the light falls. The benefits of a barn door are:

- It's inexpensive
- It attaches directly to light, no extra equipment involved
- It does not alter the quality of the light

Umbrellas: Umbrellas (FIGURE 5.12) are very popular with portrait photographers because of the soft quality of light they help produce. You have a variety of sizes to choose from, but there are a few other things to consider, too. The inside of umbrellas is generally white, which produces a very soft quality, or silver, which produces a slightly harder look. Also, some umbrellas have the option to be used as a "pass-through" light modifier. It's common to see an umbrella set up to have light aimed into it and then have the light bounce back out, but some models provide the option to allow the light to pass through. This simply creates a different, even softer quality of light, because the light is being diffused as it's spread out over the surface of the umbrella. The advantages of an umbrella:

- It's relatively inexpensive
- It comes in multiple sizes
- It's compact
- It gives you multiple options for light quality
- It attaches directly to light, no extra equipment involved

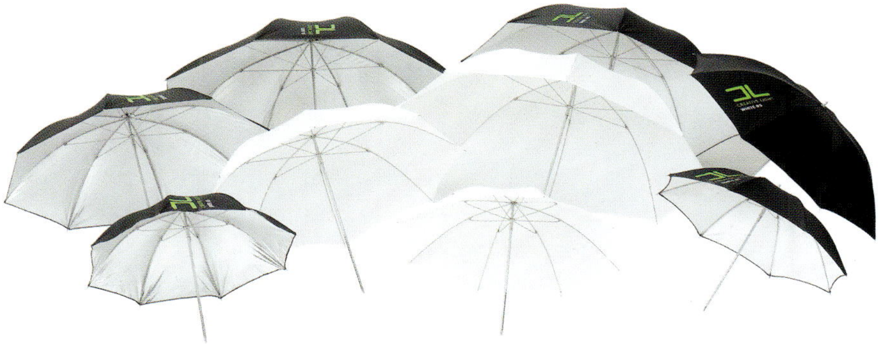

FIGURE 5.12 An assortment of umbrellas.

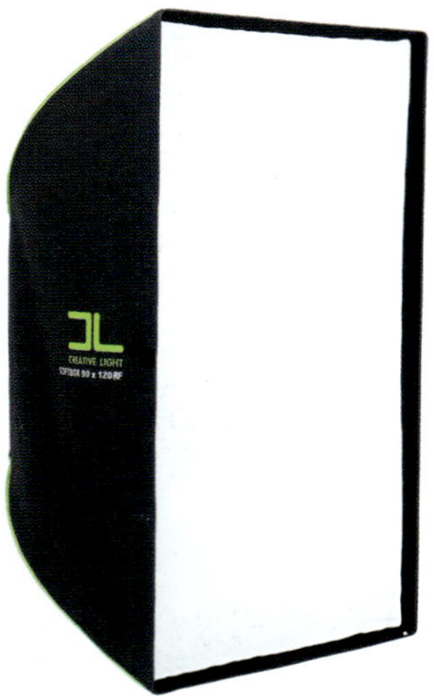

FIGURE 5.13 A typical softbox.

Softboxes: These are used to direct and soften light. The design is pretty much the same regardless of their size and shape; it consists of a fabric-like box that is black on the back and sides and uses one or multiple diffusion baffles in the path of the light (FIGURE 5.13). A softbox:

- Offers excellent light control (placement)
- Can be expensive depending on size and quality
- Collapses for portability
- Requires extra equipment (a speed ring) to attach to light

Diffusion panels: These are similar to softboxes in that they have a diffusion baffle, also called a scrim, between the light and the subject. However, diffusion panels are two-dimensional; there is no enclosed box. A diffusion panel:

- Can be homemade or purchased
- Makes it easy to change the quality of light by changing the scrim or the distance of the light from the scrim
- Requires additional stands for use

Reflectors: Most strobe lights come with or have a built-in reflector. This is what creates the even, round circle of light. Standard reflectors produce a hard-edged quality; however, soft reflectors, or "beauty dishes," are available. A reflector:

- Is generally included with studio strobes
- Has a hard-edge quality, unless it's a beauty dish or some other specialized version
- Is often required to attach accessories (barn doors, grids, as in FIGURE 5.14)

Sync Cords and Radio Slaves

These two items pertain to studio strobes and not speedlights or continuous lighting. All lighting equipment needs a way to interact with the camera. Speedlights, which attach to the hot shoe on top of the camera, are automatically triggered via the camera's electronics. Often you'll see a photographer use a cord to connect the speedlight to the hot shoe, but it is the same principle. Continuous lighting, once turned on, works like the sun; it is simply there and ready to use.

Studio strobes are a little different; we need a method that allows the camera and strobe to communicate. Otherwise, how will the strobe know when the shutter is triggered?

Sync cords are the first option. These are inexpensive cords that connect between the camera and the generator. Inexpensive, yes, but there are some drawbacks. Photographers have always joked that Murphy's Law requires that a photographer must own more than one, because if you only have one it won't work. The second issue is the cord itself, which limits the distance a photographer can stray from the generator. Also, the cord has been known to trip a few people. But the most important reason why these may not be the best choice is the camera's electronics. Today's DSLR cameras are loaded with sensitive electronics, and sync cords require a small current to travel between the generator and the camera. This connection has been known to cause problems with the camera's electronics.

Radio slaves are the preferred option when working with digital cameras and studio strobes. Radio slaves have two components: a transmitter, which transmits a wireless signal from the camera to the generator; and a receiver, which receives the wireless signal and tells the generator when to fire. Some newer generators have built-in receivers. Albeit more expensive than sync cords, radio slaves are a much safer and more convenient option (FIGURE 5.15).

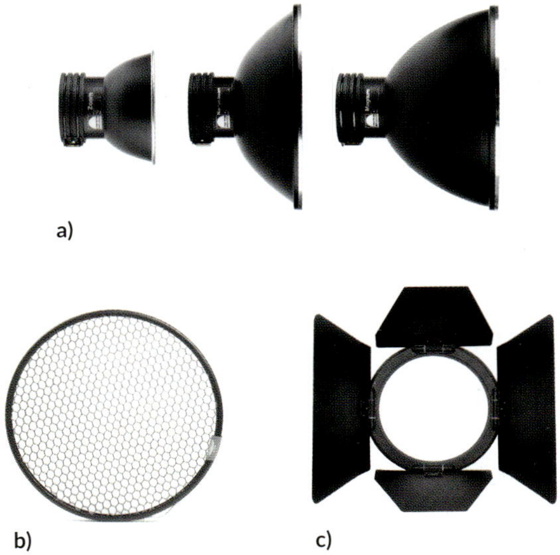

FIGURE 5.14 **a)** Variations of three reflectors. The different depths and sizes modify the light from the strobe head. **b)** A honeycomb grid attaches to the reflector to narrow the beam of light. **c)** Barn doors also attach to the reflector, and help control the spread of light.

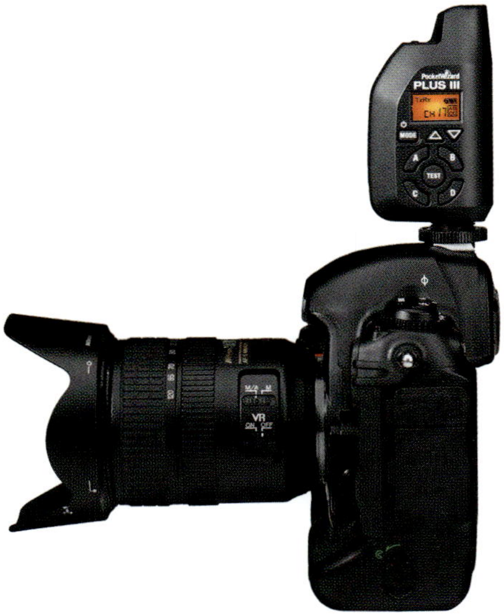

FIGURE 5.15 A radio slave attached to a camera hot shoe.

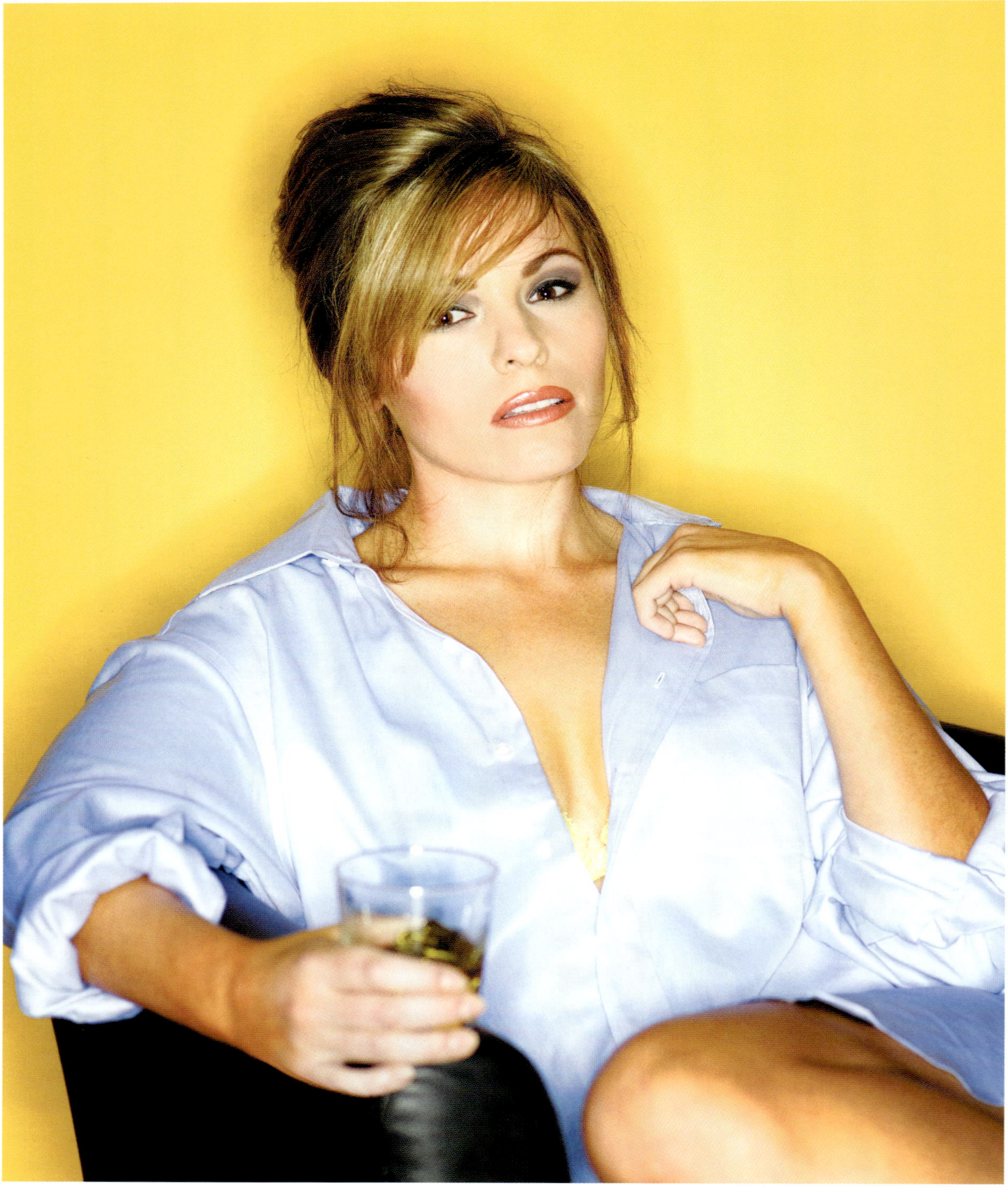

a)

ISO 50, 1/125 sec., f/4 , 150mm lens

Comparison

This chapter's comparison is a little different because given the logistics of using the same model and stylist, we needed to photograph the model the same day (**FIGURE 5.16**). This was the only comparison shoot where each of us knew exactly what the other was thinking.

These were fun images to shoot. This session was a good example of how sometimes you need to go with the flow, and if you're lucky, it all works out. Going into the shoot we knew that one of us would focus on using soft, even lighting to create the standard pretty portrait, and the other would use a modern, hard-edge lighting style.

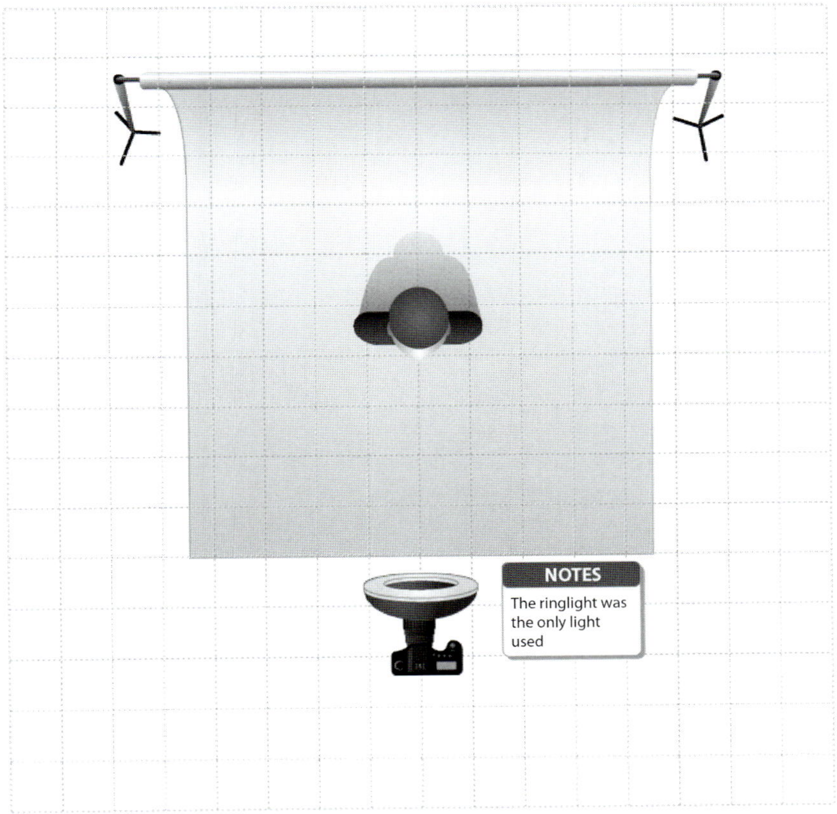

b)

FIGURE 5.16 **a)** The ring flash created hard light, as desired, for the soft sexy look she projects within the hard light. **b)** The ring flash is not only on the camera axis but, by design, surrounds the lens. **c)** Evenly balanced lighting creates a shadowless appearance and a girl-next-door look (next page). **d)** The key to this lighting setup is placing the two softboxes an equal distance from the model (page following).

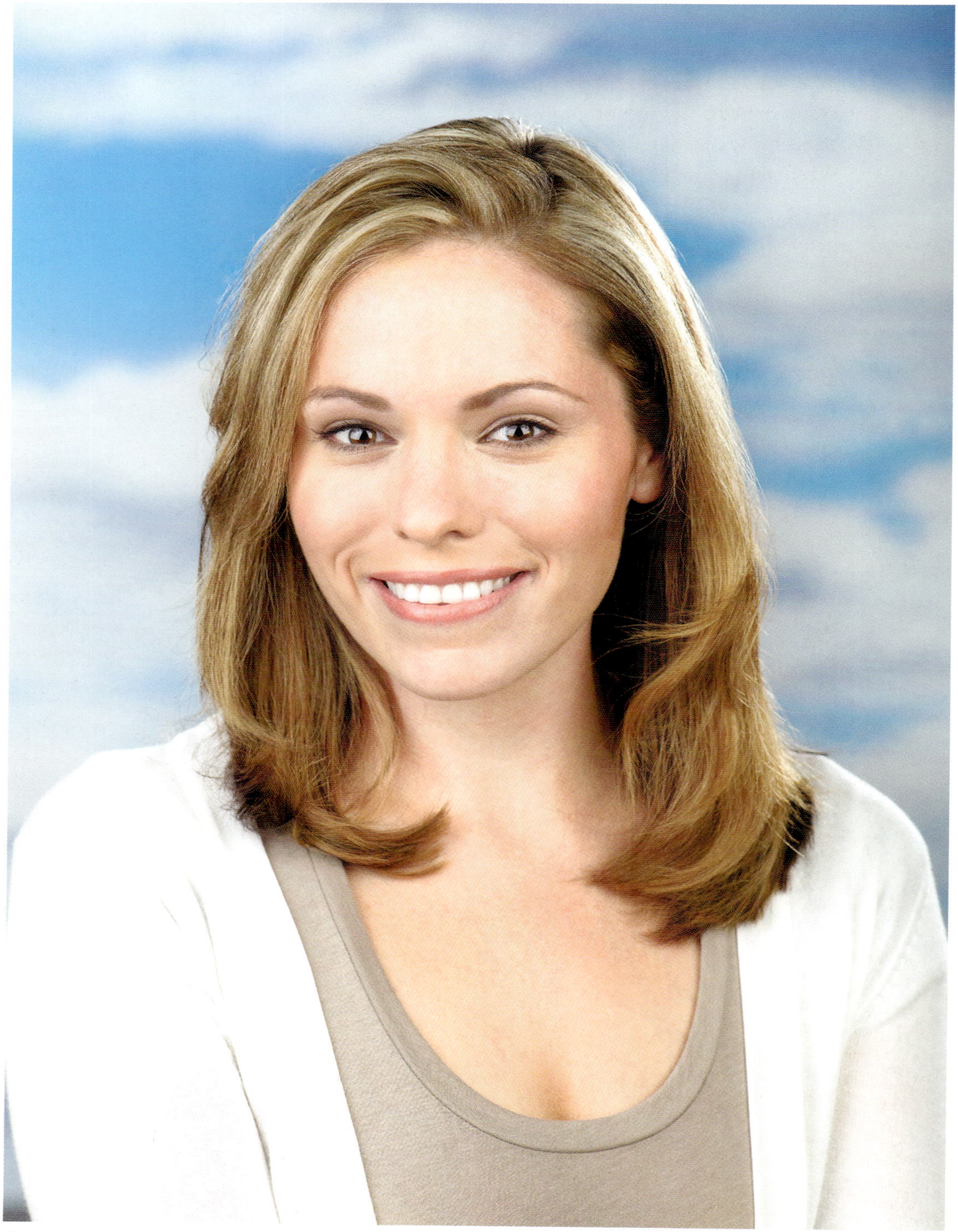

c)

ISO 50, 1/60 sec., f/8, 150mm lens

There was some confusion about wardrobe, so we didn't have the clothes we were expecting. Fortunately, we had a mix of women's clothing and a man's shirt in the studio. In both scenarios, these ended up being a much better choice than the original wardrobe.

It was interesting to see the images side by side on the computer screen with the model there. She enjoyed seeing the two different interpretations.

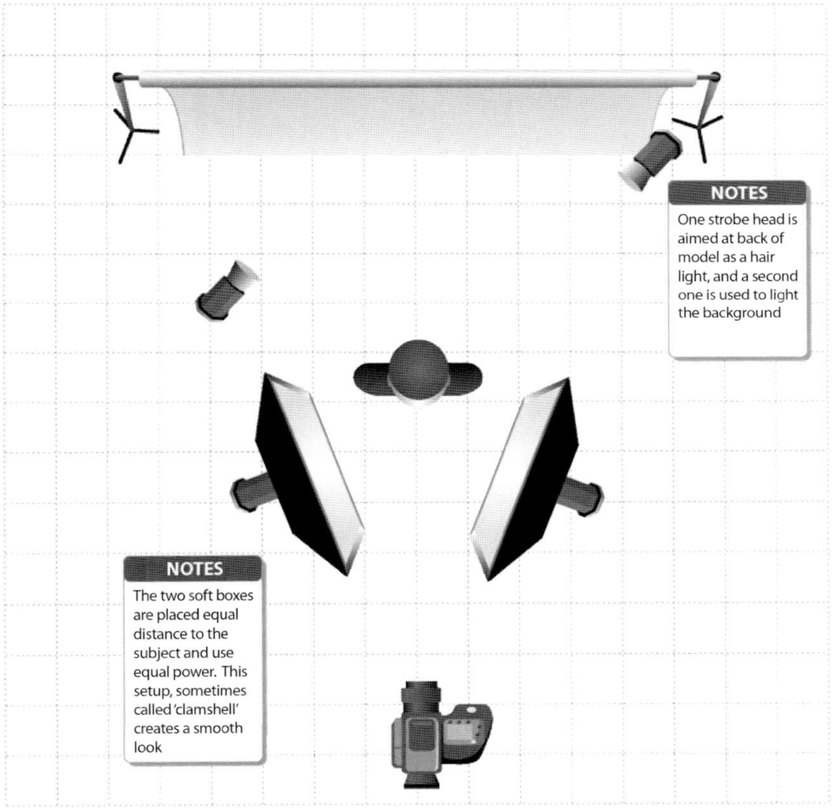

d)

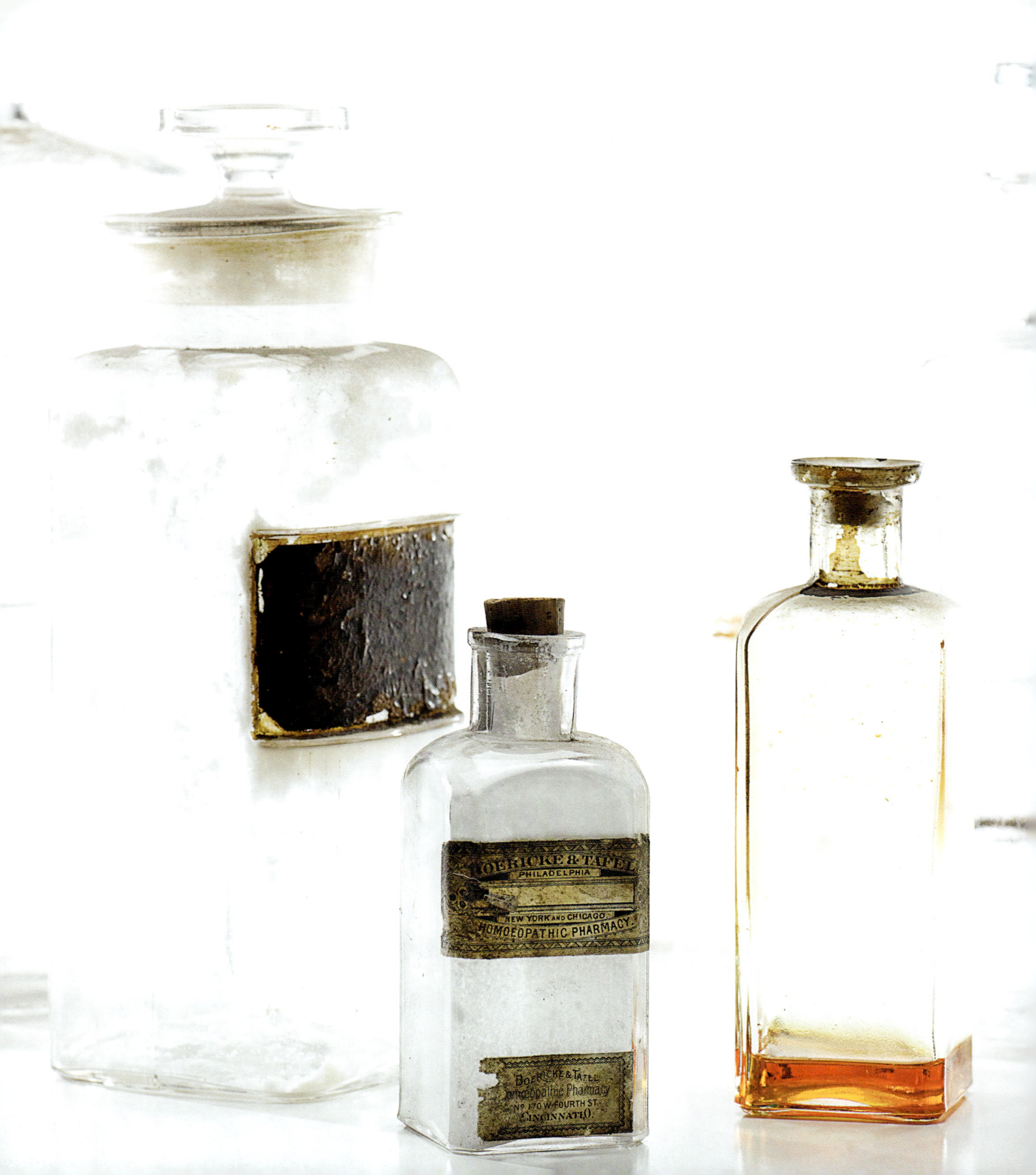
BOERICKE & TAFEL
PHILADELPHIA
NEW YORK AND CHICAGO.
HOMOEOPATHIC PHARMACY.
BOERICKE & TAFEL
omoeopathic Pharmacy
No 170 W. FOURTH ST.
CINCINNATI, O.

chapter six

DSLR CAMERAS

If there's any tool that should be considered an extension of the photographer's body, it's her camera. A race car driver has his car, a chef has his knives, a painter her brushes, and a photographer her camera. A photographer needs to know her camera inside and out because it's what connects the subject to the photographer. Much has changed in the decades since the authors became professional photographers, but the camera is still a recording device; it records a subject on film or, more commonly today, a sensor.

A good place to start this chapter is to say what it's not about. This chapter isn't designed to teach every function and nuance of modern cameras. A glance at a recent Nikon DSLR manual tallied 400 pages, in small print. We'll address camera basics, including ISO, aperture, and shutter speed, and then move on to other aspects of digital cameras, including sensors, and some key features of modern DSLRs. No camera discussion would be complete without talking about lenses and some alternatives to DSLR cameras.

ISO 200, 1/125 sec., f/22, 70mm lens

Opening Image: Photographic Equipment

Camera: Nikon D800

Lens: Nikon 70-200mm

Lighting: Profoto Acute2 and Profoto D1 monoblocks

Light modifiers: Large softbox, reflector, and zoom reflector with grid

Let's break down the lighting setup for the opening image in this chapter of the bottles:

What's unique about this setup is that no strobes are directed to the front of the subject but rather come from behind or above. Moving left to right:

a) The first strobe has a basic reflector as a modifier and is aimed directly at the background, creating the bright white background and acting as the key light for the subjects.

b) The softbox on the boom is placed directly above the set. This ensures an overall even tone and fills any hard shadows.

c) The final strobe added to the set was a reflector with a grid aimed at the back of the bottles. This strobe adds specular highlights to the bottle and some needed contrast.

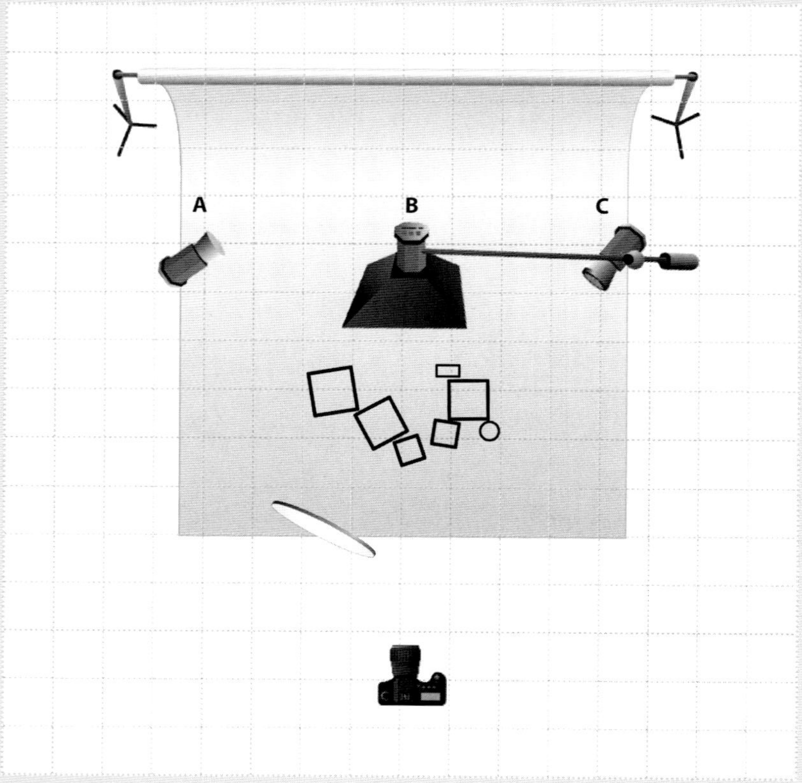

Camera Basics

The common use of the word *camera* comes from the Latin words *camera obscura*, which mean dark chamber. This was an ancient method for projecting images.

Modern cameras are simply recording devices; they take a subject and re-create it in a format that can be altered, stored, and shared via multiple output options. The basic camera principles have not changed for decades. Light, specifically that of the visual spectrum, enters a camera through a lens and is focused to be recorded. Traditional SLRs used film for recording, and modern DSLRs use sensors.

Exposure is controlled though the combination of ISO, shutter speed, and aperture. These three elements—the sensor's sensitivity to light (ISO), the speed at which the shutter opens and closes, and the size of the opening through which light passes—work together to create the desired exposure. Chapters 7 and 8 provide greater detail on how to obtain optimal exposure.

Given that cameras now come with manuals that sometimes have more than 400 pages, this is an overly simple explanation of the camera. DSLR cameras still work on the basic principles but now have much more in common with a computer than with the original *camera obscura*.

What Do the Authors Use?

This is a little like a high school test where you are given options a) through d), plus e), which covers all of the above. We pick e); we use all the options listed in this chapter, not because we're gear geeks, but rather because over time one discovers that certain tools fit certain tasks better.

That said, we both began with a single 35mm camera. Today, our combined arsenal includes DSLRs and medium- and large-format cameras fitted with digital backs. We both enjoy camera gear, but nobody can purchase everything from their wish list at once. Not only does it take time to research what to buy, but getting new equipment also requires that you have the client base, or return on investment (ROI) avenue, to warrant the investment.

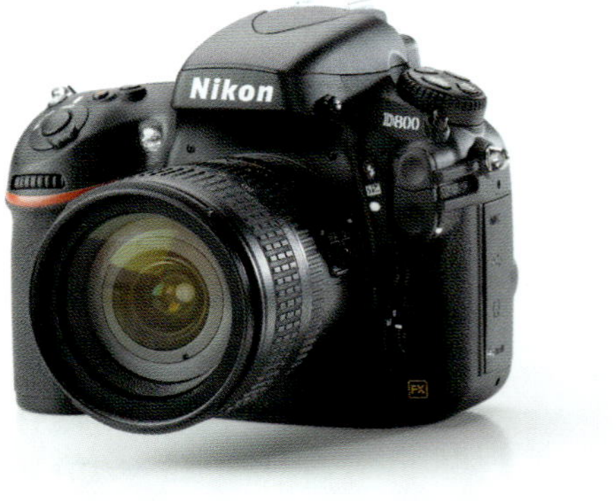

FIGURE 6.1 A modern DSLR camera with an 18mm–55mm lens.

ISO 50, 1/125 sec., f/22, 150mm lens

Today's DSLRs are electronic marvels (**FIGURE 6.1**). Each step of the image process, from the moment light enters the lens until the image is exported, is controlled, corrected, and fine-tuned to better help the photographer capture an image. Part of being a professional photographer means knowing how to work with the camera to achieve the desired results.

Sensors

The advancement to sensors from film is where the *D* in *DSLR* comes from. Most professional photographers working today prefer digital cameras over film cameras; however, plenty of photographers, especially traditionalists, and those working in fine art and alternative processes still use film. We're focusing on digital since DSLRs are the tools preferred by most professionals.

Two main topics come up when discussing DSLR sensors, size, and type.

Size: The commonly used terms are *full frame* and *cropped*. Full frame is based on the size of traditional 35mm (36 x 24mm) film. Some manufacturers use their own name instead for the size of their sensors. The FX in the bottom-right corner in Figure 6.1 is Nikon's reference to its full-frame sensor. Cameras with full-frame sensors generally create a larger file, which is one benefit, but for many photographers the lens relationship to their film camera is key. Cameras with full-frame sensors require no lens focal-length adjustment.

The degree of coverage for a 24mm lens on a 35mm film camera is the same as when using the 24mm lens on a DSLR with a full-frame sensor; no math required. Experienced photographers will appreciate this because their lenses act as expected. A cropped sensor, sometimes referred to as a DX or APS-C sensor, has a different relationship to the lenses' focal length and requires a mathematical conversion when compared with using the same lens on a 35mm film camera. An average conversion is 1.5x. Thus, a 50mm lens on a 35mm film or full-frame sensor camera is considered a normal focal length lens; however, because of the 1.5x conversion, on the cropped sensor it would have a field of coverage similar to that of a 75mm lens.

There are pros and cons in every situation. It's easy to suggest that given the conversion factor of a cropped sensor, the full sensor is better, but this is not always the case. It can be frustrating to have your wide lens suddenly act as a normal lens, but what happens on the other end of the spectrum? Many sports photographers desire long telephoto lenses, but cost becomes a factor when purchasing specialized equipment. When shooting with a cropped sensor, that 200mm lens now acts as a 300mm, and the 300mm has the field of coverage of a 450mm lens. This is why many new full-frame sensor DSLRs offer the ability to use a smaller portion of the sensor.

A side-by-side comparison is the easiest way to understand the differences between the two sensor sizes. The only camera adjustment between the two images in **FIGURE 6.2** was that the one on the left (**FIGURE 6.2A**) was shot using Nikon's FX (full frame) setting and the one on the right (**FIGURE 6.2B**) was

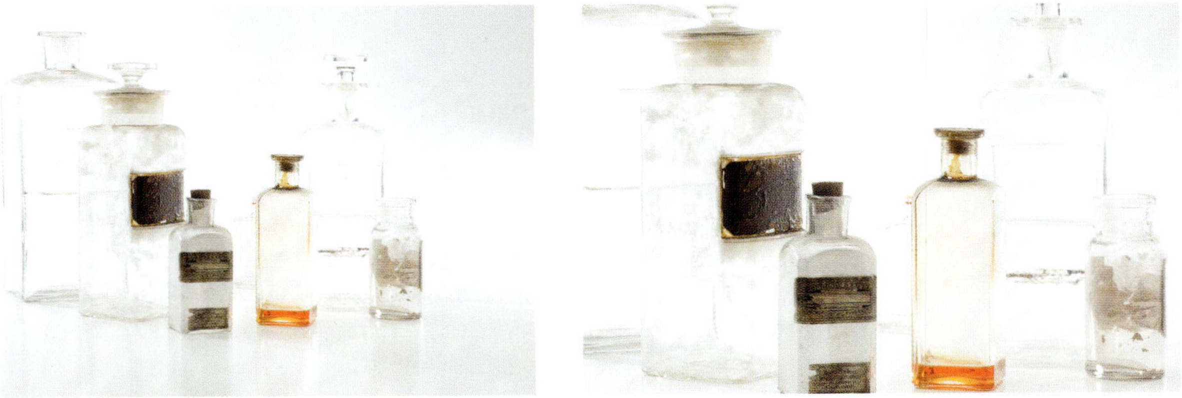

a) b)

FIGURE 6.2 **a)** The image was framed and captured using Nikon's full-frame sensor; **b)** the usable area of the sensor was reduced electronically.

ISO 200, 1/125 sec., f/22, 70mm lens

shot using the DX (cropped) setting. Some cameras allow the user to choose whether to use the full sensor or a cropped version, which is how these images were adjusted. Other parameters including focal length, distance to the subject, and exposure were left unchanged. It's easy to see how the smaller sensor cropped in.

The two more common types of sensors are CCD and CMOS. Foveon is a third; however, it is limited to a handful of cameras. Charge-coupled device (CCD) and complementary metal-oxide semiconductor (CMOS) sensors both convert light into electrons. Early DSLR cameras and high-end digital backs relied on the more-expensive CCD sensors because they produced a cleaner image with less image noise. Fortunately, CMOS technology has vastly improved, and now most cameras use this technology, which is a key reason why the cost of digital cameras has dropped.

Features

DSLRs are loaded with features, some that you'll use every day and others that get used once in a while, if at all. Again, we won't go into every option but will address some that are key for successful imagery and often save valuable time. Features specific to metering and histograms are addressed in their own chapters.

ISO: Technically, ISO is part of the exposure and metering family, but a feature unique to digital cameras is the ability to adjust ISO on the fly. Film cameras require you to change film as you desire a higher or lower ISO, but with DSLRs, you can change it with each frame (which we don't suggest doing).

White balance: Much has changed since shooting film was the only option. Photographers used to have two main choices: Purchase daylight or tungsten film, and place gels on their lights to balance the lighting's color temperature (Kelvin, or k). Now, photographers can dial it in. Well, OK, it's a little more complicated than that. DSLR cameras offer numerous white balance settings that offer everything from automatic to options based on type of lighting, Kelvin values, and the ability to set a custom temperature.

Auto can do an OK job, but it tends to provide inconsistent results. It looks for the brightest element in the scene and tries to neutralize the colors. Setting a precise Kelvin works well when you know the Kelvin value of the lighting.

High ISO Warning

It's common knowledge that raising the ISO above the camera's native setting can lead to digital noise in the shadows. That's not the only issue, though; loss of tonal range is also a concern. Raising the ISO adjusts the sensitivity of the sensor, thus affecting its dynamic range. Let's say, for example, that your camera has the ability to capture seven stops of light and detail from white to black at the native ISO; raising the ISO may lower that to five or six. There will always be situations in which this cannot be avoided, such as scenes with low light, but whenever possible, it's good to use the camera's native ISO.

Similarly, picking a specific lighting option also works well when you know the type of lighting. Although using the custom setting takes a few extra seconds, it generally provides the best results (FIGURE 6.3). With custom, you pick a neutral element in the scene, and from there, the camera will make the necessary adjustments.

Focusing options: On one hand, it's easy to use the default option of relying on the camera to focus in the center of the frame. This simply requires the user to press the shutter release halfway down, and the camera does the rest. Easy, yes, but other options should be explored, too.

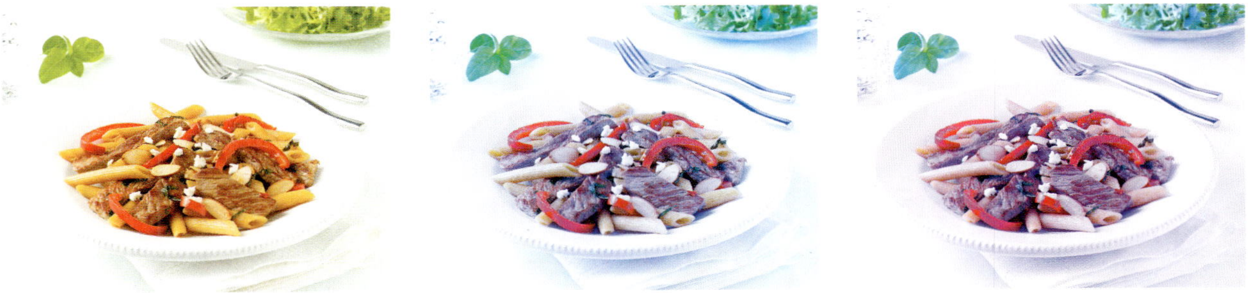

a) b) c)

FIGURE 6.3 **a)** In the image captured with the custom setting, whites look correct, with a clean and neutral tone; **b)** the tungsten setting added blue to the image, compensating for the warm color temperature; **c)** using fluorescent added magenta to the overall image.

ISO 200, 1/125 sec., f/11, 70mm lens

Most DSLRs allow the user to set where the lens focuses. This is useful when framing an image in which the subject is off center, but remember to double-check the setting. Many photographers have forgotten to check this and accidentally missed their subject. Single-servo autofocus and continuous-servo autofocus allow the photographer to tell the camera what to do when the shutter button is pushed halfway. Single-servo is perfect for stationary subjects. When the shutter is pushed halfway, the focus stays in place; moving the camera does not change it. Continuous-servo is designed to follow a subject. Holding the shutter button halfway allows refocusing as the camera is moved. A handful of other options are available, but the combination of these two provides excellent focus control.

Image quality: Entire chapters could be written about image quality. Typically, DSLRs have three main quality settings, JPEG, TIF, and RAW, each with its own subsettings. JPEG files are quick, small, 8-bit, and ready to be used straight from the camera. With JPEG files, the camera controls the processing behind the scene, which makes them ready to use. However, JPEG is a lossy format that throws away much information when the file is converted from the original higher bit depth to 8-bit. JPEGs also lose information each time they are opened and closed.

TIFFs, similar to JPEGs, are also 8-bit files that lose data when created but do not lose data when opened and resaved. This makes them a good choice when you don't want to handle the processing but also need to make edits.

Raw files are the clear winner when it comes to image quality. They retain all the information created during capture, the full 12 or 14 bits, and don't lose information when opened and closed. The greater the bit depth, the more information captured. (The following section, "Digital Backs," further addresses the importance of bit depth.) The downside of raw files is that they require postcapture processing. Common processing applications include Adobe Lightroom, Adobe Camera RAW, Apple Aperture, and Phase One's Capture One; most manufacturers also offer their own software. Although raw captures require the extra step of processing and take up a lot of space, most professionals agree the quality gains are worth it.

Movies: The worlds of still photography and the motion industry have been coming closer together for quite some time, and with the newer DSLRs they have collided. The beauty of having a single system for both still images and motion, besides the economy of owning a single set of equipment, is that many still photography traits, such as shallow depth of field, are easily achieved. The newer DSLRs don't merely have basic movie capabilities but include impressive features such as uncompressed full broadcast HD video (1080p).

Lenses

No camera system would be complete without an excellent set of lenses. If there is one rule in lenses, it's to always purchase good glass. The term *good glass* refers to the quality of the optics. It's important to remember that it's the lens that stands between the subject and the camera. Regardless of the camera, without good optics no image will meet its potential. Photographers commonly upgrade their camera bodies every few years, but a quality lens will last for decades.

Aperture/Speed

Aperture, sometimes called the speed of the lens, is a key purchase consideration. It's common to hear photographers say they own fast lenses. A fast lens is one that has a wide aperture opening, such as f/2.8 or lower, and thus allows a large amount of light to enter. The greater the amount of light reaching the sensor, the faster the shutter speed that can be used. When you're comparing lenses, the ones with the lower aperture usually have the higher price tag but tend to be worth the additional cost. Again, we always recommend purchasing good glass.

Renting vs. Buying

We strongly believe in buying the very best equipment you can afford. It is far more cost-effective to buy good equipment once than it is to replace cheap stuff multiple times. Buy only the equipment you use on a regular basis, and take great care of it. You can rent the gear that you need only occasionally.

Focal Length

Focal length is the other key consideration when you are purchasing lenses. Photographers tend to own multiple lenses to cover a range of focal lengths, but it's important to really consider your needs before you buy. For example, someone who specializes in portrait photography will have different needs than an action sports photographer. Both may use long lenses, but rarely, if ever, would a portrait photographer need a 300mm lens. Want versus need is a common internal conversation.

The following discussion on normal, wide, and long lenses is based on full-frame 35mm cameras. Those who own cropped-sensor cameras will need to consider the lens conversion, which was addressed previously, in the "Sensors" section.

Normal

The most common normal lens is the 50mm. No exact formula or number can tell us what is normal. 50mm is the standard, but a little wider or longer is still normal. The term *normal* does not mean good or bad, but rather what is normal to a person's vision. A normal lens captures roughly what our eyes see. The 50mm, preferably something fast around f/1.4, should be a staple in all photographers' camera bags. It teaches photographers how to work their cameras while not worrying about focal length; the camera sees what your eyes see. Normal lenses have an approximate angle of view of 47 degrees (FIGURE 6.4).

Wide

Wide-angle lenses have a shorter focal length and a wider angle of view. Anything shorter than normal is considered wide. Some lenses, such as a 35mm, are just a tad wider, with an angle of view around 63 degrees, while an 18mm lens has an amazing 100-degree angle of view. Another consideration is distortion. The farther lenses move from normal, the greater the possibility of distortion. Wide lenses are not a great option for product photography due to distortion.

Long

Long, aka telephoto, lenses are at the opposite end of the spectrum from wide-angle lenses. A couple of common focal lengths in these include 85mm,

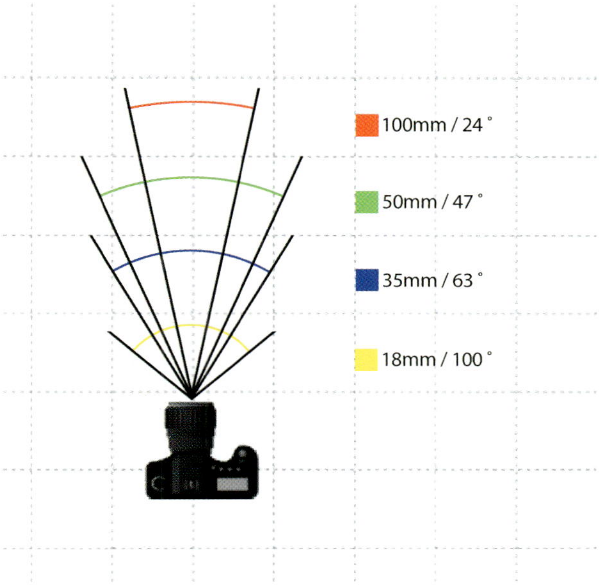

FIGURE 6.4 A diagram representing the relationship between focal length and field of view for a full-frame DSLR camera.

for portraiture, and 300mm, for sporting events. As the focal length gets longer, the angle of view gets narrower. The 1200mm extreme-telephoto lens has roughly a 2-degree angle of view. This would be a very specialized lens. The larger glass in long lenses usually translates to higher prices.

Along with angle of view, expansion and compression are considerations when choosing the best lens for a given subject. The goal of the set of images in FIGURE 6.5 is to show the angle of view of different lenses. The only change was the focal length of the lens; the distance to subject and all exposures values were unaltered. It's easy to see the difference.

The second set of images (FIGURE 6.6) takes a different approach. Now, along with changing the focal lengths, we moved the camera with the goal of maintaining the same amount of subject matter

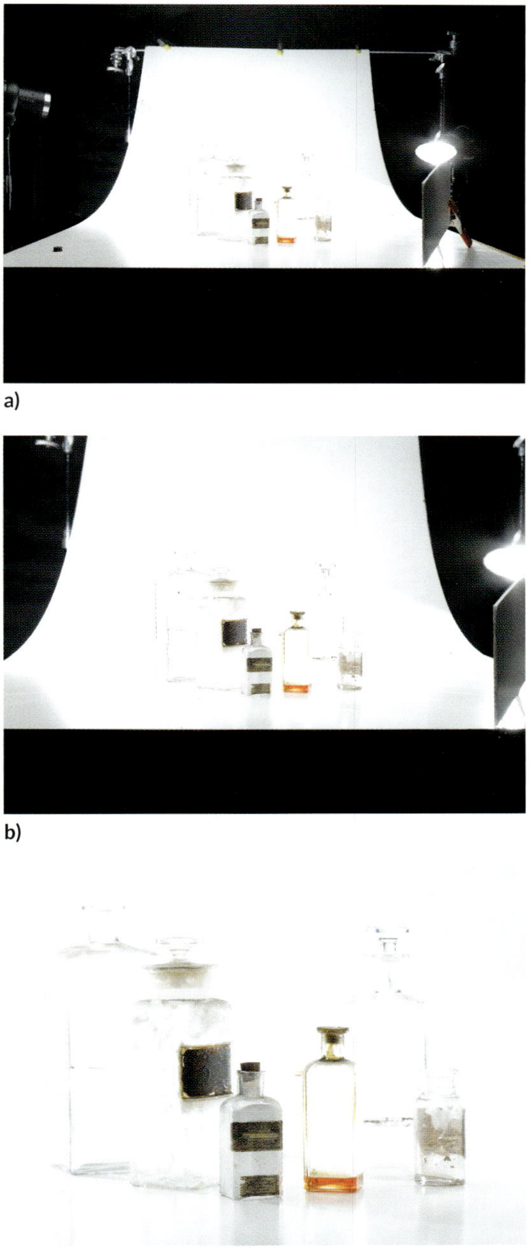

a)

b)

c)

FIGURE 6.5 **a)** The image was framed using a wide lens; **b)** framed using a normal lens; **c)** framed using a long lens.

ISO 200, 1/125 sec., f/22, 32mm, 50mm, 100mm lens

in the frame. A close examination shows how one image closely represents what is natural to the eye, while the other two either compress or expand the visual distance between the subjects.

Zoom Lenses

Zoom lenses allow for a varied focal length. The two numbers used to describe a zoom lens, such as 80–200mm, represent the shortest and longest focal lengths. On a positive note, zoom lenses offer great convenience because you don't have to carry multiple lenses; however, zoom lenses rarely have the same fast speed or quality of optics as a single-focal-length lens. Commonly, photographers will use a combination of both options.

Tilt-Shift Lenses

Opening an architectural photographer's camera bag will usually uncover a tilt-shift lens or two. These lenses are very specialized in that they provide perspective control by allowing the photographer to keep the camera level while raising, lowering, tilting, or shifting (side to side) the lens. These movements help avoid keystoning effects and convergence of lines. Product photographers also use tilt-shift lenses when it's imperative that the lines stay parallel to each other in a product shot (**FIGURE 6.7**).

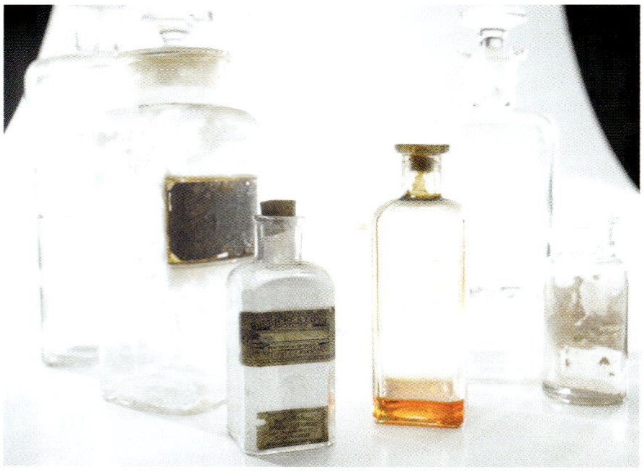

a)

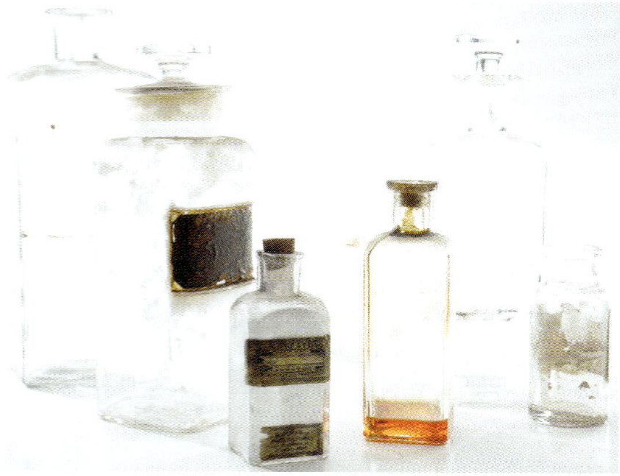

b)

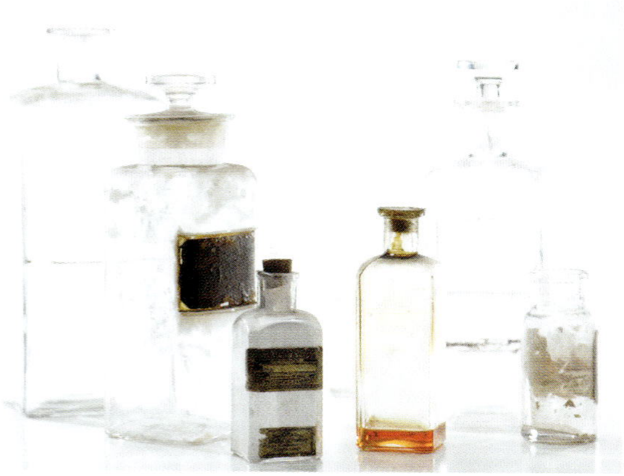

c)

FIGURE 6.6 **a)** The image was captured using a wide lens, which expands and distorts it; **b)** the use of a normal lens approximates human vision; **c)** shooting with a slightly long lens compresses the bottles together.

ISO 200, 1/125 sec., f/22, 32mm lens, 50mm lens, 100mm lens

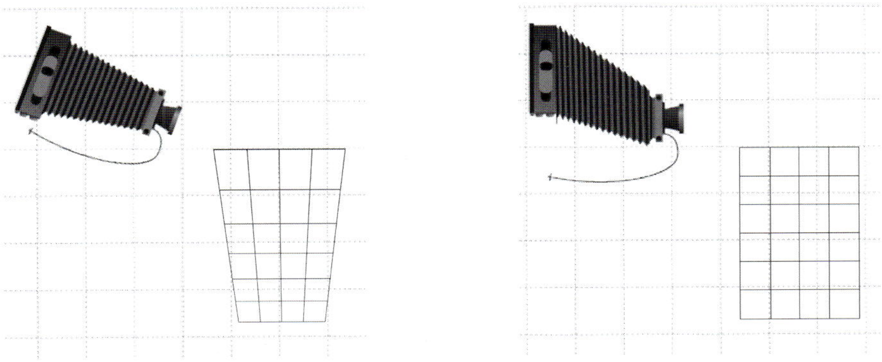

a) b)

FIGURE 6.7 **a)** This image demonstrates the distortion that happens when angling a camera with a standard lens down or up at a subject; **b)** here, the camera is parallel to the subject, and the lens is shifted: no distortion.

Other Options

DSLRs are great, but that doesn't mean they are the only option available. Traditionally, photographers referred to 35mm film cameras as small format, 2¼ cameras as medium format, and those that used 4 × 5 or 8 × 10 sheet film as large format. The small, medium, and large descriptions were based on the film size, which affected the image quality. Digital sensors changed much of that. There is still some truth in the statement that size matters in camera technology. As we previously discussed, the size of the sensor affects the relationship between lens focal length and angle of view, but larger sensors can contain more information than their smaller counterparts.

So, which option is the right choice for you? The best way to answer that question is to understand the pros and cons of each.

Digital Backs

The first place we need to start is with digital backs. Digital backs (FIGURE 6.8) aren't exactly cameras, but they are where the digital sensor is located. Unlike DSLR cameras, which have the sensor in the main body, medium-format and large-format cameras rely on an added-on digital back to capture the image.

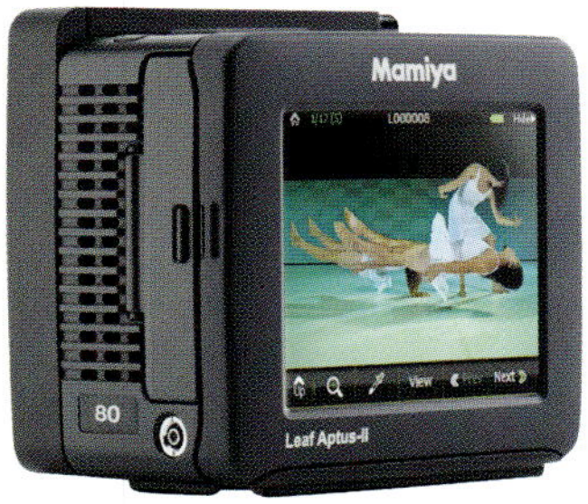

FIGURE 6.8 Mamiya 80MP digital back.

ISO 100, 1/125 sec., f/22, 150mm lens

Pros

Image quality: The number-one reason for using a digital back is image quality. Size and bit depth are the two main reasons for the increased quality. The design of digital backs allows larger sensors; some current models offer 80-plus megapixels. Bit depth is an often-misunderstood specification in camera literature. DSLR cameras capture either 12-bit or 14-bit in raw mode, while most digital backs capture 16-bit. Although this seems like a minor difference, the numbers below tell a different story.

8-bit = 256 shades

12-bit = 4,096 shades

14-bit = 16,384 shades

16-bit = 65,536 shades

An additional benefit is that digital backs can be used on a variety of equipment. The same back can be quickly switched between different medium-format cameras and even switched from a medium- to large-format camera in a matter of seconds.

Cons

Cost is a major consideration when considering a digital back. The lower-megapixel models routinely cost more than a professional DSLR, and the higher-megapixel models compete with SUVs in price. Photographers who prefer to shoot many bursts or frames in a second will find the speed limiting. Whereas some DSLRs can capture five-plus frames per second, digital backs are considerably slower.

Medium Format

Today's medium-format cameras look pretty much the same as their earlier film counterparts (FIGURE 6.9). Many of those earlier models are still in use today, but now with a high-tech digital back attached to their backside. Besides the larger film size, one of the benefits of medium format over 35mm film cameras was the ability to easily swap between different films and accessories, such as Polaroid backs. Whereas film went directly inside a 35mm camera, the medium-format camera used a film magazine that attached to the back of the body. This same principle still holds true today; digital backs attach to the back of the camera body.

Pros

Moving from a DSLR to a medium-format camera with a digital back is a rather easy progression. Both are quite portable and allow the photographer to use a viewfinder to see through the lens. Because the design of the removable back hasn't changed radically, it's easy to switch between shooting digitally, with a digital back, to film via a film magazine. For many, this is the best of both worlds.

Cons

Although these cameras incorporate sophisticated electronics, they cannot compete with a DSLR's features. Models that do add features such as multiple metering and focusing options, which are standard on DSLRs, carry a hefty price tag. The design and ergonomics of medium-format cameras require a slower pace than does the average DSLR, which isn't always a bad thing.

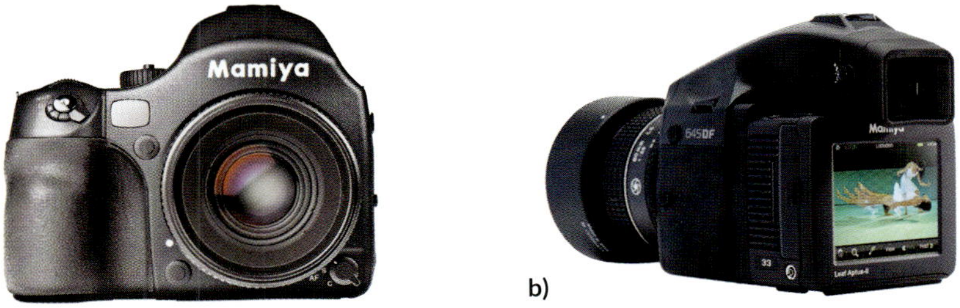

a) b)

FIGURE 6.9 **a)** Mamiya medium-format camera body; **b)** the same camera rotated to show a digital back attached.

ISO 100, 1/125 sec., f/22, 150mm lens

Large-Format/View Cameras

The thought of large box cameras with accordion bellows connecting each end conjures up visions of photographers wearing long coats and top hats. In reality, view cameras never went out of style, they have just primarily been used by commercial product and architectural photographers.

The basic design of a view camera comprises a rear standard for film and a front standard for the lens, with an accordion bellows in between. These three elements create a light-tight box where the light enters through the lens, passes through the bellows, and exposes the film on the other end. This design hasn't changed in over a century. The benefit for today's photographers is that each standard moves independently of the other (**FIGURE 6.10**). This is similar to the tilt-shift DSLR lens but offers greater range of motion and allows both standards to move.

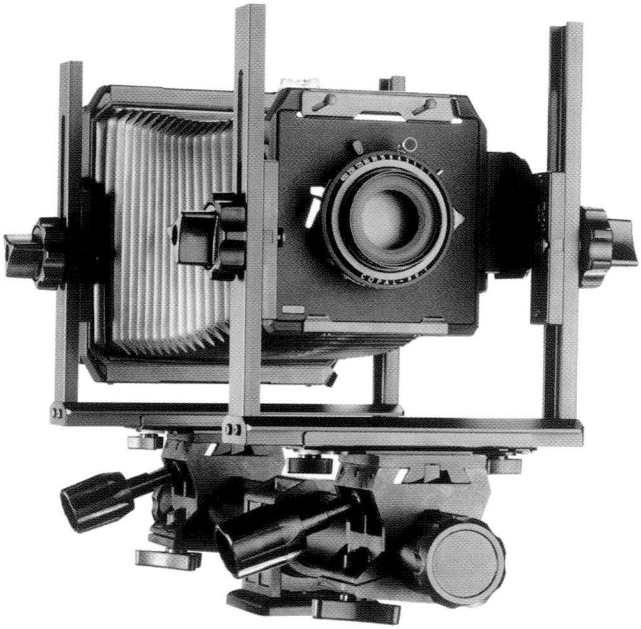

FIGURE 6.10 Typical 4 x 5 view camera.

ISO 100, 1/125 sec., f/22, 150mm lens

Pros

The primary reason for choosing a view camera is for the camera's movements. The ability to move each standard independently offers precise perspective and focal control. For many subjects this isn't important, but for those times when it is, there is no better tool for the job.

Cons

It takes time to become comfortable with the operation of a view camera. You no longer control only the focal length and focus, you must now control the movements of each standard. The simple approach is to leave each standard straight up and down, but that defeats the purpose of the camera.

When shooting film, photographers would focus on the ground glass, albeit the image was upside down and backwards, but that is now where the digital back connects. Focusing requires the digital back to be tethered to a computer and handled via live video, which takes practice but is quickly mastered.

Any Regrets?

Joe: Have you ever purchased a piece of equipment that you later regretted buying?

Brad: Yes. Many years ago I bought a Mamiya 7. It was a fantastic camera—a medium format camera that was sort of like a 35mm on steroids. I had it in my head that with that camera, I would loosen up my style and start to shoot more spontaneously because I could handhold the camera. As it turned out, it was not practical for the way I shot commercial jobs, and I was not really able to change my own personal way of shooting. I believe equipment can be a terrific aid in making it easier to shoot, but it can't make a leopard change its spots.

Joe: I know what you mean. I have a Nikon 800 that I need to use more often. I will, but it can be hard to get out there and just shoot, even when you know it's a great thing to do and an essential part of growing creatively.

Choosing the right camera is no easy task. Many questions about features, format, needs, and price should be considered, and in the end it comes down to what is simply the best fit for you, the photographer. Photographers always seem to want the latest and greatest piece of equipment, which isn't very realistic of us. There is no proof that owning equipment from one manufacturer over that of another will make you a better photographer. Making smart purchases, and learning how to maximize what you own, is far more important than what's in your camera bag.

interview **JENNIFER COUDRON**

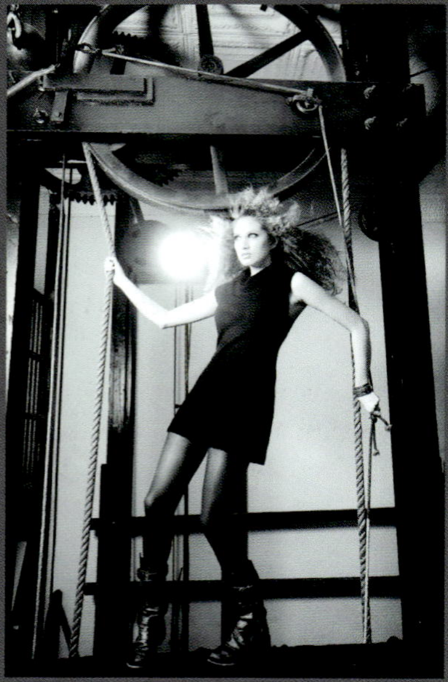

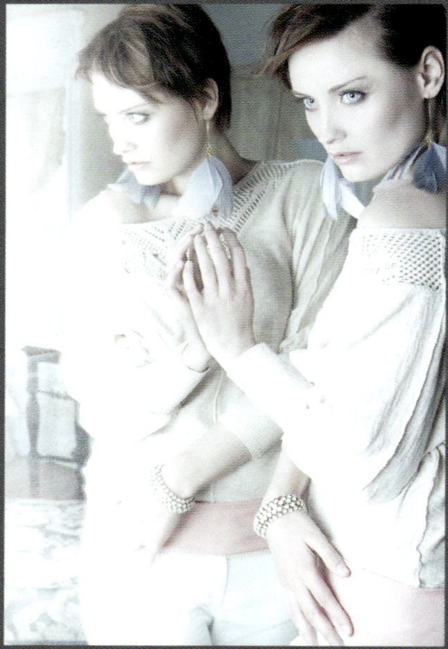

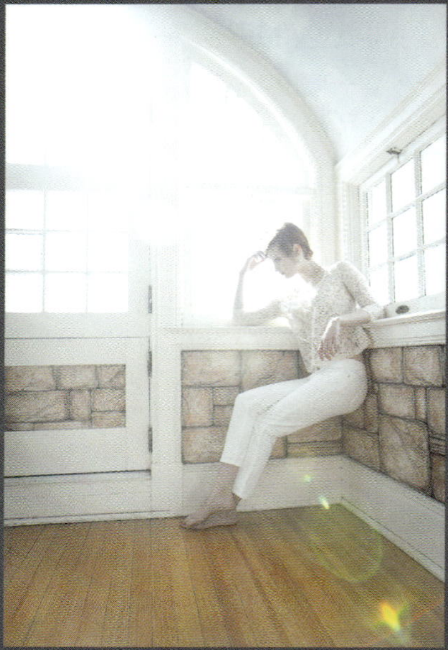

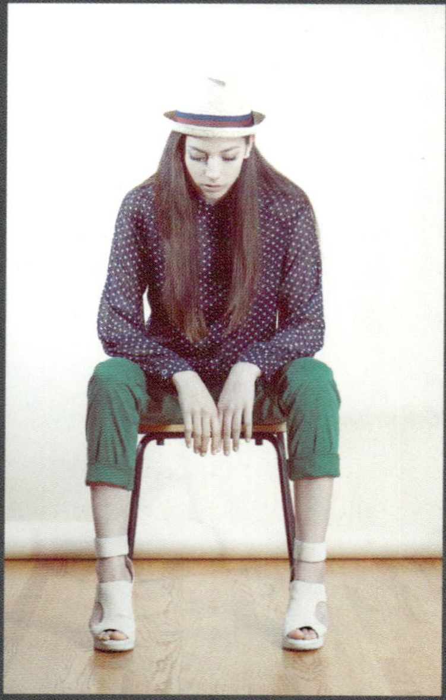

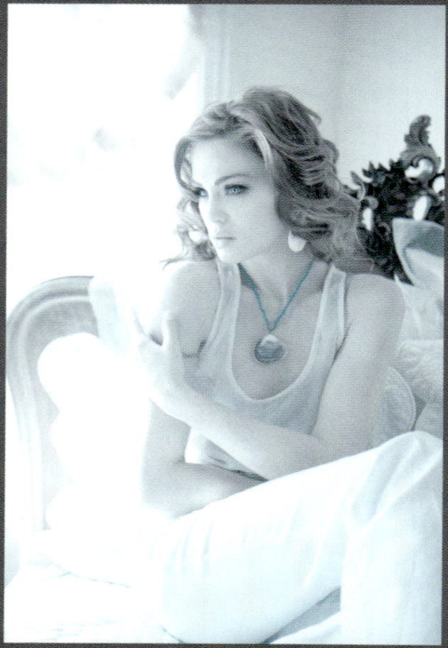

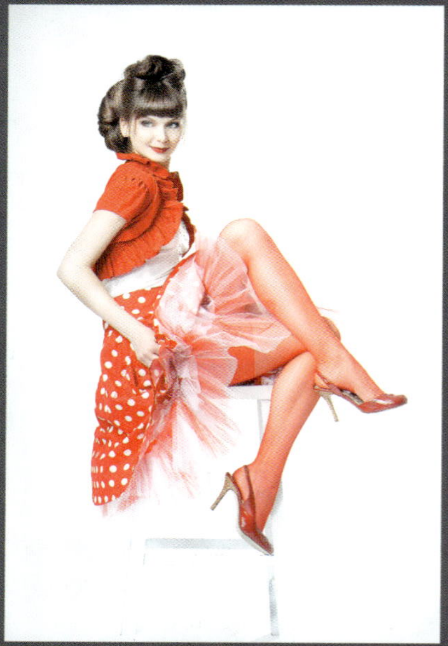

All images © Jennifer Coudron

How long have you been a professional photographer?

I graduated from the Art Institute in June 2011. My career shooting professionally began right after that, I suppose—so about a year and a half.

How did you get started?

I'd always really enjoyed photos, looking at them, and taking them as an amateur. I was doing some soul-searching while changing careers and trying to figure out what I really wanted to do next. I literally woke up one day, decided on photography, applied for school in Colorado while I was in Ohio, and moved out to Denver two weeks later.

What advice would you give to someone starting out?

You cannot shoot or practice enough. When starting, it's important to be committed and have the time to commit. I feel that those starting out should immerse themselves in photography completely. Shoot, plan, sketch, look through countless magazines, assist with and create images in as many genres as possible to find your own unique talent.

If you had to do it over, would you do anything different?

I don't think so. I worked really hard to learn all that I could. I wouldn't change a thing. Actually, I take that back—I would have saved up some more money before beginning my photographic career.

How would you define your lighting style?

Simple.

How do you decide on the type of light you will use for each shot?

I think about the mood I want to create and what kind of lighting will already be present in the studio or the space I'm shooting. However, I must admit, what I plan to do is very seldom what I actually do.

What attracted you to fashion?

When I started photography, I thought I wanted to shoot landscapes and nature and work for *National Geographic* (just as 90 percent of people want to do when they begin). One of my professors suggested I try a fashion photography class, so I did. Turns out it was a smart choice.

How do you find your models, hair and makeup artists, clothing, and so forth?

Modeling agencies, collaborative websites that offer a lot of trade for work, word of mouth. Once your name gets out there and people like to work with you, the models and artists will find you. Persistence has always worked in my favor as well.

Fashion seems like a collaborative endeavor. What are the good and bad aspects of that?

All in all, it's great. I think one of the main reasons I enjoy shooting fashion is because of the collaborative nature of it. Watching everyone's vision come to life in a powerful image is very rewarding. I would say to someone starting out, be careful and really watch every detail while shooting and take your time. Make sure the stylists and hair and makeup artists are comfortable stepping on set to make sure everything is right. Also, in the end, it is the photographer's vision; make sure it's really what you want, and don't get caught up in some-one else's vision.

Is there anything you'd like to add?

Have fun shooting; otherwise, what's the point? Continue to push yourself and try new things. If you're comfortable, you're not trying hard enough. ■

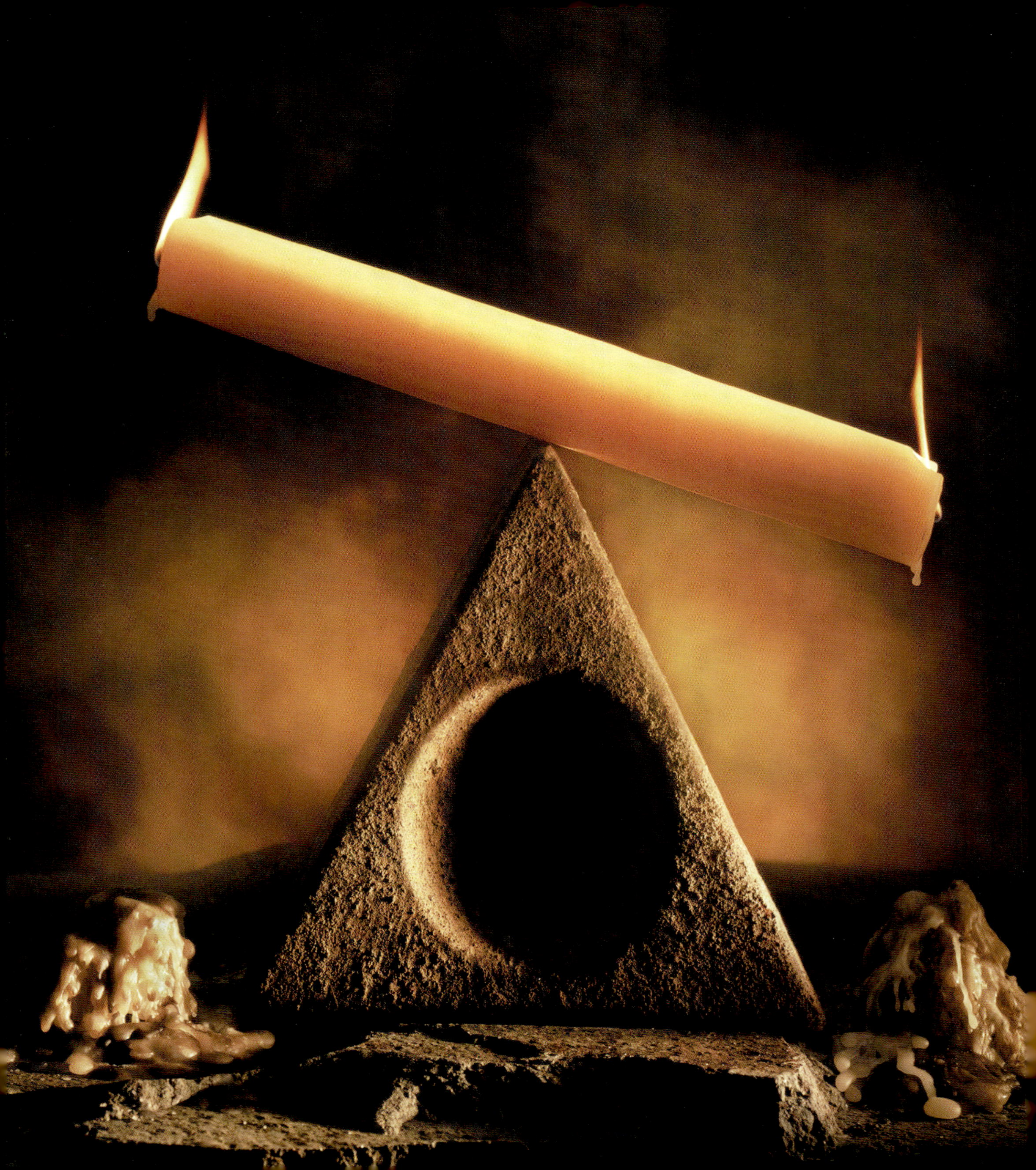

chapter seven

METERING

As a concept, metering is very simple. In practice, it's complex and can be a vexing dilemma. Metering allows the photographer to measure the amount of available and supplemental light and then calculate the proper exposure for each scene. The single most important part of creating a successful image is to expose it properly. The notion that "I'll just fix it in post-production" is a very dangerous proposition when it comes to exposure. You can make minor adjustments in post, but if you are off by very much in your exposure, the adjustments you make will compromise image quality. Properly exposing an image assures that you have captured all the information you desire within the limitations of your camera (and film, if you're using it). Depending on the scene you're photographing, you may or may not be able to capture detail throughout the entire scene.

ISO 100, 20 sec., f/16, 210mm lens

Opening Image: Photographic Equipment

Camera: Sinar 4 × 5 view camera and Kodak film

Lens: Schneider 210mm

Lighting: Norman 2000 generator and two strobe heads, Arri 1000 tungsten light

Light modifiers: softbox, grid

For the candle image on the previous page, the softbox was used for fill and the tungsten light was placed to add highlights to the subjects.

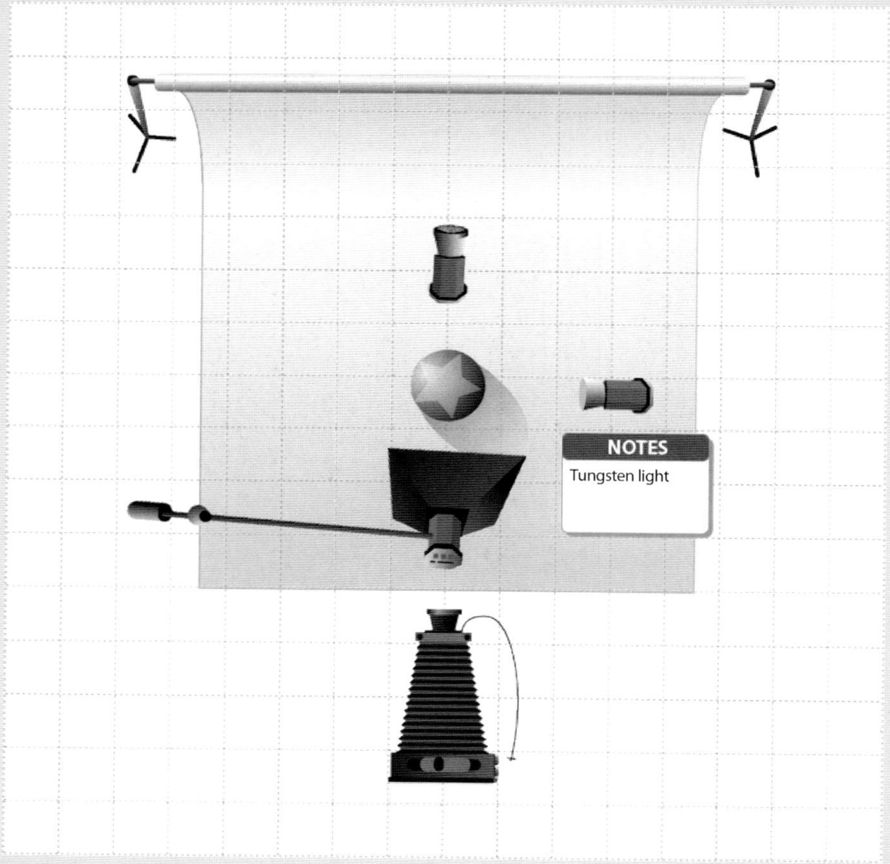

Dynamic Range

The human eye is a remarkable instrument, able to see a dynamic range that far surpasses even the most sophisticated modern camera, in part because of its iris, which automatically opens and closes to allow more or less light to strike the retina. Each camera sensor or type of film has limitations regarding the dynamic range it can capture in a single image. To put it simply, dynamic range is the amount of information that can be captured from dark to light. A camera that captures seven stops of light has a higher dynamic range than one that can capture a five-stop range; it can correctly record a wider range of tones within a scene (**FIGURES 7.1A** and **7.1B**).

Camera manufacturers are constantly trying to increase the dynamic range of their cameras, because photographers want to capture as much information as possible within a scene. It's far easier to get rid of tones we don't want than to create missing information. You can't make up tones that do not exist.

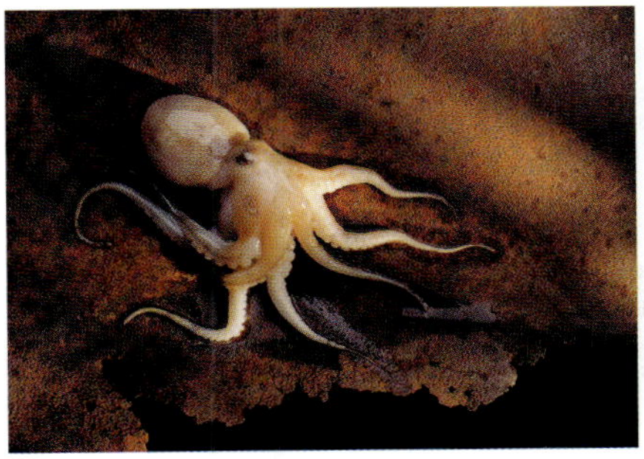

a)

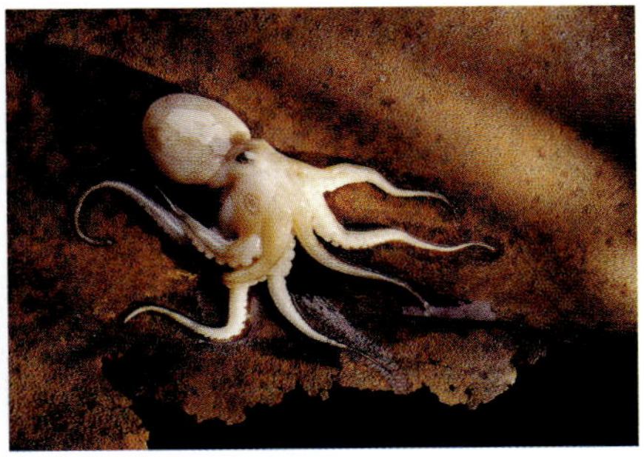

b)

FIGURE 7.1 **a)** This image represents a broad dynamic range, able to capture more highlight and shadow detail; **b)** here, decreased dynamic range results in loss of both highlight and shadow detail.

ISO 100, 1/125 sec., f/22, 150mm lens

Why Do You Still Meter?

Brad: I've seen you shoot in the studio, and given that you shoot digitally, why do you still use a meter?

Joe: It's funny; people often think that because I shoot digitally I don't need to use a meter, but I would suggest the opposite. With digital, it's really easy to lose highlight and shadow detail, and once you blow out the highlights they are gone. My style relies on highlight detail, which means that I cannot afford to lose any detail. Metering ensures that I'm able to maintain that essential highlight detail.

tip When you are considering purchasing a camera, dynamic range is an important factor. You want to compare cameras' dynamic range at their native ISO. Dynamic range decreases as ISO increases.

In terms of metering, dynamic range is important because it'll help determine how we expose the image. For instance, if we meter a scene and find that the range between our shadows and highlights is ten stops but our camera has a dynamic range of seven stops, then we will be unable to capture the full dynamic range. We'll have to make a decision to lose information and detail in the highlights, the shadows, or both. On the other hand, if our camera has a dynamic range of seven and our scene has a range of five, then, provided we expose properly, we'll be able to capture all the tonal detail in the shot.

Determinants of Exposure

Four basic elements work in concert with one another to determine exposure. Changing any one of these requires you to adjust one or more of the other elements to ensure the same exposure. Several of these were discussed in detail in the last chapter, so we'll simply review them as they relate to exposure. Choosing the right combinations will enable you to maintain your creative vision and the integrity of your image. You'll have to make compromises in any case, but you want to be fully aware of how to make them intelligently.

Practical Matters

Let's say you need to photograph 40 different pairs of black leather ski gloves on a white background. The gloves have intricate white stitching and a stitched white logo. The client wants to see detail in the leather and the stitching. You spot-meter (more on this later in this chapter) the leather and the logo and find there is a seven-stop difference. Your camera has a dynamic range of five stops, which means you will lose detail in either the blacks or the whites with your current lighting setup. You need to rent a camera that can handle this dynamic range, get more light onto the leather while keeping it off the logo, or flag the light off the logo. The other option is to take an exposure for the blacks and a separate one for the whites and then composite them in post.

Technical vs. Creative

We are not big proponents of using a camera's automatic exposure setting. Why let the camera make key artistic decisions for you? Properly exposing your film is of paramount importance but not at the expense of artistic and creative parameters. Using your manual setting will allow you to get the right exposure while still being able to control things like depth of field and implied motion.

Available Light

The first thing you need to think about is how much light there is in the scene you are about to photograph. More specifically, how much light is reflecting off the objects you are photographing? You discover this by metering the scene. A bright sunny day creates more luminance than a cloudy one does and therefore needs less exposure.

Without the use of additional lighting, available light is the one element that's hard for the photographer to control—except in the studio. There, you have almost complete control of your "available light." If you want the "sun" to be brighter, you can increase the power of your lights or move them closer to the set. If you want to use a fast shutter speed, or a small aperture opening, then you know you'll need to start with more light than if you intend to use a slower shutter speed, or a larger aperture opening, since a fast shutter speed (or a small aperture opening) will reduce the amount of light available for exposure.

ISO

The second determinant of exposure to consider is ISO (International Organization for Standardization). A film's or sensor's ISO is a measure of its sensitivity to light. This sensitivity is represented by a number, and the higher the number is, the more sensitive the sensor is to light. Common ISOs are 50, 100, 200, 400, 800, and 1600. A doubling of the ISO number relates to a doubling of the sensor's sensitivity; therefore, a sensor set to ISO 200 is twice as sensitive to light as one set to ISO 100, and because of this, it

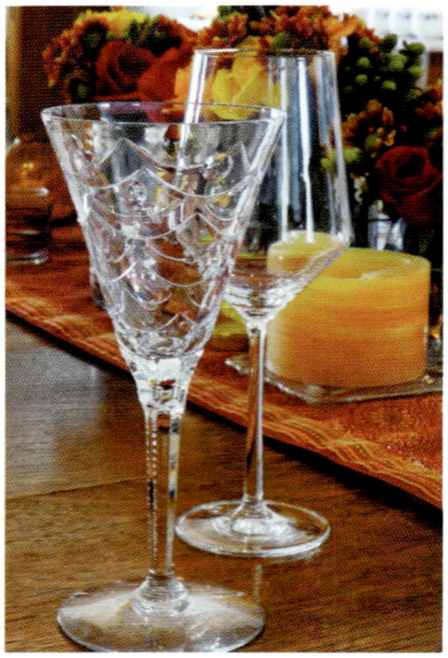

a)

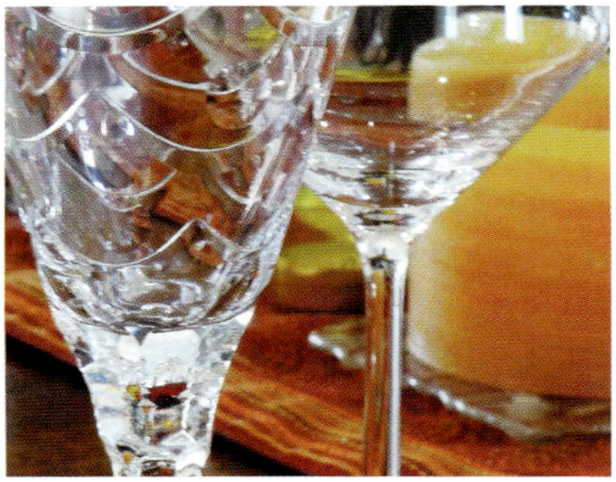

b) ISO 100, 1/60 sec., f/4, 150mm lens

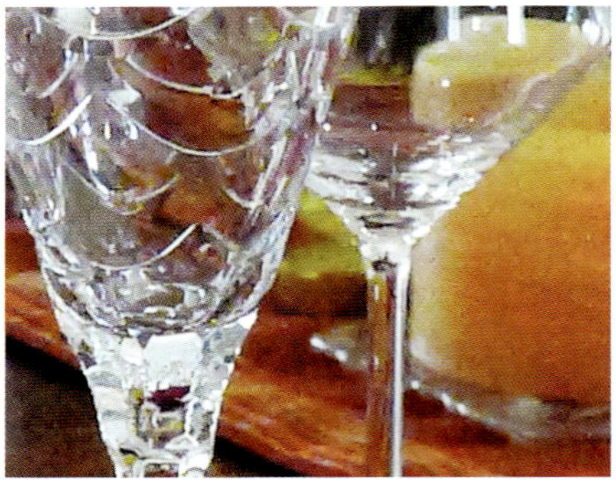

c) ISO 1600, 1/1000 sec., f/4, 150mm lens

FIGURE 7.2 **a)** Overall image; **b)** the detail image shows very little noise using a lower ISO of 100; **c)** in this detail, increasing the ISO to 1600 results in greater noise, especially in the shadows.

needs half as much light to make the same exposure. This halving/doubling relationship can be confusing, but it's a key component to creating properly exposed images that also meet your creative desires. You will see the same relationships occur with apertures and shutter speeds.

Choosing the correct ISO will be determined by many factors. The higher the ISO, the more noise you will see in your images (**FIGURES 7.2B** and **7.2C**), and the lower the dynamic will be. If you need an image with no noise and a wide dynamic range, then you'll need to use a lower ISO and use the other three determinants to compensate when calculating your exposure. Low ISOs work well when photographing scenes where there's considerable light or the object is relatively stationary. In order to get the proper exposure for a fast-moving object in low light, you'll need to use a higher ISO. You should make sure to run tests with your cameras to become aware of how much noise you can expect at various ISO settings. Different cameras will create different degrees of noise.

Necessary Compromises

What if you need to freeze the motion of a beverage splash with limited light and you can't have a noisy image? Your client wants the entire image in focus as well. The simplest solution is to get more light so you can use a fast shutter speed and a low ISO. If you can't get more light, a compromise will need to made. There may be some noise in the image or you may need to have part of the image out of focus due to a wider aperture. Sometimes you can't accomplish everything desired in a single image.

Aperture

Apertures and shutter speeds control the amount of light that strikes the sensor or film. Like the iris in your eye, apertures do this by opening and closing a diaphragm, thereby limiting the amount of light that passes through to the sensor. The wider the opening is, the more light passes through; the smaller the opening, the less light. The size of the opening is referred to as an f-stop. It is imperative that you memorize all of the full f-stops you may encounter using most lenses. They are:

1.4, 2, 2.8, 4, 5.6, 8, 11, 16, 22, 32, 45, 64

As we move from left to right, the opening of the aperture gets smaller, with each aperture letting in half as much light as the previous number. F/16 lets in half the light of f/11, f/4 lets in twice the light of f/5.6. This relationship becomes important because it allows you to pick aperture, shutter speed, and ISO combinations that give you the correct exposure while still enabling you to control creative aspects of your images, such as depth of field.

Shutter Speed

Shutter speed also helps determine exposure by controlling how long light is allowed to strike the sensor. The longer the shutter is open, the more light strikes the sensor. If you haven't already, you also need to memorize the common full stop shutter speeds. They are:

1 sec., 1/2 sec., 1/4, 1/8, 1/15, 1/30, 1/60, 1/125, 1/250/, 1/500, 1/1000, 1/2000, 1/4000

As we move from left to right, we are halving the amount of exposure by halving the amount of time that the shutter is open to allow light to strike the sensor. For instance, 1/60 allows half as much exposure as 1/30, and 1/250 gives twice the exposure of 1/500. Selecting the correct shutter speed will enable you to not only expose properly but also control motion in your images.

tip Most modern cameras and lenses also have half- and third-stop settings, allowing for even greater exposure control. Check your manual to fully understand your camera's capabilities.

Equivalent Exposures

There is a vast array of ISO, aperture, and shutter speed combinations that will give you the exact same exposure. These are referred to as equivalent exposures. In most instances you will have selected an appropriate ISO and

EQUIVALENT EXPOSURES

f-stop	1.4	2	2.8	4	5.6	8	11	16	22	32	45
shutter speed	1/1000	1/500	1/250	1/125	1/60	1/30	1/15	1/8	1/4	1/2	1 sec.

note It is important to remember that the chart above is hypothetical. Each image will have its own set of equivalent exposures depending on the amount of light in the scene.

will then use equivalent aperture and shutter speed combinations to expose your image correctly.

The chart above shows a possible series of equivalent exposures. If you meter a scene and your meter reads f/16 at 1/8, you could choose any one of these combinations and get exactly the same exposure. This can be a difficult concept to grasp thoroughly, so let's spend a little more time with it.

Shooting f/16 at 1/8 produces exactly the same exposure as f/22 at 1/4–f/16 @ 1/8 = f/22 @ 1/4.

An aperture of f/16 lets in twice as much light as does f/22. In order to get the same exposure, then, we need to let in half as much light with our shutter speed; 1/8 is open half as long as 1/4, allowing half as much light, thereby balancing our equation. To see if you understand the concept of equivalent exposures, try solving this equation using the chart above: f/2.8 @ 1/250 = f(x) @ 1/15.

(Double-check your knowledge: The answer is at the end of the chapter.*)

You hate math, especially fractions, so why do you need to know this? Because different combinations will enable you to control the aesthetic aspects of your images while still exposing them correctly. For instance, let's say that you want to throw the background of your shot out of focus.

Strobe vs. Continuous Light

Just a reminder that the concept of equivalent exposures discussed above works with continuous lighting and not strobes. When using strobes, you control the exposure with aperture and the intensity of the strobes. As mentioned, the intensity can be changed by adjusting the power of the light or its position relative to the subject. Shutter speed is not a factor in exposure when using strobes.

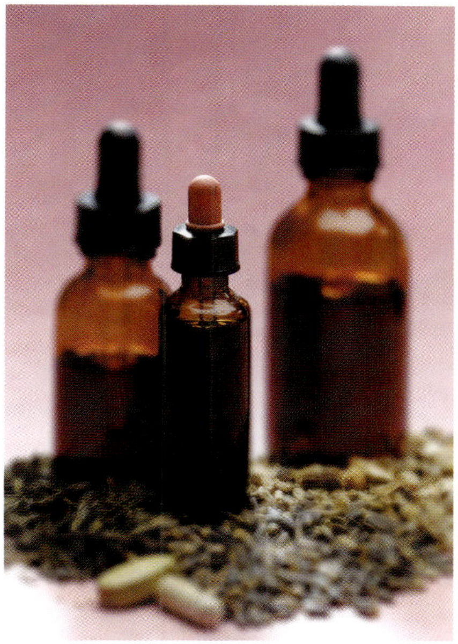

a) ISO 100, 1/60 sec., f/5.6, 210mm lens

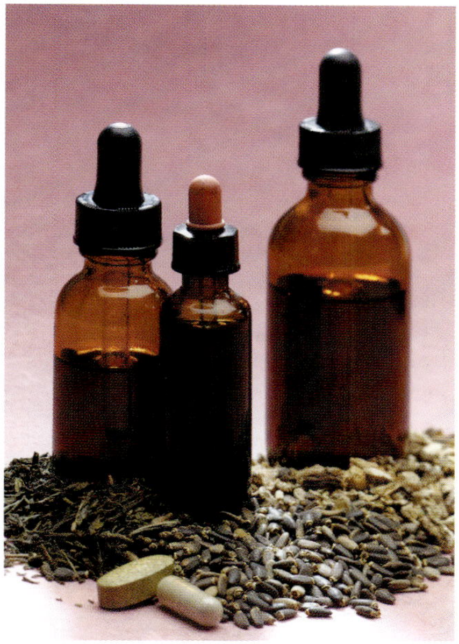

b) ISO 100, 1/4 sec., f/22, 210mm lens

FIGURE 7.3 Both images are equivalent exposures, but **a)** this one has a very narrow depth of field, whereas **b)** this one has greater depth of field.

Choosing f/5.6 @ 1/60 or f/22 @ 1/4 will both expose the image correctly, but using the f/5.6 exposure allows you to have the background out of focus, whereas the f/22 exposure doesn't (FIGURES 7.3A and 7.3B).

Bracketing

Bracketing is sort of the opposite of equivalent exposures. Instead of producing the same exposure, bracketing will give you a range of exposures (FIGURES 7.4A–E). When exposure is especially important or tricky to figure out, bracketing the exposures provides a range of them to ensure that one of the exposures will be appropriate. It's the quintessential "save your butt" technique. The advent of digital, and the ability to see your images on an LCD as you shoot, has diminished the need for bracketing, but it can still be a lifesaver in certain situations.

One of the great things about bracketing is that it can provide you with a "better" exposure than the "correct" exposure. Sometimes an exposure that is slightly lighter or darker than the normal choice will be more pleasing or have more emotional impact.

FIGURE 7.4 **a)** Two stops underexposed, **b)** one stop underexposed, **c)** normal exposure, **d)** one stop overexposed, **e)** two stops overexposed.

ISO 100, 1/125, various f-stops, 150mm lens

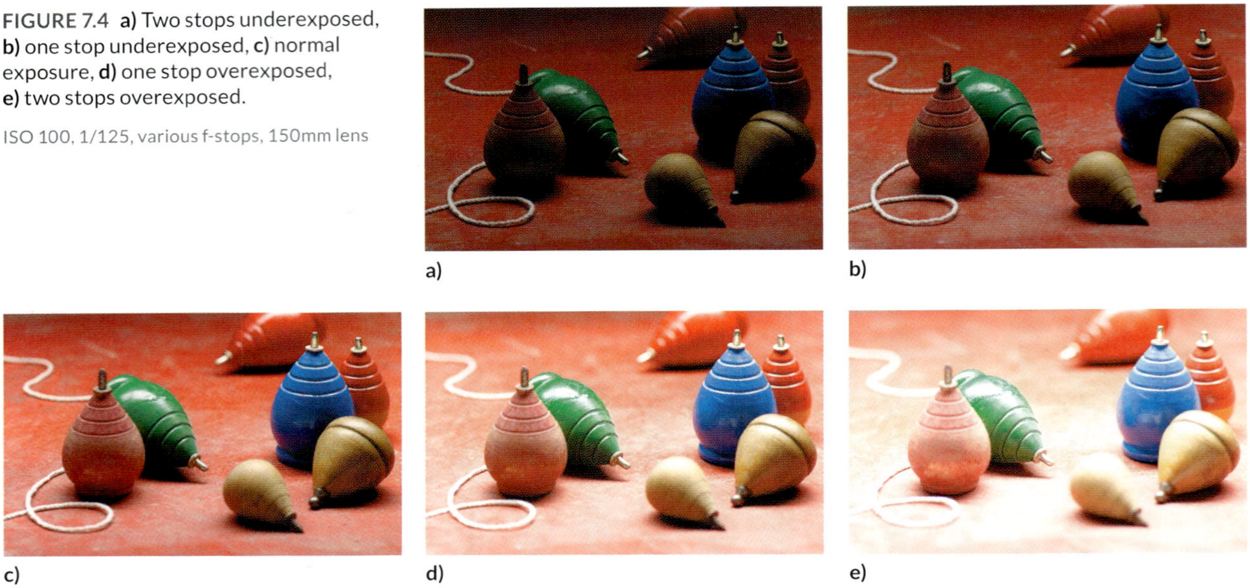

Types of Meters

Meters measure the light in a scene. Exposure meters do not recognize color; they are only metering tonal values from black to white and the gray tones that lie between. In many scenes a relatively even distribution of all of these tones will occur. After measuring the light, meters then average this information to produce an overall exposure of middle, or 18 percent, gray. As long as you are photographing an "average" scene, most metering methods will work reasonably well (FIGURE 7.5). In this image you can see that the white background is balanced by the dark clothing, and that there's an array of gray tones in the skin. Together they make up an average scene.

The images below (FIGURES 7.6A and 7.6B) show another image that has a range of tones and would be considered an average scene. The wide variety of tones from dark to light all balance each other to create an average scene of 18 percent gray.

Unfortunately, a lot of subjects are not average, and you'll need to pick the right meter and method to assure that you expose your images properly. We'll explore these situations below and in the next chapter.

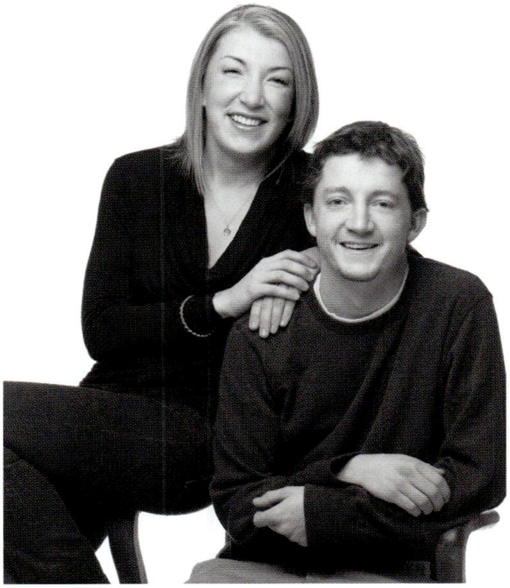

FIGURE 7.5 The tones in this image are evenly distributed between darks and lights.

ISO 100, 1/125, f/11, 150mm lens

Reflected vs. Incident

There are two types of light meters: reflected-light meters and incident-light meters. As the name implies, reflected meters measure the light reflecting off of the objects in a scene. All in-camera meters are reflected meters.

If you're photographing an average scene, reflected meters do a good job of evaluating this information to provide the correct exposure. Light objects reflect more light than dark objects do. If what you're photographing has a majority of light or dark subject matter, you can get an erroneous meter reading. We'll examine this problem in greater detail in the following chapter.

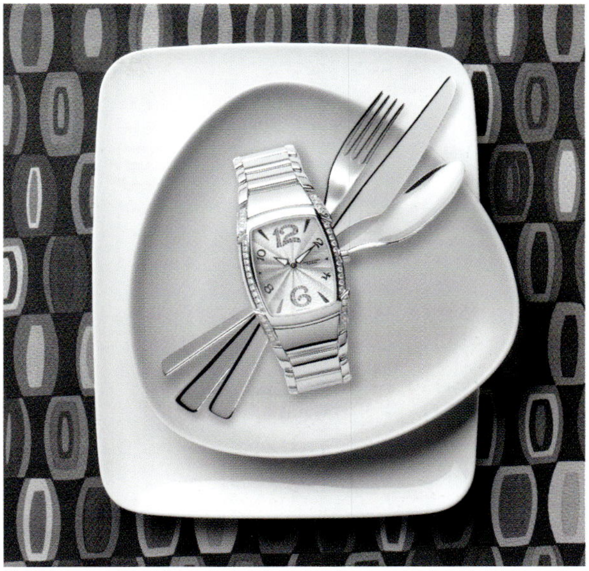

a)

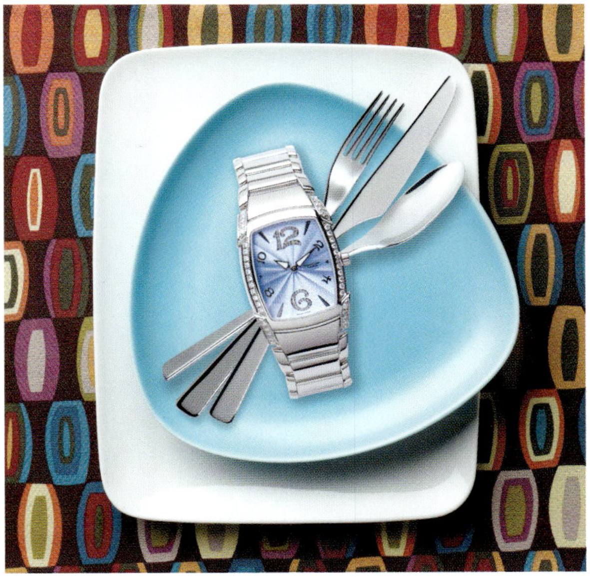

b)

FIGURE 7.6 **a)** In this version of the image, the tones are evenly distributed between darks and lights. **b)** This is the same image in color. It takes a while to learn to translate color values into tonal values.

ISO 100, 1/125, f/22, 210mm lens

tip If you intend to become a studio photographer, consider buying a meter that's capable of metering strobes as well as ambient light. Obtaining a meter that's suitable for all your lighting needs is worth the extra cost.

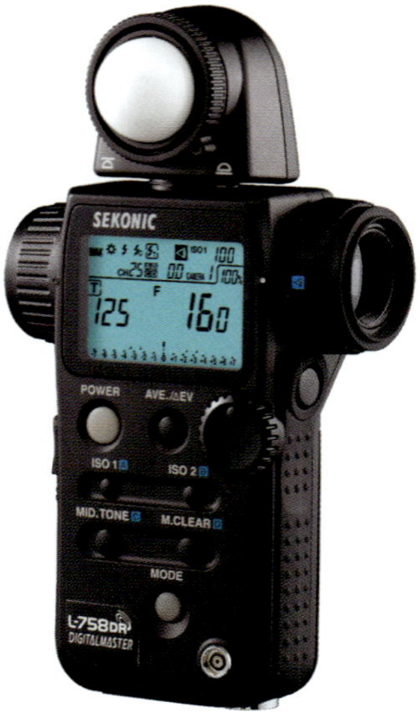

FIGURE 7.7 A handheld meter in incident mode, with the integrated sphere covering the light sensor.

You can avoid this problem in two ways. The first is to use an incident meter to measure the light falling on the scene as opposed to reflecting off the scene. You place an integrating sphere over the light sensor, and the light falling on the sphere is then averaged to produce an exposure for middle gray (FIGURE 7.7).

The actual subject matter doesn't come into play, because you are measuring the light striking the scene as opposed to the light reflecting off the scene.

Another way to avoid subject failure is to use a gray card and your camera's or a handheld reflected meter. A gray card is a piece of cardboard that's 18 percent gray. By metering only the card, you're exposing correctly for middle gray. All the other tones in the scene will then also be exposed and rendered properly. This method of metering is very accurate and is used a great deal in studio situations.

In-camera vs. Handheld

Virtually all modern cameras have in-camera light meters. Used properly, they provide very accurate exposure calibration. The one major exception is large format: These cameras don't have an internal meter. When shooting with a large-format system, you can determine correct exposure with a handheld meter by using either the incident setting or the reflected setting metering off of a gray card.

Handheld meters are more versatile than in-camera meters and are a vital piece of equipment for most professional photographers. Handheld meters have different metering modes, including ambient light and various strobe settings.

Mind the Dome

It's important to make sure that the light hitting the dome is the same as the light in the scene you're photographing. If you're standing in shade with your meter, but the scene you are photographing is flooded with light, you'll get an inaccurate reading. Also make sure to point the dome directly toward your camera to get the proper reading.

Metering Modes

Metering modes for your in-camera meter vary depending on camera manufacturer and model. It's important to thoroughly understand these modes for your individual cameras, as they can greatly assist you in getting the correct exposure in a variety of situations. Yes, we're telling you to read your manuals. It'll pay off, we promise. Then experiment with the different modes in different situations. Because you'll be using a handheld meter or you'll meter off a gray card in a studio situation, you won't need these modes there. You'll control your lighting and then make precise exposure decisions. For this reason, we'll only briefly cover the three main in-camera meter modes.

Matrix or Multisegment Metering In this mode, the meter is metering various zones (segments) of the image and then averaging them together to give you a good overall exposure. Depending on your camera, it may give priority to the zone that is in focus. Matrix metering will be the default mode for most DSLR cameras and works well in most situations, especially when you are photographing an average scene.

Center-Weighted Metering Sometimes you'll be better off metering less than the entire scene. Perhaps you're photographing a portrait and the sun is behind your subject; using the matrix mode will underexpose your subject due to the bright surrounding background. By emphasizing the subject in the center of the frame, the center-weighted mode will give you a better exposure for your subject.

Spot Metering Spot metering works well when you have a small subject within the scene, and you want to make sure that it's correctly exposed. Spot metering is similar to center-weighted, but it's metering a smaller spot in the center of the frame or your focus point. It can work well for wildlife photography when the animal is small within the frame.

The images below (FIGURES 7.8A–C) were taken with the same lighting. Each was shot with a normal exposure setting, but the metering modes were different. You can see how they differ, with the spot-metering mode being the brightest because it is exposing for the shadow area of the pumpkin.

In all modes, the camera is making an educated guess as to the proper exposure. Modern camera meters are increasingly sophisticated, but they can be fooled. The more you experiment and the more you understand the strengths and weaknesses of each metering mode, the more successful you'll be at achieving the proper exposure.

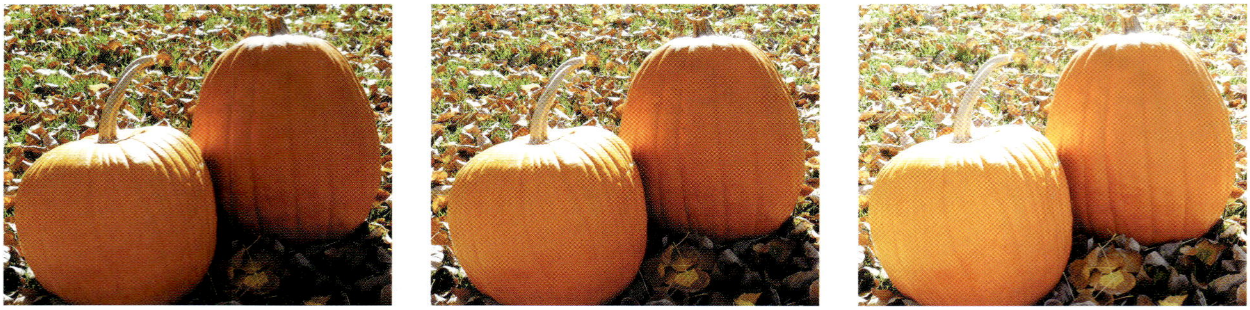

a) b) c)

FIGURE 7.8 **a)** Matrix metering—good overall exposure, although the fronts of the pumpkins are a little dark, **b)** center weighted—this is the best exposure for this image, although the highlights on the tops of the pumpkins are blown out, **c)** spot metered—the fronts of the pumpkins have good detail but the shot is generally overexposed.

ISO 80, various f-stops, f/8, 35mm lens

Priority Modes

In addition to the modes we just discussed you can also give priority to either the aperture or shutter speed settings when considering exposure. You can also control both in manual mode or give up all decisions in auto mode. We recommend using manual settings whenever possible and avoiding auto mode at all costs. In manual mode you have control over both the shutter speed and the aperture. You can control both depth of field and movement. In a studio situation where you are controlling the light, the manual mode makes the most sense.

There are times when you'll be shooting, the light may be changing as you shoot, and choosing a priority mode will be expedient.

tip Remember that you want to shoot at 1/ lens focal length for your slowest shutter speed if you are handholding your camera. Regardless of the length of your lens, you don't want to shoot slower than 1/60 sec. with a handheld camera.

Aperture Priority

You choose aperture priority when controlling depth of field is more important than how you deal with movement. In this mode you select the aperture and the camera automatically picks the corresponding shutter speed for a correct exposure. As the light or the scene changes, the aperture remains constant and the shutter speed fluctuates.

Shutter Priority

You would want to use shutter priority when you want to control motion, picking a slow shutter speed to blur movement and a fast shutter speed to freeze motion. In this mode you choose the shutter speed, and the camera automatically picks the corresponding aperture for a correct exposure. As the light or the scene changes, the shutter speed remains constant and the aperture fluctuates.

In this chapter, we've introduced you to the many things that can influence metering and exposure. As your career develops, you'll find yourself in a number of different circumstances, and you'll invariably blow some exposures. Learn from your mistakes and move on. Most of the studio photographers we know can set up their strobes, adjust the power and their camera settings, and take an exposure that's within a half stop of normal without ever using a meter. There's no substitute for experience. Study your manuals, get out and apply the information, experiment, and have fun.

*The answer to the equation we asked you to solve in "Equivalent Exposures" is f/11.

Comparison

This chapter's comparison was the first one we did and was instrumental in forming much of the content in this book.

We batted around a lot of subjects before settling on the idea of photographing forks (**FIGURE 7.9**). What we liked was that they're simple objects and open to interpretation. As often happens, Joe went clean, new, and light, while Brad went old and dark, scouring antique stores looking for the perfect old fork. We were in the studio together when we shot these, and it was fun to see how some of the elements were similar (red object and the fork sitting on the edge of something), while our lighting approaches were vastly different.

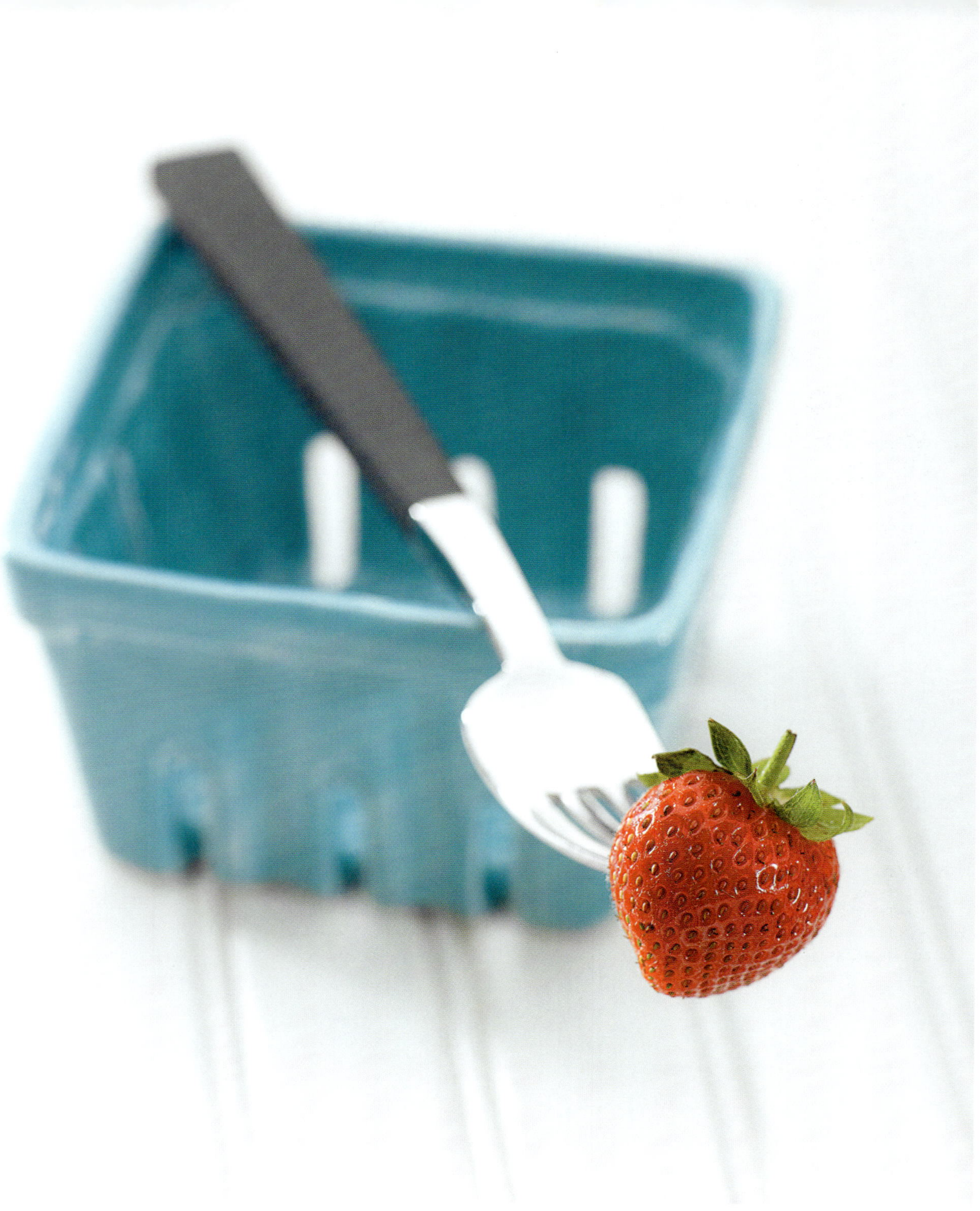

a)

ISO 50, 1/125 sec., f/8 , 100mm lens

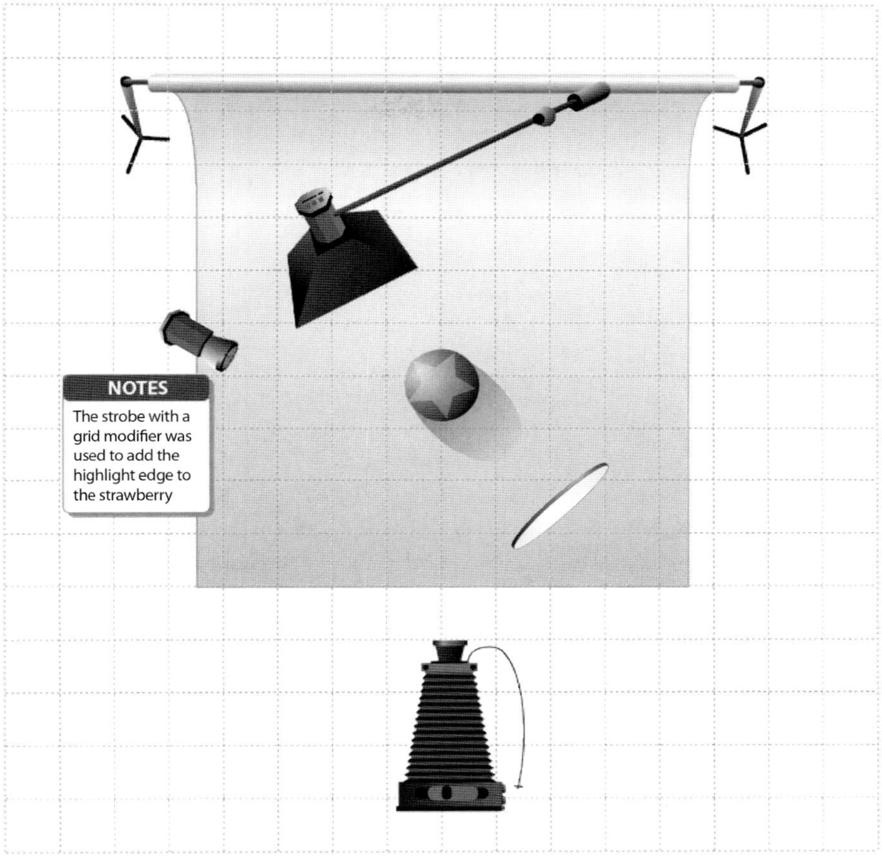

b)

FIGURE 7.9 **a)** A high-key approach was used to accentuate the clean, sleek lines of the fork and the appeal of the strawberry; **b)** notice the grid modifier that was added to create specular highlights on the strawberry; **c)** rustic props called for warm light painting to add highlights and texture to the fork (next page); **d)** a softbox was underexposed by 1 1/2 stops, and then highlights were added using a flashlight (next page).

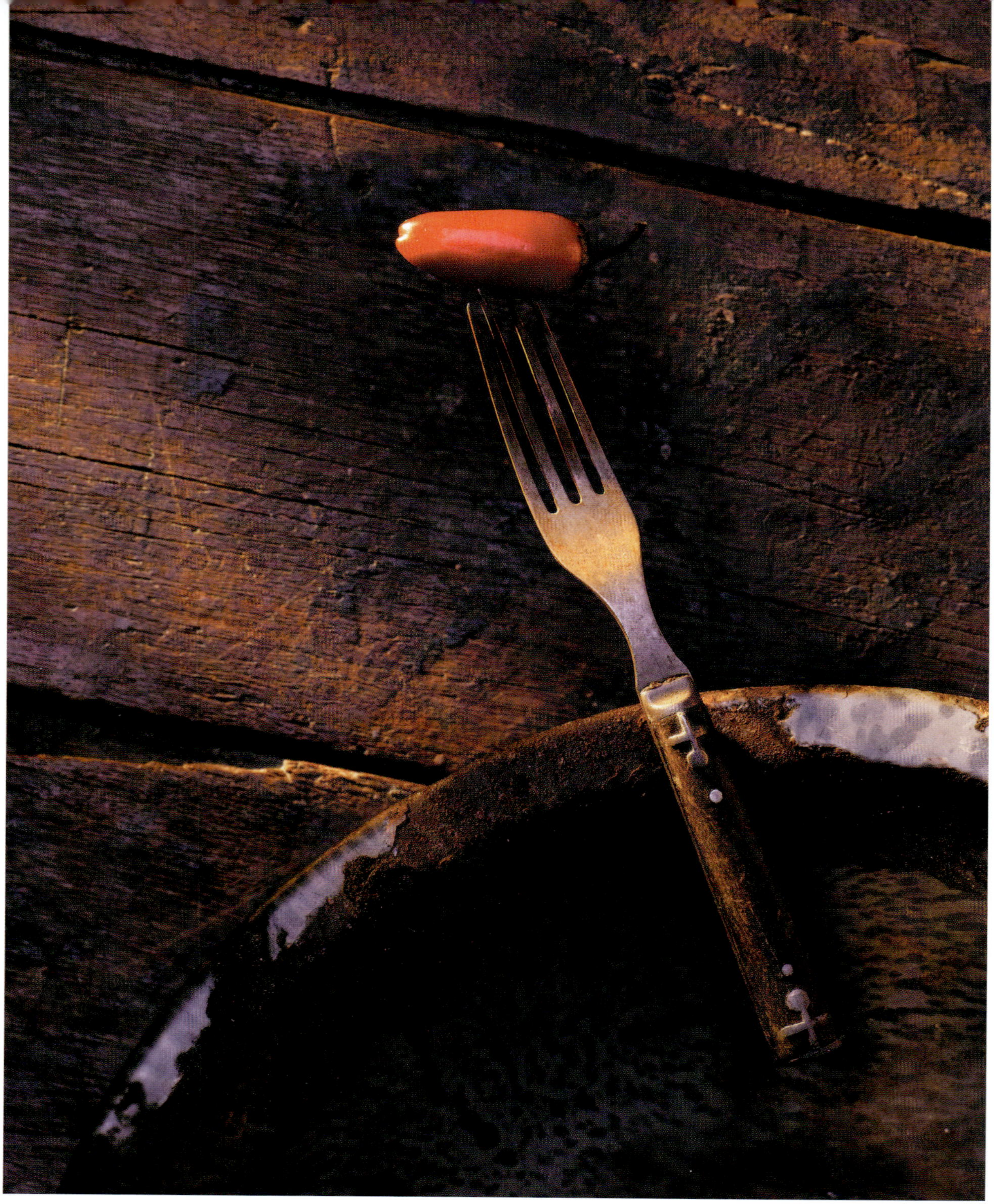

c)

ISO 50, 20 sec., f/11, 150mm lens

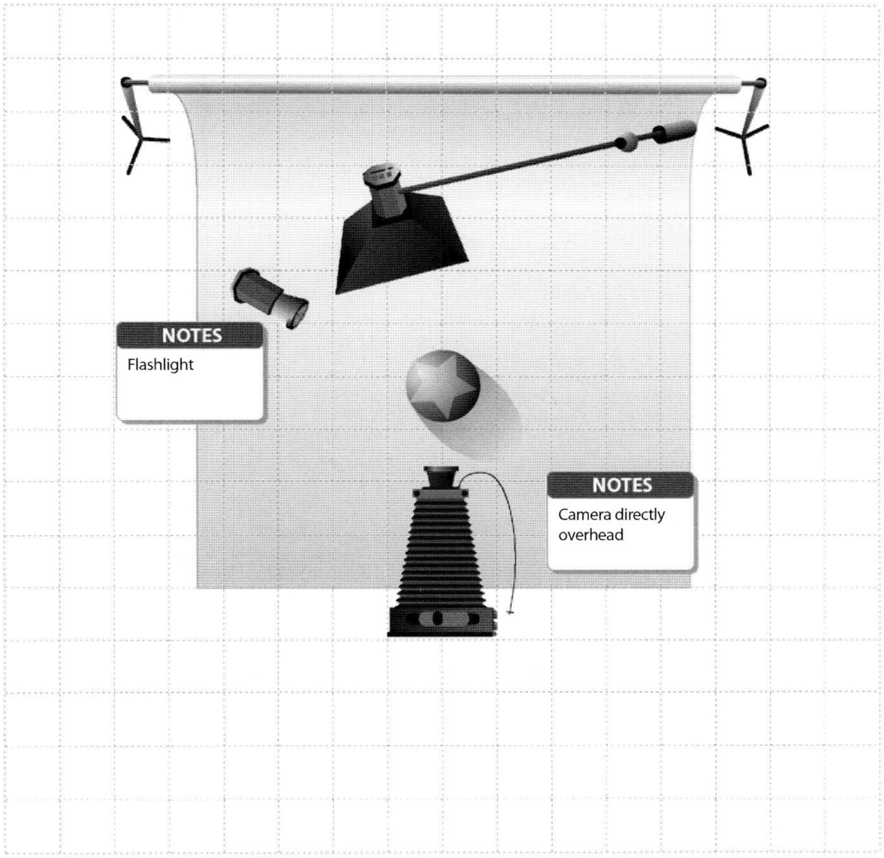

d)

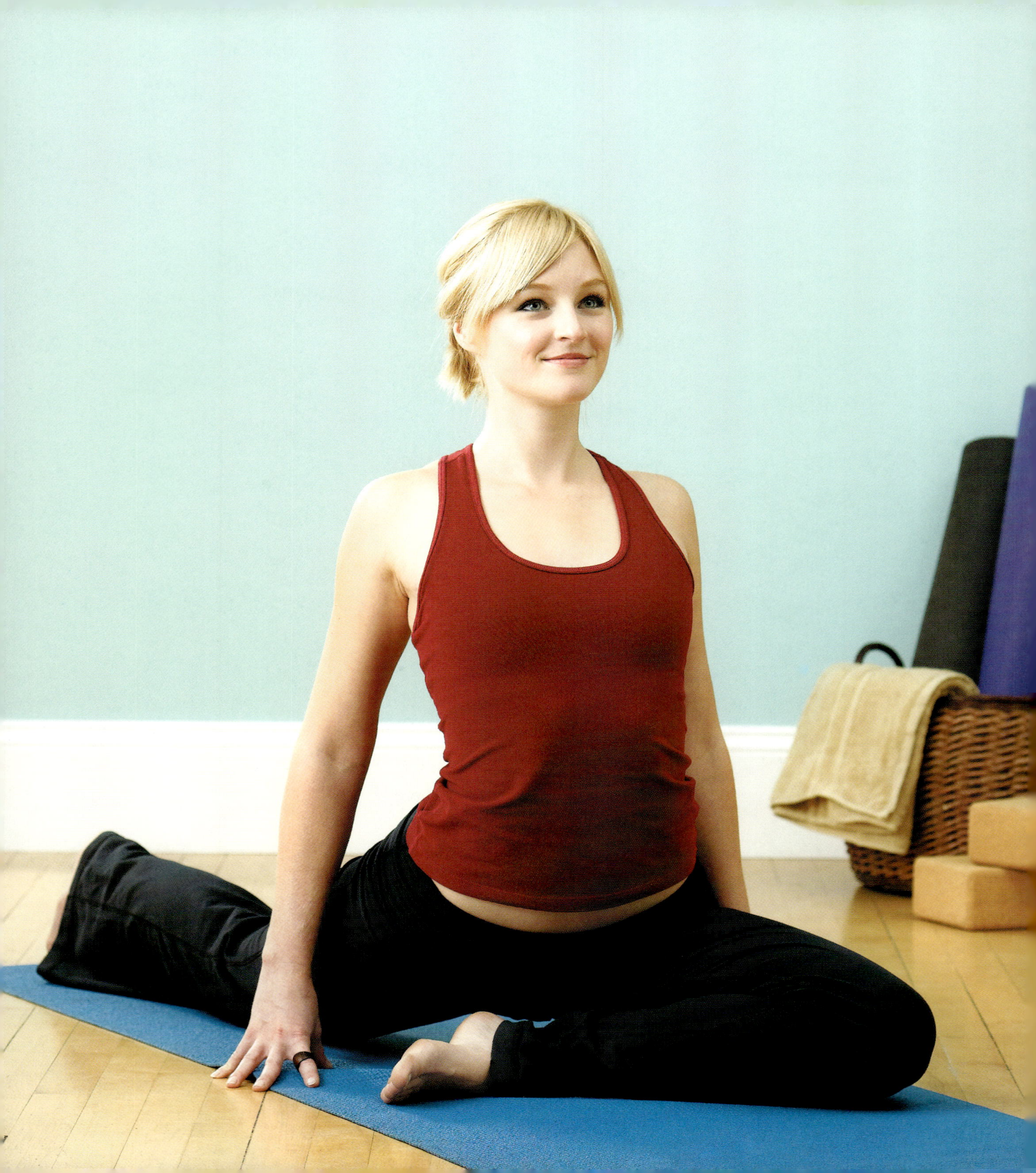

chapter eight

READING A HISTOGRAM

Reading something, whether it's a book, a magazine article, or the newspaper, usually involves gaining new information and learning something. The same is true with the relationship between histograms and photographs. We read histograms to gain a more comprehensive knowledge of the photographs we take. The ability to analyze this information, as it relates to your individual images, will help you consistently expose images properly.

ISO 50, 1/60 sec., f/8, 150mm lens

Opening Image: Photographic Equipment

Camera: Mamiya 645afd with Leaf Aptus-II digital back

Lens: 150mm

Lighting: Profoto Acute2 2400 and 1200 generators and three strobe heads

Light modifiers: 6 × 6 silk, 4 × 8 foam core

This lighting scheme for the yoga subject on the previous page was designed to emulate window light.

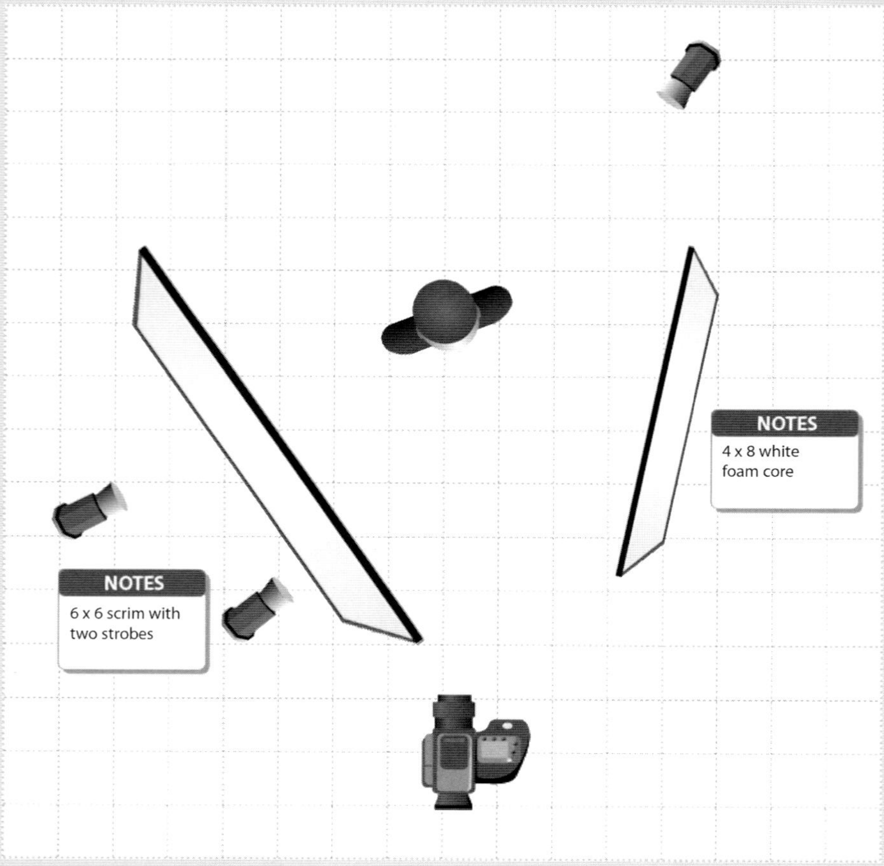

What Is a Histogram?

A histogram is a graphic representation of your image. It's a map that helps assure that your image's final destination is where you wanted to end up. By looking at the image and then at its histogram, you'll be able to analyze whether or not you have the proper exposure to reproduce the image the way that you want.

Histograms enable you to see precisely which tones are captured within an individual exposure and how much of each tone there is. In an 8-bit RGB image, the horizontal axis in a histogram represents tonal values from 0 to 255, black to white. The vertical axis represents how many pixels of each tone there are.

Imagine that the pixels are children's building blocks, stacked one on top of the other. In the histogram in **FIGURE 8.1**, you can see that pixels are distributed throughout the tonal range from 0 to 255, with more pixels having a tone around middle gray (128) and another peak at a lighter tone (around 200).

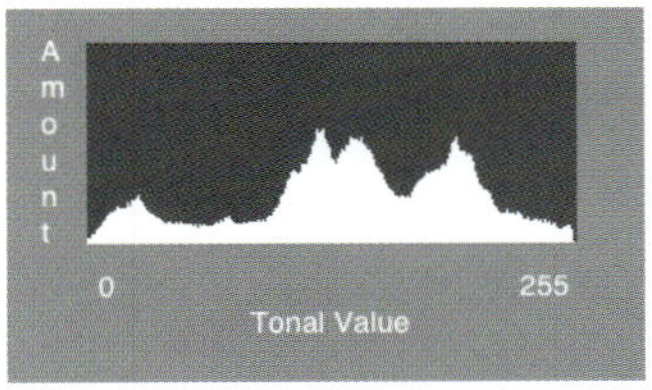

FIGURE 8.1 The tones in this image are distributed between darks and lights, with a few peaks representing more pixel information at those tones.

Most cameras and post-production software will show histograms representing the overall image as well as each individual channel: red, green, and blue. In this book, we'll just be concentrating on the histograms that represent the overall exposure.

At some point you may hear someone say, "Wow, that's a great-looking histogram." The truth is, a statement like that has no meaning because histograms are neither good nor bad; they simply are what they are. They represent the pixel information that has been captured in an individual image. The histogram itself isn't right or wrong, but it can give you feedback about whether or not you have exposed a particular scene correctly. Let's look at a few examples (**FIGURE 8.2A** and **8.2B**).

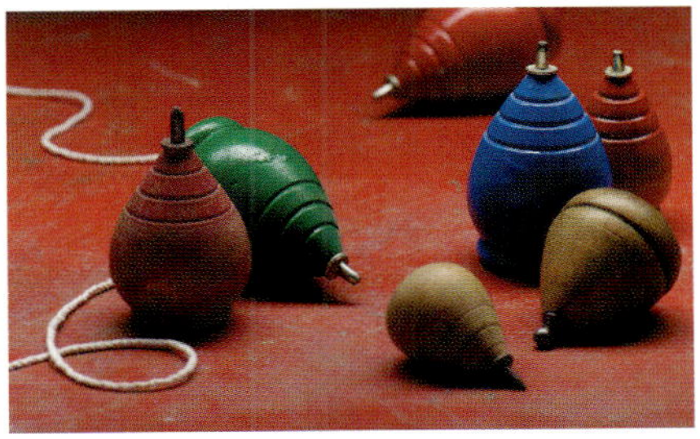

a)

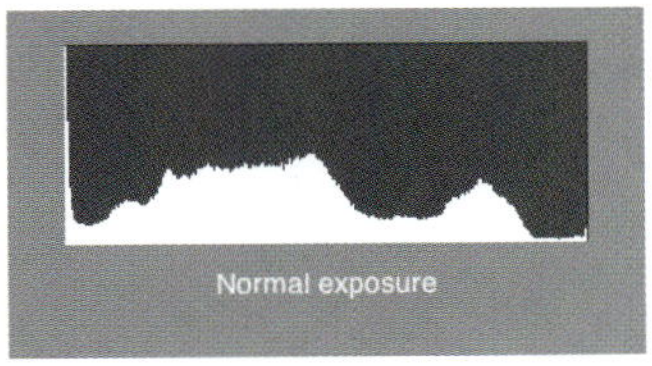

b)

FIGURE 8.2 **a)** A normal exposure and **b)** its corresponding histogram.

ISO 100, 1/125 sec., f/8, 150mm lens

The most important thing to keep in mind when it comes to reading a histogram is to look at the scene you're photographing and then make sure the histogram you're reading corresponds correctly to that scene. In other words, does the pixel information make sense? Is it what you would expect to see? More importantly, do you have the amount of information you need throughout the image, especially in the shadows and highlights? For the example above, the answer is yes.

You'll notice that there's a spike along the left edge, and because of this we can assume that there's some information in the deep shadows that was not captured. Here's where interpreting the histogram becomes important. For this shot we didn't care that some shadow detail wasn't captured in our normal exposure. We have a good overall range of tones, and the fact that some of the darker shadows won't have detail is fine. In fact, it actually adds to the overall mood we were looking for in this shot.

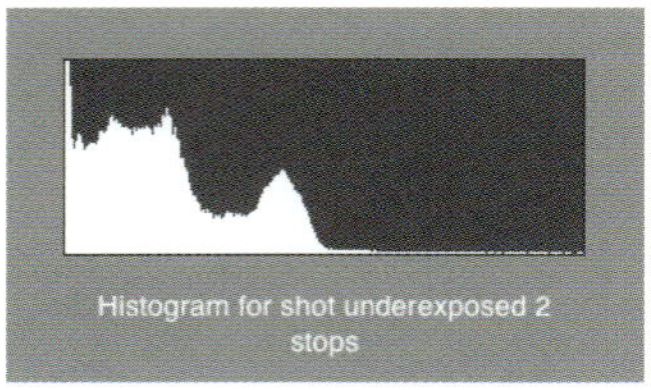

FIGURE 8.3 A histogram representing two stops of underexposure.

What if we're photographing the same scene, but instead of seeing a histogram like the one in Figure 8.2, we see this histogram (**FIGURE 8.3**)?

An image with this histogram would have virtually no information in tones brighter than middle gray. We can also tell that a substantial amount of information has been lost in the darker tones. The distribution across many tones that we saw in Figure 8.2 has shifted significantly to the left, toward and beyond 0. When you see such a severe cutoff along the left edge, you know that much of the information in the photograph has been pushed to 0. This means there'll be no detail in those areas; they will simply be black. There may be times when losing all this information would not be a problem, but that's not the case here, as you can see in **FIGURE 8.4**.

FIGURE 8.4 An image that's underexposed two stops.

ISO 100, 1/125 sec., f/16, 150mm lens

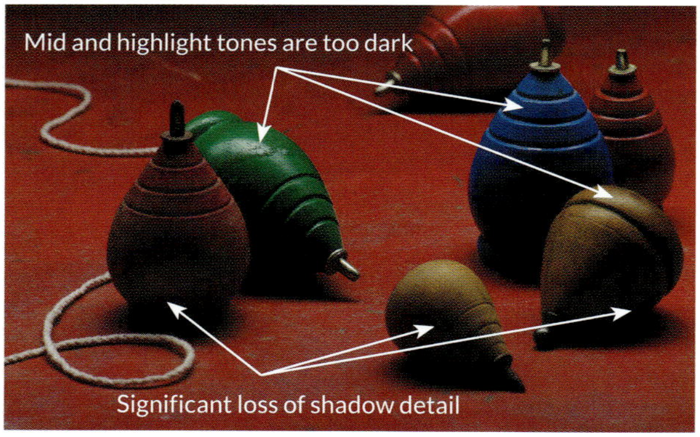

It is pretty clear that the overall image is too dark. The highlights and midtones are muddy due to the fact that the image was underexposed. Considerable amounts of shadow information have been lost; the shadows are all blocked up with little or no detail. By looking at the histogram, you would be able to tell that this scene is underexposed without even seeing the image on the camera's LCD.

The next photograph shows the results of overexposure (**FIGURE 8.5**). This image received two more stops of exposure than the correct normal exposure.

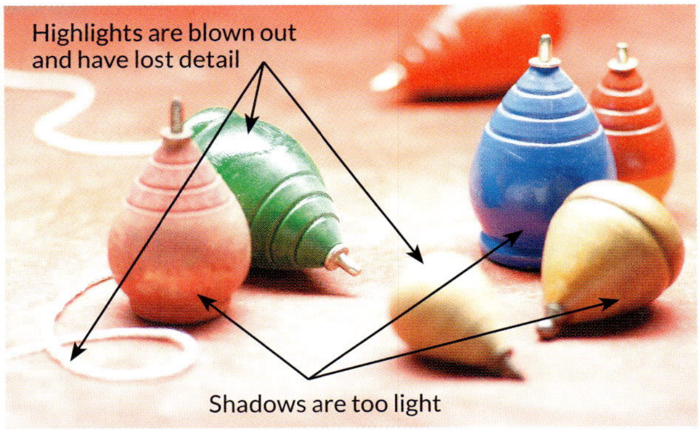

FIGURE 8.5 The same subject, overexposed two stops.

ISO 100, 1/125, f/4, 150mm lens

Here we see that the pixel information has moved dramatically to the right (**FIGURE 8.6**). Much of the highlight information has moved beyond 255, which means that by overexposing this image, important highlight detail has been lost. The rich midtones are now washed out and the entire image is too bright.

FIGURE 8.6 The histogram for the image overexposed by two stops.

If you set up the image of these tops in the studio and saw this histogram on your camera's LCD, you would know that your exposure was incorrect. Many cameras have an additional feature to aid with proper exposure. They have the ability to show areas within the shot that have highlights or shadows that are being clipped. Clipping means that pixel information is too light or dark to maintain detail; it falls outside the 0 to 255 parameters. The areas that are being clipped are indicated by a solid or blinking color (**FIGURE 8.7**). This can be extremely helpful when you are trying to decide if your image is properly exposed.

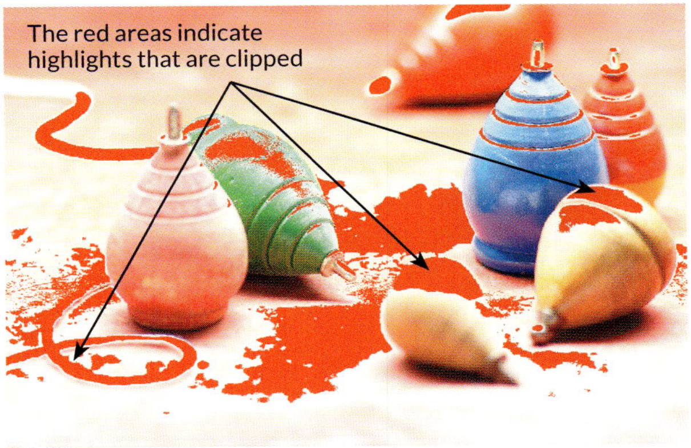

FIGURE 8.7 This image shows the clipping warning activated. The solid red areas indicate highlights that are being clipped, meaning that detail in these areas is gone.

Losing detail in essential parts of your images is unacceptable and will require adjustments in exposure, lighting, or both. As mentioned in discussing Figure 8.2a, at times we don't mind losing shadow (or highlight) detail. But if our client needs to see detail throughout the image, then we must make adjustments. In an image short on shadow detail, these could include more exposure, as long as the highlights don't blow out. Or we could add a little overall fill light to the image to open up the shadows, while maintaining highlight detail and the same overall exposure (**FIGURE 8.8A** and **8.8B**). These kinds of compromises are common when you're working within client and reproduction constraints. Just because the image looks great on your monitor is not an assurance that it'll reproduce the same way on other media.

FIGURE 8.8 **a)** A normal exposure; **b)** whereas this shot has the same exposure, a little front fill was added to open up the shadows.

ISO 100, 1/125 sec., f/8, 150mm lens

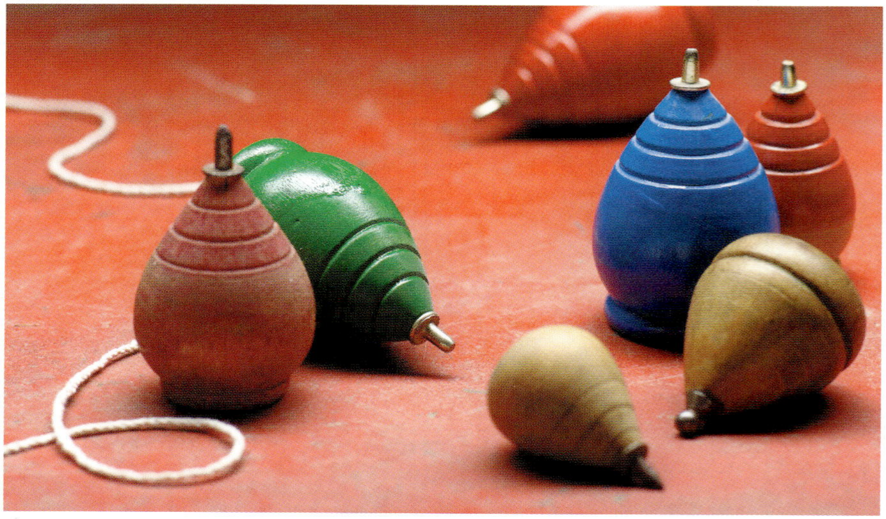

a)

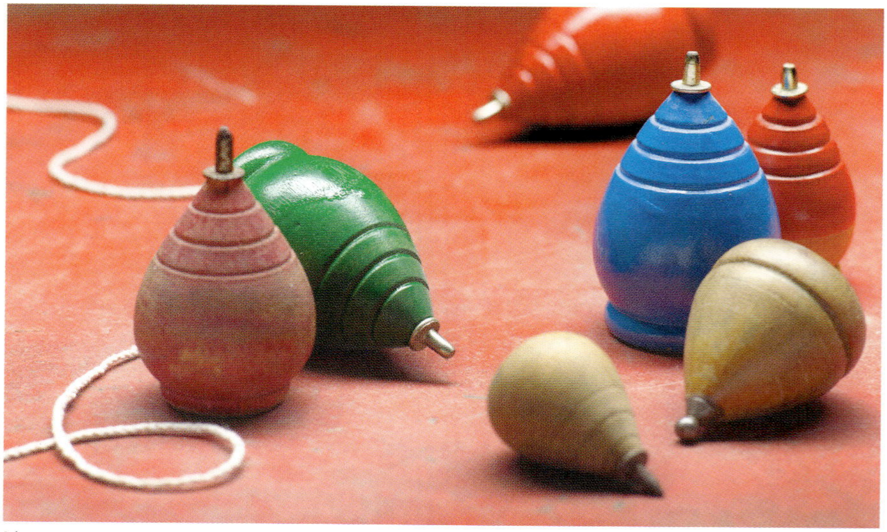

b)

Why Are Histograms Important?

In the previous chapter we mentioned that there are times when you can't capture all the tones present in a scene in a single exposure. Sometimes you will have to lose shadow detail to maintain highlight detail or visa versa. Cameras with higher dynamic range make it easier to maintain detail over a greater range of tones, and DSLRs have a wonderful tool to previsualize the final image: the LCD on the back of the camera.

Here's the problem—a lot of pictures look good on the LCD. But LCDs can be incredibly deceptive when it comes to getting a true reading of the final image. The image on the LCD can be greatly affected by the ambient light. Images look brighter when the ambient light is dark and darker when the light is brighter. Sometimes it can be very difficult to see the image at all in direct sunlight.

Relying on what the LCD shows can lead to improper exposures. Carefully examining the histogram will enable you to more accurately determine if you are exposing your photos in ways that are appropriate for the images and for your personal interpretation of each scene.

Although the LCD has limitations for judging exposure, it is a good tool for reviewing composition—but again, make sure not to let it interrupt the flow of your shoot.

Chimping

Chimping is the bad habit of looking at the LCD after every image you take. Let's say you're photographing a model, and after every shot you stop to look at the screen. The momentum of the shoot is killed. The energy is lost. Models are like strobe packs. They store up energy and then release it when the shutter is pressed. You have to get in a rhythm, and stopping to check out your LCD all the time stops this from happening. Once you get your shot set up, take an exposure, look at the LCD, and check your histogram. Make adjustments, if needed, and then shoot, only occasionally checking the LCD for any changes. Concentrate on what is in front of you, not on the back of the camera.

Subject Failure

Your in-camera meter will do a reasonably good job of metering most average scenes. On many occasions, however, the subject matter will not fit neatly into a tonally balanced average scene. At times the scene itself is predominantly dark or light, or the main subject is darker or lighter than the background. These situations can "trick" your meter into rendering an incorrect reading. Remember, your camera's meter analyzes the light reflecting off a scene, averages it, and then provides the correct settings for an 18 percent gray, or neutral, exposure. *Subject failure* refers to those times when scenes are not middle gray. We have always thought the term was a misnomer. The subjects are what they are; the failure occurs when we don't correctly read the scene and analyze the corresponding histogram.

Using your incident meter or metering off a gray card will greatly reduce exposure problems even when subject failure is an issue. We'll examine ways to compensate for subject failure when you are forced to use your in-camera meter. This will also help you to better understand metering and exposure in general.

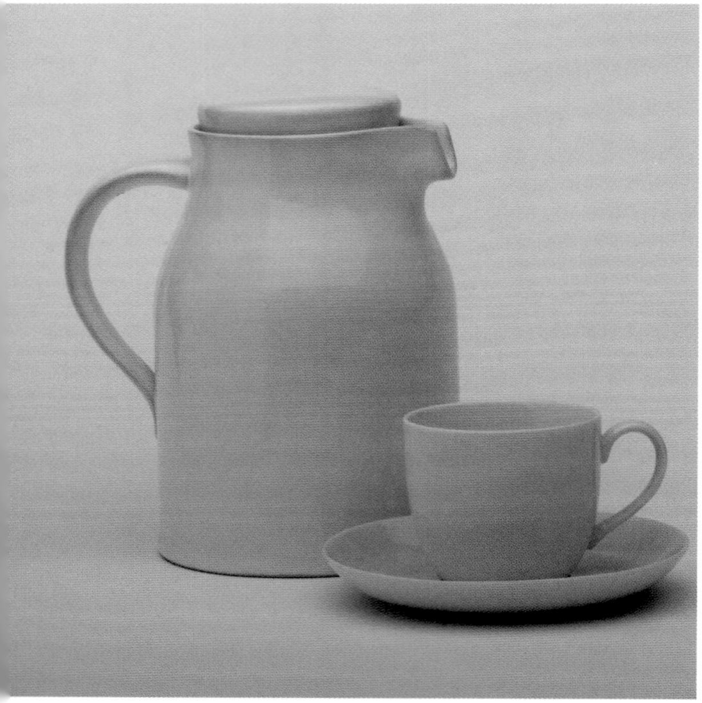

FIGURE 8.9 An image exposed according to the meter reading.

ISO 50, 1/125, f/11, 150mm lens

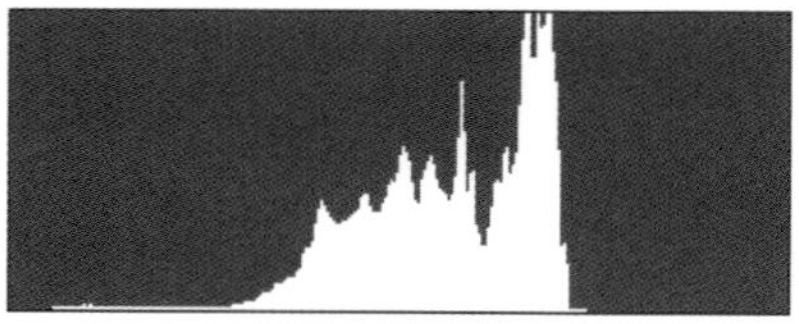

FIGURE 8.10 The histogram for an image exposed according to the meter reading.

High-Key Scenes

High-key scenes occur when the subjects in a scene are brighter than 18 percent gray (think a white bunny in a snowstorm—a white subject against a white background). Your camera's meter would gather the light reflecting off the subject and background and give you a meter reading that would turn this bright scene into one that is middle gray. In other words, the meter would give you a setting that would produce an underexposed image. The tonal values should be brighter than 18 percent gray, but the meter's exposure put these values at or around 18 percent gray.

The image on the left (**FIGURE 8.9**) is a high-key scene exposed using the in-camera reflected meter reading. You can see that the photo is gray on gray, not white on white. In order to expose this image properly, we need to overexpose from what the meter tells us is the correct exposure. How much we need to overexpose is determined by how bright the actual scene is. In general, we will need to overexpose by between one-half and two stops.

Looking at the original histogram (**FIGURE 8.10**), you can see that most of the pixels are gathered around middle gray. This indicates an incorrect exposure for this particular scene. We would expect to see pixel information primarily in areas above 18 percent gray. The pixels would correspond to the scene itself, white on white.

Increasing the exposure provides tones that are appropriate for the scene being photographed. **FIGURE 8.11A–F** includes images and their corresponding histograms as exposure was increased from one to two additional stops in half-stop increments. You can see how the values in the images

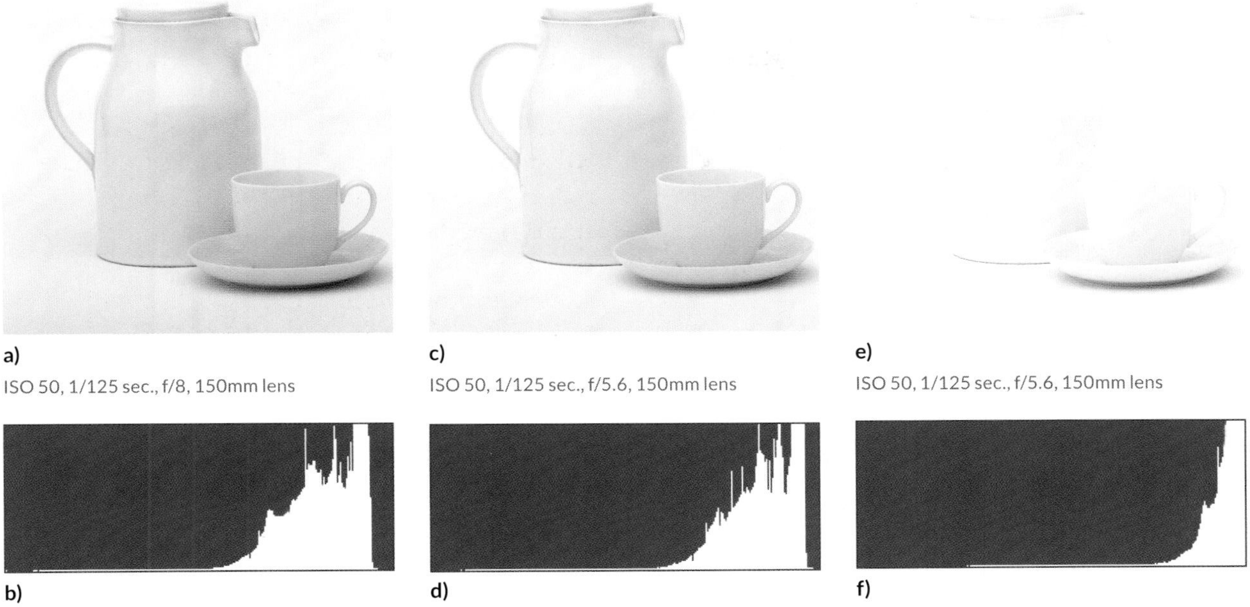

FIGURE 8.11 **a)** An image with +1 stop exposure; **b)** the histogram for +1 exposure; **c)** +1 ½ stops exposure; **d)** the histogram for +1 ½ exposure; **e)** +2 stops exposure; **f)** the histogram for +2 exposure.

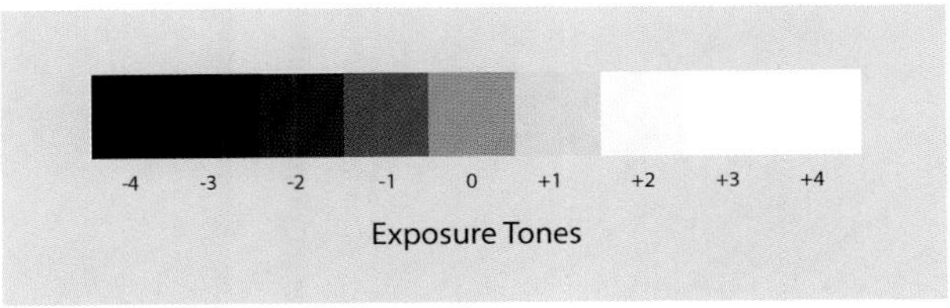

FIGURE 8.12 These tones represent one stop, plus and minus, exposure increments.

become brighter as exposure increases and that each histogram reflects these increases in exposure. Increasing the exposure by one stop over the meter reading makes the image brighter, but not quite as bright as it needs to be, whereas increasing it by two stops creates an image that's too bright, resulting in the loss of too much highlight detail.

FIGURE 8.12 is a graphic representation of what happens to tones in an image as you increase and decrease exposure.

In our example, the meter places the tones' average at or about zero. In order to get them to be white but maintain detail, adding one to three stops of exposure will be sufficient. Each subject will require a different amount of exposure compensation to render it properly. Our example looks best with right around one and one-half stops more exposure.

Low-Key Scenes

A similar thing happens with low-key scenes. A low-key scene has a majority of dark subjects; most of the scene is darker than 18 percent gray (think a black poodle sitting in a mound of coal—a black subject against a black background). In this case, your camera's meter is going to turn a dark scene into a scene that's closer to middle gray. Your meter reading will create a scene that's overexposed.

Using the in-camera meter, FIGURE 8.13A and 8.13B demonstrate how objects that should be black are rendered too light due to the meter's overexposure. The corresponding histogram also shows how tones that should be to the left of 18 percent gray have moved significantly to the right. When you know that your subjects do not constitute an average scene, you realize that you'll need to underexpose from what the meter is telling you in order to properly place the tones where they belong.

Decreasing the exposure provides tones that are appropriate for the scene being photographed. In FIGURE 8.14A–D, images and their corresponding histograms illustrate what happens as exposure is decreased by one and one and one-half stops. The tonal values in the images become darker as exposure decreases, and each histogram reflects the decrease in exposure. Underexposing from the meter reading by one and one-half stops places the tones where they should be for the subject. This is the proper exposure for this subject, but each subject will be a little different.

Backlit Scenes

Often the most difficult subjects to meter are backlit scenes. Imagine you're standing on a beach looking at a strikingly beautiful sunset. Your fiancé suggests that you take his picture standing in front of the sunset, which means he'll be in shadow in front of a bright background. If you have your meter set to matrix mode, the meter will end up underexposing your fiancé in order to

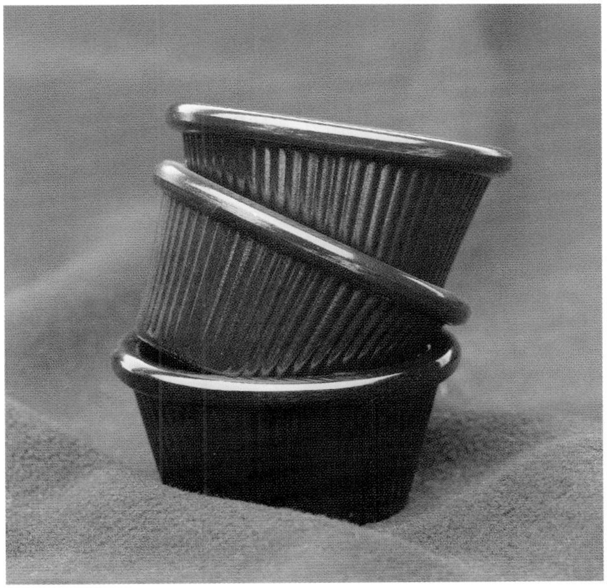

a)

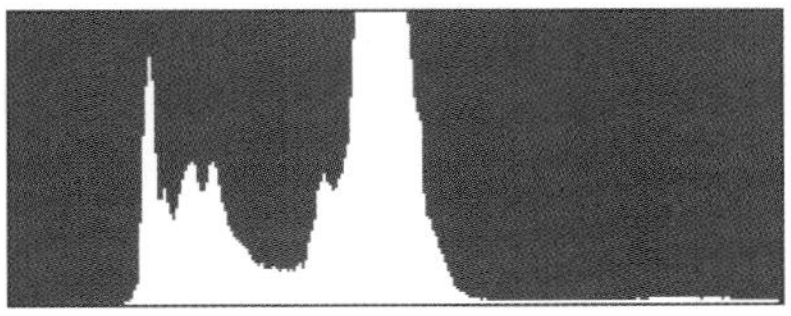

b)

FIGURE 8.13 **a)** An image exposed according to the meter reading; **b)** the corresponding histogram.

ISO 50, 1/125 sec., f/11, 150mm lens

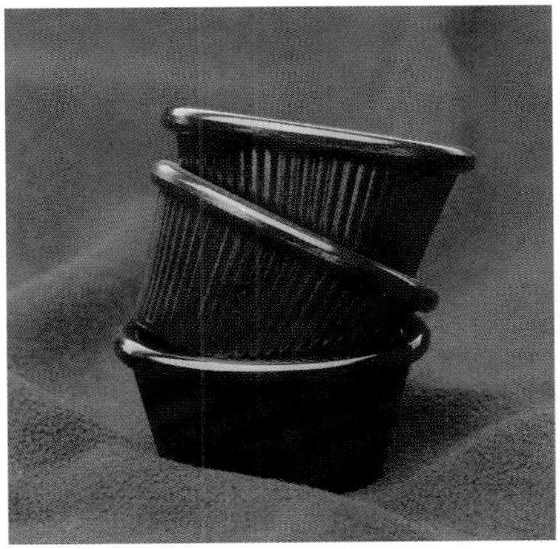

a)

ISO 50, 1/125 sec., f/16 1/2, 150mm lens

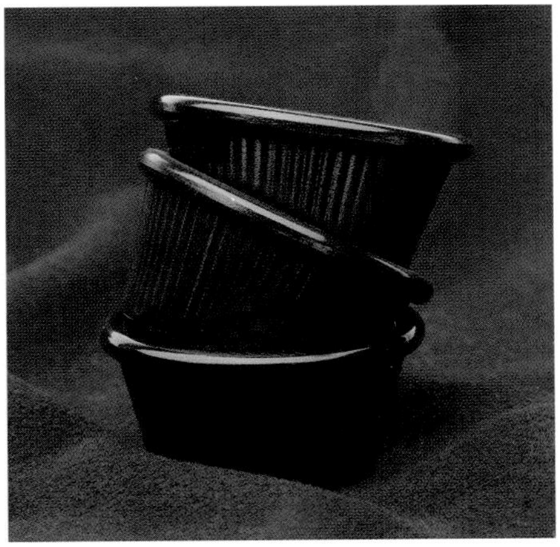

c)

ISO 50, 1/125 sec., f/16 1/2, 150mm lens

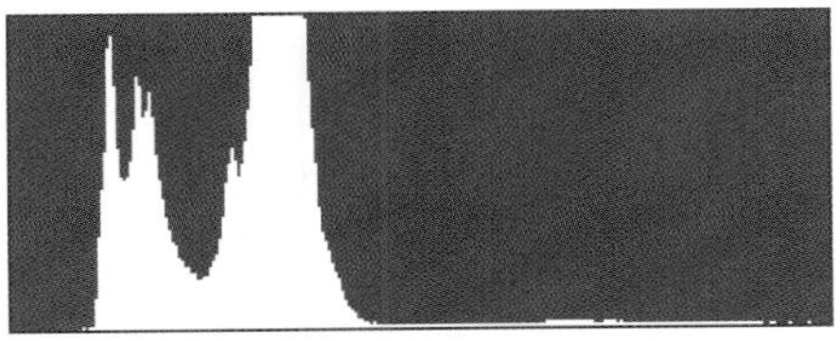

b)

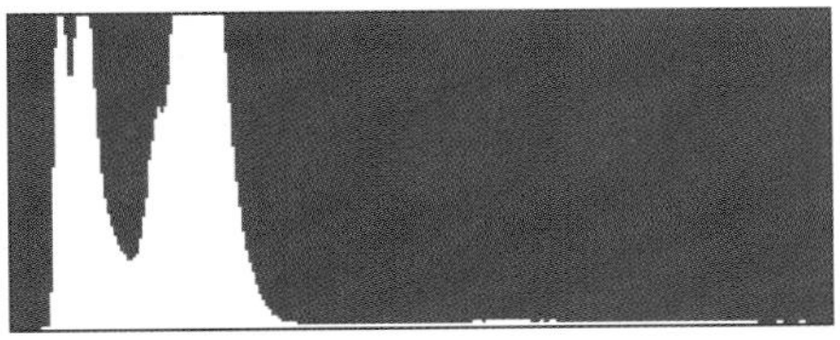

d)

FIGURE 8.14 **a)** An image with one stop less exposure and **b)** the corresponding histogram; **c)** this image has –1½ stops exposure, and **d)** the –1½ histogram.

more properly expose the bright background. What's more important, your handsome fiancé or the beautiful sunset? We can't answer that question, but without additional lighting you're going to need to compromise.

Doing what the meter tells you should give you a decent, if slightly washed out, sunset, but your fiancé will be significantly underexposed. If you set your mode to center weighted or spot meter, and meter your fiancé, he will be better exposed but your sunset will be completely overexposed and washed out. It is possible to compromise a little; here's how.

With your camera in the matrix-metering mode, meter the overall scene. Let's say this gives you a reading of f/22 at 1/125 sec. Now move in very close to your subject so that his face fills the frame and note what the exposure reading is. In this case, let's say f/11 at 1/125 sec. You have not taken an exposure yet, but you have the information necessary to calculate the exposure that will split the difference. The proper reading for the background was f/22, and the proper reading for the subject was f/11. Return to the original place where you were taking the picture and split the difference between your two exposures, giving you some detail in both your subject and the background. You will set your camera to f/16 at 1/125 sec. for this final image.

tip Although there is detail in the tree, the dark areas are washed out due to overexposure and lens flare. This can be an interesting technique, but you have to make sure you control how much and where it occurs within the image.

FIGURE 8.15 A–C shows a specific example of this process. Figure 18.5a was shot using the meter reading of the entire scene (f/6.3 at 1/640 sec.) You can see that the tree has very little detail. We moved in close to the tree and got a meter reading to correctly expose the tree. Moving back to our original position, we then took the shot in Figure 8.15b (f/6.3 at 1/125 sec.). In this image you can see we have detail in the trunk, but the rest of the image is completely overexposed.

In order to maintain some detail in the highlights and shadows, Figure 8.15c (f/6.3 at 1/320 sec.) essentially splits the difference between the two exposures. This exposure is a compromise between the first two exposures, and it enables us to have detail in the tree without completely blowing out the sky and washing out the trunk.

tip Some people love this control while others find it somewhat stifling. As you start your photo career, the way your personality fits with various types of photography will be a major area to explore.

Natural light can be some of the most beautiful light there is, but backlit situations illustrate the potential need for supplemental lighting. Having a fill card, speedlight, or other additional lighting will enable you to balance the light between the subject and the foreground. In the studio you can maintain a greater level of control when balancing various lights.

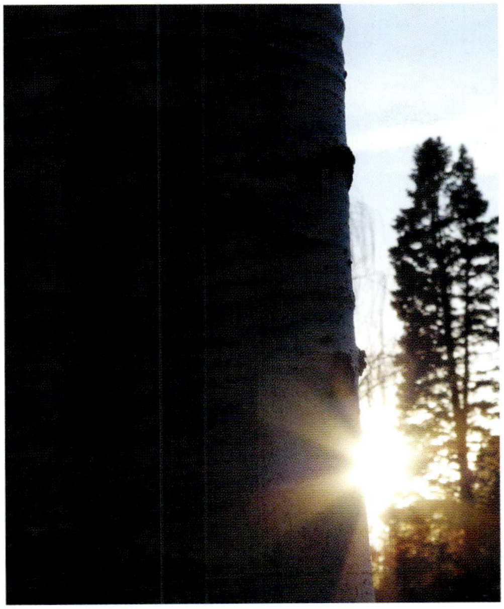

a)

ISO 400, 1/640 sec., f/6.3, 65mm lens

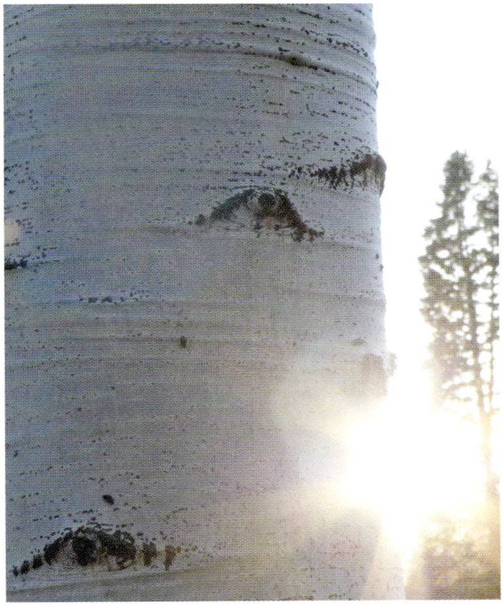

b)

ISO 400, 1/125 sec., f/6.3, 65mm lens

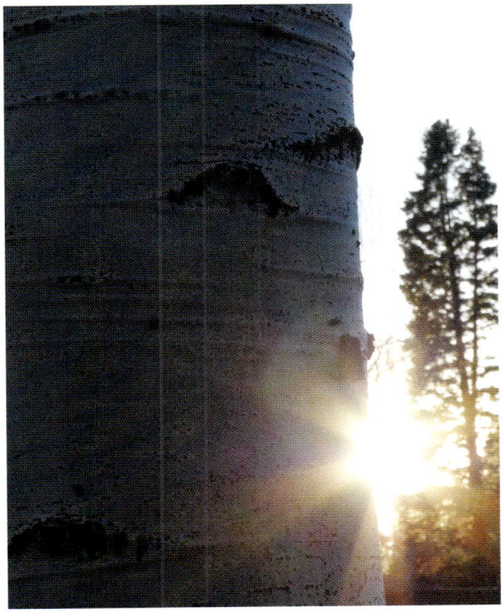

c)

ISO 400, 1/320 sec., f/6.3, 65mm lens

FIGURE 8.15 **a)** An image shot according to matrix mode meter reading; **b)** exposure for the tree trunk only; **c)** this exposure splits the difference.

Prioritize

The technique above, splitting the difference, can come in handy, but it should not be used all the time. We're back to deciding what's important in a shot. Sometimes having the main subject in silhouette will provide the most dramatic and appropriate result, while at other times you'll need the main subject to have detail, and you won't care if the background is overexposed. The choices are yours.

Maintaining Histogram Integrity

Why do I get all these gaps in my histogram?

The reason we've spent so much time concentrating on properly exposing your images might help you avoid having to ask this question. When you expose your images correctly, you will see a smooth continuous-tone histogram that corresponds to the image. There will be no breaks in the histogram. FIGURE 8.16A and 8.16B shows a low-key image that was properly exposed.

The image is relatively dark, but that's a result of the subject matter rather than the exposure. The histogram shows a majority of the pixels stacked in the lower tonal values, and this is what we would expect. The gradations from dark gray to black are smooth and consistent, and there's relatively little noise throughout the image.

In FIGURE 8.17A and 8.17B, we see an image that's underexposed and a histogram warning that too many pixels are located in deep shadows or off the graph entirely.

This image is about one and one-half stops underexposed. In the digital world it has become far too common to feel like that's no big problem—"I'll just fix it in post." We hear that all the time. In fact, we've said it ourselves, and inevitably we regret that assertion.

So let's "fix" the above image and look more carefully at what happens. In FIGURE 8.18A and 8.18B we added a curves adjustment layer to the underexposed image and brightened it by about a stop to a stop and a half. If we don't look too closely, the picture itself doesn't look too bad; the histogram is our

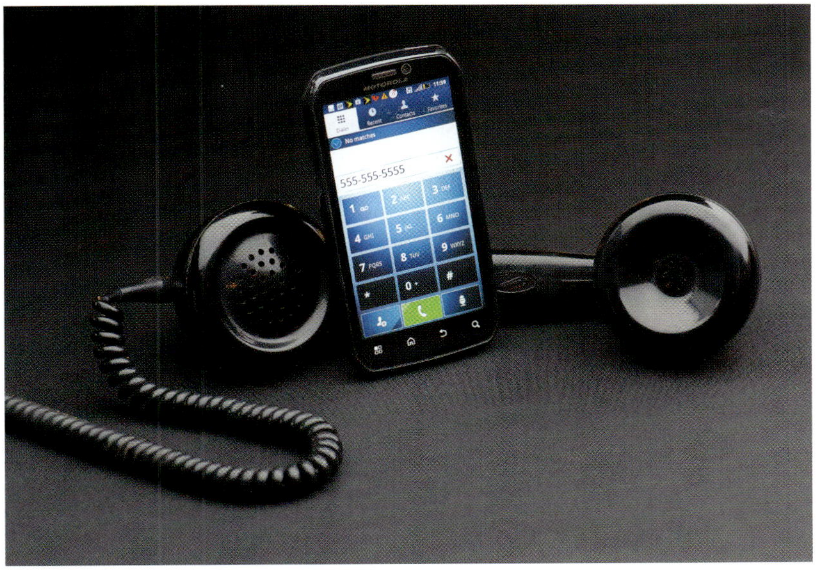

a)

b)

FIGURE 8.16 **a)** A properly exposed scene; **b)** the corresponding histogram, indicating minimal problems.

ISO 50, 1/2 sec., f/11, 150mm lens

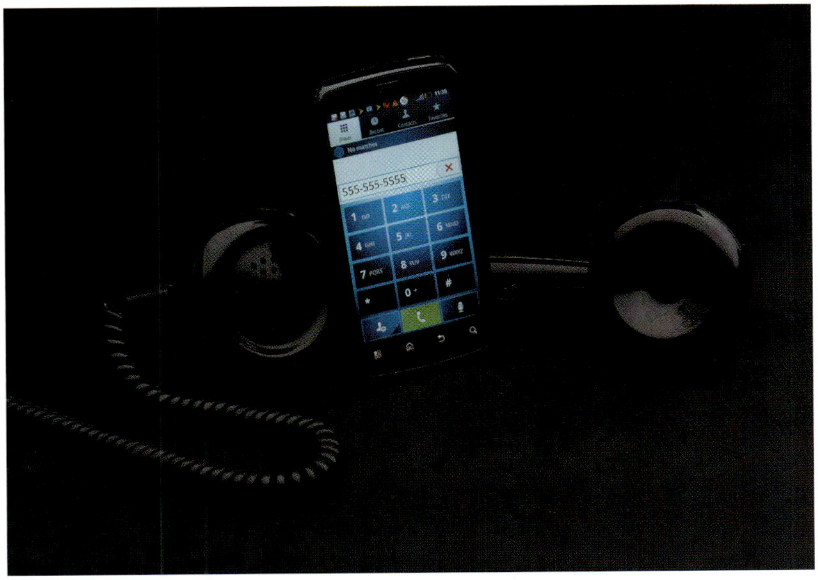

a)

b)

FIGURE 8.17 **a)** The underexposed scene; **b)** the corresponding histogram, which reveals underexposure.

ISO 50, 1/2 sec., f/16, 150mm lens

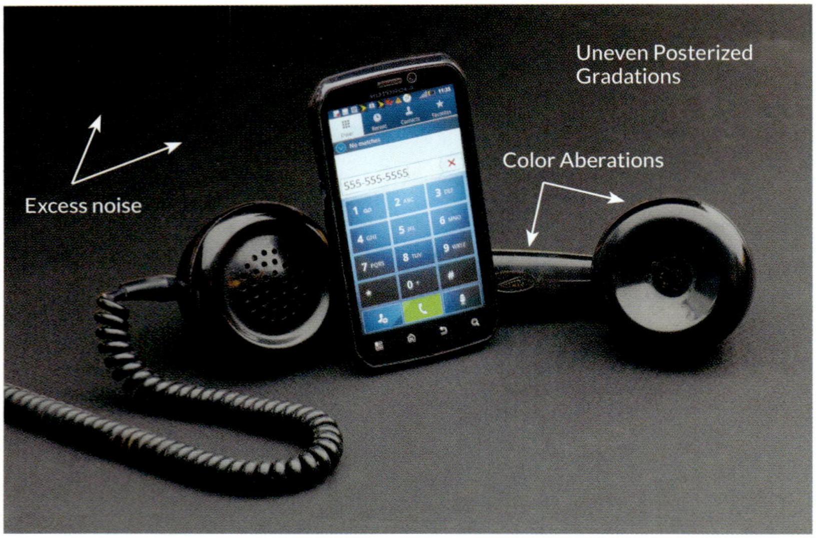

a)

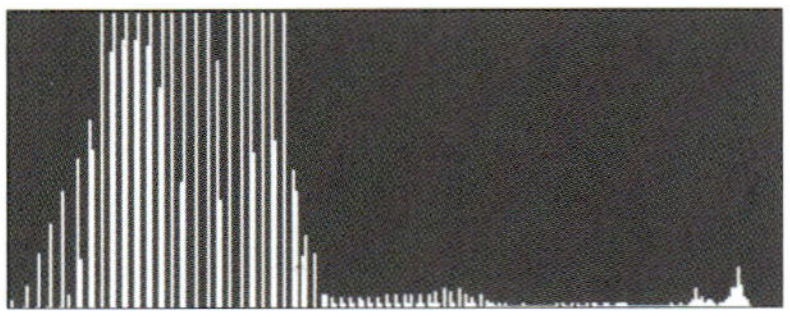

b)

FIGURE 8.18 **a)** The image after Photoshop adjustments; **b)** the corresponding histogram, which shows significant problems.

ISO 50, 1/2 sec., f/16, 150mm lens

first clue that this image has significant problems. This histogram is a mess. Major gaps throughout represent tones devoid of pixels. The black lines in the graph do not contain pixels. When we added the curve adjustment, Photoshop moved pixels across the horizontal axis from left to right, brightening the image, or increasing exposure after the fact. The problem is, there are a limited number of pixels, which need to be stretched over a wider area.

Imagine you have built a bridge out of rope and short 2 x 4 boards to cross a small stream. The boards are right next to one another, parallel to the streambed, with no gaps between them. Later the stream becomes wider, and because you have no more lumber, you are forced to separate the boards in order to cover the width of the stream. If the gaps remain small, you can still step from board to board, but as the stream widens so do the gaps, until you can no longer cross safely. The same is true with making adjustments to your images. Small changes are usually OK, but larger changes can lead to significant image degradation.

When you "fix it in post," you're moving pixels from one place on the graph to another. In the case above, all the pixels were shifted significantly to the right. Because certain tones no longer have corresponding pixels, the gradations are no longer smooth, resulting in bands of discrete tones.

In addition to unwanted posterization, you will also find an increase in noise and other unwanted effects, like color aberrations. Remember, garbage in, garbage out. If you want a beautiful final product, you need to start with a perfectly exposed image.

Histograms are a much more reliable way to read how your final images will turn out than looking at the LCD on the back of your camera. Learning to properly meter will help you to create images that will be easy to work with, but your camera's meter can be fooled by subject failure. In order to ensure that you have all the information required and desired, you will need to be able to read your histograms and then make the appropriate exposure corrections. This is an area that takes concerted effort and practice to master, but better final images will make it worth it.

Screen vs. Prints

Don't be fooled. It is possible for your adjusted images to look pretty good on your computer monitor only to fall apart as prints. We have seen students go to print their final graduating portfolios thinking that their images look great. It is not until they produce a print that they notice posterization in their images, especially in areas like smooth gradations in the sky or studio backgrounds.

interview BRIAN MARK

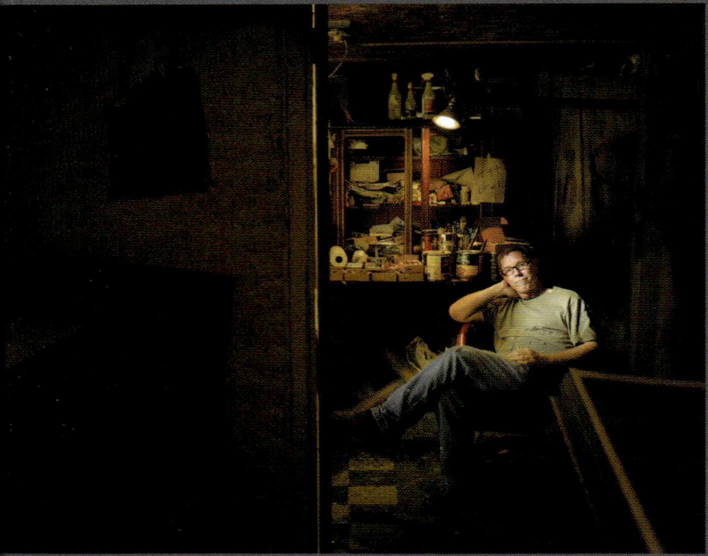

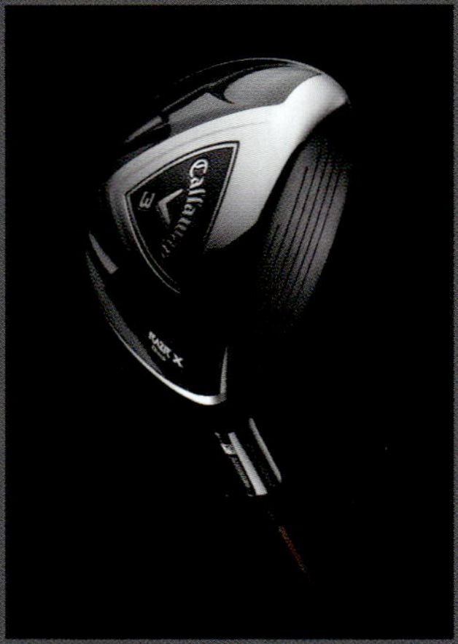

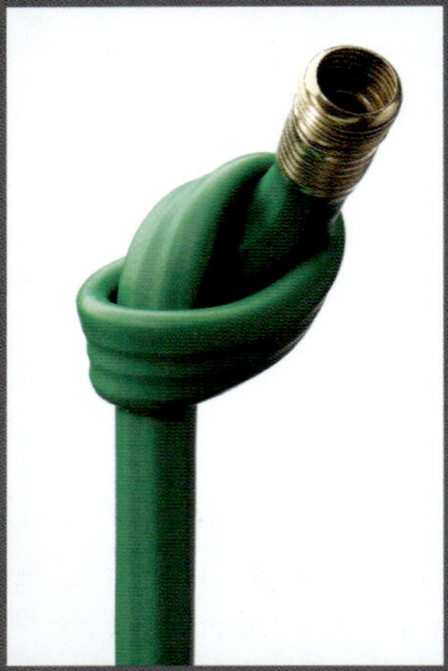

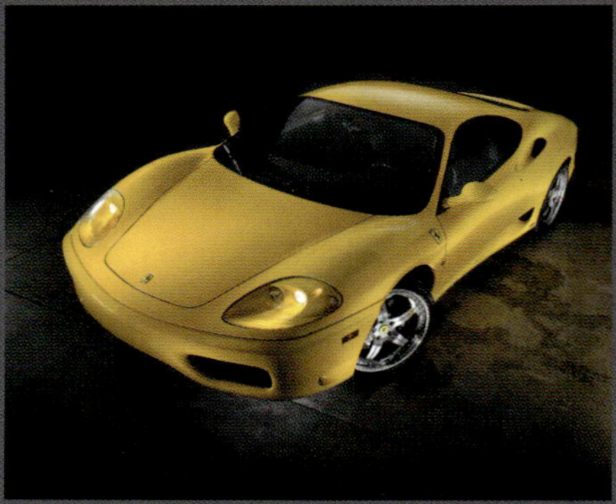

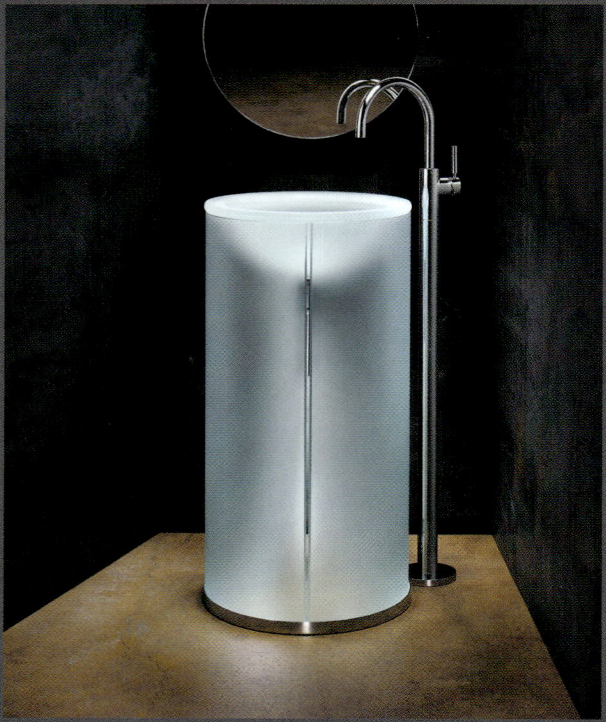

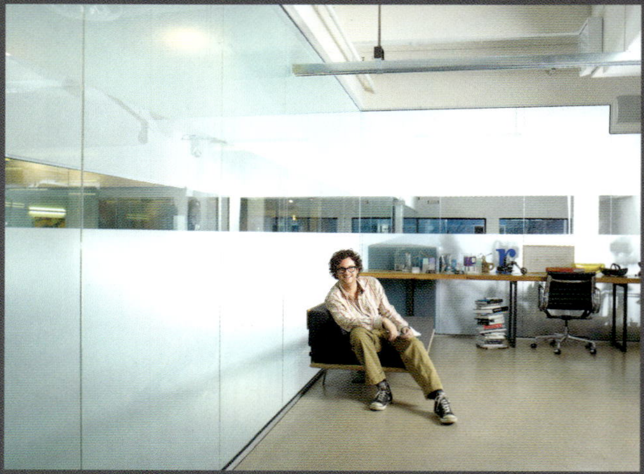

All images © Brian Mark

How would you define your lighting style?

I like drama in my photos—a nice, rich black and lighting to show texture and shape. Sometimes the object or person dictates how the light should be, but I always try to give it some extra punch. I have often found that images get more interesting the more I take away. The more I pare things down to their essence, the more impact they have.

How did you get started?

My father got me interested in photography way back, and I figured maybe I could do it for a living. I went to photo school, assisted, and then started out on my own in Denver. I had a live/work studio for years before moving into my present studio.

You said you assisted; was it helpful and why?

I assisted for a New York photographer (Hunter Freeman) when he had just moved to Denver. It was a great experience because it showed me firsthand how a professional studio was run. It's one thing being able to create a nice photograph, but to create photos with client specifics, budgets, deadlines, and tight workflows day after day is another story. I find that I don't always like the prospect of the business side of profession, but once I get started I enjoy various business-related tasks.

If you were starting out today, would you do anything differently?

I had an amazing start during a time when wonderful commercial photography was being done. Today, well, it's a much different environment both technically and philosophically. My approach today would be different. There are a lot of directions for photographers to venture into; I think lifestyle and motion are really interesting. It is really important for people starting out to be aware of new trends and opportunities. Right now, motion is the next wave. Being a stylist (hair, makeup, or food) is a great thing; no overhead and you get paid really well! All the stylists I know are always booked solid.

Do you have one overriding style of lighting, or do you use a wide variety of techniques?

Lots of techniques. The subject usually dictates the light I will use. For instance, shiny objects usually look best with broad light and textural objects work well with harder lights. I will often combine both and then retouch distracting hot spots if needed.

What are your favorite things to shoot and why?

I love to take photos of all kinds of things. I guess I don't have favorite things, but I do have favorite clients. I enjoy clients who hire me to do what I do best. They expect me to work within certain parameters, but they don't feel the need to micromanage every step as we create the image. They give me freedom to do what I do.

Do you have a favorite of your images shown here? Why?

I like some images because of my experiences when shooting them. However, those experiences don't necessarily translate to great images for others, so I choose images that don't need me there to talk about them. I do like shooting things that are challenging. For instance, the shot of the sink was very difficult. The sink by its very nature presents many challenges. It is transparent but also reflective, so you see the sink, what's behind it, and what's reflected in it all at once.

Anything else you would like to add?

The business of being a photographer is often a much different experience than just creating imagery, but you can't be in business if you don't create great images. I really enjoy the process of it all... and it's the best thing to be paid for something you enjoy. ■

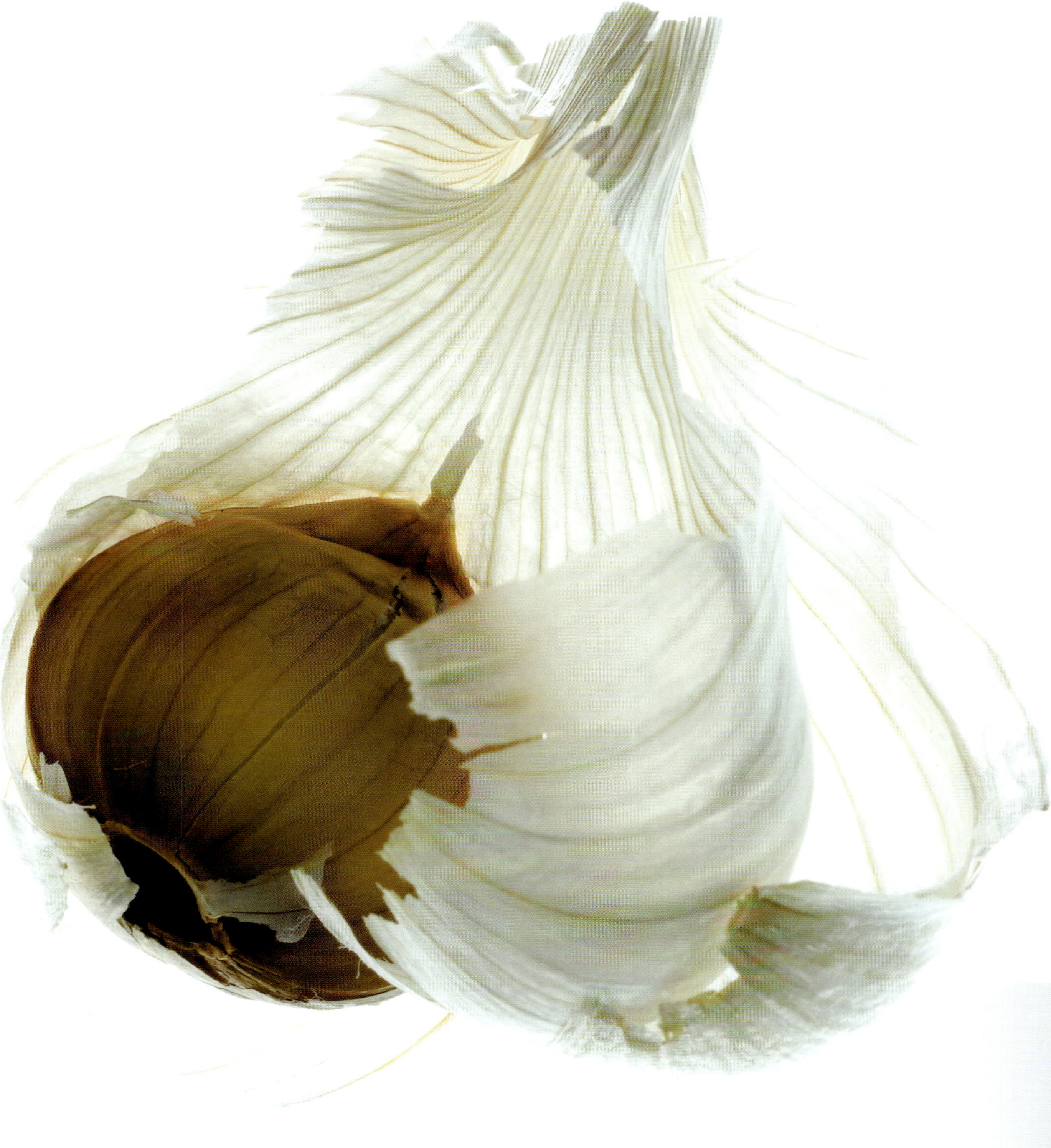

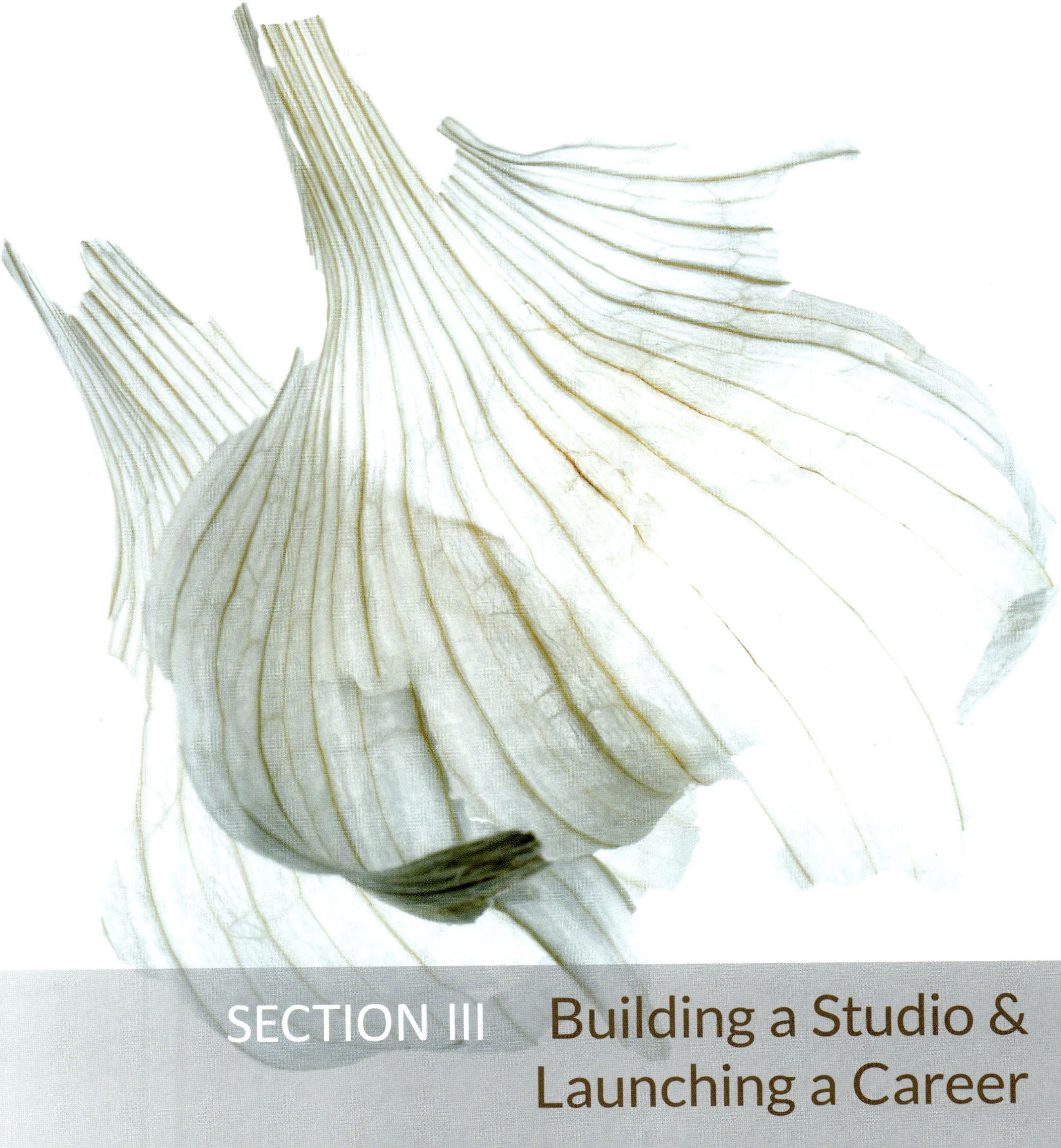

SECTION III

Building a Studio & Launching a Career

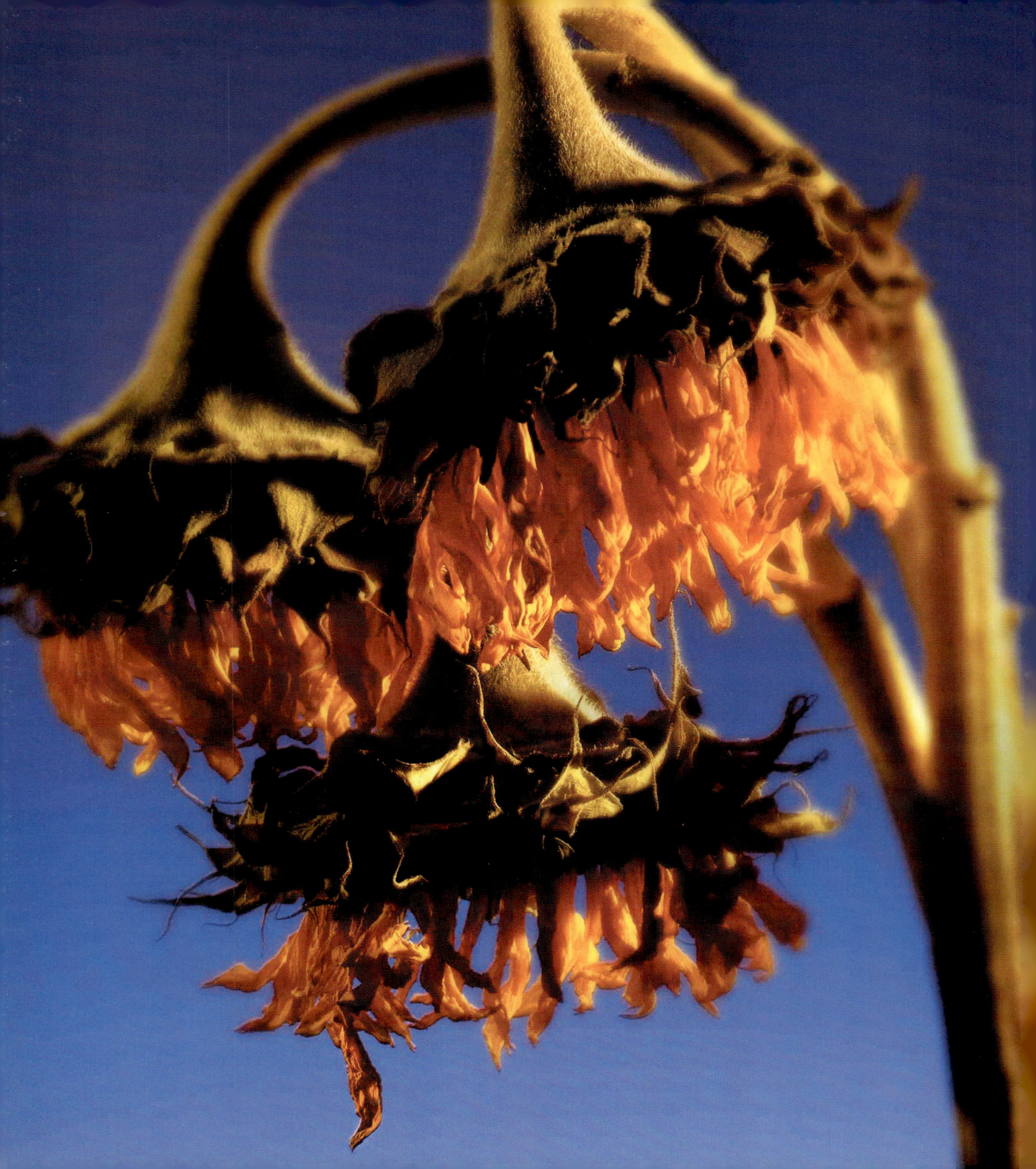

chapter nine

GETTING STARTED WITH $500

Even with tremendous photographic skills, it can be a daunting task to actually start a career in photography. We often take our students on field trips to established photographers' studios and see the look of panic in their eyes as they try to figure out how they will ever be able to afford the equipment they see in these studios. Don't worry; only the independently wealthy start their career with a completely decked-out studio. You can succeed in the competitive world of commercial photography with just the basics. When you start out, you need to have the bare necessities of equipment, a professional attitude, and a competitive spirit. You need to find ways to work harder and leaner than more-established photographers.

ISO 50, 1/2 sec., f/5.6, 150mm lens

Opening Image: Photographic Equipment

Camera: Nikon D800

Lens: Nikkor 150

Lighting: Nikon Speedlight SB-800, Aluminum clip-on incandescent light

Light modifiers: Blue gel on speedlight, reflector

For the image of the previous page, the incandescent light was used to add warm highlights and to lend texture to the petals.

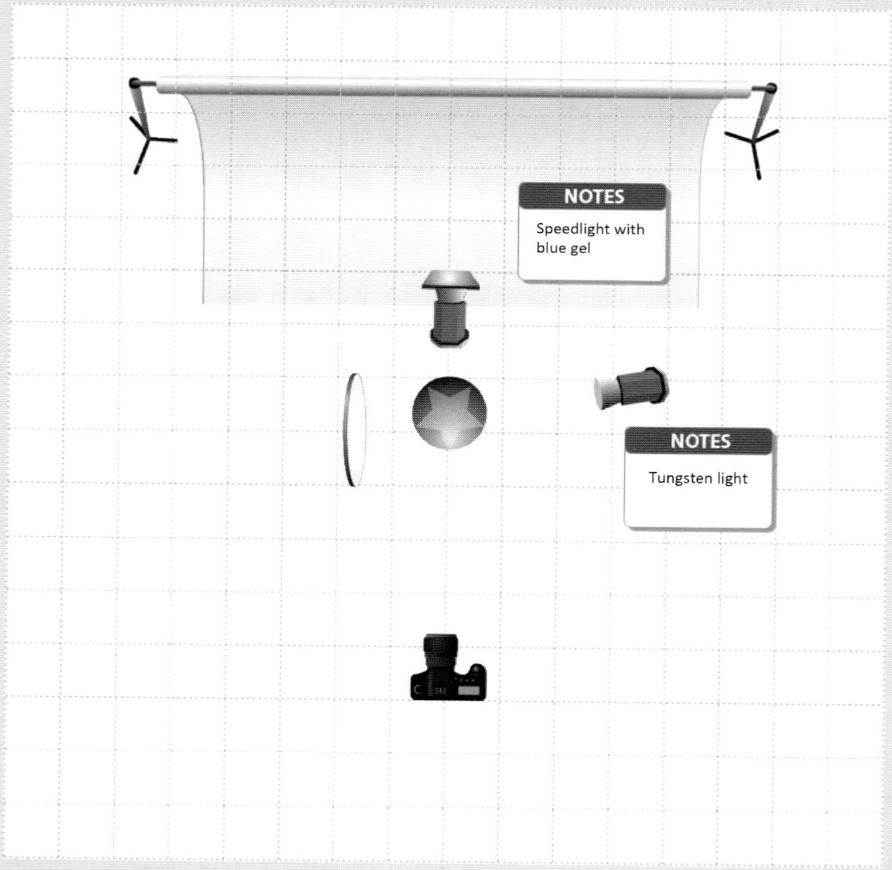

The final section of this book is dedicated to finding smart, economical ways to build a studio and launch your career. What will you need to get started, and what will you need to add as your work and your clients get more sophisticated? For ease of illustration, we've broken this up into three distinct categories. In reality, though, your growth will follow a more continuous and organic path than these concrete stages. As your career develops, expectations will increase as well; both you and your clients will expect more from your work. As your business and finances grow, you'll be able to upgrade your equipment and your studio to match and exceed these needs.

When are you going to feel confident that you're ready to open a studio and start your career as a professional photographer? Probably never. Starting your own business is a lot like getting married or having children. You can come up with a long list of rational reasons why you shouldn't do it, but in the end it's a leap of faith. If you wait until you are 100 percent sure that you are ready to go, you'll never get off the starting line. That being said, you can do plenty of things to make sure that you're as prepared as possible to be successful. We'll examine several of these throughout this chapter.

Equipment

Having fancy new gear and a beautiful studio are not essential to getting started or creating compelling images. The most important things you will need are a willingness to experiment and a drive to not settle for images that are substandard. You can create amazing images with inexpensive lighting equipment in a modest working space.

Studio

We're going to make a couple of assumptions here: You already own a suitable DSLR camera and lenses, and you have a space in which you can shoot. This space can be a garage, basement, or section of your apartment. It doesn't have to be huge or very elaborate, but it should be clean, orderly, and organized so that you can quickly and easily find what you need. Higher ceilings are better, but if you are shooting tabletop work, a 10 × 10 room with 8-foot ceilings will suffice. For portraits, it is nice to have a slightly longer space so that you can get more room between your subject and your background. It's nice to have a neutral room color so that light reflecting off the walls, ceiling, or floor does not create a colorcast in your shots. You could also put up gray

What Are You Going to Shoot?

It's vitally important that before you start setting up a studio and buying a bunch of equipment, you spend time deciding what it is that you want to photograph. If you love shooting big elaborate sets, you're going to need a lot more space than if you love shooting smaller tabletop images. Using a 4 × 5 camera to photograph still lifes makes sense, but it would be a bad choice if what you love photographing are small children. We believe that clients respond positively to images that photographers were passionate about shooting. Figure out what you love to shoot and then set up a studio that will accommodate that work.

seamless paper to cover brightly colored walls. The floors need to be solid enough so that you don't get camera shake if people are moving within the space. Use a table or rolling cart to store and organize materials like tape, A-clamps, mirrors, blocks, small reflectors, and props. Shelving or cabinets are essential to help you organize your equipment and to keep things off the floor so that they don't get damaged.

You'll need to be able to make the space dark. It doesn't have to be pitch black, but you have to be able to get it dark enough so that any window light is not strong enough to affect your exposures. It's ideal if the room is a dedicated space used just for photography, but you can certainly use other rooms as long as you can easily move things out of the way and give yourself enough space to set up and place lights where you need them to be (FIGURE 9.1).

Lighting

tip Remember, the larger the diffuser the softer the light will be, resulting in broader highlights, softer shadows, and more gradual gradation between the two.

Chapter 5 discussed many of the various lighting options you have at your disposal; however, we're assuming at the moment that you only have 500 bucks. So as nice as it would be to have some high-end strobe equipment, that's simply not going to happen. The great thing is that you can still create beautiful and compelling lighting. In the illustration below, we show a homemade lighting kit that you can create for under $50. It includes two aluminum clamp lights, 75- and 150-watt light bulbs, PVC pipe and elbows for the scrim frame, and a white shower curtain liner for diffusion material. You can make a variety of sizes of diffusers by simply using longer or shorter pieces of PVC and different-size diffusion material (FIGURE 9.2).

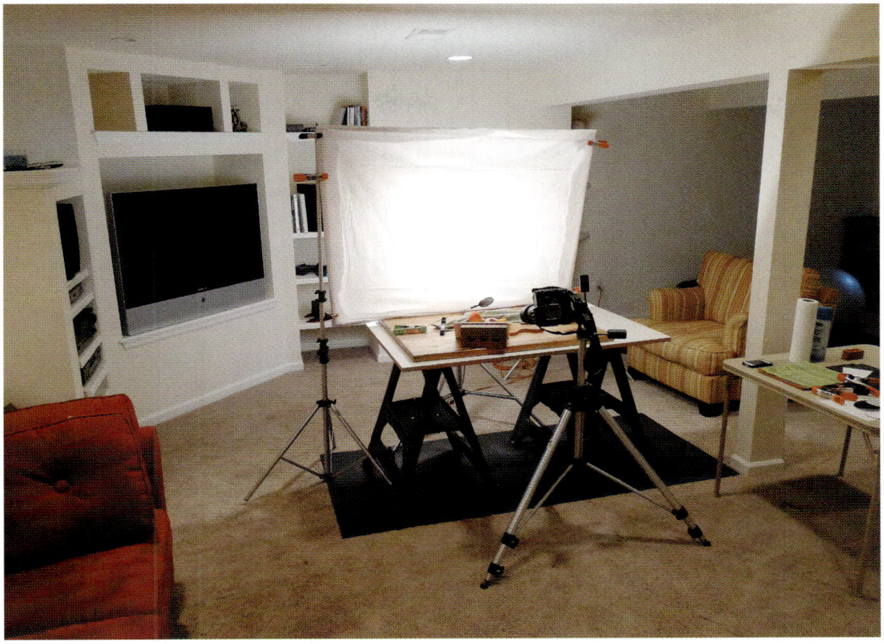

FIGURE 9.1 This is the type of studio you can easily set up in your home.

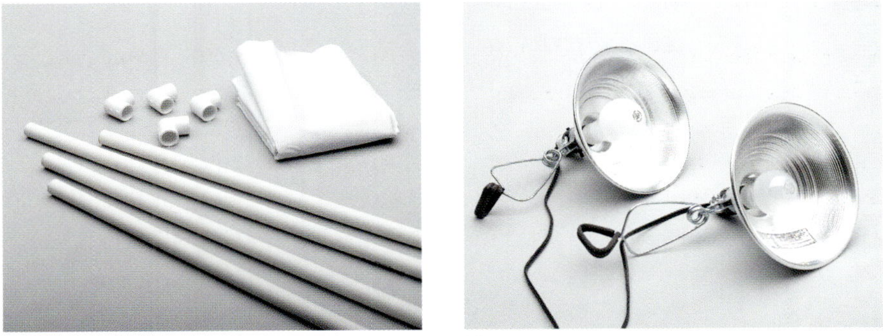

a) b)

FIGURE 9.2 **a)** An inexpensive lighting kit created with hardware store materials; **b)** clip-on lights—use various-powered bulbs within manufacturer's guidelines.

All these materials can be found at your local hardware store. You can use the lights with or without the diffusion material to create a variety of effects. Because these lights are continuous light sources, they work well when photographing objects that don't move. If you need to freeze action or you're photographing people, it may make more sense to use strobe lighting.

A variety of small, compact, and relatively inexpensive strobe lights called speedlights are made by specific camera companies as well as independent

A Unique Studio

If you feel as if your studio space is insufficient, this should make you feel better. Joe once had a student who was a long-haul trucker and used the back of her truck as a studio space to successfully complete her class assignments as she drove cross-country.

lighting manufacturers. These lights vary in price from around $50 to over $1000. Most use AA batteries, although some have separate auxiliary battery packs to extend the number of shots you can take before you need to replace batteries. These lights are small and lightweight and can be used in the studio or on location (**FIGURE 9.3**).

They can be placed in the hot shoe on your camera (**FIGURE 9.4**), thereby putting them directly on the camera axis. In this configuration they work well as fill lights or help you reduce dimension, texture, or both in your subject. As you can see in the example (**FIGURE 9.5**), the light is harsh and does not create much texture. It is not "pretty" light and is not the best choice for this subject—but that doesn't mean that it couldn't work for other subjects. Advertising and editorial photographers have been using this flash-on-camera "snapshot aesthetic" effectively for several years.

You can also use sync cords to move the lights away from the camera axis. Before purchasing a speedlight, make sure that it can be attached via a sync cord to the camera so that you can get the light off the camera axis (**FIGURES 9.6A** and **9.6B**). Purchase a sync cord that's long enough to give you latitude in terms of where you can place the speedlight.

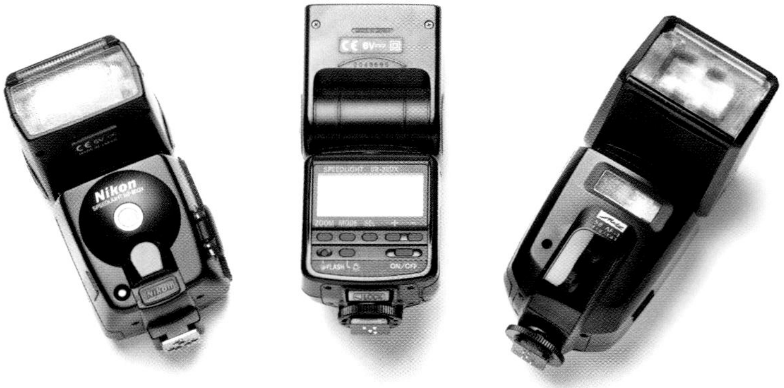

FIGURE 9.3 Examples of available speedlights.

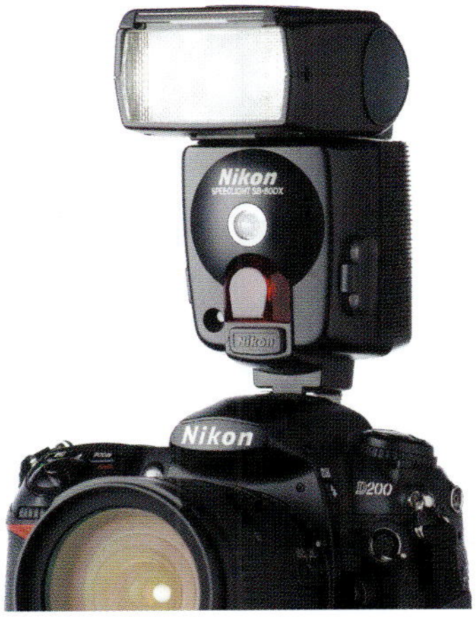

FIGURE 9.4 A speedlight attached to a hot shoe on the camera.

ISO 100, 1/60 sec., f/11, 110mm lens

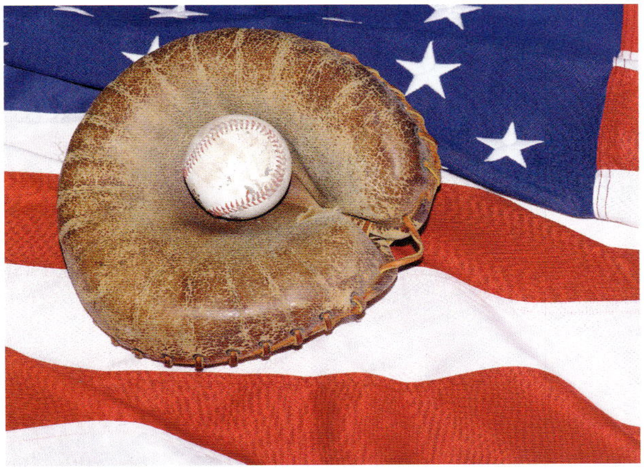

FIGURE 9.5 The speedlight was on the camera axis.

ISO 100, 1/60 sec., f/11, 110mm lens

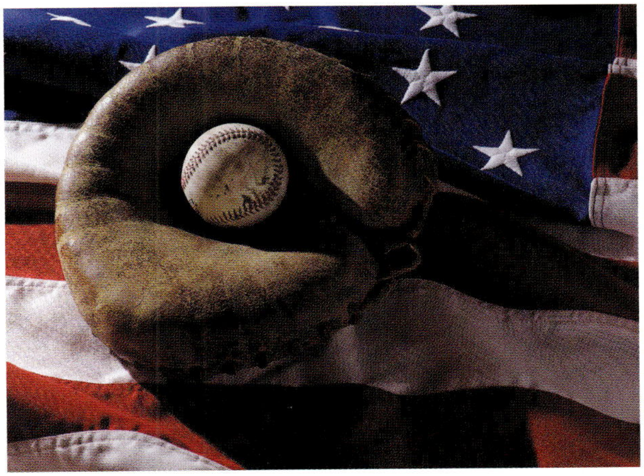

a)

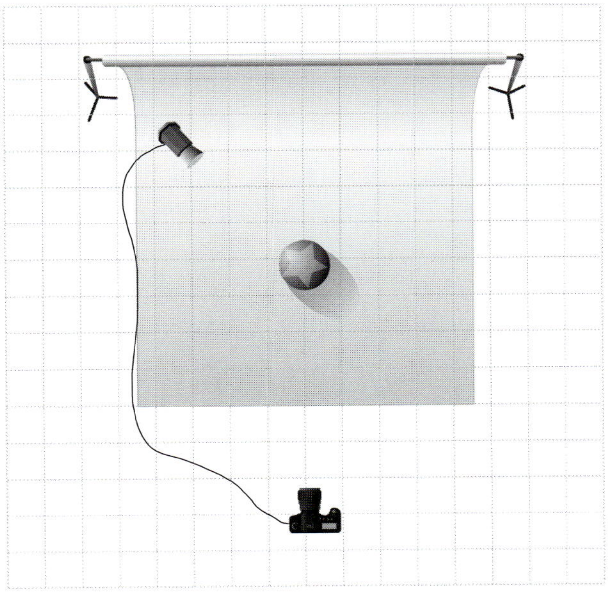

b)

FIGURE 9.6 **a)** For this image, the speedlight was moved off the camera axis to create more dimension and texture; **b)** placing the light behind and slightly above the subject creates a more dramatic effect than having the light directly on the camera axis.

Homemade Light

We once knew a student who took a Bundt cake pan, cut four holes in it, and placed four inexpensive speedlights within the pan, thereby creating his own ring light, which he used to light unique, contemporary portrait images. Now that's creative!

Many lights will sync with other flash units so that you can use multiple speedlights in a single setup. Additional speedlights will not need cords as long as they are capable of slaving off the light that is connected to the camera. In order for one light to slave off another light, its sensor must be able to "see" the other light's light. Depending upon how you have your lights placed, this can sometimes be tricky, and you may need to adjust which light you sync to the camera and which lights are slaved.

tip The faster the object is moving, the shorter the flash duration will need to be to freeze the movement. Catching the movement as it slows down will let you get away with longer flash duration. For instance, if you catch a splash at its apex before gravity reverses its motion, you can use a flash with a longer flash duration.

Speedlights can be used just the way you use the clamp on tungsten lights. Without any diffusion, they are point source lights, but you can also put diffusion material in front of them to create a softer diffused light. All the same theories discussed in earlier chapters apply to the speedlights. Many of them have a very short flash duration, so they can be used to freeze movement, even relatively fast movement such as splashes, pours, and spills.

Grip Equipment

Grip equipment refers to anything that holds or modifies lighting as well as tools that can assist with backgrounds, surfaces, props, and so on. Like most things photographic, grip equipment can be very expensive, but there are ways to make your own and save money.

tip You can buy a lot of grip equipment used and save a bunch of money. Keep your eyes open for things like light stands and other grip equipment. You can often find it on the Internet, at garage sales, or in used-camera stores.

Stands

Stands are used to hold lighting as well as reflectors, flags, and scrims. They come in a variety of heights and sizes designed to hold items of various weights and sizes. Some, such as C-stands, have arms or other attachments that allow you to place lighting and modifiers more precisely. You can also purchase reticulating arms that attach to clamps that can be clamped onto

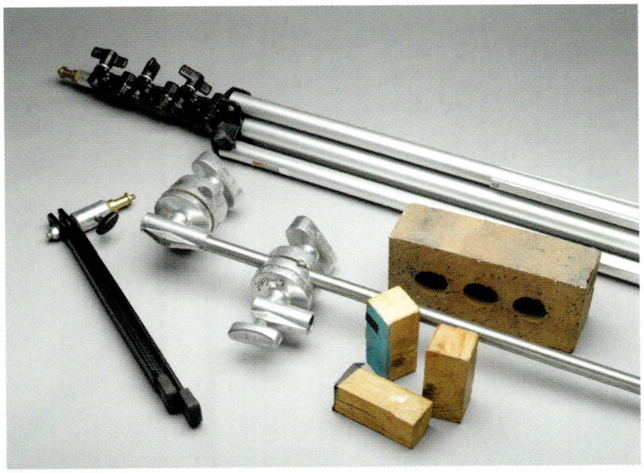

FIGURE 9.7 Examples of various stands and grip equipment.

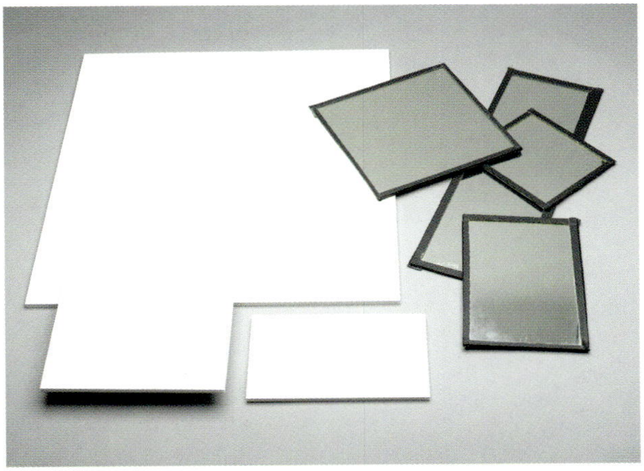

FIGURE 9.8 Examples of inexpensive light modifiers (reflectors, such as bounce boards and mirrors).

the edges of the set or stands and used to hold reflectors or flags (FIGURE 9.7).

Reflectors/Fill Cards

Reflectors refer to anything that can be used to bounce light back into the scene. In your studio you should have the following: a series of different-size mirrors, from about 2 × 2 inches to 12 × 12 inches; various sizes of white foam core; and both silver and gold chrome coat (FIGURE 9.8). These materials can be used as fill cards or to create harder, more specular edge lights and fill light.

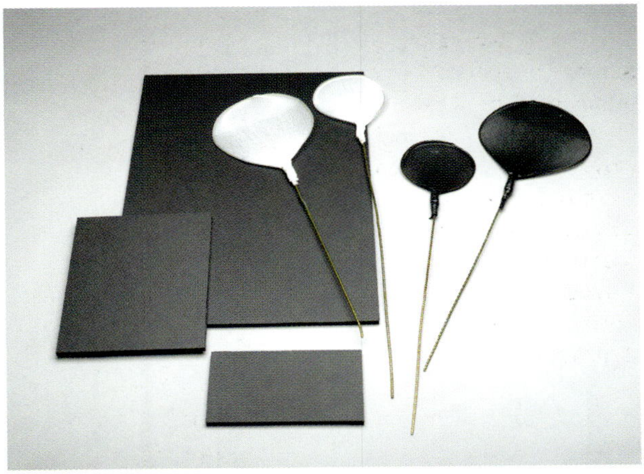

FIGURE 9.9 Various flags and gobos.

Flags or Gobos

Flags (aka gobos) are used to take light away from parts of an image (FIGURE 9.9). It's possible to remove all or part of the light depending on the type of material you use. In your studio you should have the following: various sizes of black foam core and various sizes and densities of scrim material. You can make your own scrims by using heavy gauge wire such as coat hangers and then covering them with semi-opaque material such as black nylons or other mesh materials. You can create these in a variety of shapes and sizes for almost no money, thereby enabling you to subtract light from areas of the image (FIGURES 9.10 and 9.11).

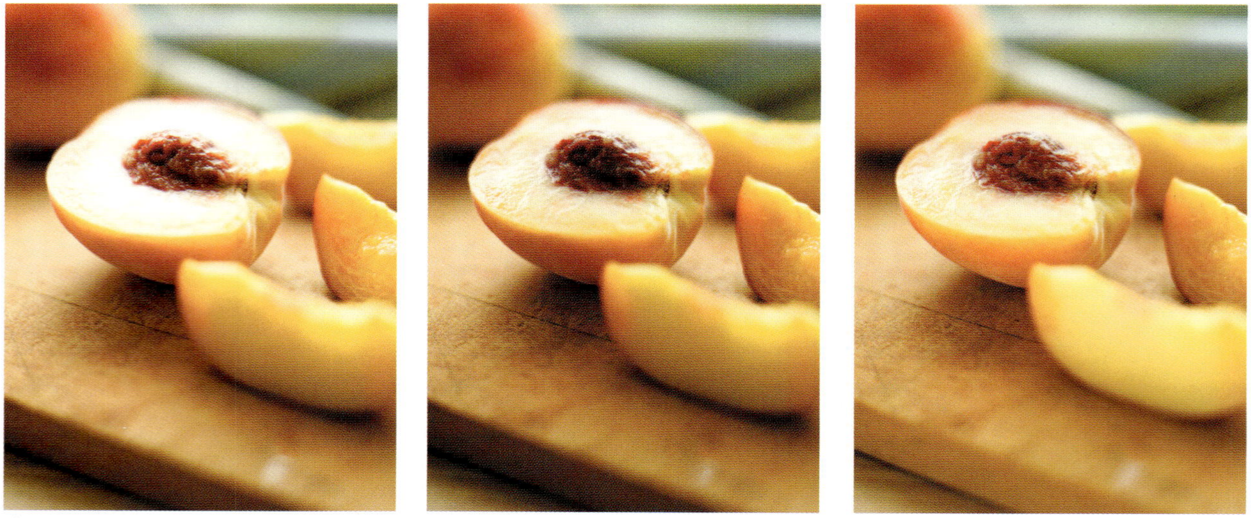

a) b) c)

FIGURE 9.10 **a)** A straight shot using no flags and no reflectors. Notice the hot highlights on the top of the peach and the darker shadows on the front of the peaches. **b)** One of the black nylon dots was used to subtract light off the top of the peach. **c)** A flag was used to subtract light from the top of the peach and a fill card bounced light onto the front of the peaches.

ISO 100, 1/125 sec., f/5.6, 150mm lens

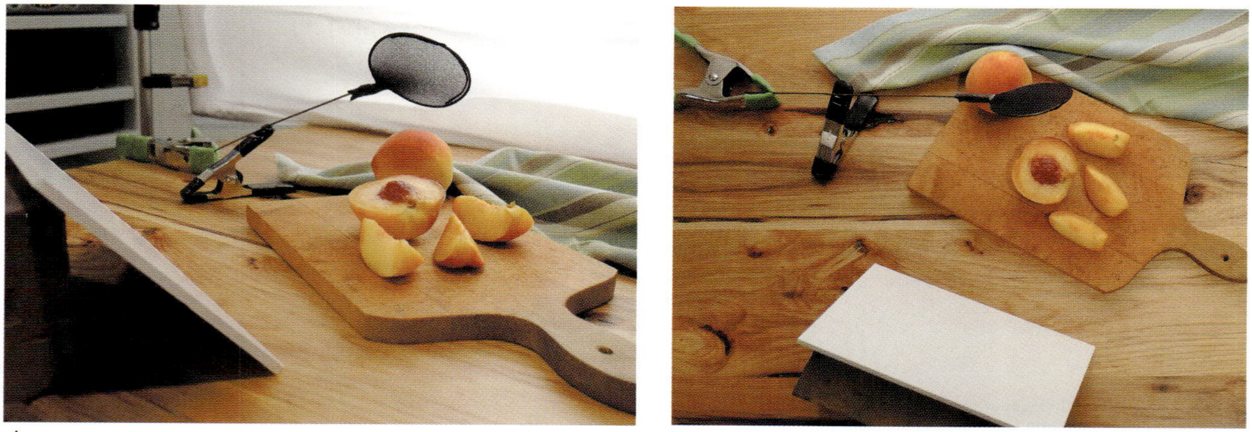

a) b)

FIGURE 9.11 **a)** and **b)** Overviews of how and where the flag and fill card were used.

Miscellaneous

Depending on the types of things you like to shoot, you may also need some or all of the following:

- Sawhorses to support tabletop surfaces
- A piece of 4 × 4 plywood on which to place surfaces
- Bricks and/or wooden blocks to support props, reflectors, and flags
- A-clamps to hold reflectors
- Scissors, tape, tweezers, Q-tips, and fishing line to suspend or hold props
- A variety of tools to build, repair, or modify sets and props

Budgets

When you start out, it's rare to get an opportunity to work on the biggest and best jobs. What is important is that you're getting an opportunity to photograph work that will be published and that you're getting paid an amount commensurate to the work itself (**FIGURE 9.12**). It is essential that you do not undercharge for your work when you are starting out. Most photographers love what they do and often undervalue the work that they produce. We've heard many a photographer say, "I love what I do and I'd do it for free." It's great to love what you do, but don't give it away; that's bad for the industry and bad for you as you begin your career.

Determining what an image is worth is a difficult aspect of being a commercial photographer. As your career develops, it becomes easier (we'll be discussing some resources that can help you make this judgment in upcoming chapters). In the meantime, you'll need to do some research to learn about the going rates for various types of photography. Every market is different. A studio portrait produced in Des Moines, Iowa, will be valued differently than one produced in Manhattan.

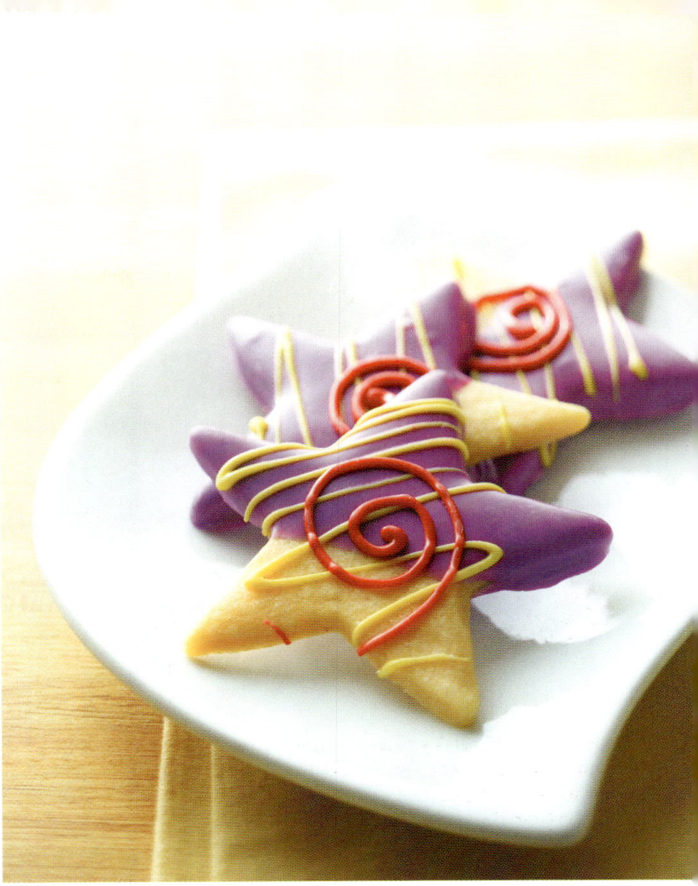

FIGURE 9.12 You can produce beautiful images on tight budgets.

ISO 100, 1/125 sec., f/8, 100mm lens

Joining a local chapter of an organization like ASMP (American Society of Media Photographers) can help you determine appropriate rates for different kinds of work. It's not foolproof. We suggest that you start by asking the client what his or her budget is. On several occasions over the years, we've learned

Finding Work

Finding potential clients can be difficult. When you begin, you'll probably be working directly with smaller clients; larger clients often have an advertising agency or design firm to produce their promotional materials. Find small local businesses that need photographs for their brochures, ads, or websites. Produce a simple but professional printed portfolio that you can show to potential clients. You can send printed promo pieces or emails that include photographs, or you can contact clients by phone in order to try to set up an appointment to show them your printed portfolio. In addition, you should create an easy-to-navigate website that showcases your best images. This should lead to opportunities to meet with potential clients, show them your work, and express the enthusiasm you have for what you do.

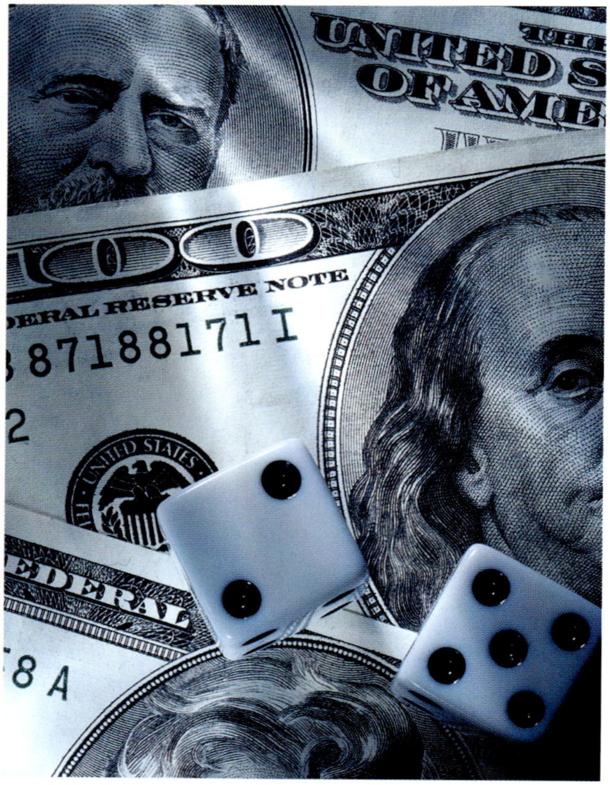

FIGURE 9.13 Proper research can lead to winning bids.

ISO 100, 1/125 sec., f/22, 150mm lens

that the client's budget actually exceeded what we initially would have charged for the job. By asking first we were able to agree to a budget that was higher than our initial estimates (FIGURE 9.13).

You also need to know your bottom line. What's it going to cost you to produce the job, both in terms of actual hard costs and the costs of running and maintaining your studio? How much money do you need to make to break even, and how much profit do you expect to make? Obviously, you may not be able to charge as much as more established photographers, but you need to charge what's in line with the rest of your market. If you become labeled as the "cheap" photographer, it can be very difficult to move beyond that label into bigger and better-paying work.

tip Working as an assistant for an established photographer not only gives you great insight into how to set up, light, and successfully complete a commercial photo shoot, but it can also give you information about how to charge for similar work.

Expectations

Once you accept a job, the expectations are always going to be high. The client doesn't care that you are new to the business; they will still expect you to come through with high-quality work. It's important that before you bid on or accept any job, you're confident you have the ability and the equipment to deliver work that will meet or exceed the client's expectations (FIGURE 9.14). This will be true throughout your career, but it's especially important that you don't get in over your head, fail to deliver, and establish a poor reputation at the beginning of your career. It's fine to be nervous about an upcoming job and it's actually good to continually challenge yourself and stretch your comfort zone; however, you do not want to take on work that is clearly above your capabilities.

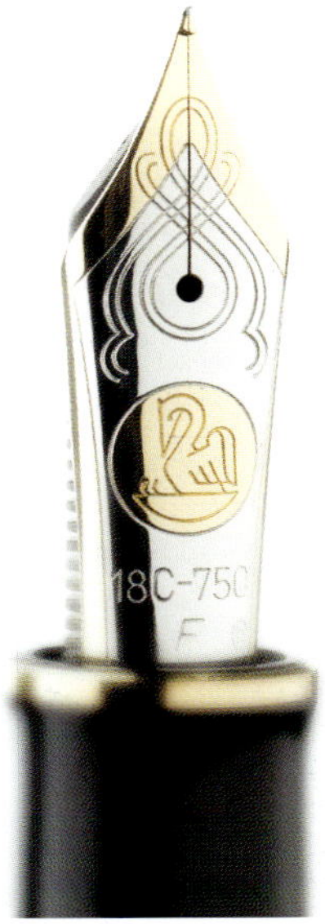

FIGURE 9.14 A simple yet professional image that pleased the client.

ISO 50, 1/125 sec., f/22, 210mm lens

One of the most immediate limitations you will face is your shortage of equipment and perhaps lack of an appropriate studio space. For a lot of the work you'll initially use homemade lighting setups, and shooting in your garage may work fine. Let's look at a couple of areas that you do need to be concerned about.

Your Studio

Shooting for friends and people who are fully aware of your shooting situation and conditions will be fine. They know what to expect and may be perfectly happy sitting on a couch in your basement as you photograph their product. There will also be clients who don't feel the need to be with you while you take the pictures. They may ask you to come pick up whatever needs to be shot and then deliver the images back to them when you're done. This is a great situation for those of you who might not have an ideal space to bring clients. If clients are at the shoot, it's important that you are a good host. You may not have a big, fancy studio, but you must have a comfortable place where the clients can observe what's going on while also being able to do their own work. Food, beverages, and a professional experience need to be provided.

It's important to realize that for certain clients, coming to your home and spending the day in your garage while you photograph their products will not meet their expectations. This doesn't mean that you shouldn't go after that job in the first place. Depending on where you live, you may be able to rent studio space for the day as well as any additional equipment required to successfully complete the shoot. These additional expenses can be passed on to your client as the cost of doing business. It may mean, though, that the fees you're charging for your services will need to be lower in order to compete with more established photographers who have the necessary equipment and space to complete the project.

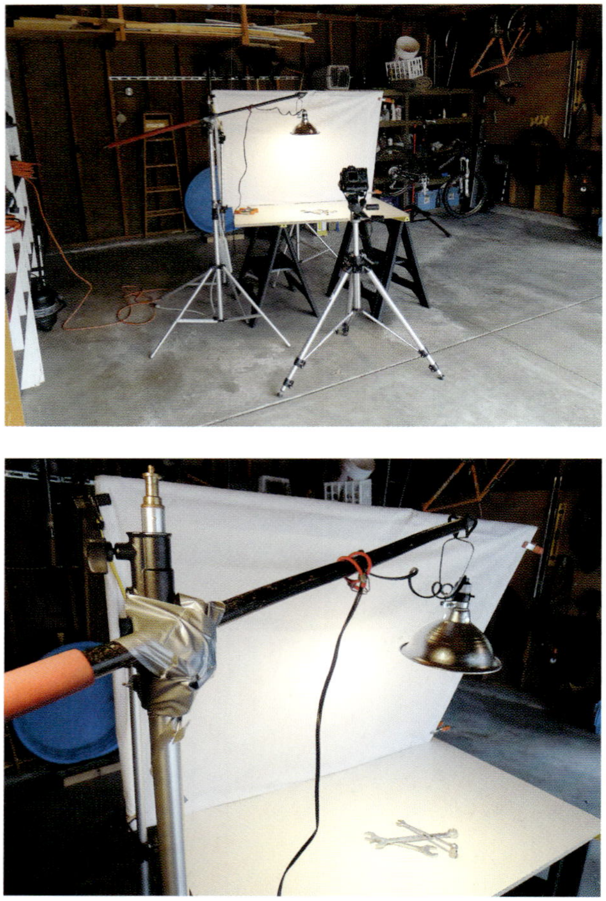

FIGURE 9.15 This type of setup doesn't meet the level of professionalism necessary if clients are attending the shoot.

Equipment

The ideas listed above that apply to your studio also apply to your equipment. If you're duct-taping broom handles to your dining room table in order to hold flags or scrims, you probably don't want the client to witness that. It doesn't mean it can't work—it's just that you won't look professional, and that seeming lack of professionalism will make the client nervous (**FIGURE 9.15A**). They're coming to you because you are the expert, and they'll expect you to be confident and professional in all you do. Once you have clients attending your photo shoots, you need to make sure that the gear you have reflects the level of photography you are trying to produce. As your career progresses and your client list increases, you'll be able to purchase equipment that will make you a more efficient and better photographer.

Budget

We've already discussed what you can expect in terms of budgets as you start your career, but here we want to talk about what the client's budget expectations will be. Perhaps the most important thing to keep in mind is that it's essential that you feel comfortable talking to your client about all things pertaining to the job, including money.

The truth is, regardless of whom you're working for, they want to spend the least amount possible in order to get the results they're looking for. Most clients don't fully understand why photography is so expensive. Part of your job is to educate them about why you charge what you do for your services, as well as the expenses that will be incurred during the shoot. If you know that you're going to need to rent a special lens or purchase particular props or cast a special model in order for the shot to be successful, then make sure you explain all of

You Don't Need the Latest and Greatest

The photographer I assisted in Los Angeles gave me a great piece of advice. He suggested quite forcefully that I keep my overhead as low as possible while first starting out. It is a difficult balance to keep your overhead low while also needing a certain amount of equipment to be effective and to look like you know what you're doing.

Neither of us believes in buying every new photo gizmo that comes along. We think you should save your money and buy only the equipment that's absolutely necessary to create the images you make. That said, ever-increasing advances in technology make this philosophy difficult when it comes to things like digital cameras and computers. With those you'll need to update your equipment more often to keep pace with technology.

With most of the rest of your essential gear, though, you should be able to purchase quality merchandise that will last the length of your career. Only buy the equipment that you're going to use on a regular basis and rent the items you will need only occasionally.

this to the client. Don't fall into the trap of trying to do things as cheaply as possible if it means you will end up with results that you or the client will be dissatisfied with.

Once you tell a client a job will cost *X* amount, then you are pretty much locked in to that sum unless *they* request changes that will directly affect the cost. Such changes could include increasing the number of shots they need, deciding you should shoot in additional locations, or requesting more elaborate props or sets.

If, as you prepare for a shoot, you realize you forgot items or underbid certain things, you'll be better off in the long run to eat some of those costs yourself in order to make sure that the shots are successful and meet the expectations of your client. We've all heard horror stories from clients about photographers who promised one thing and then delivered something far different. Remember, you told them what the job was going to cost. It's a bad idea to try to cut corners midway through, because most likely you will not get the results that will ensure that the client will come back to you or refer you to others (**FIGURE 9.16**). You might not make quite as much money on that particular job, but if the client is happy and comes back to you with additional work, you'll be ahead in the long run. It's easier to keep a current client happy than it is to find a new client.

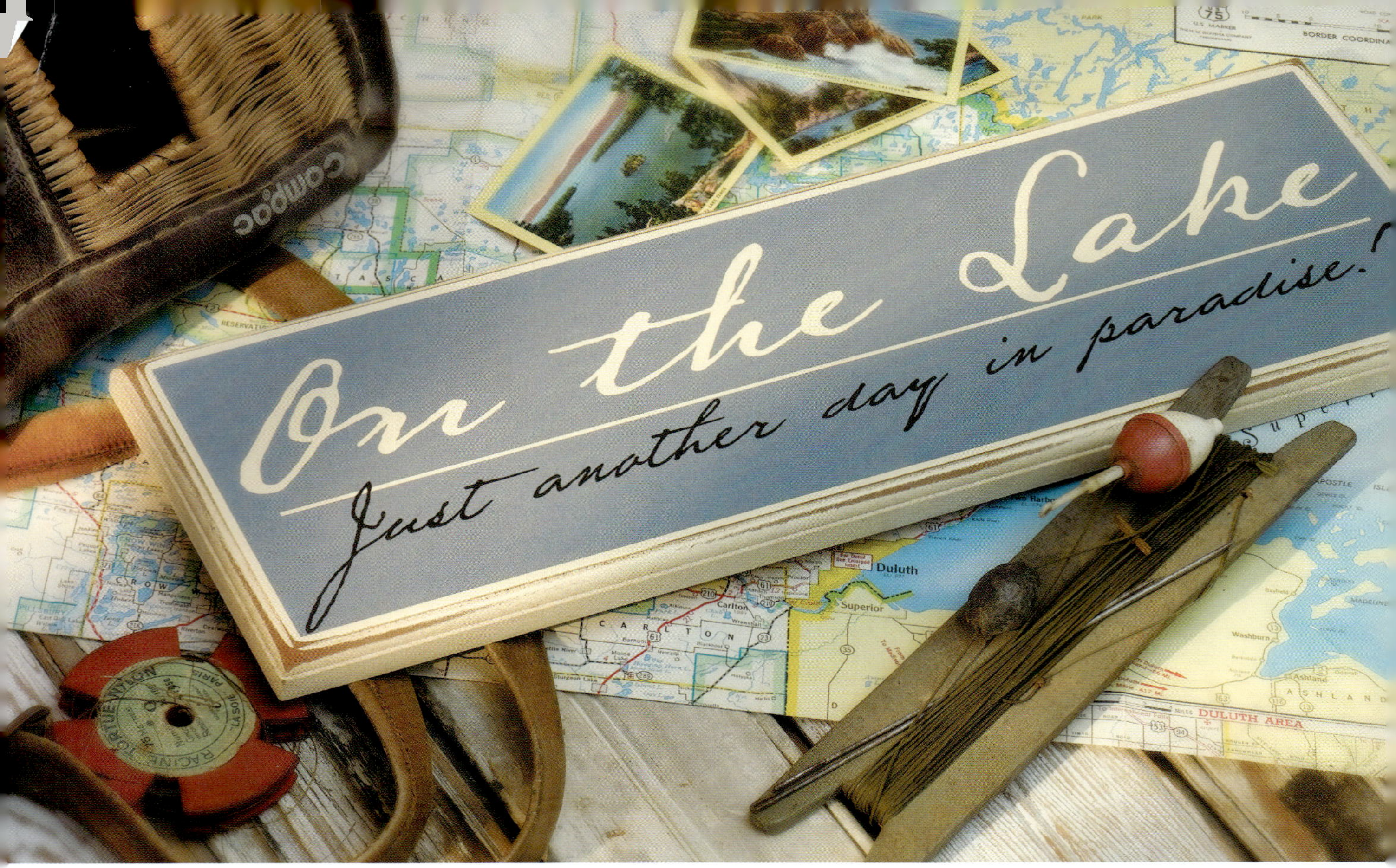

FIGURE 9.16 Still life shot that needed props not originally budgeted for.

ISO 50, 1/125 sec., f/16, 150mm lens

Expectations for Your Career

For whom do you want to shoot? Where do you want to live? How much money do you want to make? How successful do you envision yourself being? Do you want to own your own business or work for someone else? What are your priorities in life?

These and a host of other gripping questions are probably swirling around in your head as you are making the decision to become a professional photographer. Understand that there may be certain limitations to all that you hope to accomplish. This is not necessarily a bad thing, if you are willing to address some of the issues at the beginning of your career.

If you want to shoot national fashion campaigns, live in Denver, and make $300,000 a year, for instance, you need to realize that that's probably not

The Importance of Communication

Let's say your client makes some changes that you feel warrant additional compensation. It's not OK to wait until after the shoot and include these costs in your invoice without having discussed it with the client. If you know that you need to charge more for additional work or changes that a client has requested, bring this to the client's attention immediately. It may be that when they hear how much more expensive what they want is going to be, they'll decide to forgo the changes and stick with the original estimate.

Imagine how you'd feel if you were getting your car repaired and you said, "As long as you're putting new tires on, would you mind balancing them as well?" expecting that there would be minimal or no charge associated with this work. When you went to pick up the car, you learned that they charged you $50 per tire to balance them and no one bothered to tell you this when you made the initial request. Most clients are not unreasonable as long as they know what to expect—and as long as they have the option of declining the extra options and cost.

going to happen. Likewise, if you want to shoot for *National Geographic* and make it to every one of your kids' soccer games, recitals, and school functions, that's probably not going to happen either. You can shoot fashion in Denver, but most likely it won't be national work and you won't make $300,000 a year. The models and support staff don't live in Denver, and neither do the clients. The choices you make at the beginning of your career will have a lot to do with the success you have during your career. In order to get to where you want to be, you must first know where you want to go—and you must be realistic about the possibilities.

It's been our experience that the students who have been the most successful in their postgraduate careers have had a clear understanding of what they wanted to do after they graduated. The great thing about a career in photography is that there are so many options. You can be your own boss or you can work for someone else. You can work in the studio or on location or both. You can specialize in photographing architecture, food, fashion, products, or people. You can have a career as a photojournalist, an advertising or editorial photographer, a consumer portrait photographer, or a fine art photographer. You can spend half your career doing one of these, get bored, and then move into a different kind of photography. What's important here is that you determine what your goals are and then set up the necessary steps to reach those goals.

tip It's a good exercise to sit down with a piece of paper and write out a Statement of Career Intent. This is just a short paragraph that clearly, succinctly states what you want your career to be. Where do you see your career in five years, and what steps do you need to take to get you there?

Statement of Career Intent Example

"After graduation in June, I will be moving to Los Angeles to assist photographers specializing in celebrity portraiture. I plan to work for several photographers for the first year so that I can gain a broad variety of knowledge about lighting and working with celebrities, magazines, and publicists. I will be a full-time assistant for one photographer during the second year in order to obtain insights about marketing, bidding, and producing photo shoots. During these two years I will continue to refine my own portfolio and develop contacts within the industry. I will start to market my own work to magazines and directly to movie and music producers and corporations. In five years I will have my own small studio where I can produce work as well as shoot on location."

Taking Stock of Yourself

This is not a self-help book, and it's outside the scope of this work to assist you with in-depth soul-searching and intense behavior modification, but you do need to recognize your strengths and weaknesses and how these may affect your ability to be successful within the competitive professional world of photography. Let's examine a few areas to look at before deciding that photography is the career for you. These will apply more to those of you who decide that you want to go into business for yourself, but they're relevant to any career in photography.

- **You need to be self-confident.** As mentioned earlier, clients are coming to you because you're the expert. You need to know what you're doing and you need to be able to portray this confidence.
- **You need to be positive.** No one will want to work with you if you're complaining about the state of the industry or whining about the particular job you're working on. You need to be patient, too. Your career is not going to fall into place overnight, so you have to understand that it will take time for your business to grow. You also need to be patient in dealing with clients and their expectations. You can set your boundaries with clients without making them feel ignorant or combative.

- **It's imperative that those around you are supportive of your career choice.** You'll encounter difficult times as you start out, and those closest to you need to understand that. You'll need to be self-motivated. This will be especially important for those of you who want to go into business for yourself. If you know that you'll get to work at 10, take a two-hour lunch, and leave the studio at 3:30, you'll have a difficult time creating a successful business.
- **You need to do the research.** For those of you who want to start your own business, resources are available to help you get started. Organizations such as the Small Business Administration counsel startup businesses to help improve the chances of success. They and other career counseling organizations do great work for little or no cost.
- **You need to reach out.** For those of you who want to work for someone else, whether that's a corporation, a newspaper, or some other entity, you will need to research these possibilities and then send a cover letter and résumé and hopefully get an opportunity to show your work. Even when companies are not hiring, it's not a bad idea to try to make contact and get on their radar screen for when they are hiring.

What's important in all this is to be honest with yourself and evaluate your strengths and weaknesses, consider whether you can correct the weaknesses, and then plan a career path that'll maximize your strengths and minimize your weaknesses. Owning your own business is not for everyone, and working for someone else can often be difficult and trying as well. The truth is a career in photography is not for everyone, and that's OK. Your teachers, friends, and family can help you honestly evaluate if it's a career suited for you. It isn't the easiest career out there, but it can definitely be one of the most rewarding.

interview JAKE POTTS

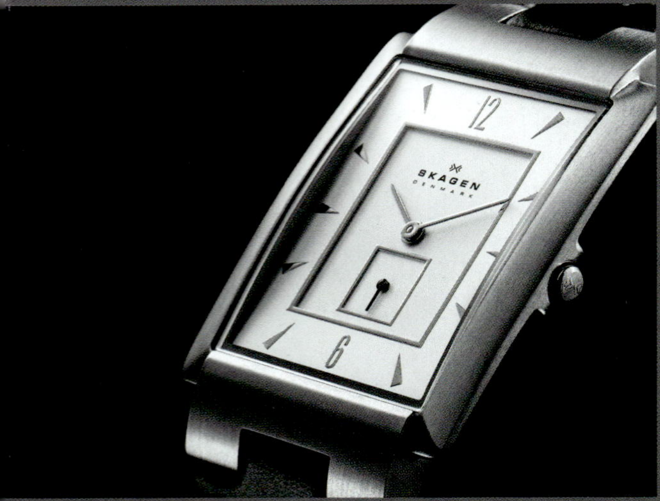

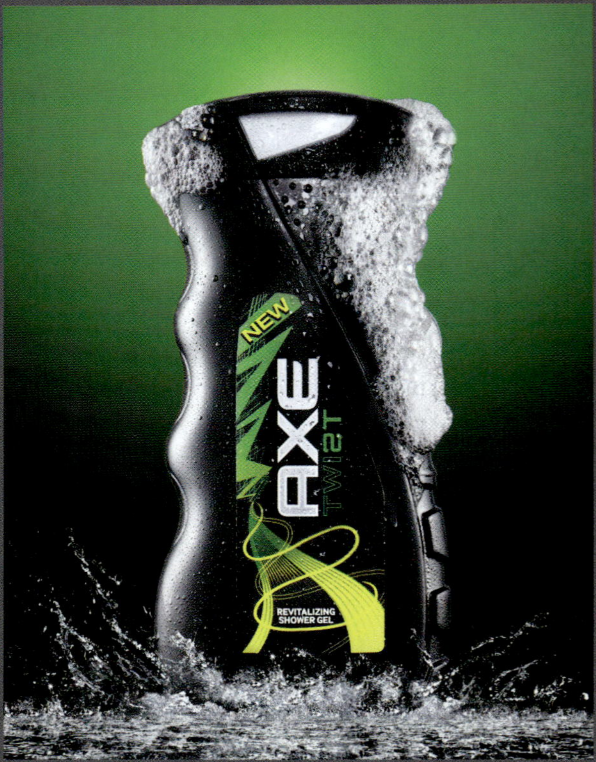

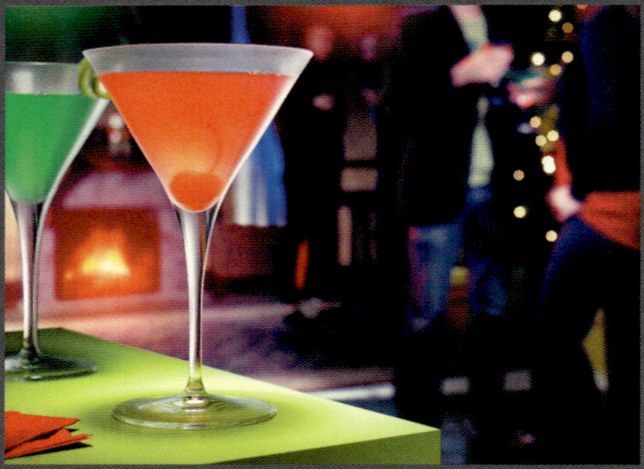

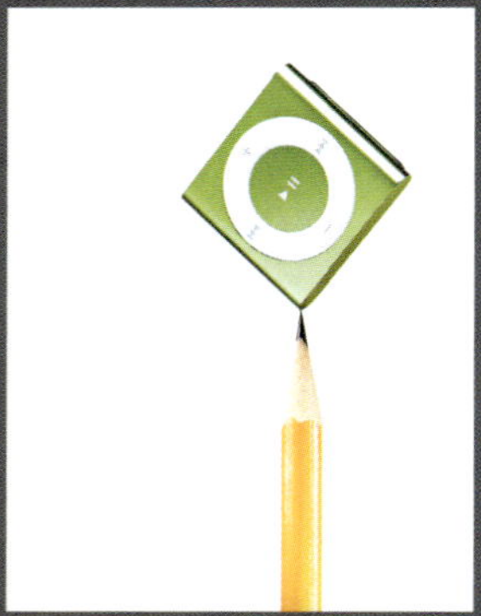

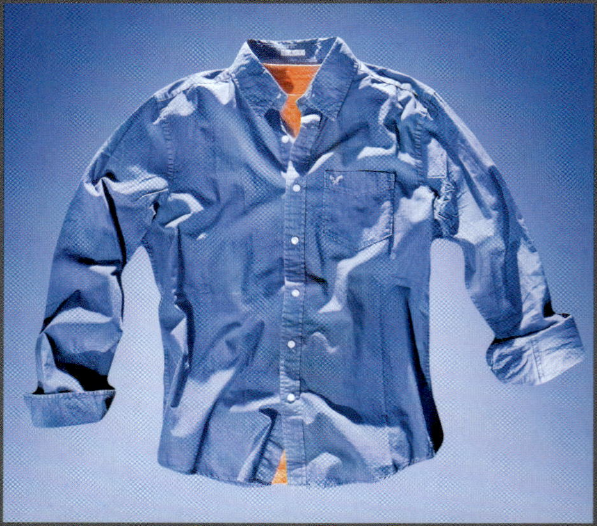

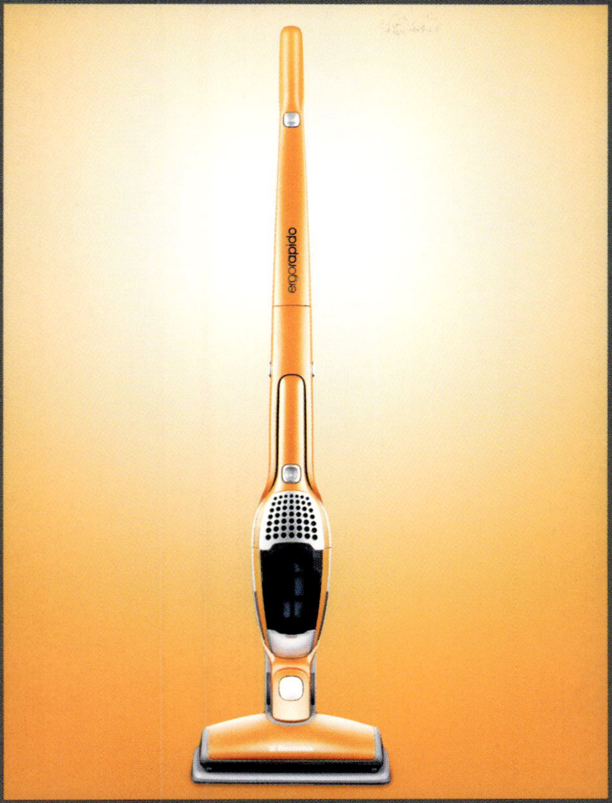

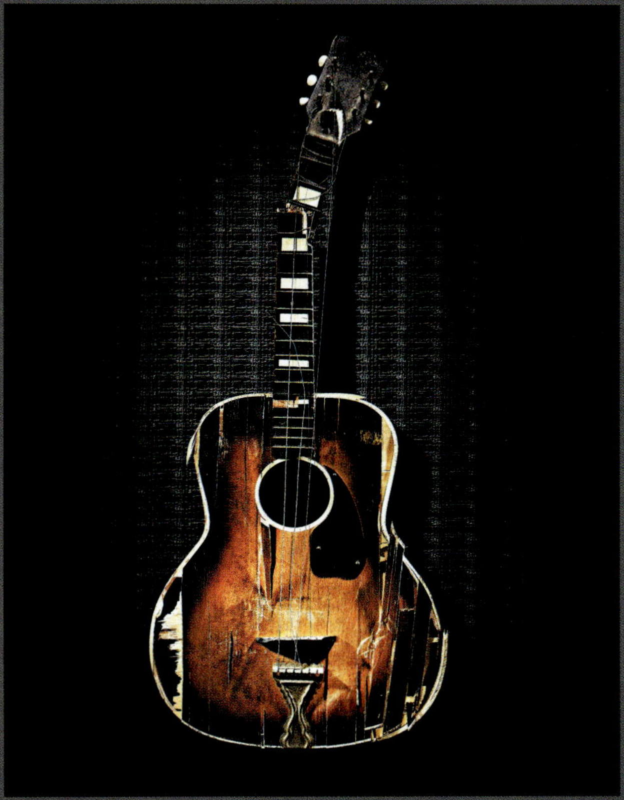

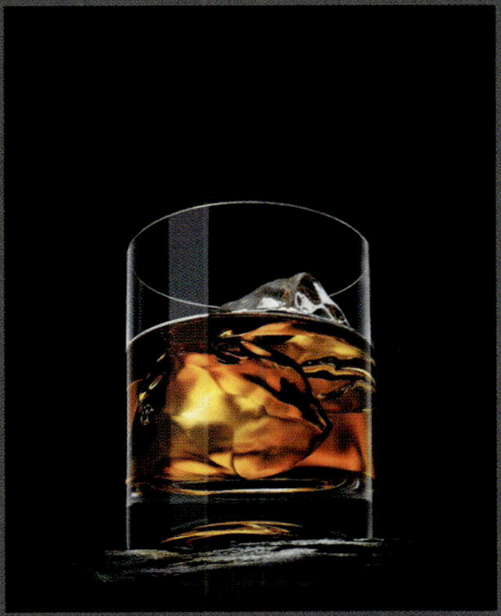

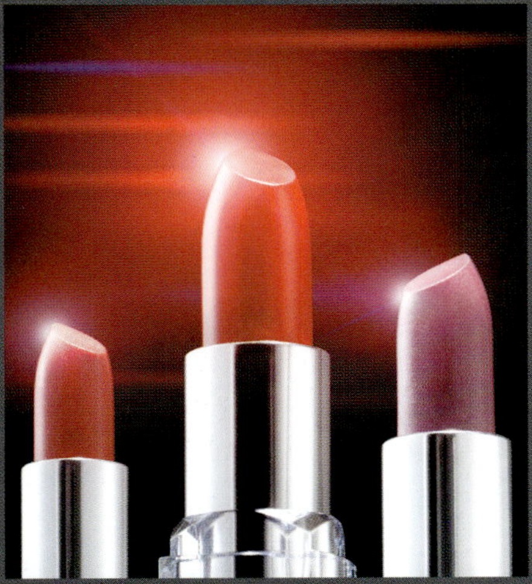

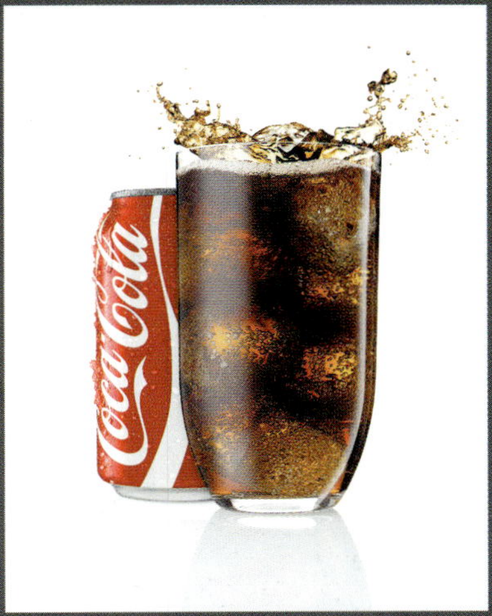

All images © Jake Potts

How long have you been interested in photography?

I think I've always been a visual person, but my interest in pursuing photography as a career only came about a few years back.

Do you have formal training?

I received a Bachelor of Arts from the Art Institute of Colorado in March of 2011.

What was the best part of your photo education?

Without a doubt, the people. I met a group of friends who really pushed me to think and create in ways I could have never done otherwise. We had these healthy competitions each week in critique, always trying to outdo each other. I knew I had to work hard because they were going to work hard. Sometimes they would win, sometimes I would. Either way, we were all creating really strong images.

What did you find to be the most frustrating parts of being in school?

A lot of really cool ideas for projects were pitched by students that never came to fruition. Most of the time it was due to lack of effort. School is the time to take risks and if you fail, at least you went down trying something really awesome. If I had known they weren't going to do it, I sure would have.

If you had to do it over, would you do anything different?

Hindsight is always 20/20. There are things I could have done better, but all those hours I put in while in school prepared me for when I graduated. I tried to make the most of the time I had while I was a student.

How did you make the transition from school into the profession?

About six months before graduation I started looking for an internship. I made a list of places I'd love to work, both locally and nationally. I decided to start at the top of the list and work down until someone would take me. With some effort, I landed an internship at the studio I had ranked number one. I put life on hold for a couple months, moved a few states over, and worked full time as an intern. I used that opportunity as a two-month interview. I wanted to give them every reason to hire me. With a little bit of luck (and good timing), they decided to keep me on staff at the end of my internship.

Your lighting is very crisp and clean and precise. How would you define your lighting style?

I think that's an accurate description. I usually approach a shoot with a pretty solid idea of what I'm trying to achieve with the lighting. However, I do spend some time experimenting until I see something I like. Every once in a while, something will move on set or a light doesn't fire and I stumble on something that works a lot better. I love when that happens.

What advice would you give to someone just starting out in the field?

If I could give a single piece of advice, it would be to make sure that your attention to detail is spot on. The way you present yourself and your work speaks more than the work itself.

I assume many of these images have been composited. What's your take on trying to get the image in a single shot versus compositing elements together?

There are a lot of great things about photography today, especially all of the tools at our disposal. I think it all comes down to knowing how to best use time. Some things are best to take care of on set, and some things are best taken care of in post-production. I think clients are used to the idea of compositing now. If the final image will be composited, I will quickly strip it together to make sure it works, and to give the client a more concrete view of what the finished image will look like.

What would be your dream assignment?

That's a tough one. I really don't know, but it would probably involve helicopters.

Is there anything specific you would like to add?

I think it's important to always shoot personal work. Once you begin making images for other people, it's hard to make images for yourself. Balance is healthy, and required. ■

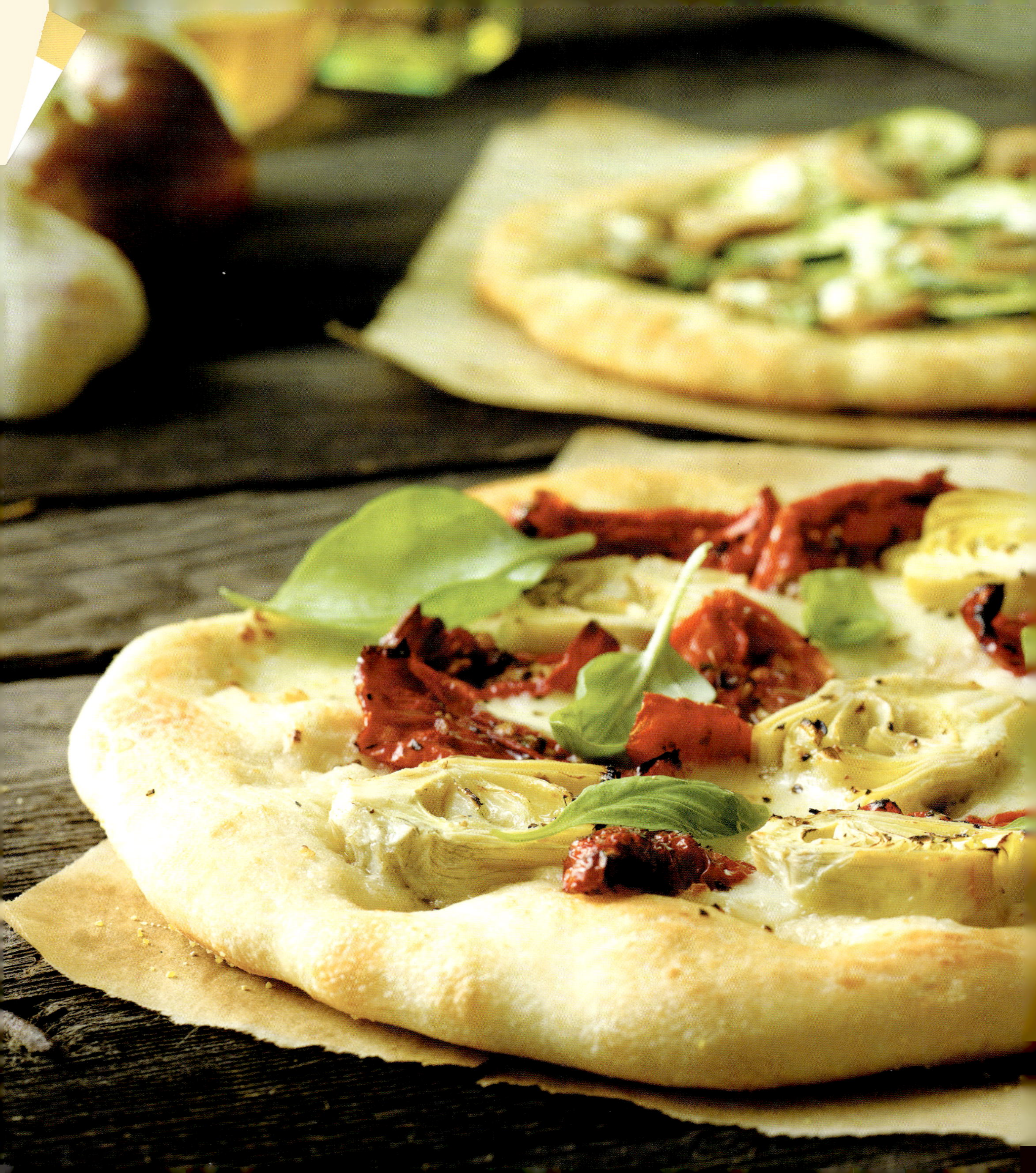

chapter ten

A WORKING STUDIO

The decision to build a studio represents a fun and exciting time in your career. Entering this phase means that you've had some success with a basic setup, shot some paying jobs, and most importantly, have some happy clients. You've decided that photography is a viable career for you, and you're ready to take the next step.

The "Getting Started" phase, in Chapter 9, required more of a time commitment than a financial one, but now it's time to invest some money. Don't worry, we aren't talking about leveraging your house, but you do have to start thinking carefully about your return on investment (ROI). Purchases should always serve a need, and in business that means growth, generally financial.

ISO 50, 1/60 sec., f/5.6, 100mm lens

Opening Image: Photographic Equipment

Camera: Sinar 4 × 5 view camera with Leaf Aptus-II digital back

Lens: Schneider 100mm

Lighting: 2400ws Profoto Acute2 and Profoto Compact Flash 600ws monoblock

Light modifiers: Large scrim, small softbox, gobo, and white fill card

Working with food, especially pizza, requires a team of people. This shoot included a food stylist, a food stylist assistant, an art director, a photography assistant, and a photographer. The goal of the image on the previous page was to convey a naturally lit, rustic feel.

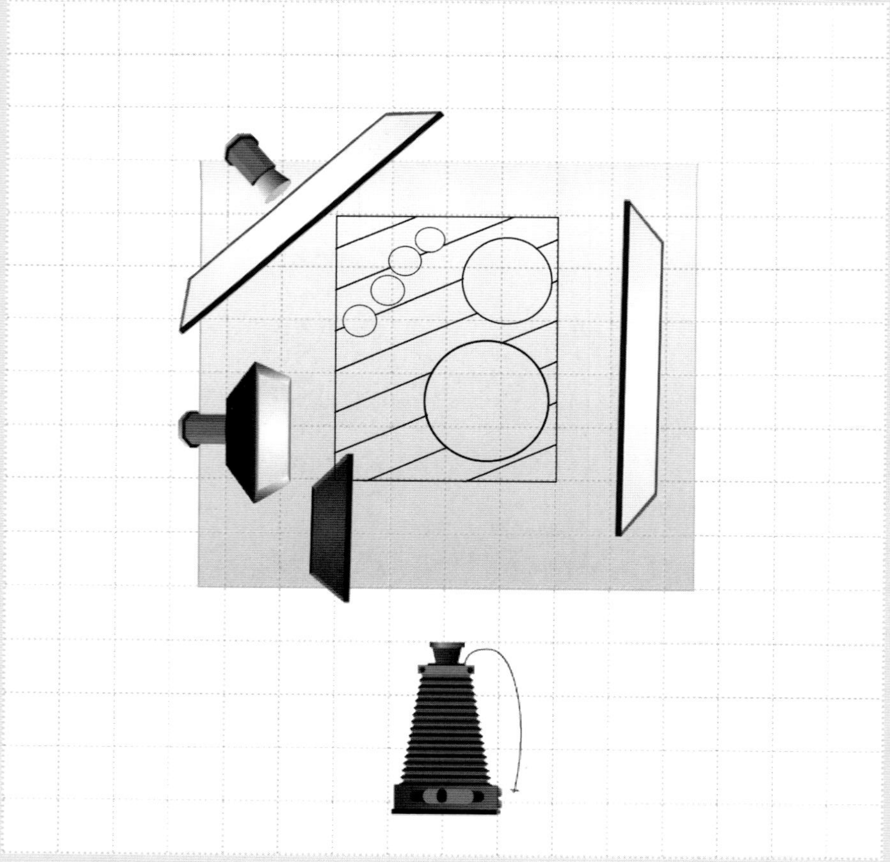

Investing requires a leap of faith. There are no guarantees that any business will be successful, but in every business, the time comes when you have to make the decision to invest in your future. What does it take to move out of the basement or garage and into a situation where you can shoot larger projects in an environment suitable for working side by side with clients?

This chapter will not only address your equipment needs but also discuss some nuances of business that arise at this point in your career. Whether the issue is equipment, budgets, or expectations, moving a career forward requires a close examination at every phase.

Equipment

By now you probably have the basics: a suitable DSLR with lenses, a tripod, and an array of stands, clamps, and miscellaneous items such as tabletops and fill cards. As you move into the professional world, not only does your style have to progress, but your equipment must also meet the demands of your work.

Studio

Taking that leap in your career often means working more collaboratively with clients. This could simply mean that they want to hang around while you shoot or that they're more hands-on on set. Either way, they'll be there when you're shooting. Although you might be comfortable setting up shop in your house, you have to consider it from your client's point of view. Ask yourself whether as a client, you'd consider it a suitable location.

The answer could be yes or no, so let's take a look at some considerations. Many artists and photographers have conjoined residence and studio locations, often called live/work space, where they conduct their business. From a cost standpoint, having a single overhead expense is rather attractive when starting a career. But for this to work, you must maintain a clear division between the two; your client won't feel comfortable if he senses he's encroaching on your personal space.

Joe's Path

Although I've been a professional photographer for decades, I still remember each step of the journey. Like most of you, when I began I couldn't afford to run out and purchase the equipment that I read about in magazines (the Internet didn't exist at the time). My initial tools were hardware-store clamp on lights, and blue light bulbs that I purchased from an arts and crafts store; I later learned that the blue of the glass mixed with the tungsten inner workings produced "daylight," or white light.

It wasn't till college that I was exposed to studio strobes, and even then there was no way that I could afford a set. After college, I worked as a photography assistant, and on weekends I went back to shooting small projects in my living room using the same hardware-store lights from years earlier. It took time, but I eventually reached the point when it was time to decide whether photography would be a hobby or a job. After deciding I wanted to make it my career, I knew that I needed to purchase some professional lighting equipment. My first lighting set was a used Norman 2400ws pack with two heads, which I just sold last year.

As my career grew, so did my arsenal of equipment. Each purchase, which covers items addressed in all three chapters of the "Building a Studio & Launching a Career" section, was carefully thought out with a focus on how it would help me achieve my next goal, whether financial or stylistic (**FIGURE 10.1**).

FIGURE 10.1 Lighting for me has always been about creating a natural look. I never want the viewer to think how an image was lit, but just to simply see the subject. For the lighting set up for this image I tried to replicate diffused soft-light coming through kitchen shades.

ISO 50, 1/60 sec., f/5.6, 100mm lens

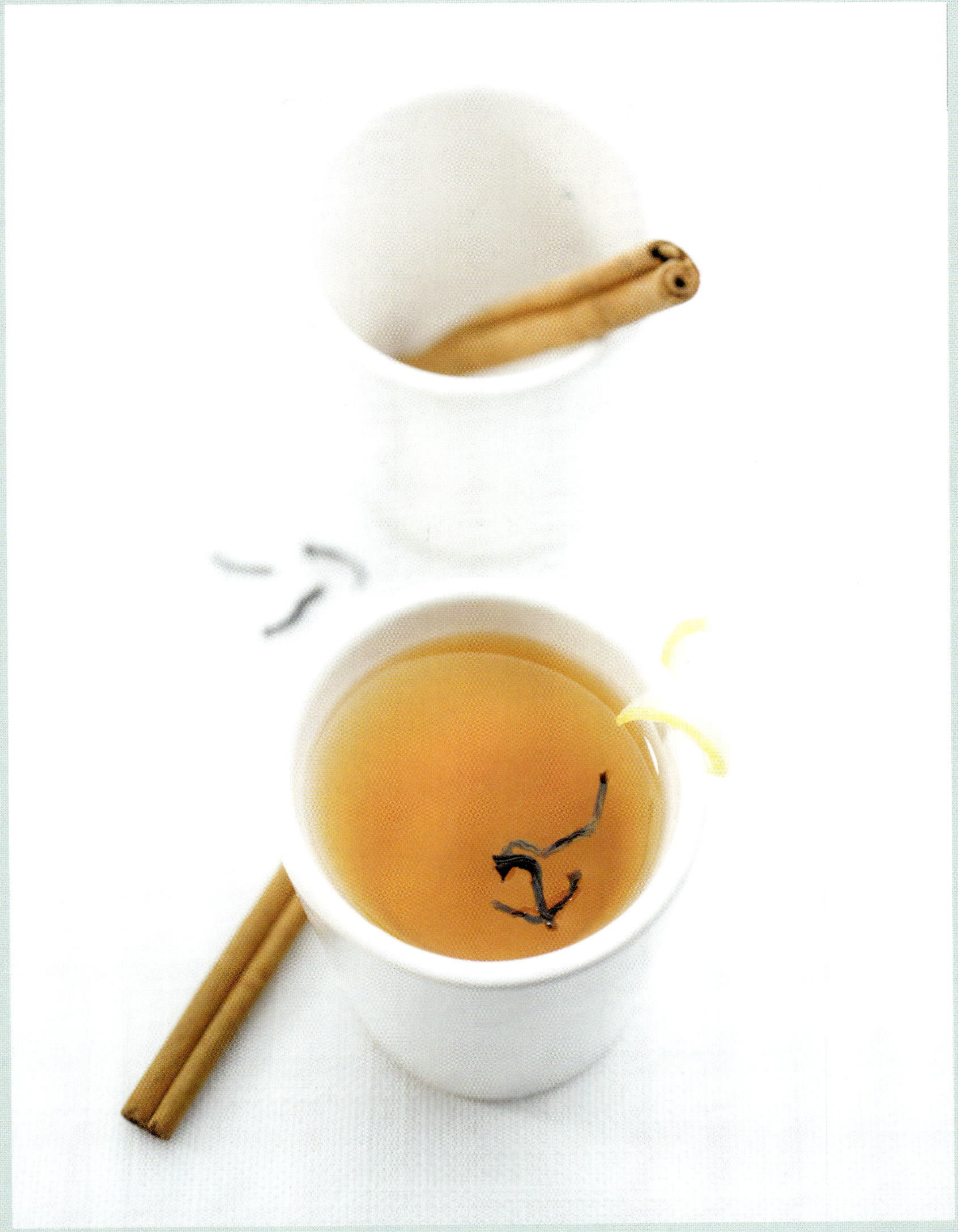

Best Studio Features

Joe: We've both worked in numerous studios; are there any studio features you couldn't live without?

Brad: I love a studio with a white ceiling, because I like to bounce light off it to create a broad, even fill light. I also love having a garage door to make loading and unloading equipment easier. Because I sometimes use long exposures, a good, solid floor is a must. The best ever was a freight elevator to get props and equipment out of the basement.

Joe: I have to have a large kitchen with tons of counter space for food prep.

Two other smart choices are either sharing studio space or renting space on a per-need basis (FIGURE 10.2); each option has its own set of pros and cons. Sharing space is a great way to divide overhead costs among multiple people. There's also something to be said for the creative energy that can be found in a group environment. Still, anyone who has siblings knows that sharing means you give up privacy. Keep in mind that you may see your studio mates more frequently than your significant other.

Renting space on a per-need basis means that you pay only for what you need, which is nice because your cash flow directly corresponds to how busy you are. This also means the studio won't have your personality and style, though. Availability is another issue to consider; will the studio be available when your clients want to shoot?

What you photograph is paramount when considering studio space. Are the needs of a photographer who specializes in tabletop jewelry the same as those of someone who photographs cars? Probably not. The smart approach is to assess your current needs and those of the foreseeable future and spend your money wisely. Don't let ego tell you that you need a 3000-square-foot studio when 800 will do. You need something that fits your style of work, budget, and clients—nothing more, and nothing less.

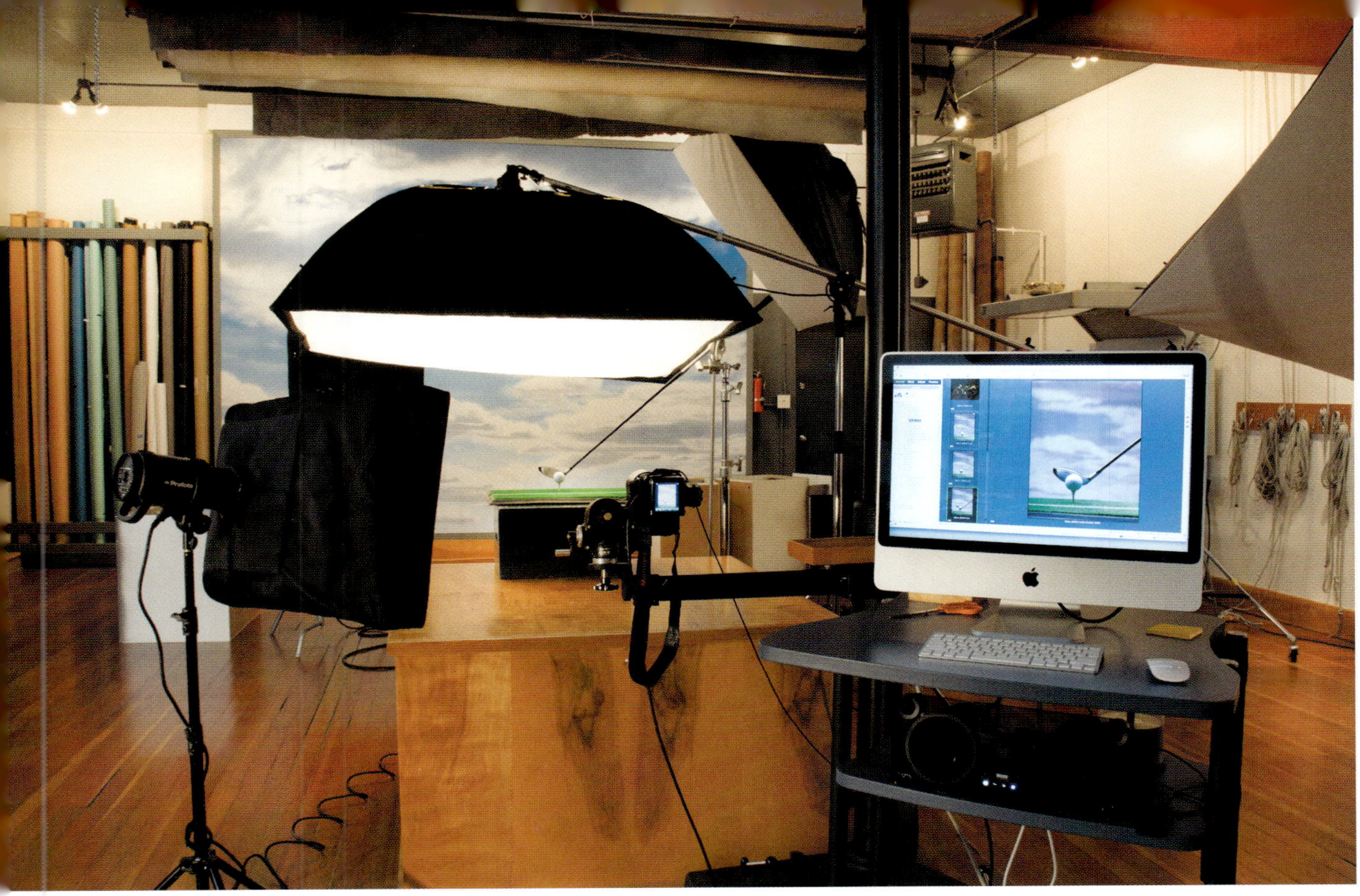

FIGURE 10.2 This image shows the studio and lighting setup for the golf ball and club image shown in Chapter 4, Figure 4.4. The lighting consists of a mix of monoblocks, generators, and strobe heads with softbox light modifiers.

ISO 200, 1/30 sec., f/16, 35mm lens

Lighting

You've reached the stage in your journey where hardware-store aluminum clamp lights, 150-watt light bulbs, PVC piping, and a shower curtain simply won't work; you need to invest in professional equipment. This would be a good time to look back at the section in Chapter 5 called "Lighting Equipment," and again think about your needs versus wants.

In the following section, we use the terms *generator, strobe pack,* and *power pack* interchangeably.

Let's take a look at a handful of lighting options and their uses.

Monoblocks

Monoblock (aka monolight) strobes (**FIGURE 10.3**) are self-contained, all-in-one units that include the power pack (generator) and strobe head together. This portable package is easily transported for studio and location shooting. Having fewer cords to stumble over, because there's no cord connecting the strobe head to the generator, is an added benefit.

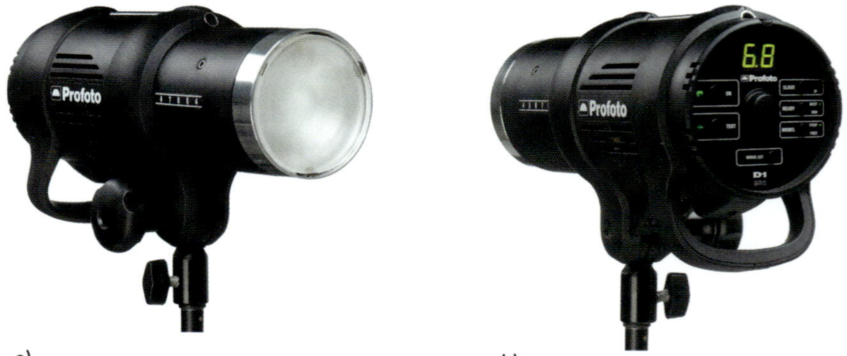

a)

b)

FIGURE 10.3 **a)** Front side of a Profoto monoblock, showing the built-in reflector with glass cover; **b)** the digital controls are a good hint that this is a combination generator and flash-head light.

Monoblocks generally don't offer the upper-end power range (watt seconds, or ws) of stand-alone generators, but depending on what you are shooting, this may be sufficient. Weight is something to consider; because monoblocks are a combination of generator and strobe head, they are heavier than a single head. This isn't an issue if you're using a regular stand, but take care when using a boom. If you place one on the end of a boom, you'll want to use a counterweight and purchase a monoblock unit that offers a remote method for adjusting its settings. The power and modeling light controls are on the back of the unit.

Monoblocks are commonly used by photographers who specialize in people photography and are a lower-power option for product photographers. These are also a good option for small table-top setups where not much power is required (**FIGURE 10.4**). Expect to pay anywhere from $500 to $1500 per unit depending on power output. A good option when getting started is to purchase a kit that includes two or three monoblocks and stands, and possibly a light modifier or two. Buying kits is cheaper than à la carte purchases.

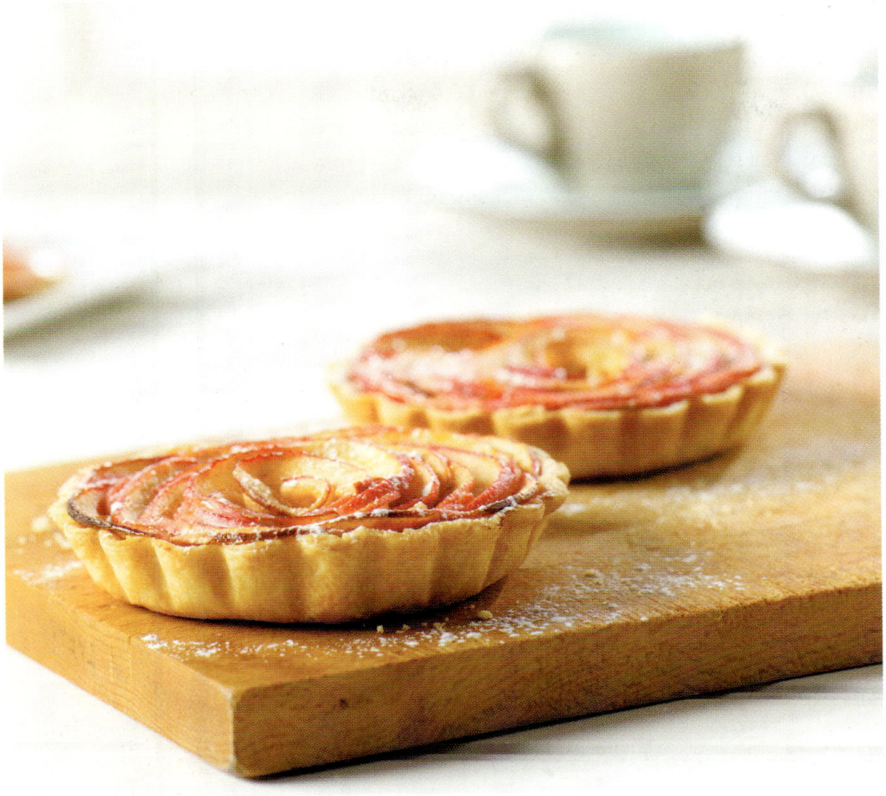

a)

FIGURE 10.4 **a)** This apple-tart image was captured as an option for the apple comparison the authors were working on. The "hero," or final, image is in Chapter 2 (Figure 2.19a). **b)** How the image was set up and lit: The main light source was a monoblock with an octagon-shaped softbox. **c)** The back side angle reveals another monoblock, which provided the look of light daylight coming in from the window.

ISO 50, 1/60 sec., f/8, 150mm lens

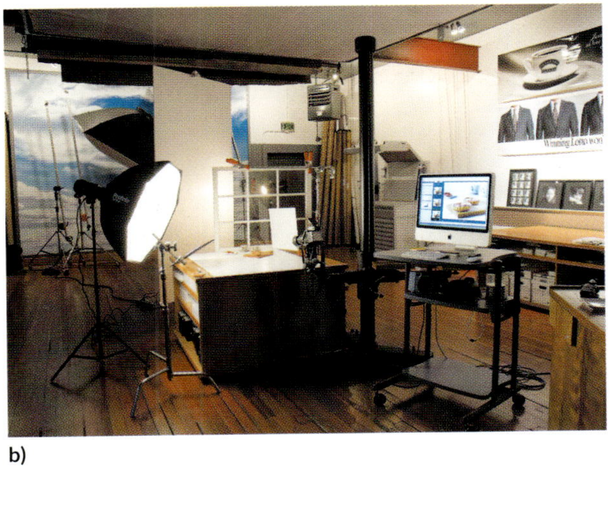

b)

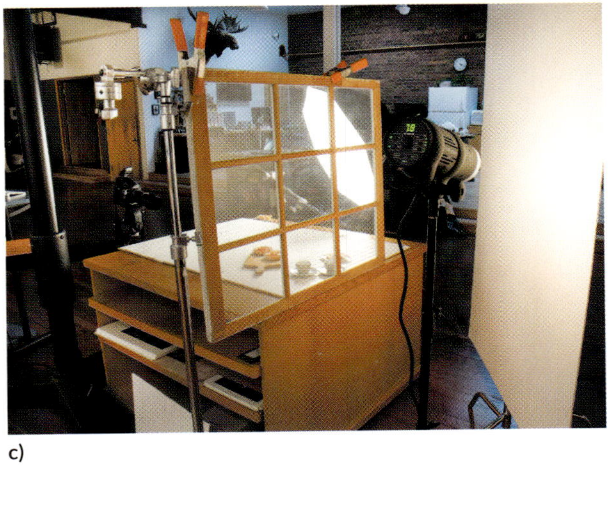

c)

Not All Monoblocks Are Created Equal

As you learned in Chapter 5, two benefits of strobes over tungsten lighting are the instantaneous burst of light and the daylight (5500 Kelvin) color temperature. It's easy to imagine that it's important for flash after flash to produce the same color temperature; nobody wants to edit a handful of images in which one frame looks good and the others have either a warm (yellow) or cool (blue) tint. Inexpensive monoblocks are notorious for using a rheostat method for controlling power output. This acts similarly to a household lamp attached to a dimmer switch, where as you rotate the dial not only does the light change brightness but also changes color temperature. The dimmer the light, the warmer the appearance. When shopping for a monoblock, make sure the color temperature changes less than 200 degrees Kelvin between the highest and lowest setting.

Generators and Strobe Heads

The longtime workhorse of photography studios is the generator combined with the strobe head. Unlike the monoblock, this setup consists of two separate components, the generator, which produces the power, and the strobe head, which delivers the burst of light. These are connected via a cord (FIGURE 10.5). A great benefit to this setup is that you can connect multiple strobe heads to a single generator. The number of heads and how the power is distributed depend on the features of the generator (FIGURE 10.6). Having all the controls in a single location can be a great convenience. It's common to see photographers place the strobe back close to their tripod when shooting to allow quick power adjustments.

A large variety of generator options is available, all affecting price. Power, or watts, is the first difference you'll notice when researching generators. Some have an output as low as 600ws, while others are 4800ws and above. It's safe to say that the generator with the higher output will cost more when all other features are equal.

Other factors that affect price are durability, control, and flash duration. Durability is rather straightforward, but what about control and flash duration? Control consists of two key elements: how power is divided among strobe heads, and the precision with which the power can be adjusted.

FIGURE 10.5 Here we have a single strobe head connected to a generator. Although only one head is connected, this unit accepts up to four of them.

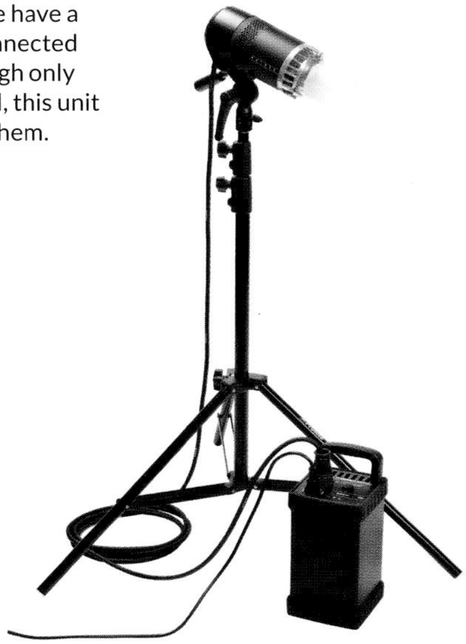

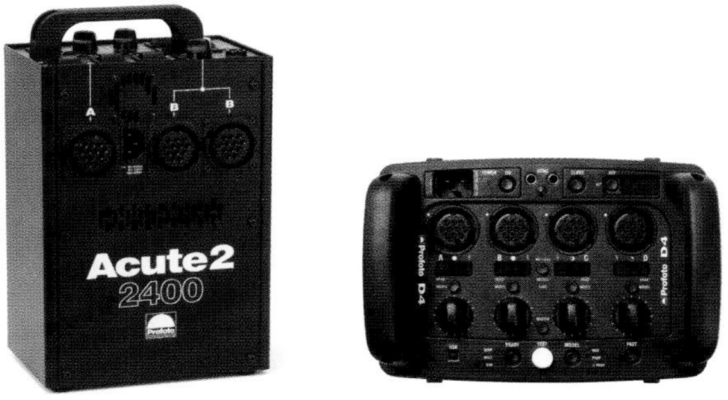

a) b)

FIGURE 10.6 **a)** The Profoto Acute2 allows the user to connect up to three strobe heads. This number varies depending on the model and manufacturer. **b)** Each of the four strobe heads and controls are available in one simple location.

Asymmetrical adjustment means that each head can be controlled individually and thus may have different output. Symmetrical adjustment means that each head will have the same output. It's best to purchase generators that offer both options. This can be beneficial when you need identical power from two strobe heads to light a background evenly while using a third with a different power setting to light a model.

The other control consideration is how precisely the power can be adjusted. Let's use a 2400ws pack as an example. It's preferable to be able to make adjustments in small intervals throughout the range of the pack. For example, some packs may allow options of 300ws, 600ws, 1200ws, and 2400ws, while others may allow any increment up to 2400ws.

By design, all strobes have a relatively short flash duration, but as addressed under "Flash Duration," in Chapter 5, in certain cases—such as stopping the movement of water—an extremely short duration is required (Figure 5.5).

With such a wide range of features—power output (ws), durability, control, and flash duration—it's easy to understand why many different products, and a multitude of price points, are available on the market. Many manufacturers follow a model similar to that of a car manufacturer such as Toyota, where Toyota, Lexus, and Scion are all part of the Toyota line of cars but offer a different level of features. A quick review of one strobe manufacturer's line of generators showed three unique 2400ws options, ranging from $2000 to $12,000. Although it might be wonderful to own the most expensive equipment, you need to ask whether it is necessary. Owning a Porsche 911 Carrera sounds great, but it probably wouldn't serve your needs if you lived on a farm.

As your career progresses, you'll learn what features are must-haves. The more specialized your career, the more you may need something that is found only on the most expensive units. For example, if your career is based on capturing the release of liquid as a soda can is opened, then you'll need to purchase a generator with extremely short flash duration, and that generally means the higher-priced units.

Speedlights

Pretty much a staple in every location photographer's camera bag is one or more speedlights. These are commonly directly attached to the camera's hot shoe or slightly off camera via a dedicated cable.

In the past few years, several accessories have come to market that enable studio and location photographers to simultaneously fire multiple speedlights and even use many of the speedlights' automatic features, such as through-the-lens (TTL) metering (FIGURE 10.7).

The automatic features and low cost of speedlights make them a good option for photographers early in their careers, but there are some drawbacks.

QUALITY VS. QUANTITY

I can either blame or thank my father, but I learned a long time ago that spending my money on a few high-quality items is a better choice than purchasing many lower quality pieces. It may seem like a good investment at the time to purchase multiple strobe packs and a handful of inexpensive strobe heads, but quality gear will outperform and outlast the cheaper items. In Chapter 6, I mentioned the importance of purchasing "good glass," and what holds true for lenses also applies to lighting gear. Make sound investments that will last for years.

—JOE LAVINE

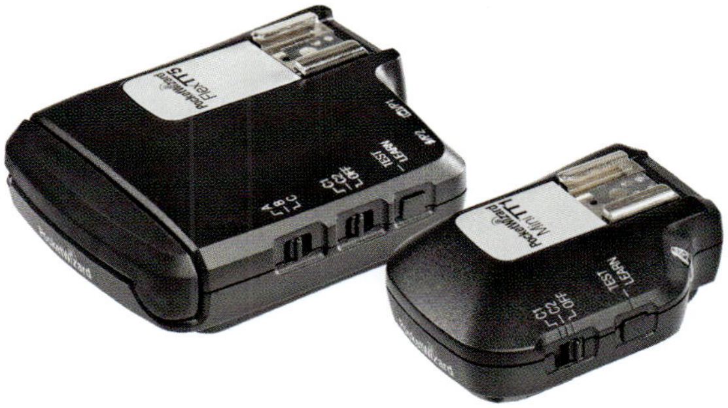

FIGURE 10.7 PocketWizard's MiniTT1 and FlexTT5, which allow simultaneous firing of numerous speedlights.

Three issues that stand out are power, quality of light, and lack of a modeling lamp. The small size of speedlights makes them easy to pack and move around a set, but they cannot compete with the power (ws) of studio strobes. Also, the size of their light source provides a hard quality of light. Of course, light modifiers such as scrims, umbrellas, and softboxes can be used to soften the light, but these options absorb some of the light, which then causes issues with their limited power. The third issue, which for many is the largest, is the lack of modeling light. Studio photography requires paying attention to fine details, and the lack of modeling light means there is much trial and error.

Speedlights' compact size and affordability make them an excellent addition and backup to any studio setup. There are plenty of times when large studio strobes become cumbersome and you need a small amount of light in a tight location, or simply a little kick of light on a background or hair light on a model.

Think long term, and trust in your future. Don't purchase cheap equipment just to purchase a lot of equipment. You can start small and build up over time. You'll want to consider your future wish list when making purchases today, and buy into a system. Buying lighting gear is similar to purchasing camera gear in that you obtain cameras and lenses from the same manufacturers. A great thing about a studio strobe is the vast array of optional accessories, but remember, accessories from one manufacturer may not work with accessories from another. Fortunately, options such as monoblocks, generators, and strobe heads tend to be part of a system that shares accessories. This is a great benefit when building one's arsenal of lighting gear.

Grip Equipment

The definition of grip equipment doesn't change as you move forward in your career, but the quality and amount does. When you're just getting started, clients respect your ingenuity in making a clamp out of duct tape, but at some point you need to demonstrate that you have the proper tools for the job. Grip equipment won't make you a better photographer, but it will allow you to work efficiently, and clients appreciate that time is money.

You'll never stop purchasing grip equipment, but where to start? Here are some items that are considered must-haves; some have been discussed in earlier chapters, and others are new and addressed in greater detail.

- **Stands:** There is no such thing as too many stands. It's a good idea to have a variety of sizes ranging from ones that hold a light inches off the floor to those that reach the height of your ceiling, or at least twelve feet (FIGURE 10.8). A starting point would be to own a stand for each light, a couple for fill cards and gobos, and two more for background support. If you shoot using large (aka heavy) light modifiers it's wise to own a couple of heavy-duty stands such as C-stands.
- **Clamps:** A-clamps are the starting point, but a couple other styles can simplify your life. Manufacturers each have their own names for specialized clamps, but two favorites are ones that attach to a stand and clamp down on almost anything, and clamps designed to attach to a tabletop and hold a light (FIGURE 10.9).

FIGURE 10.8 **a)** Standard floor stand; **b)** example of heavy-duty stand.

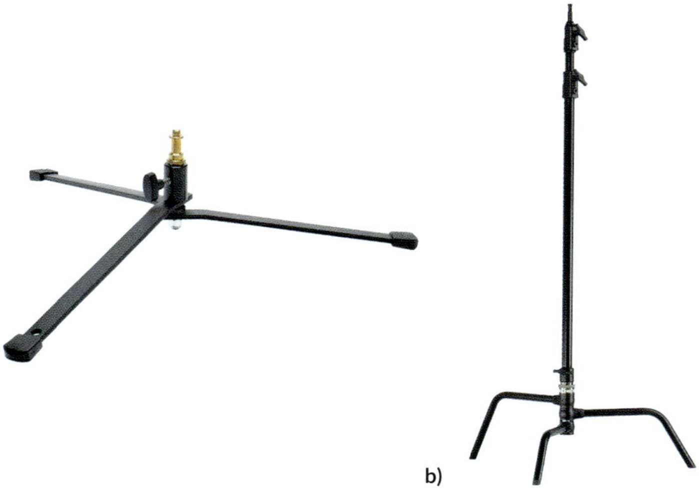

a)

b)

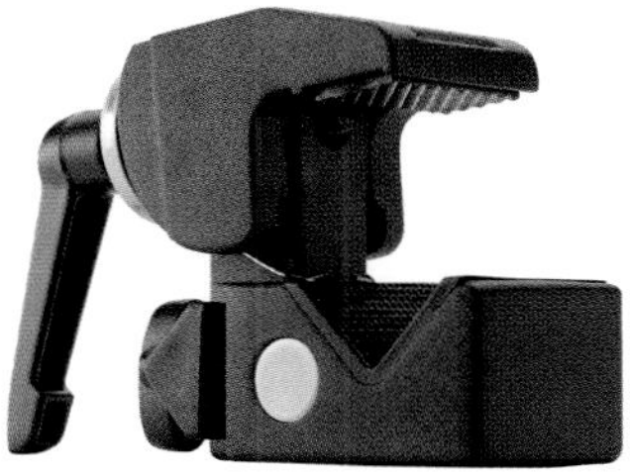
a)

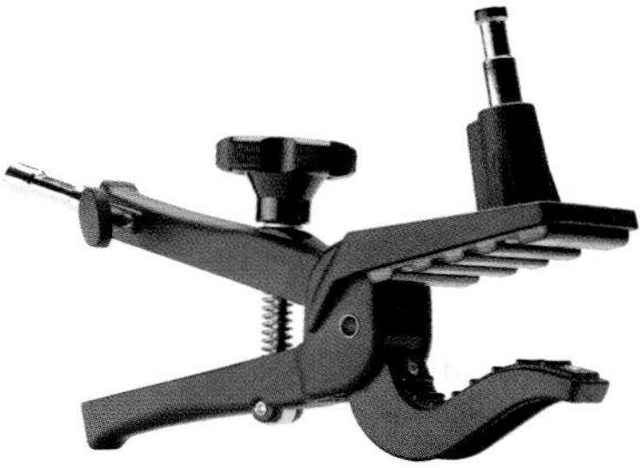
b)

FIGURE 10.9 **a)** Sometimes called a super or magic clamp, this style attaches to the top of a stand; **b)** being able to clamp a light directly to a table is great when working with limited space.

- **Extension arms:** Part of controlling light is being able to strategically place a fill card or gobo wherever is needed. The last thing a photographer wants is to know where light needs to be added or subtracted and not have the means to control it. This is where extension arms are indispensable (FIGURE 10.10). These come in numerous sizes and options, including straight, flexible, and those with multiple pivot points, to meet almost any need.

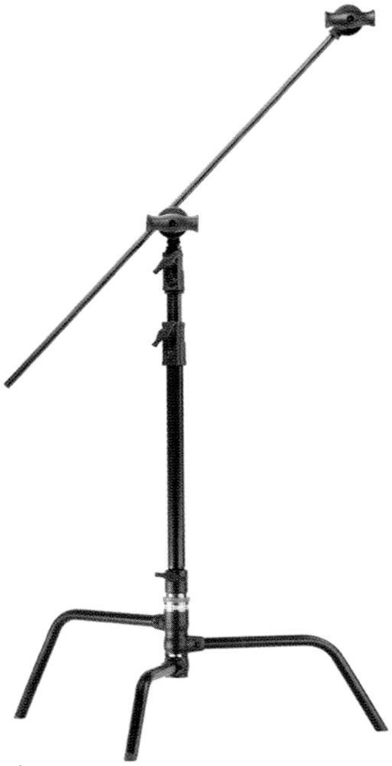
a)

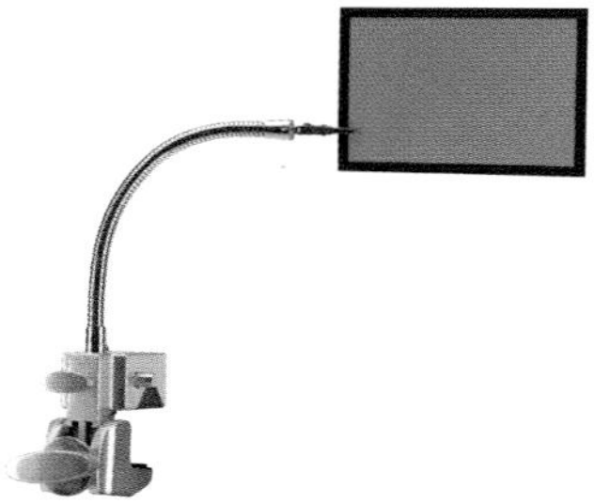
b)

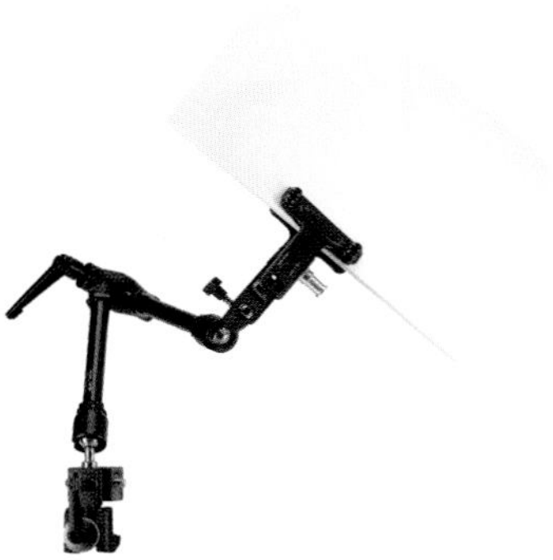
c)

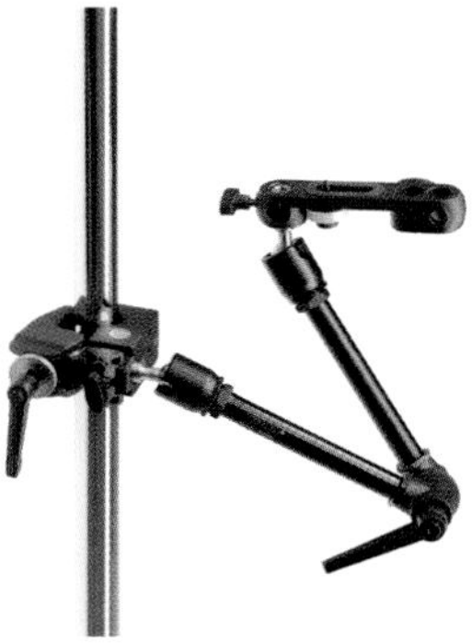
d)

FIGURE 10.10 **a–d)** Just a handful of the extension-arm options available.

What's Your Must-Have?

Joe: Brad, all photographers have that single piece of grip equipment that they can't live without. Mine is my Matthew's Dots and Fingers kit (different size gobos and flags), which I use on almost every shoot to control light. What is yours and why?

Brad: It is a common piece of equipment, but I would have to go with C-stands. They are so versatile and there really is not a good substitute. I remember being very excited when I purchased my first couple C-stands. I bought them used, and they just made everything so much easier and more efficient.

It's good to start with a few basic grip equipment items, but over time you'll make additional purchases based on need. You'll be setting up for a project and discover that you're missing just the right tool to fit something where you need it. Although you may not have it for that shoot, those are the moments when you realize it's time to place an order for a specialized item.

Budgets

Money is never an easy topic or discussion. The good news is that if you're talking about budgets, then you're also talking about paying clients, and that's not a bad thing. This point in a photographer's career is where understanding budgets is the most crucial. As you become more established, working with budgets becomes second nature, but for now it might require some practice to figure out how to handle a budget.

Unless you are independently wealthy, the investment you've made in equipment signifies that this is a career and not merely a hobby, and therefore making money is important. Chapter 9 addressed the need to know what it costs to break even—what some people call the dollars required to keep the lights on. The equipment cost leap from Chapter 9 to Chapter 10 means that this number has changed. Again, as a career it's more than keeping the lights on. Plenty of resources are available to help an emerging photographer determine how to price a job. Here are a handful of options:

Software

Blinkbid (blinkbid.com) and fotoQuote (cradocfotosoftware.com/fotoQuote-Pro/) are two software programs that allow users to import data needed to help determine the worth of an image. This information includes, but isn't limited to, specialty, placement, rights, demographics, and usage.

Professional Organizations (National)

Large professional organizations are a wonderful resource for getting an overview of best practices. Whether you have questions about acceptable file formats or budgets, these organizations pull data from a large volume of professionals. There're numerous options, so researching the best fit takes some time. A few common ones are the American Society of Media Photographers (ASMP), Advertising Photographers of America (APA), and Professional Photographers of America (PPA).

tip Having a pitch planned when making business calls to introduce yourself and show your work will reduce much of the initial stress. It'll help you sound confident and professional, which is what every client is looking for.

Local Groups

Get to know your local professional community. Whether it's local charters of national organizations, your city's Chamber of Commerce, or a local artist league, these smaller organizations are helpful in understanding your unique market. As mentioned earlier, a studio portrait produced in Des Moines, Iowa, will be valued differently than one produced in Manhattan.

Expectations

Working as a professional photographer is filled with expectations. Each project requires a balance between those that are self-imposed and ones from the clients. It's the balance all professionals strive to achieve.

Self-Imposed Standards

The most successful photographers tend to place higher expectations on themselves than others place on them. This is good. This is a sign that you care about what you do and are always looking to improve. Nobody's ever going to say that working in the arts is easy; it's not. It's said that you are only as good as your last job, and that's the truth. People in this industry have short memories; you could have done nine wonderful shoots in a row for

tip Don't demand perfection; it's impossible to obtain, and trying to achieve it will often lead to disappointment. Instead, strive for excellence, with a goal of improvement on every new project.

them, but if the tenth doesn't go well, that's the one they remember. That's OK. Use it as a motivator to make the tenth better than the ninth. There's a lot of competition, but being pushed to excel will have rewards. If you improve on the tenth, and your competitor does not, then you'll be the one who stands out. Self-imposed high expectations are a must for all successful photographers.

Working with Clients

tip Hosting a photo shoot is like hosting a party; you want to make sure your guests enjoy themselves and want to come back soon.

You want your clients to have high expectations of your work. Clients place a lot of faith in the photographers they hire. The concept or vision for an image has been discussed, debated, and often languished over for a period of time before it is entrusted to a photographer to reproduce. At some point, a creative director, an art buyer, an art director, a graphic designer, or someone else entrusted with decision-making power determines that you are the right person for the project. They place their trust in you. They expect you to produce results.

Again, this is good. It means they're confident in your skills and aesthetic.

The roles clients take during a photo shoot can vary dramatically. Let's take a look at three different scenarios and the possible pros and cons of them.

Scenario 1: This client prefers to discuss a project at great length before the shoot and then trust the work to be carried out in her absence. While this provides a more relaxed atmosphere for the work, you get no direct

The Next Level of Clients

This may seem like a scary step in the process, but now is the time to market beyond small local businesses and go directly to the people who handle the hiring for larger companies. This means contacting marketing firms, design firms, advertising agencies, and in-house marketing departments of companies. Don't get caught thinking that you aren't ready or that these groups hire only photographers who have been in business for years. The truth is, companies require all levels of photographers, from those just getting started to ones with international reputations. The idea is to get your foot in the door, do a good job, and steadily work toward becoming a well-known photographer. These are the clients who really understand the value of photography and will allow you to not only keep the lights on but grow your business.

feedback. You never really know whether what you're doing meets her expectations until you submit the work.

Scenario 2: During the shoot the client is at the studio but takes a hands-off approach, generally commenting on the images only when you ask for input. The input is great to have, but you may feel as though someone's keeping an eye on you. A balancing act is required: How relaxed can you be, and how much input should you ask for and expect?

Scenario 3: Some clients prefer a more hands-on approach. These are the ones who are always near the set or computer and routinely provide their feedback. They make suggestions and are curious why you make certain decisions. This type of client takes a lot of ownership of the project and makes his opinions known.

So, which is better? Each scenario provides unique challenges. You'll discover which style fits you better, but the key is to be prepared to handle anything that you encounter. You probably can't afford to turn down the clients whose style doesn't mesh easily with yours, so you have to learn to be flexible.

Working with clients will have challenges. Realize that each project requires a team; that will help you understand that a lot has to happen for a photo shoot to come to fruition. Don't be surprised if, no matter how clear your

STRIVING FOR MORE

Early in my undergraduate days, I was young and arrogant and thought my work was better than my classmates'. When we posted our assignments around the room for our peers and instructors to judge, I felt my work stood out. I couldn't believe it when other work earned higher marks than mine. I recall following the instructor into his office and demanding an explanation, and in a quiet voice he made it very clear that if I did not improve, regardless of whether my work was the best in the class, he would continue to reduce my scores. I was furious and said it wasn't fair. I lost the argument, and although it took a couple of years for me to realize it, I eventually understood that he was right. I learned to always strive to improve from shoot to shoot. I know that I wouldn't have experienced the success that I've enjoyed in my career if it had not been for that conversation. Thank you, Mr. Lerner.

—JOE LAVINE

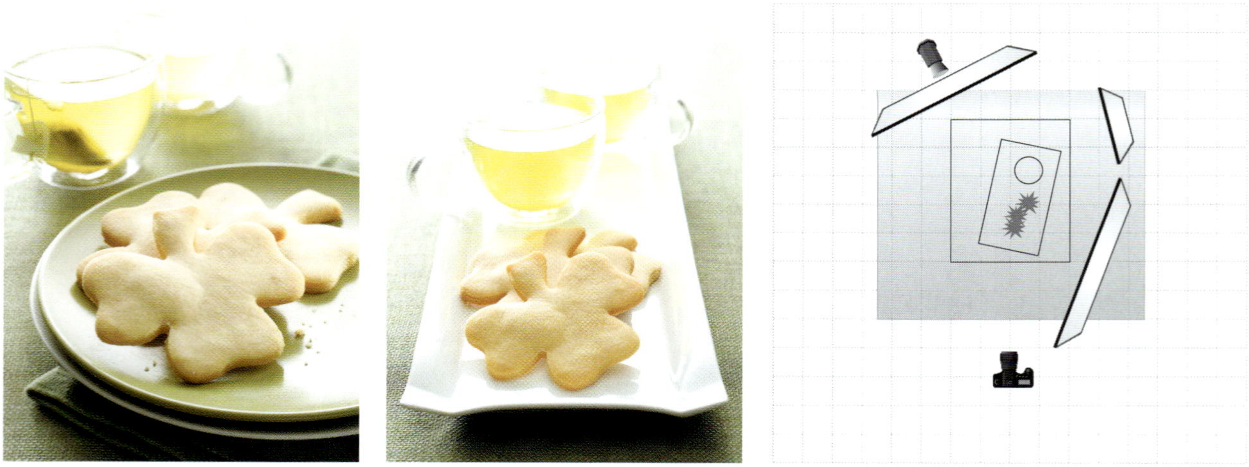

a) b) c)

FIGURE 10.11 **a)** The original client concept was to place the cookies on a green plate with tea in the background; **b)** option two replaced the green plate with a rectangular white plate in hopes of making the cookies stand out; **c)** a simple lighting setup using a scrim, a single strobe, and two white fill cards; **d)** the final version combined latte art with a white plate to better convey the concept of St. Patrick's Day.

ISO 50, 1/60 sec., f/11, 80mm lens

vision when you start, you need to produce a few options through a process of discussion and experimentation to reach the final image (**FIGURE 10.11**). This is not weakness or lack of artistic integrity; it's called working with clients.

Career Path

There is nothing "single" about a career. A career is a journey and not a single day, a single photo shoot, or even a single year. You've passed the first hurdle of "Getting Started," and now is the time to evaluate where you are today and where you would like to be tomorrow, even if "tomorrow" is actually years down the road. Taking the time to routinely reevaluate who you are as a photographer and where you want to go in photography is imperative. Professional photography is a wonderful but demanding career, which makes it essential to do the style of work you enjoy in the location where you wish to live.

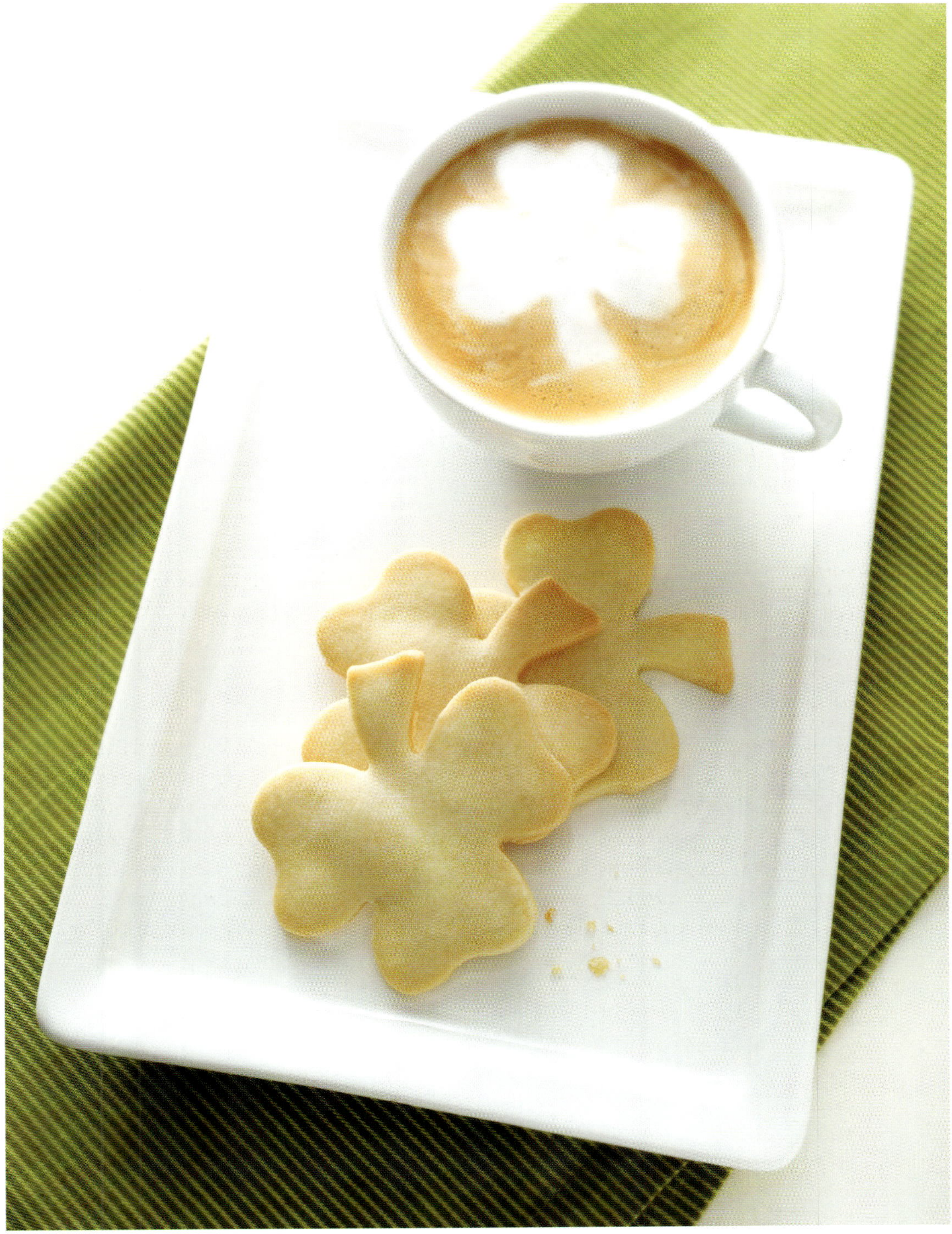

d)

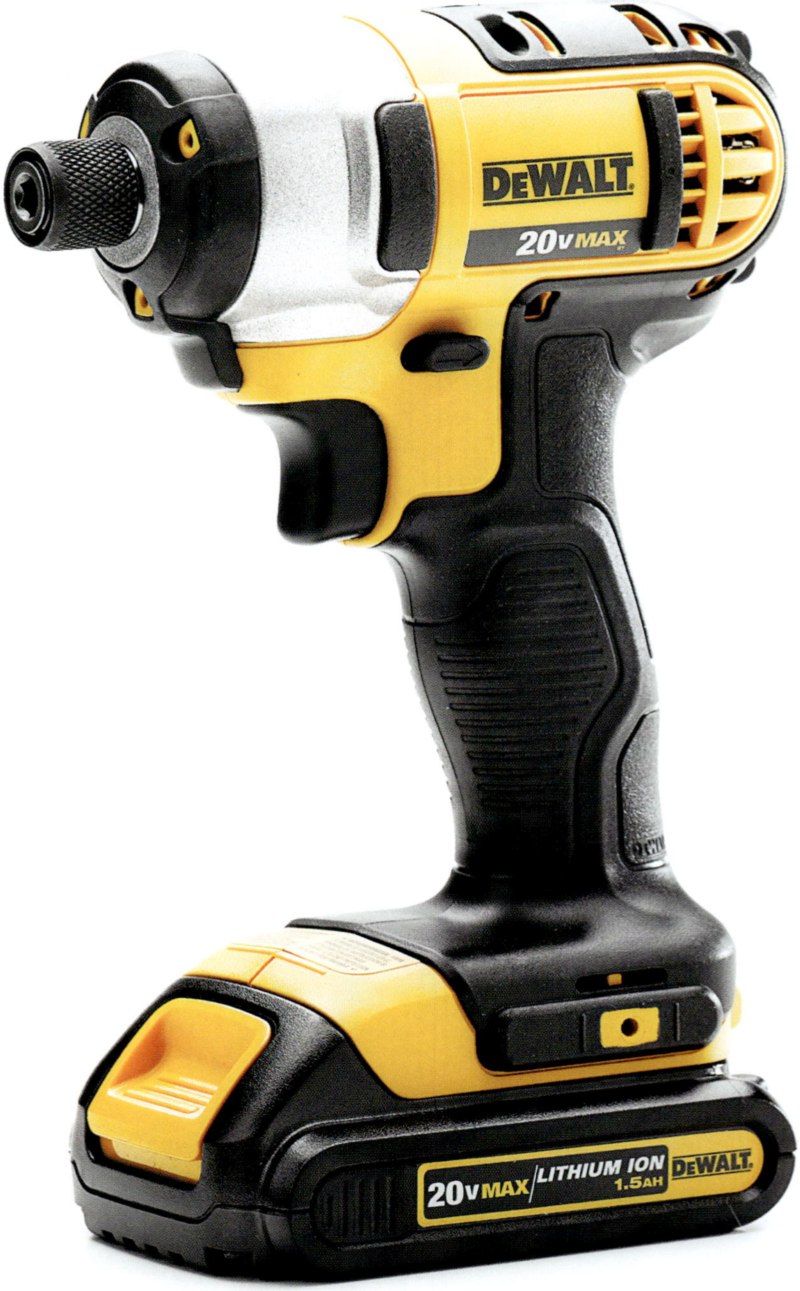

a)

ISO 50, 1/125 sec., f/16, 150mm lens

Comparison

For this chapter's comparison, we decided to use a common household drill. The guidelines were simple; we had to use the exact same drill, but Joe would shoot a clean product image, and Brad would capture more of a product lifestyle shot. The results demonstrate two common client needs (**FIGURE 10.12**).

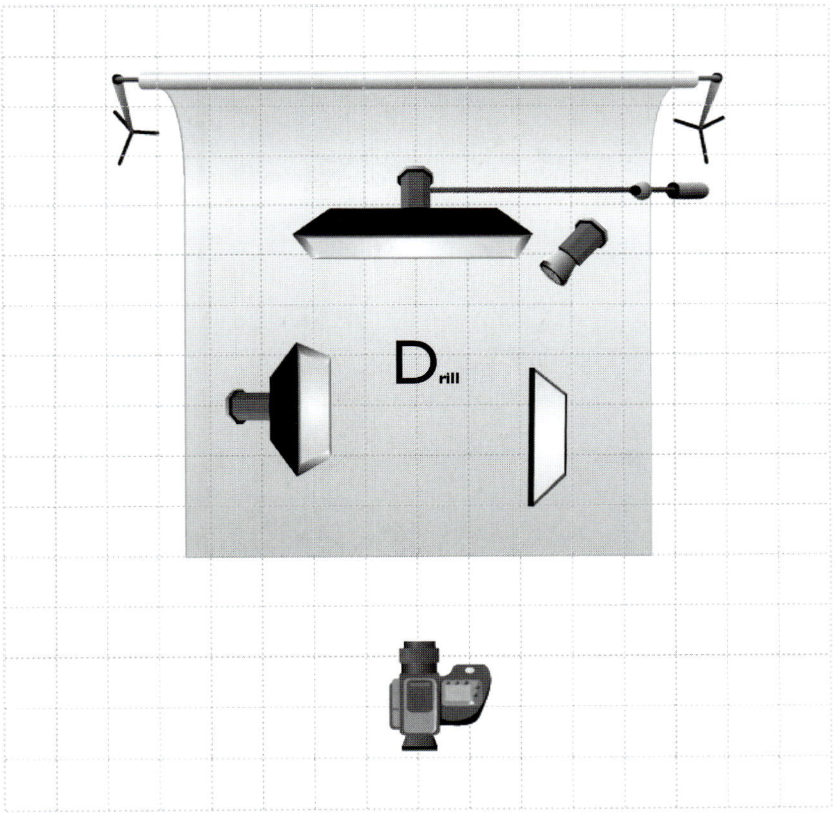

b)

FIGURE 10.12 **a)** The clean product shot on white allows the viewer to see all the small details without the distractions of a background; **b)** the lighting diagram for the image on white; **c)** manufacturers often like to showcase their products in a believable environment (next page); **d)** a diagram showing lighting for the look of a workshop (next page).

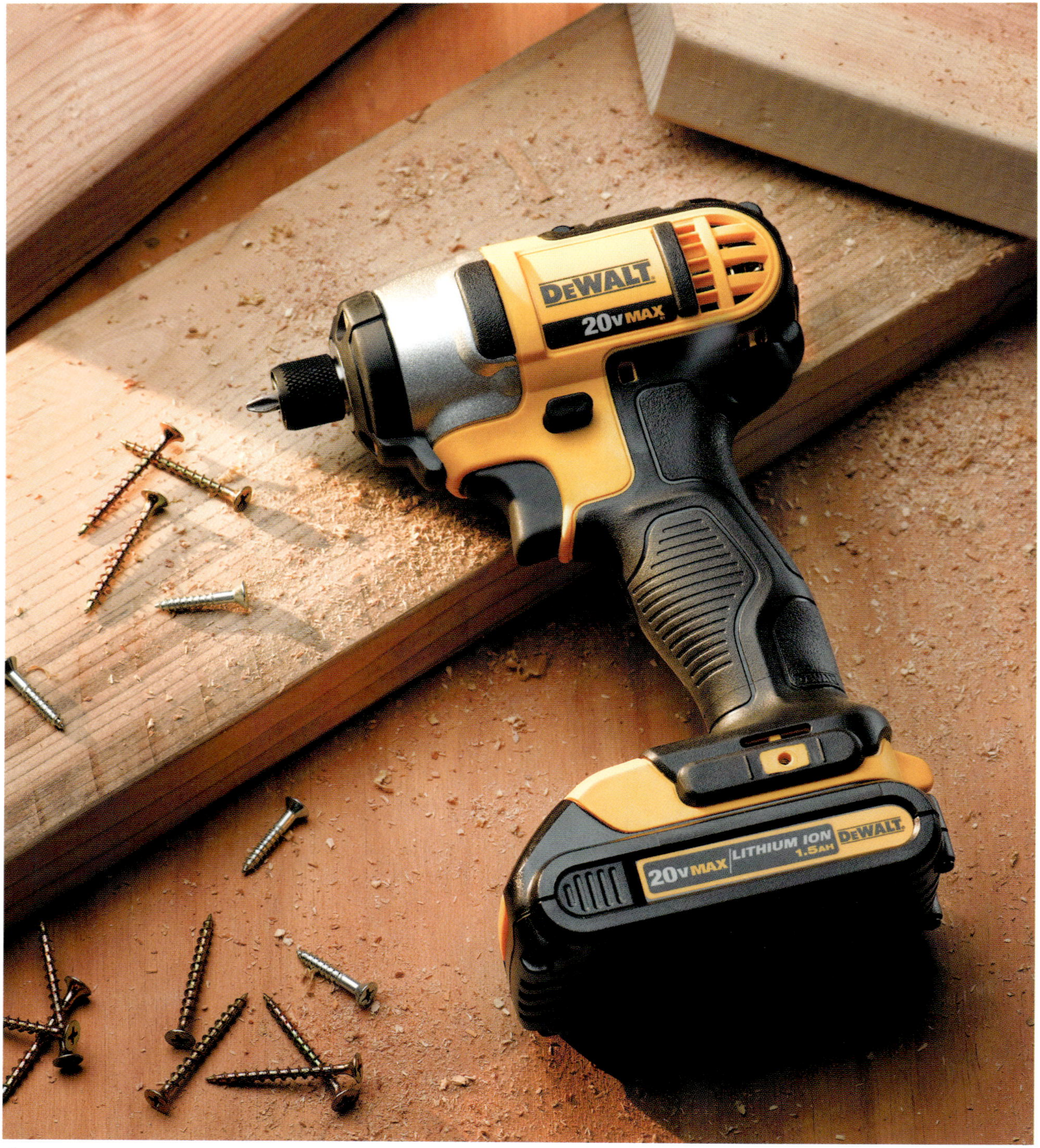

c)

ISO 50, 1/2 sec., f/11, 150mm lens

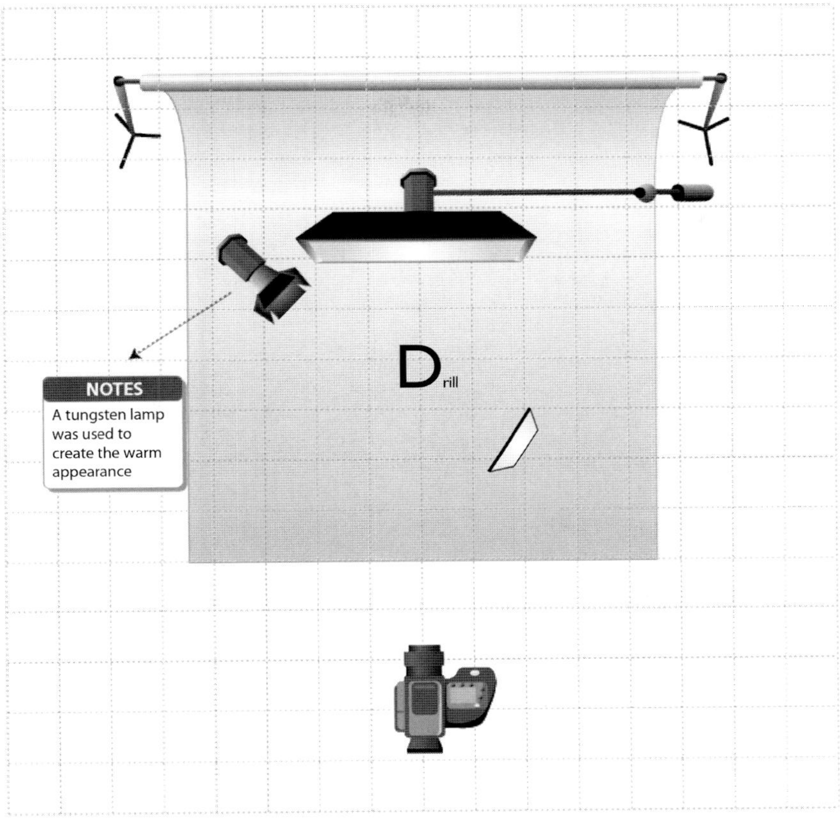
NOTES
A tungsten lamp was used to create the warm appearance
Drill

d)

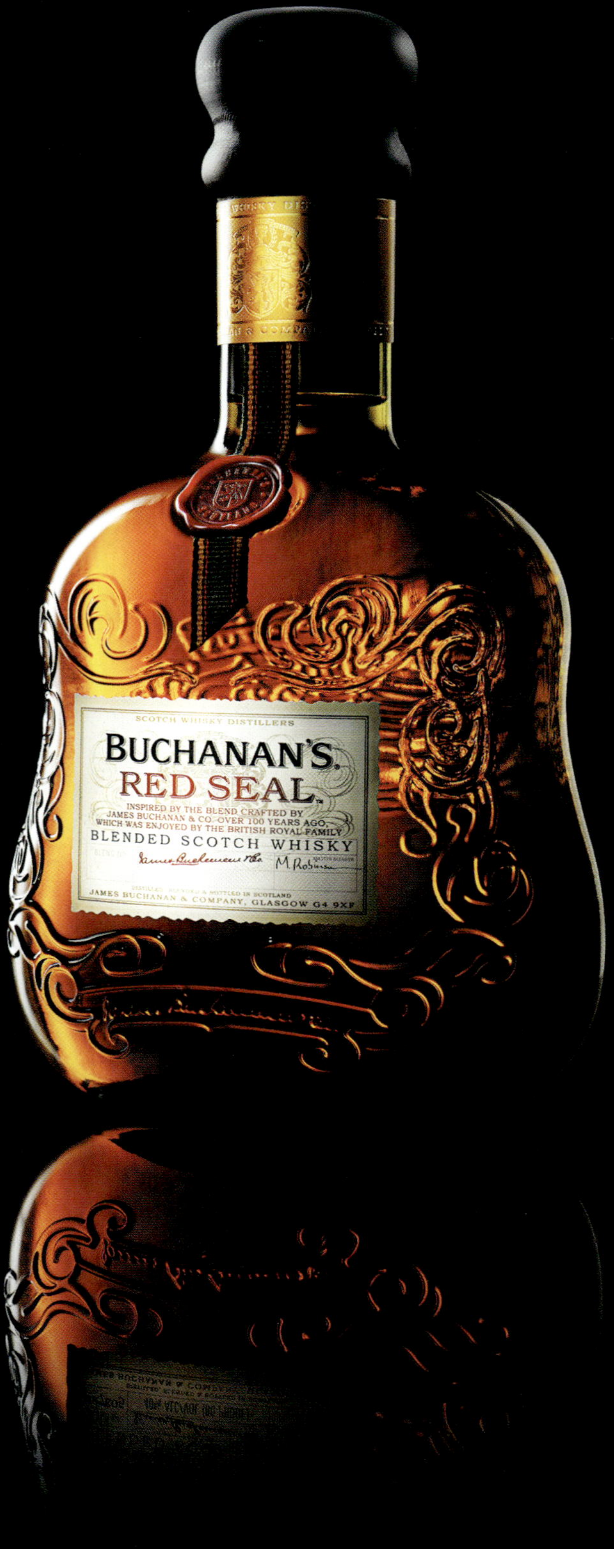
SCOTCH WHISKY DISTILLERS
BUCHANAN'S.
RED SEAL
INSPIRED BY THE BLEND CRAFTED BY
JAMES BUCHANAN & CO. OVER 100 YEARS AGO,
WHICH WAS ENJOYED BY THE BRITISH ROYAL FAMILY
BLENDED SCOTCH WHISKY
JAMES BUCHANAN & COMPANY, GLASGOW G4 9XF

chapter eleven

SUCCESS

Oh, this is a tricky word! What does it mean exactly? That's a very personal question: What does a successful photography career mean for you? As much as this can vary from person to person, one thing is constant—it's easier to reach that goal if you have a good idea of what it looks like, what it tastes like, what it is. Getting to where you want to be professionally is directly tied to what you want to achieve personally. What will you be willing to give up? What compromises are you willing to make between work and the rest of your life?

There is no right or wrong. This chapter will explore what to do when you reach this plateau, and that's all it is, a resting point when you have reached a modicum of success. So now where do you go?

Image © Martin Wonnacott

Opening Image: Photographic Equipment

Camera: Sinar p3 with Sinar eVolution 75 digital back

Lens: Sinar 90

Lighting: Profoto D4 generator and two strobe heads, Profoto ProZoom Spot

Light modifiers: 6 × 1 softbox, 20-degree grid, reflector cards

Multiple lights and reflectors were used to create this elegantly lit product shot on the previous page.

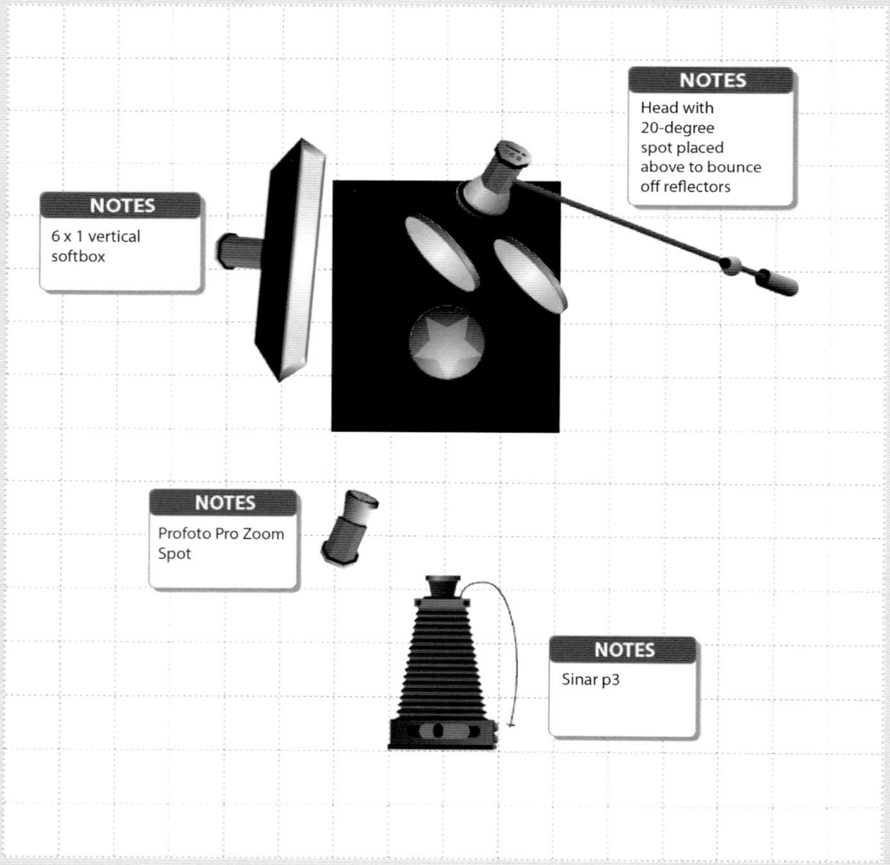

Things Are Good

Let's assume that you've been in business for quite a few years and you've put together a career very much like what you initially envisioned. You're shooting for clients you enjoy and the budgets are good. You have a cool studio and equipment that meets your needs. Most important, you've developed a style that is recognized and sought after. Sounds pretty good, don't you think? It is good—but it can also be a trap. Every career has several phases, and all of them have pluses and minuses. When you start out you are super eager but pretty poor.

You then move on to building a business that is exciting and nerve-racking, due to equipment and studio expenses and sometimes to client expectations. Eventually, you get to a place where work comes in consistently, money is less of a worry, and the work itself is satisfying. The key at this point is to make sure that work remains fun and gratifying.

You'll get jobs you do for the money, and hopefully you'll land some work you do for the love of it. The key to a long, lucrative, and satisfying career is to achieve as much overlap between the two as possible (**FIGURE 11.1**).

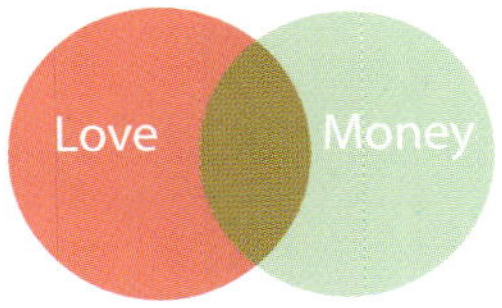

FIGURE 11.1 The more overlap you have between work done for love and work done for money, the happier and more productive you'll be.

The Trap

We know that the prospect of having a solid, stable career sounds like it has nothing but upsides, and to a certain extent that's true. Here's the rub. Creative people with a strong personal style are often pigeonholed. As long as you're happy producing work within that style, and as long as the market

NERVOUS IS THE NEW NORMAL

My best friend at photo school started his business before I did. I'll never forget his response when I asked him how it was going. He said, "Well, let me put it this way. When I don't have work I'm pretty nervous that I'll never make it in this business, and when I do get a job, I'm nervous that I'm going to screw it up. So all in all, I'm pretty nervous all the time." Just for the record, he has gone on to be a very successful lifestyle editorial shooter in L.A.

—**BRAD BARTHOLOMEW**

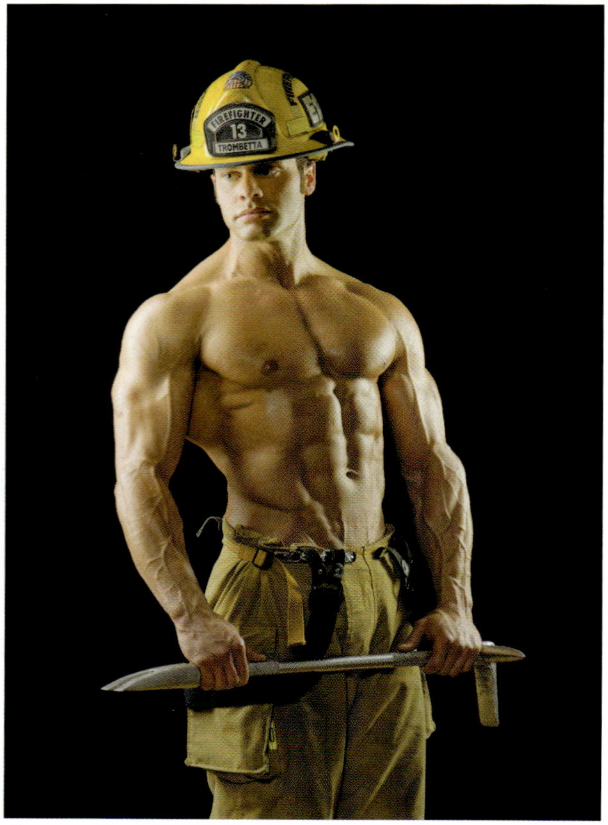

a)

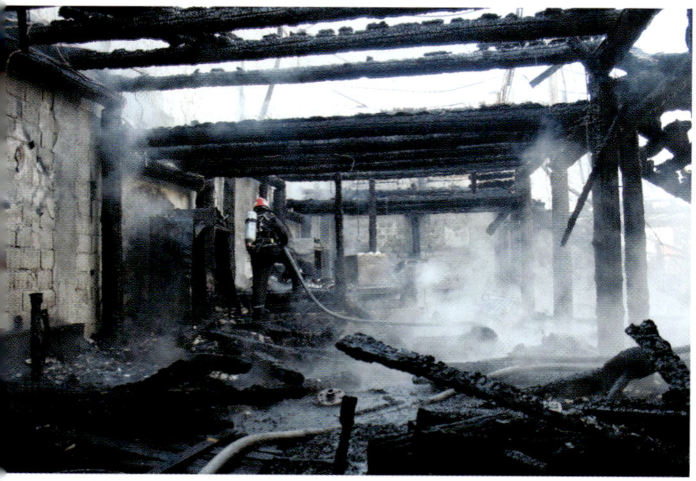

© Shutterstock

b)

demands that style, life is good. Trouble can arise if the market shifts or you become bored with producing that type of work.

One of the reasons we've stressed the need for constant experimentation is that it will help you remain fresh and engaged with the work you produce. The willingness to constantly look for new ways to express yourself will help you keep your work marketable, and it will lead to personal and professional growth (**FIGURES 11.2A–C**).

On the other hand, there may be times when you would love to take your work in new directions but the market consistently requests images produced in your tried-and-true style. This is true for artists working in a number of different genres. More than likely you've gone to a concert performed by your favorite artist or band, only to be disappointed that they mainly played songs off their new album that you felt didn't compare to their classic work. But how are they supposed to grow as artists if everyone wants the same old things (**FIGURE 11.3**)?

You want to overlap work done for money with work done for yourself, but given a choice, in the long run, you'll be better off doing what you love more of the time. People will respond to quality work that comes from your passion. Make sure that you balance this with creating images that speak to the marketplace and you are halfway there (**FIGURE 11.4**).

FIGURE 11.2 **a)** This image was shot in the studio using a simple lighting setup; **b)** we bought a stock shot to use as a background; **c)** here's the final composited image.

ISO 100, 1 sec., f/16, 150mm lens

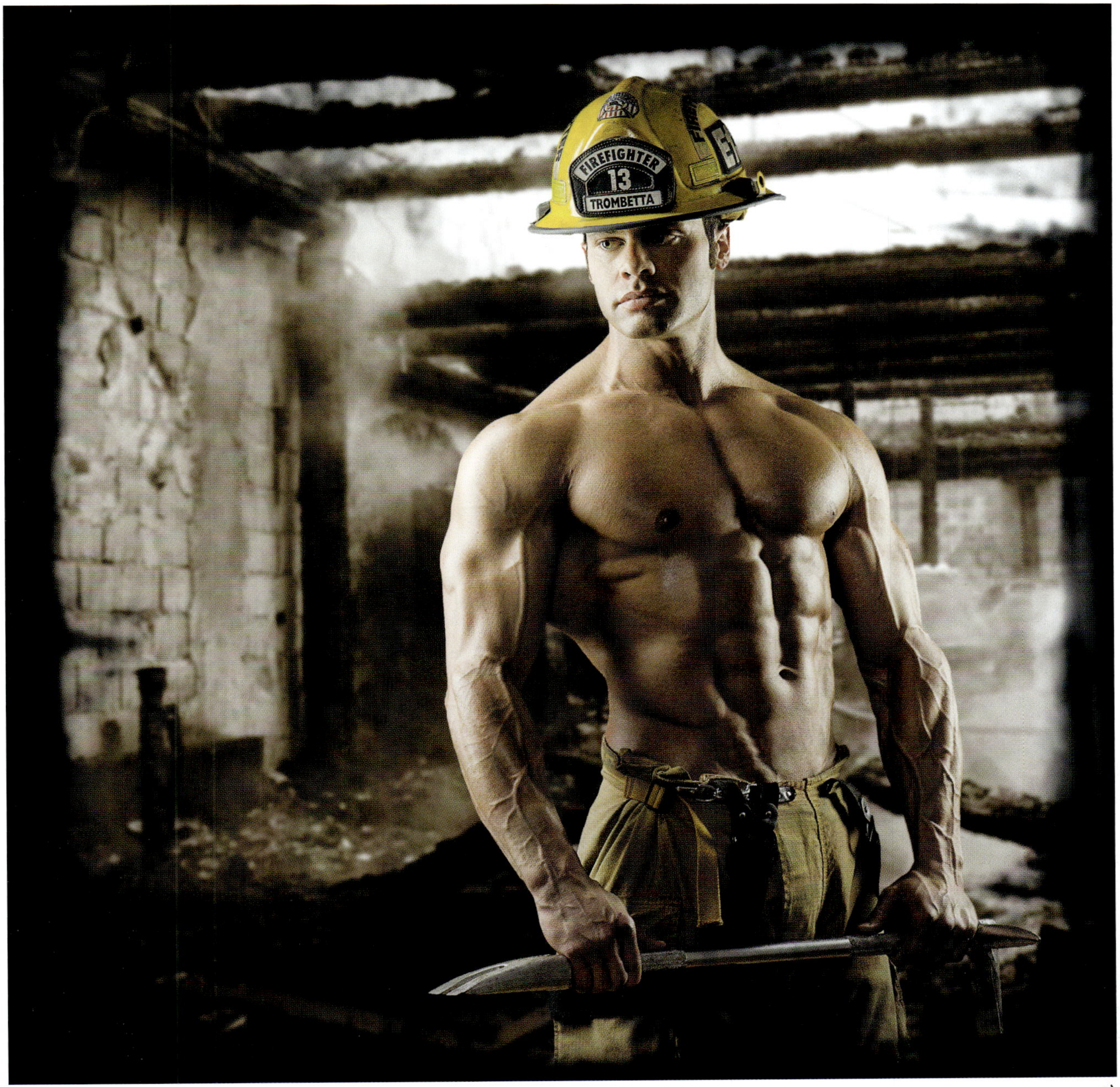

c)

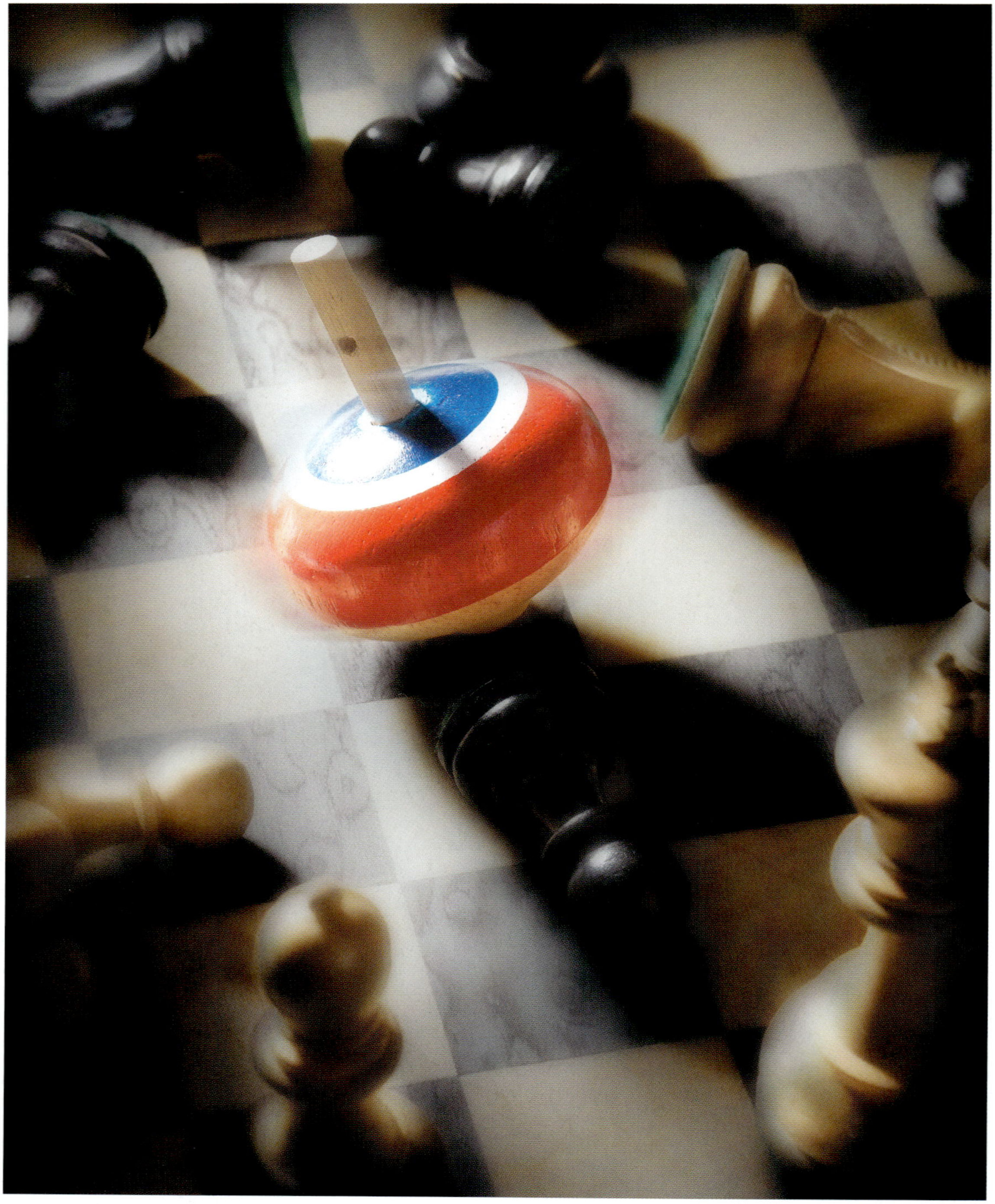

FIGURE 11.3 This image represents a change in style that allowed for technical and creative growth.

ISO 100, 1/2 sec., f/16, 100mm lens

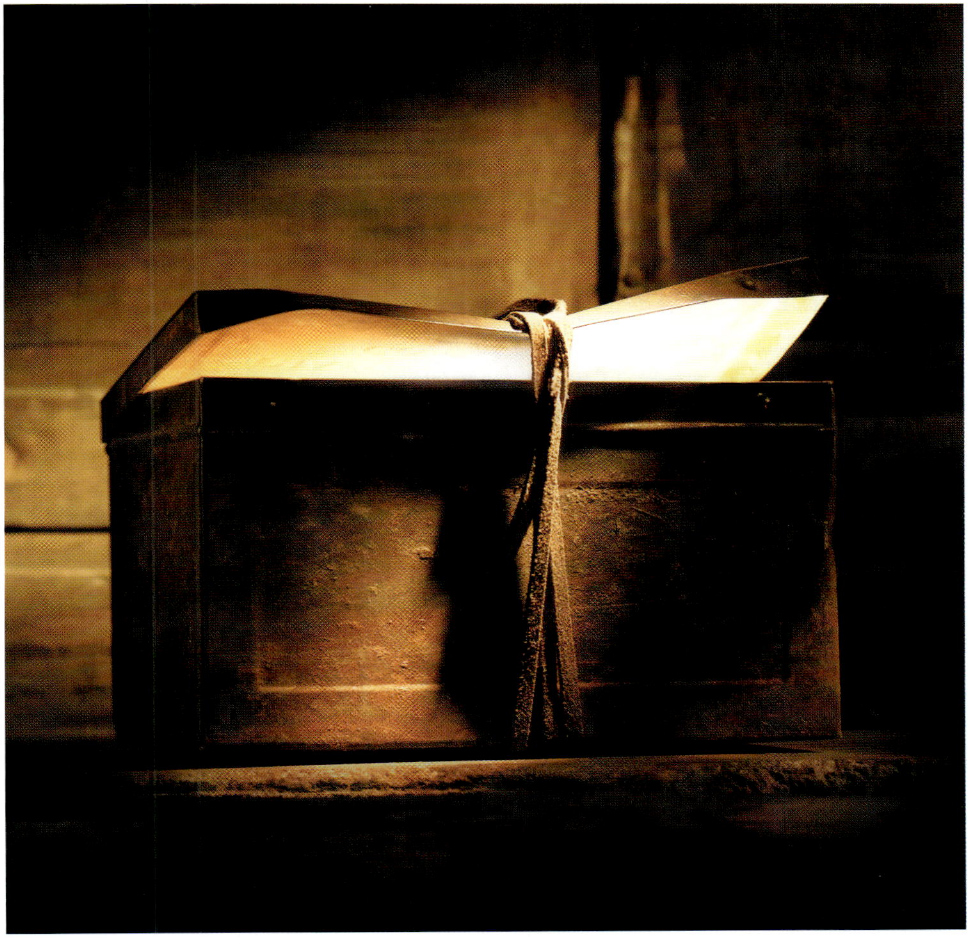

FIGURE 11.4 When this image was shot, Brad used the kind of light that he loved to create and that the market embraced. With time, his style had to evolve to continue to speak to his market.

ISO 100, 30 sec., f/16, 210mm lens

CHANGING DIRECTION

For more than a decade I've been fortunate to work on a firefighter calendar to benefit the local Children's Hospital here in Denver. In the past, all of the photos were shot on location, with the hunky firefighters doing heroic things (Figures 11.2A and 11.2C). For this calendar, we wanted to go in a different direction. The firefighters were shot in the studio and then composited with existing burned-building images. I'd never done anything quite like this, so I needed to do some research and take test shots before we moved forward. This project gave me a chance to experiment and grow professionally, and the hospital thought the resulting images were very effective.

—BRAD BARTHOLOMEW

Marketing

The other half is marketing. Some would say that marketing is responsible for more than 50 percent of success. You must *continually* market yourself. How you choose to do that will depend a great deal on the kind of work you are doing. Obviously, a consumer portrait photographer working in Memphis is trying to reach a different audience than a product photographer working in New York. Knowing your audience and targeting your marketing materials to them specifically will help you carve out a portion of the market.

Branding

As your business grows and your clients become larger and more sophisticated, you'll need to separate yourself from your competitors. The way to do this is to establish a unique brand for your business. This will include, but is not limited to, a logo, a color scheme, the personal style and emotional content of your work, and a well-defined lighting style. You want to make sure that you take a careful look at your work and yourself and then create a brand that reflects both. If your work is dark and moody, then a logo and color scheme should be employed that relates to that tone. If your work is clean and slick, then a very different set of choices will be used to define your brand (**FIGURE 11.5**).

The easiest way to think about branding is to look at major corporations and how they present themselves to potential clients. Check out the competitors in any major consumer product market; every company is trying to establish

ARTISTS' DILEMMA

I know two very successful painters. They both produce beautiful, compelling work. Each has experienced being a victim of his own success. They want to create images different from previous work that sold well. The galleries push them to continue to produce salable work, while they would prefer to move on to new uncharted territories. This exemplifies the need to constantly do work for yourself to keep motivated.

—BRAD BARTHOLOMEW

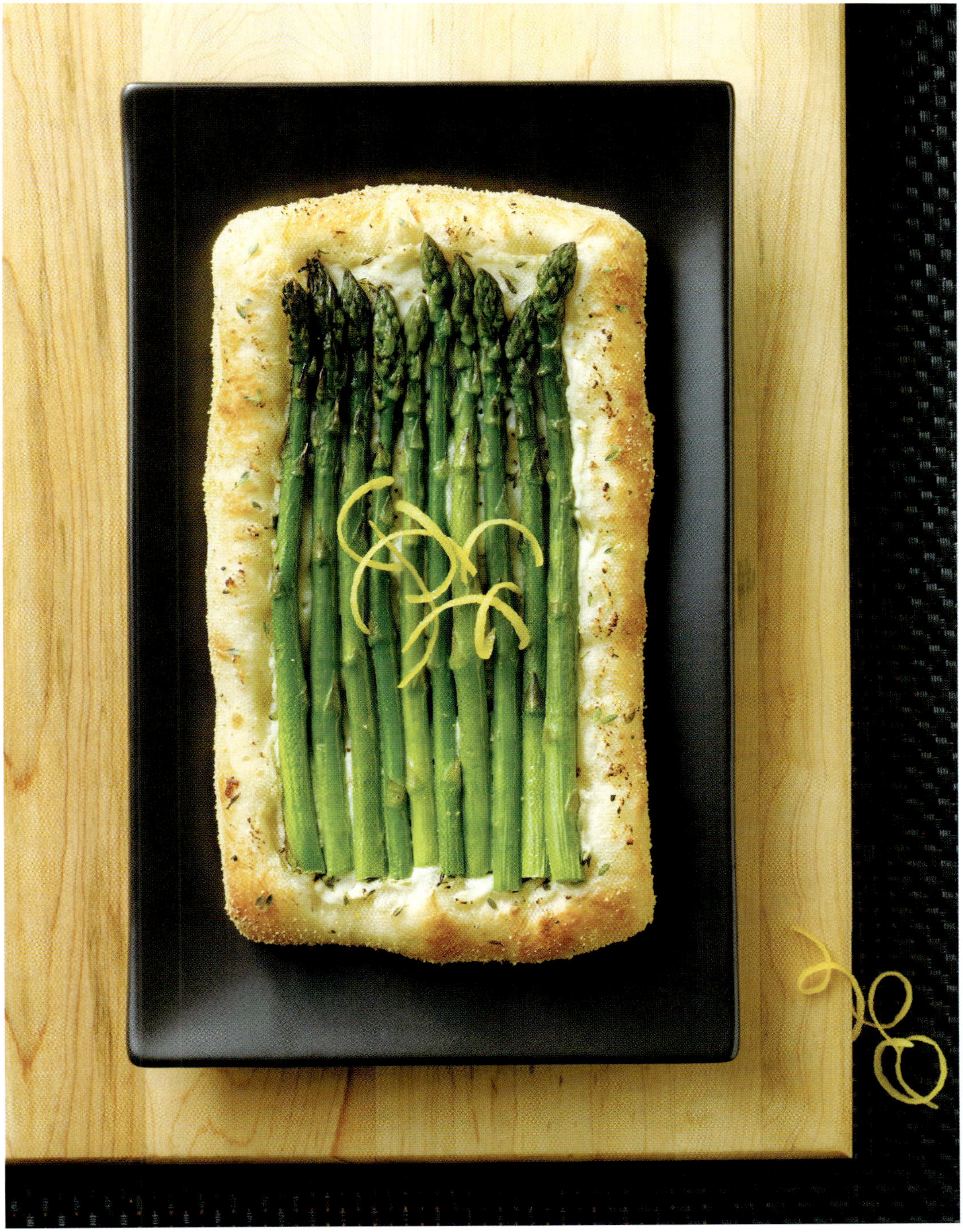

FIGURE 11.5 This shot is very clean and precise, and the branding should reinforce that style.

ISO 100, 1/125 sec., f/16, 100mm lens

QUIRKY BRAND

I once had a student who produced really fun, bright, and quirky work. She created a portfolio that consisted of a refurbished Barbie doll carrying case. She gutted the inside and lined it with velvet and then placed her images inside. For 99.9 percent of my other students, this would have been a monumental mistake, but it worked for her because it matched her personality and her work.

—BRAD BARTHOLOMEW

loyalty from its consumers or potential consumers. Each manufacturer produces trucks that are supposedly tougher than the other brands. Research shows that if you purchase one truck over the others, and the product reasonably meets your expectations, you'll be reluctant to switch to a different company. You'll also defend your choice to others and pass your preference on to future generations.

The likelihood that your photography business will extend for generations is slim, but nonetheless, the lessons you can learn from major corporations are important. Produce work that meets or exceeds clients' expectations and they'll be hesitant to look elsewhere (FIGURE 11.6). Most freelance photography businesses are small and rely on the expertise of just a few individuals, but establishing loyalty and strong relationships with your clients will help ensure that your business grows and thrives. There's an adage that it's easier to keep an old client than find a new one. In the interview at the end of this chapter, Martin Wonnacott reinforces the importance of treating clients well several times.

Ways to Reach Your Audience

The most important piece of your entire marketing strategy is you. The way you present yourself and your work will be the key ingredient for your success. You must be positive and upbeat. No one wants to work with a gloomy, depressing photographer. The days of the moody "artist" are behind us; there are far too many really talented people for clients to have to put up with some jerk with a camera.

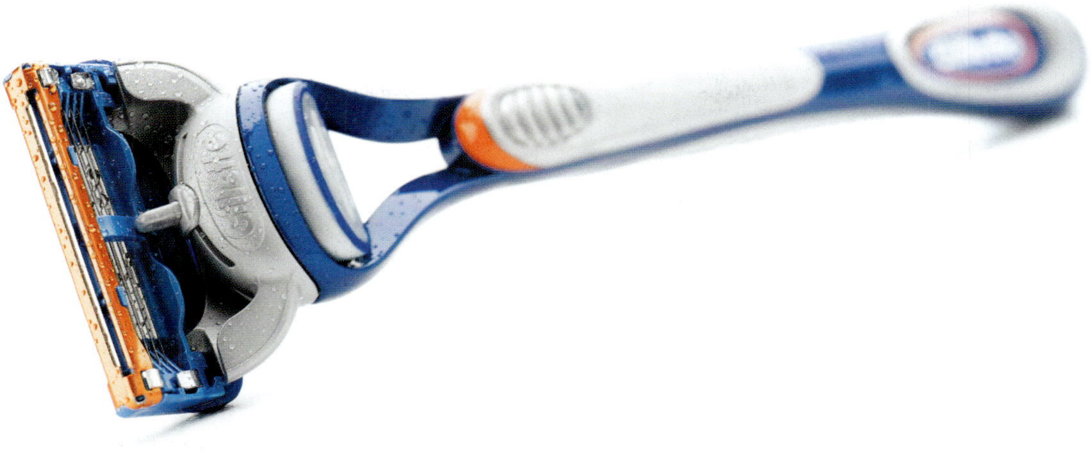

FIGURE 11.6 Here we see a deceptively simple-looking shot, which was actually harder than it looks to make. The client will return if you can meet or exceed expectations, especially with what appear to be pretty straightforward photos.

ISO 100, 1/125 sec., f/11, 100mm lens

After you, the next most important component will be your portfolio. The definition of what constitutes a portfolio has radically changed in recent years, as a direct result of the rise of digital. Portfolios used to be prints or color transparencies. Now portfolios also include iPads, other electronic devices, and, of course, your website. A clean, well-designed, easy-to-navigate, and quick-to-load website is an essential part of your marketing plan. No one has time to wait for a clunky site to open. You want your site to be an introduction to you and your work. Let your personality come through.

You can use an about-me page on your site as a way to introduce yourself to people who'll see your site but not have the time to meet with you in person. Even with a terrific site, there's still no substitute for getting an opportunity to sit with an actual potential client and review your work. It gives clients a chance to get to know you better and decide if you'll be a good fit for the work they need produced.

Brad's Path

I wasn't someone who always knew that he wanted to be a photographer. I came to the party a little late. I was out of college with a BA in psychology, and I knew I didn't want to pursue that, but I was unsure of what I did want to do. I attended a photo class at a local college while taking a year off in the beautiful Rocky Mountains. I loved it and decided to go to the Art Center College of Design in Pasadena, California. I worked at a job I truly hated for 18 months to save some money for school. My wife and I moved to Pasadena, and she put me through school.

After Art Center, I assisted in L.A. and then moved to Denver, where I opened a freelance commercial photo business and started teaching. I rented studio space for about seven years. I shared my first studio with two other photographers. It was a huge warehouse type of space, and my share of the rent was $300 a month! After about two years of that I moved into a space that I rented by myself. Those first two years were really rough, and I thought about giving up many times. At one point I had $13 in my business checking account. The next few years brought steady growth in clients and budgets. After being in business for seven years I bought a building and moved my studio there.

The next decade was probably the most satisfying, both creatively and business wise. It was fun to work on a variety of local and regional accounts and some national catalogs. My family was always a priority, so I tended to be out of the studio by 6 p.m., and I hate working on the weekends. I found that I really love teaching, so I took on more classes and scaled back on shooting. I still do both and find them both rewarding (**FIGURE 11.7**).

FIGURE 11.7 This image involved shooting the man in the studio and the storm from the roof of the studio. The images were combined, and the water in the umbrella was added in post. This is one of Brad's favorite images in his portfolio.

ISO 100, 1/125 sec., f/11, 150mm lens

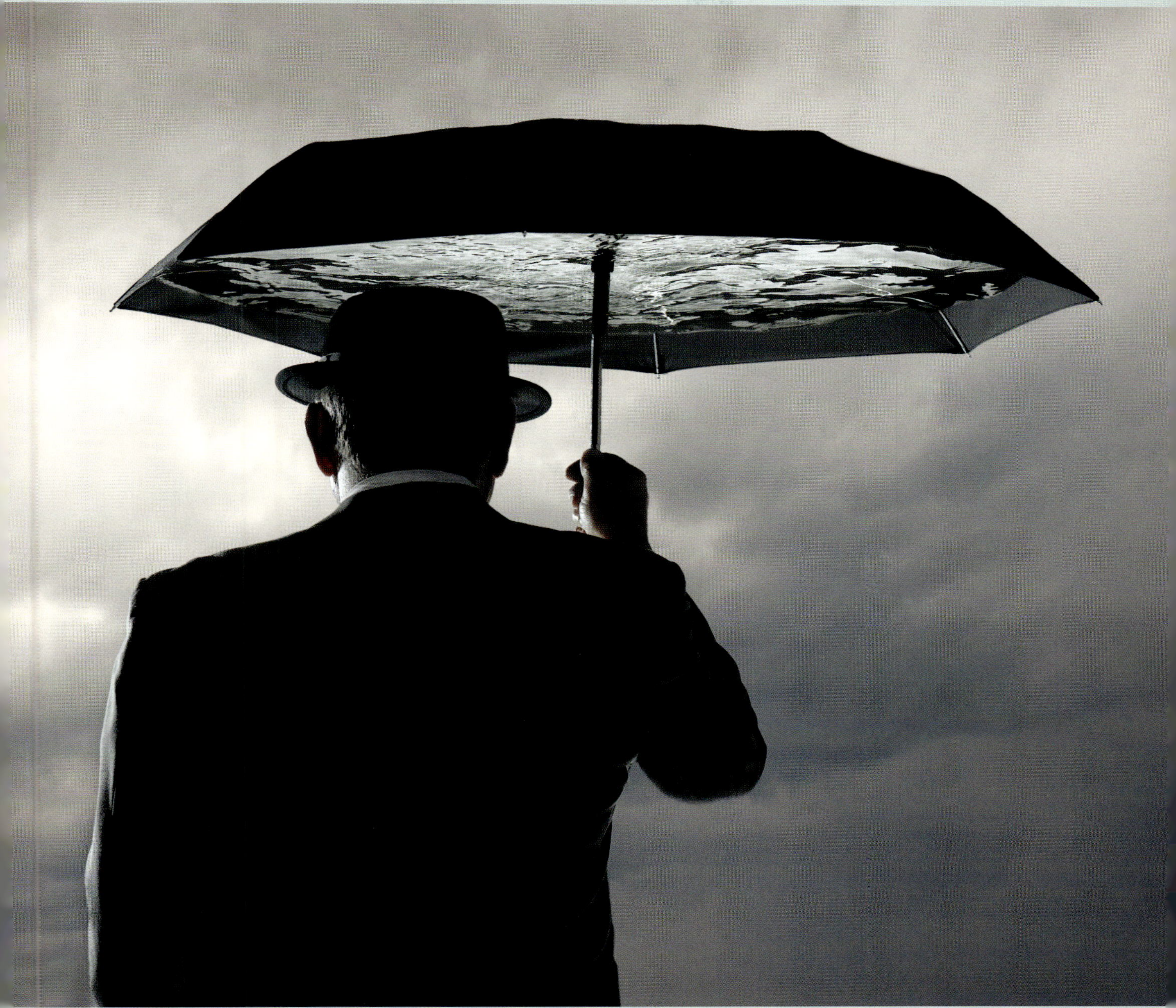

Having a blog is another way to connect with a wider audience and get them interested in what you're doing (**FIGURE 11.8**). The key to a good blog is that you need to update it on a regular basis. The same is true of your website. If someone is interested in your work and returns to either, only to find them exactly the same, they'll lose interest.

It's not unusual to update a blog at least once a week, and remember, it's not all about you. A blog gives you the chance to show people what you are interested in. Linking to other sites is also a key way to increase your search engine optimization, or SEO (which means when people search for certain photography-related terms, you're more likely to pop up in the results—and, maybe some of the other sites will even end up linking to you, too, which will enhance your SEO more). It also adds value to your own blog. For every item about you, you should have approximately five things that aren't. Your blog should be branded the same way as all your other marketing materials are.

There is no escaping social networking. Facebook, LinkedIn, Twitter, and a host of other sites have become invaluable tools for reaching your target audience. You want to make sure that you keep your business and personal sites separate, though. There's no need to have clients know what you were up to over the weekend. Many sites cater to very specific demographics that you can tap into and use to create a buzz about your work. People can find out about your work when they go to Pinterest, 500px, or any number of other sites.

A Sample About-Me Statement

I have been photographing subjects from the mundane to the sublime for 25 years. I have always tried to treat each subject with enthusiasm, respect, and a sense of whimsy and wonder.

My specialty is not specializing. I have been fortunate to photograph people and products, in the studio and on location. I shoot for advertising agencies, design firms, and directly for clients.

I believe in the collaborative nature of commercial photography, uniting inspired ideas. I am pleased when, at the end of the project, the client will say, "Well, that was enjoyable," as if they are surprised. As if previous photo shoots were painful experiences. Pushing to create strong, conceptual, beautiful images can be stressful and difficult, but in the end, we're taking pictures. It's supposed to be fun.

[This sample statement was adapted from Brad's site—create your own!]

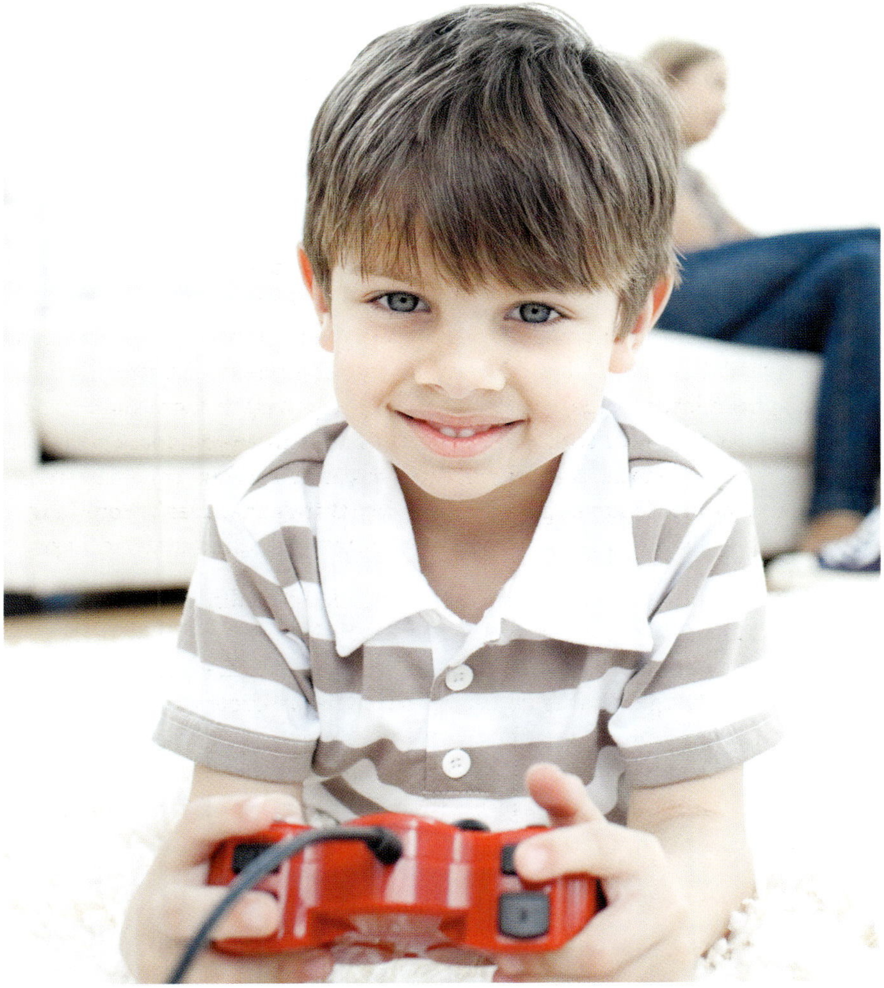

© Shutterstock

FIGURE 11.8 Add your latest and greatest images to your blog, or use new work that is outside what you normally do to gauge reaction to it.

ISO 100, 1/125 sec., f/4, 150mm lens

The truth is that by the time this book is published, there'll be a host of new networking sites, and many others will have become passé. It can be exhausting trying to keep up with what works and what doesn't. You can't be everywhere, but you should pick a couple of sites that cater to your clientele and then contribute regularly. Starting and then not contributing any more does more harm than good.

Companies like Agency Access can supply mailing lists of potential clients. These cater to people who want to work with advertising agencies, but lists exist for everything from women with newborns to new homebuyers. Many can send email blasts for you to specific targeted markets. Email blasts are a good way to show your latest work to specific people you would like to work with (**FIGURE 11.9**). You can do the same thing with postcards and other forms of direct mail.

In addition to all of the above, simple things like handing out business cards and staying connected to national and local organizations are still effective ways to network. Don't limit yourself to photography groups; look for other groups that could benefit from your work as well. If you're an architectural photographer, for instance, you may want to join the local chapter of the American Institute of Architects or a similar group. This would help you get a chance to network with a specific group of people who need your services.

These are just a few marketing ideas. What's most important is that you'll need to formulate an overall strategy and a budget. The most successful photographers realize that they have to put money into a cohesive and comprehensive plan. They'll set aside money, say, 10 percent of their previous year's profit, and dedicate it to marketing for the upcoming year. As your business grows, so will your marketing budget, enabling you to target bigger and more sophisticated clients (**FIGURE 11.10**).

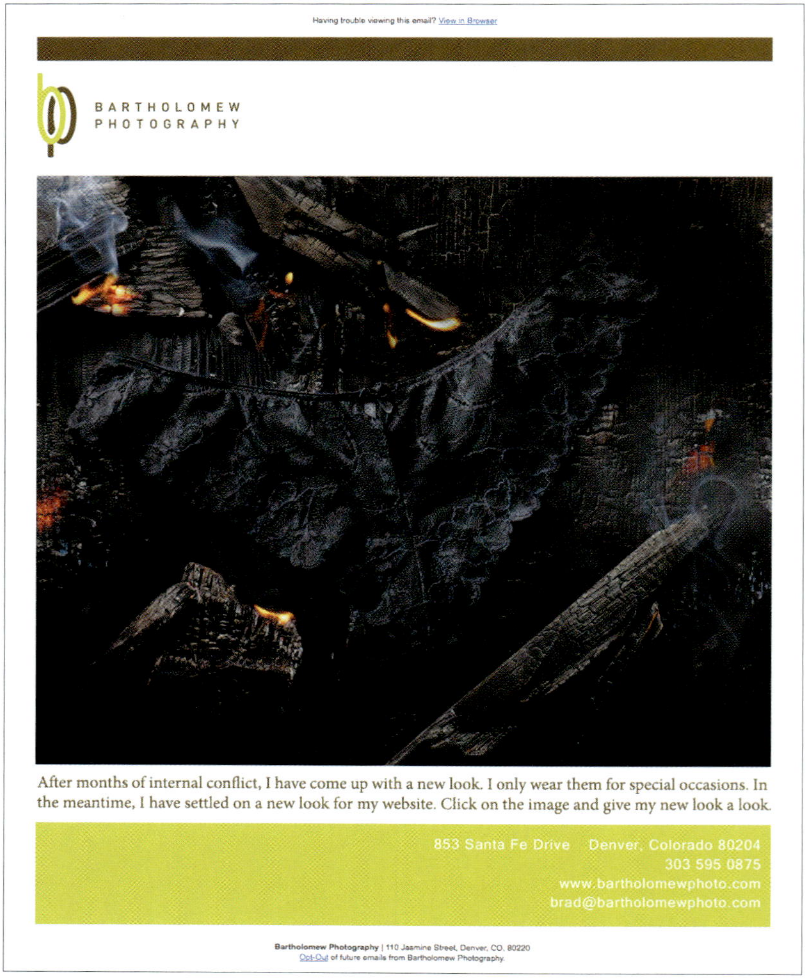

FIGURE 11.9 An example of an email blast. Adding a short caption is helpful in explaining the image and piquing interest.

ISO 100, 1 sec., f/16, 150mm lens

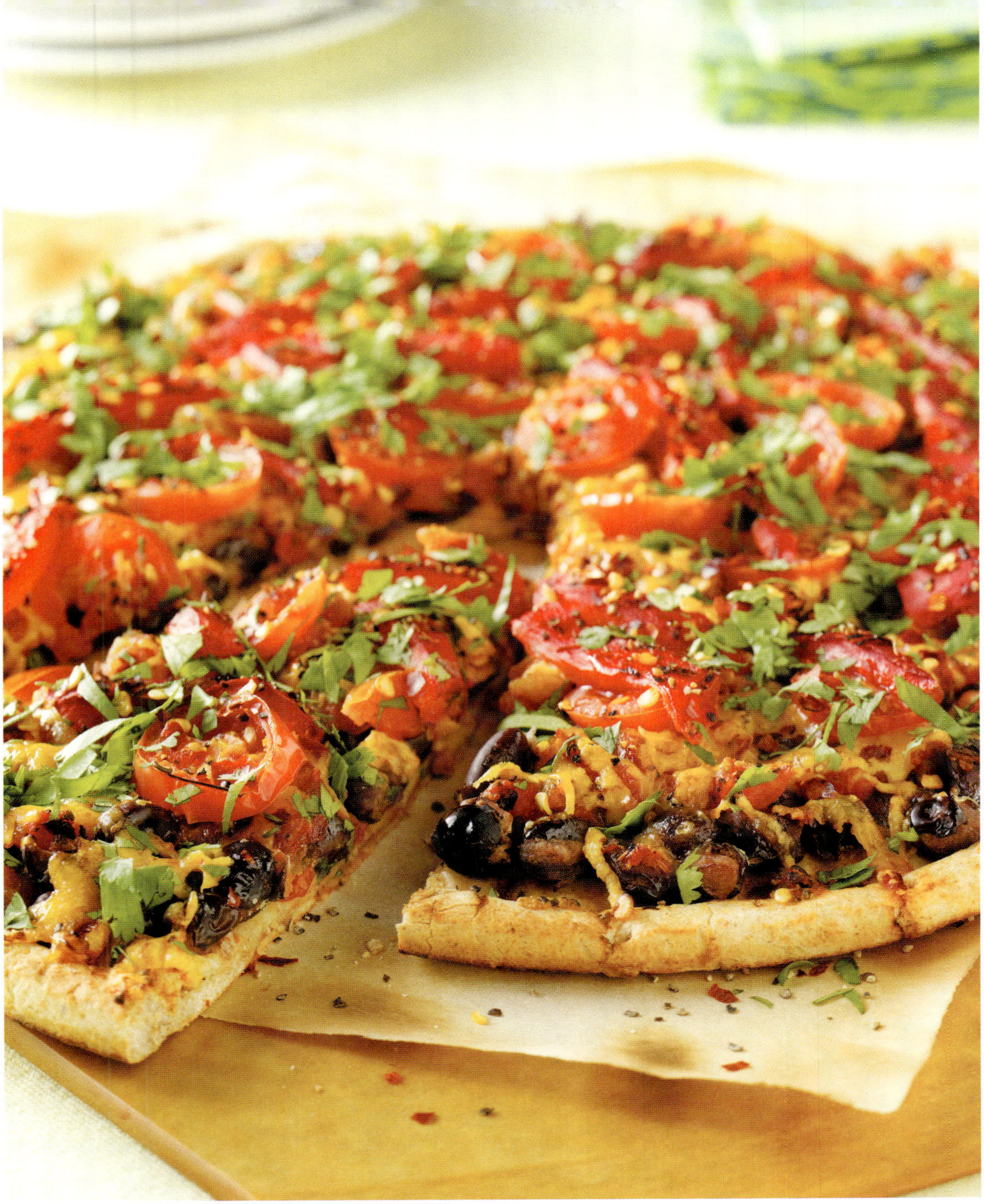

FIGURE 11.10 Working for national restaurant chains requires attention to detail and extraordinary support staff, including food stylists and assistants.

ISO 100, 1/125 sec., f/16, 100mm lens

Once you have a plan in place, you need to adhere to it. Remember, it takes time and consistency before you'll see the results of your efforts. Set up specific dates when you'll be sending out materials or updating sites. Having a great plan does you no good if you don't implement it. Then monitor your results and revise your plan accordingly.

High-End Equipment

Chapter 10 discussed most of the significant advancements you will make regarding equipment, but there are some things to examine as you reach higher levels of success. It's important to reiterate that none of this is one size fits all. Depending on your specialty and which regions of the country you work in, your clients will have different needs and expectations.

Studio

We have heard art directors say that they don't care what the studio looks like as long as the photos are great. We simply don't believe that. It does matter. It's like saying that you don't care what a restaurant looks like as long as the food is good. That may be true if you just want to grab a quick burger, but if you're paying serious money for a meal, you want the whole experience to be exemplary. You would be disappointed if the place was dirty or freezing cold.

The same is true for your business. When you're working on big jobs, you can be assured that people from the agency will be there, and so will their clients. At that point your studio is not only a reflection of you, but also an indication of the agency's judgment in selecting you in the first place. Martin Wonnacott makes a great point in his interview when he says, "They will remember the experience of working with you more often than the images you created together."

The key here is to make sure that at a minimum, you have attended to their comfort. As your budgets get bigger, there'll be expectations that your surroundings will become nicer. You want to make sure that form follows function (**FIGURES 11.11A–C**). Don't create some fabulous space that doesn't accommodate the way you shoot. It might seem cool to have a pool table or arcade games, but if they use up functional space, they become counterproductive.

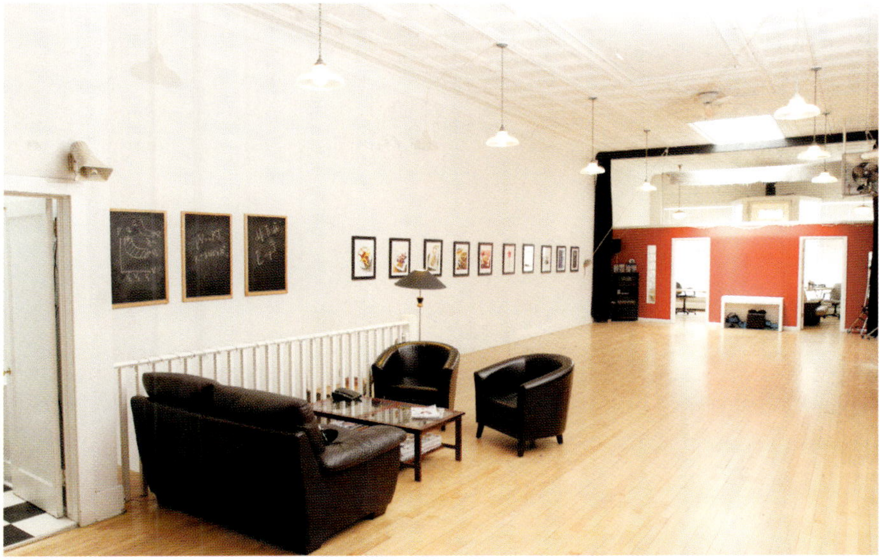

a)

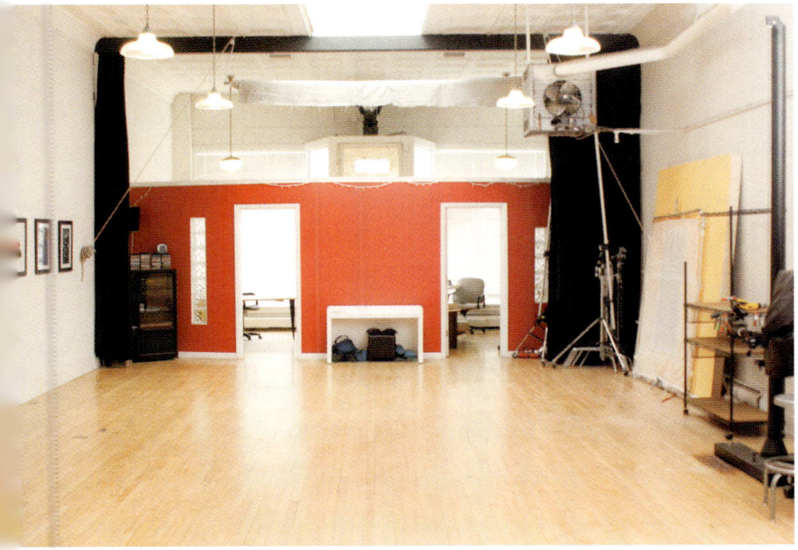

b)

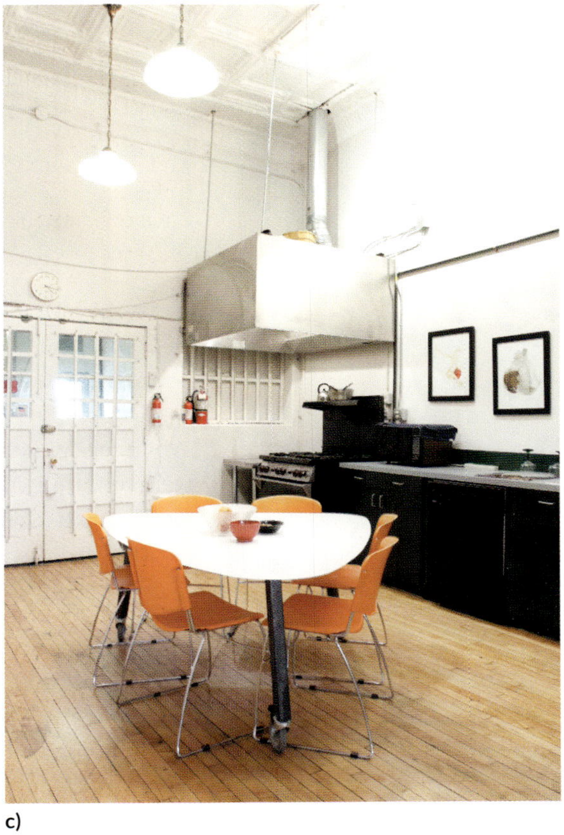

c)

FIGURE 11.11 a–c) Various views of a comfortable and functional studio.

MANAGE YOUR OVERHEAD

On my last day of assisting, my boss sat down with me and asked what my plans were. I was moving from L.A. to Denver and planned on renting a studio and getting started ASAP. He looked me square in the eyes and said, "Keep your overhead low, manage your expenses." This was coming from Richard Noble, one of the most successful commercial photographers of his generation. Even for him, a lot of overhead could become oppressive. After owning my studio building for almost 20 years, I recently sold it. I was teaching more, and it just didn't make sense to continue to maintain that amount of overhead. I miss the space, but I don't miss the expenses. I rent a studio by the day and pass these expenses on to clients. What a concept!

—BRAD BARTHOLOMEW

As with most things, there's a balance. You want to create an impressive space, but you need to not overspend. If the investment you make can help you land larger accounts with bigger budgets, then it's money well spent. This gets back to the idea of return on investment, and it should guide all your decisions as you become more successful. In fact, it'll help drive your success.

Lighting

The same idea applies to your lighting equipment. There is no reason to spend a ton of money on gear that doesn't make you more efficient or enable you to create the type of light you need to enhance your style. Let's look at one example. Let's say that as your career has progressed, you've moved from doing general still life images to specialized images, in particular spills, pours, and splashes (**FIGURE 11.12**).

It may be that the equipment you used previously can no longer handle your present needs. It's not that it isn't still great equipment. It's just that your current shots require more refined results. As an analogy, you could punch a hole in a piece of plywood with a hammer, but a drill will give you better results. In order to freeze splashes, you need equipment capable of producing very short flash durations. Strobes that can do this are quite expensive. While you were experimenting and adding images to your portfolio, it made sense to rent this equipment, but as all types of splashes become more of your commercial work, there'll come a time when purchasing the equipment makes both economic and logistical sense (**FIGURE 11.13**).

As your expertise increases, you'll be expected to work more efficiently. This is where you want to put your money. Things that can make you more efficient will pay for themselves. You'll be able to get more work done and look more professional as you do it (**FIGURE 11.14**).

There are also times when the quality of light you desire can only come from a specific piece of lighting equipment. If that look is a sometime thing, then rent the equipment, but if it is integral to your style,

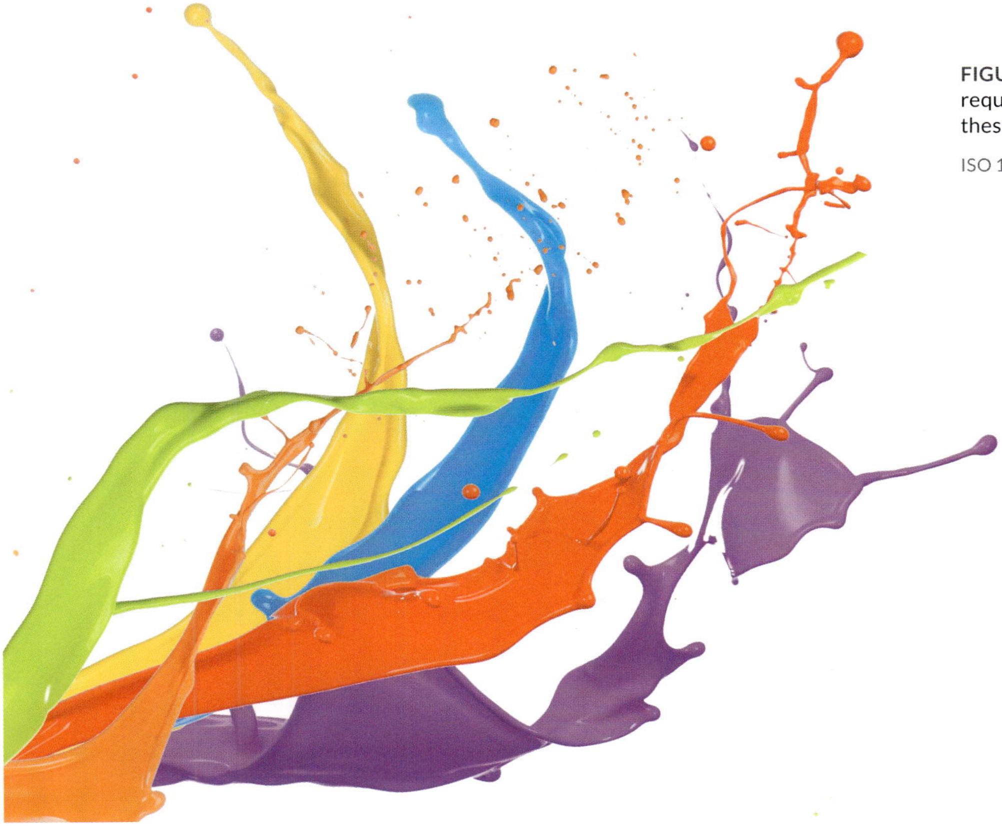

© Shutterstock

FIGURE 11.12 This image required specific gear to achieve these results.

ISO 100, 1/125 sec., f/16, 210mm lens

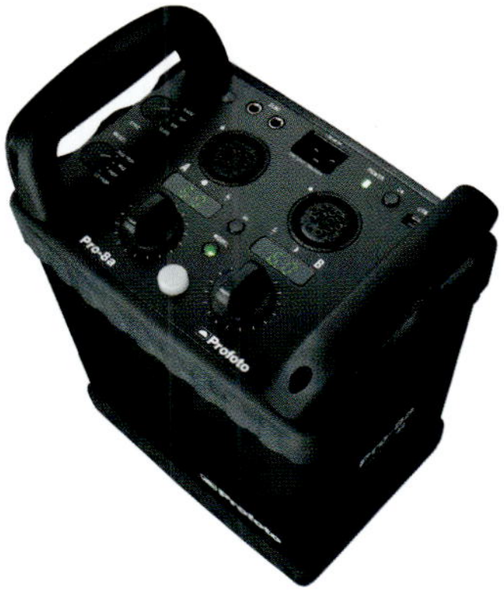

FIGURE 11.13 This is one example of a strobe generator capable of freezing fast-moving objects.

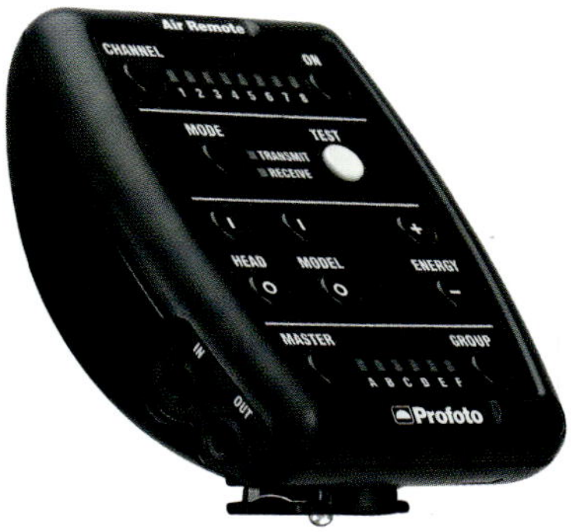

FIGURE 11.14 This amazing little thing, the Air Remote, allows you to adjust your strobes from your camera or from across the room, saving time and effort.

FIGURE 11.15 A large parabolic reflector is ideal for creating a unique quality of light suited for people and fashion shoots.

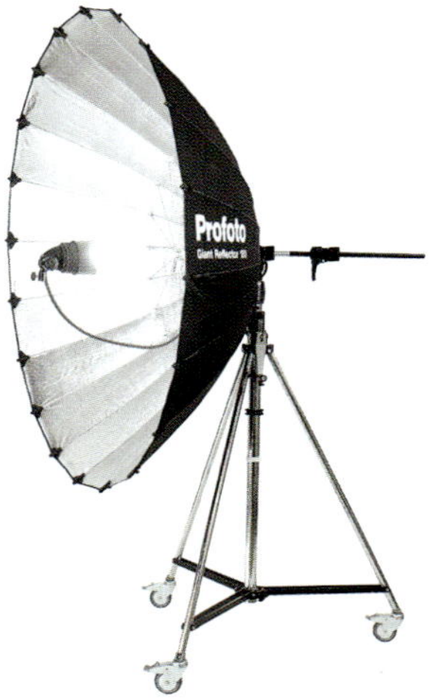

you should probably buy the gear. The shower curtain plus PVC pipe softbox created pretty nice light, but it may not be what you ultimately want. It also might not strike in-studio clients as terribly professional. Certain lights and modifiers just create special light (FIGURE 11.15).

Grip Equipment

When it comes to efficiency, grip equipment is a sound place to spend money. By its very nature, it's designed to make a photographer's life easier. Chapter 10 covered this pretty thoroughly. As your budgets increase and shots become more complicated, you'll just end up needing more of it. Companies like Matthews make stuff for still, film, and video photographers that you never knew existed (www.msegrip.com). When we look through their catalog, we could spend a ton of money—if we only had a ton of money. It's worth becoming familiar with all the equipment that's available so you can add to your grip kit as needed.

Budgets

The last area to discuss is budgets. As mentioned earlier, although we broke this section into three chapters, it works more as a continuum than as distinct levels of success. It's not as if you go to bed one night and then wake up the next day to realize that you have "made it." It's imperative that you value your work throughout your career and that you know what the going rate is for what you do.

Just because you love what you do doesn't mean that you should undervalue it. Joining organizations and assisting can help you learn some general guidelines. Asking your clients what they can afford can work at times. If your fees have remained the same but your skills have improved, try asking for more money. If your clients balk at the new rates, you can pull back. This is more art than science and can be confusing and frustrating. We read articles in national industry magazines quoting rates from New York and L.A. that simply don't apply to what we can charge in Denver. Ask advice from friends in the industry. As the jobs become more complex and you need more help, your bids will need to grow as well (**FIGURE 11.16**).

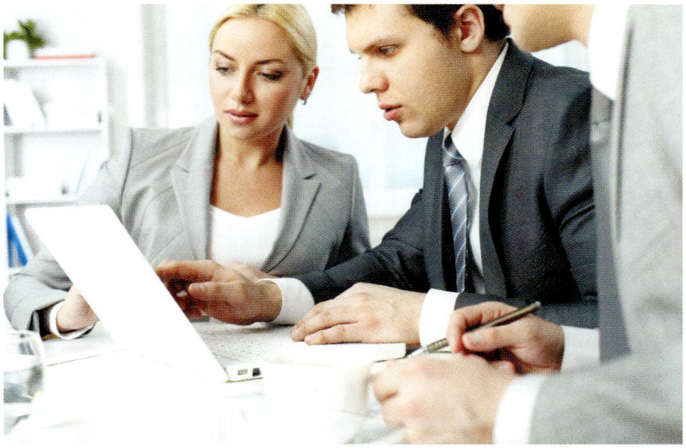

© Shutterstock

FIGURE 11.16 Reps can help you open up markets you may not be aware of.

ISO 100, 1/125 sec., f/8, 100mm lens

Market Value

What's the going rate for what you do? If the number one draft choice in the NFL came into the league saying, "I just love playing the game so much I'd play for free," the rest of the players would crush him. Number two's salary is predicated on number one's, number three's on number two's, and so on, so if number one is willing to play for less than the market value, it ruins it for everyone else. If you undervalue yourself, you devalue the entire market.

Representation

Once you reach a certain level, you may want to consider getting representation. Artist reps have connections within the industry; they get your work in front of the people who are hiring. When you first start out, you have a lot of time to market yourself, but as you get busier you'll find less and less time to do this. If you become so busy shooting that you can no longer market your own work, you may think that you don't need to market yourself any more because you keep getting tons of work. This is shortsighted. People you are working with will move, clients will go out of business, and sometimes, despite your best efforts, they will move on to other photographers.

You simply have to continually market yourself, and a rep can help with this. They also will know what jobs are worth and can help you bid jobs. They take a percentage of your fee for their services. This varies by location, but it's usually between 25 to 35 percent. That may seem like a lot, but remember, you are getting 65 to 75 percent of a job you wouldn't have known existed—and it may well be a better-paid one than you would have found on your own.

Bigger budgets will bring greater expectations from your clients—and from you. Embrace these expectations. Continue to experiment and grow as an artist (**FIGURE 11.17**).

Conclusion

Lighting is the key ingredient to creating compelling images. In order to light something correctly, you must first understand the subject thoroughly, and you must know what you're trying to say about it. Blindly setting up your lights, hoping that you'll come up with something great, isn't a sound strategy. There are no rigid formulas for any of this. There are guidelines and principles, but as soon as you think you have the answers, you need to revise the questions.

We hope that this book has helped you discover some of the things to ask and ways to go about finding possible answers. You must understand your equipment and how to use it to meter light so that you capture all the information you need to render the scene the way you intended to. There aren't shortcuts

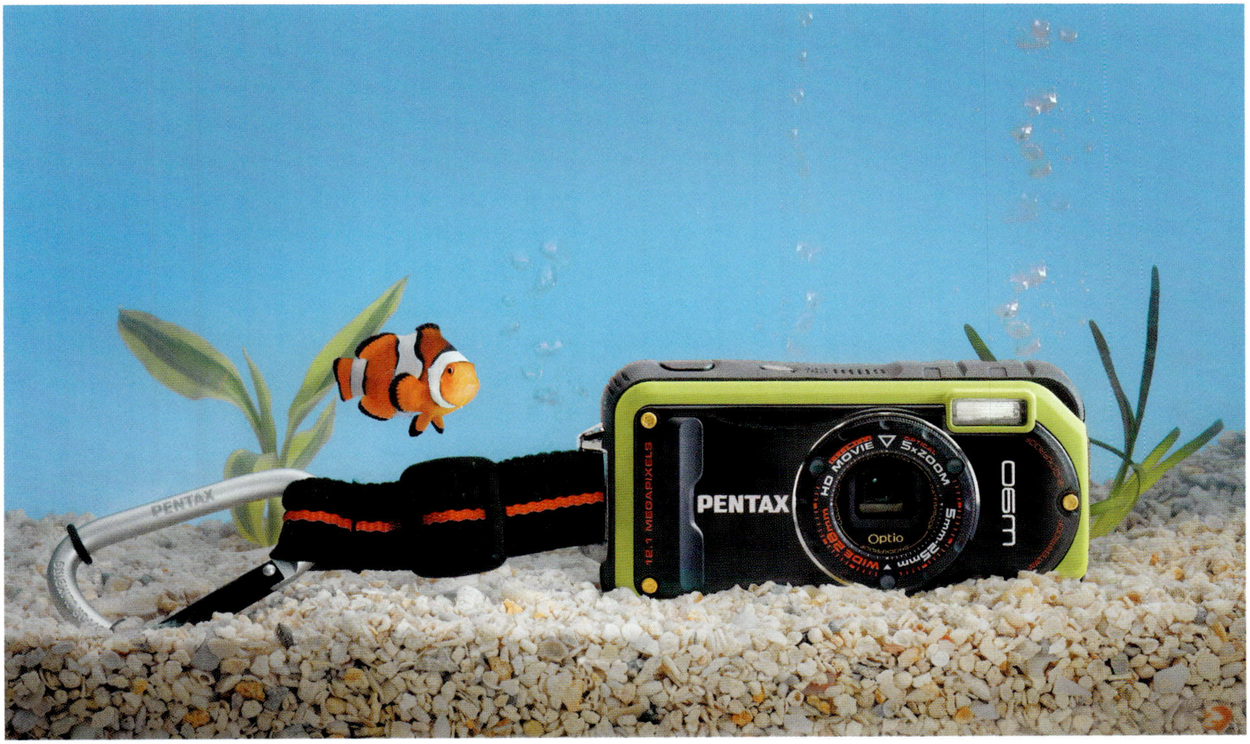

FIGURE 11.17 Shooting a camera underwater with a fish requires a lot of help and experimentation.

ISO 100, 1/125 sec., f/4, 100mm lens

for this process. It takes time, patience, and a lot of practice. A willingness to persevere when frustrated and continually explore new techniques will reap great rewards.

For those of you who decide to make a career out of making photographs, we hope that we've given you some insights into the perils and joys of the business. We were really happy, when reading the answers in the interviews, to see how often the word *fun* was used. Both of our about-me pages on our websites use that word. This is a great industry filled with wonderful, creative people. It *is* fun. We wish you great success as you experiment and develop your own styles of lighting right.

interview

MARTIN WONNACOTT

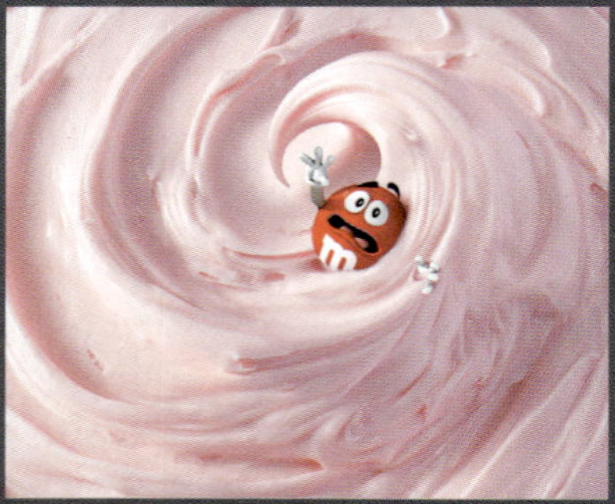

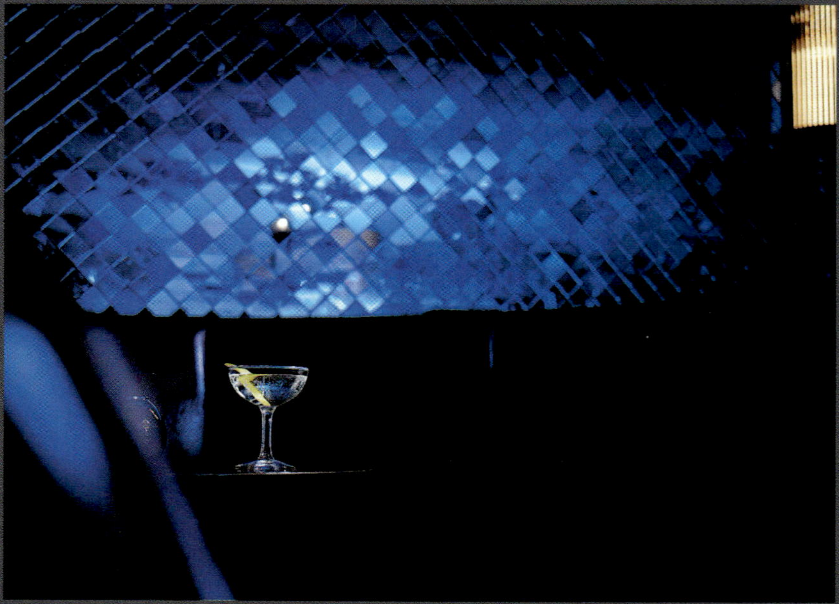

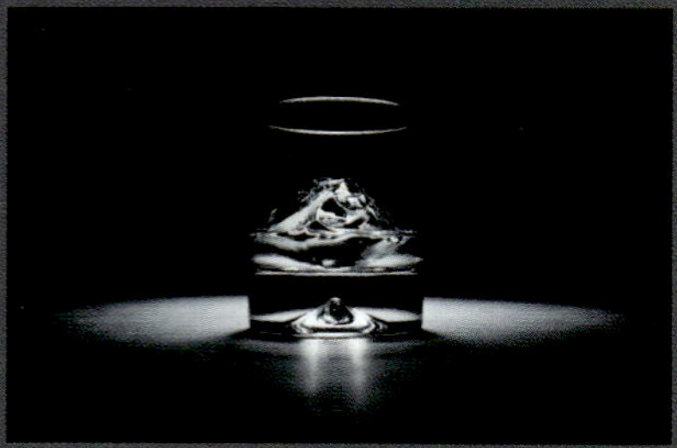

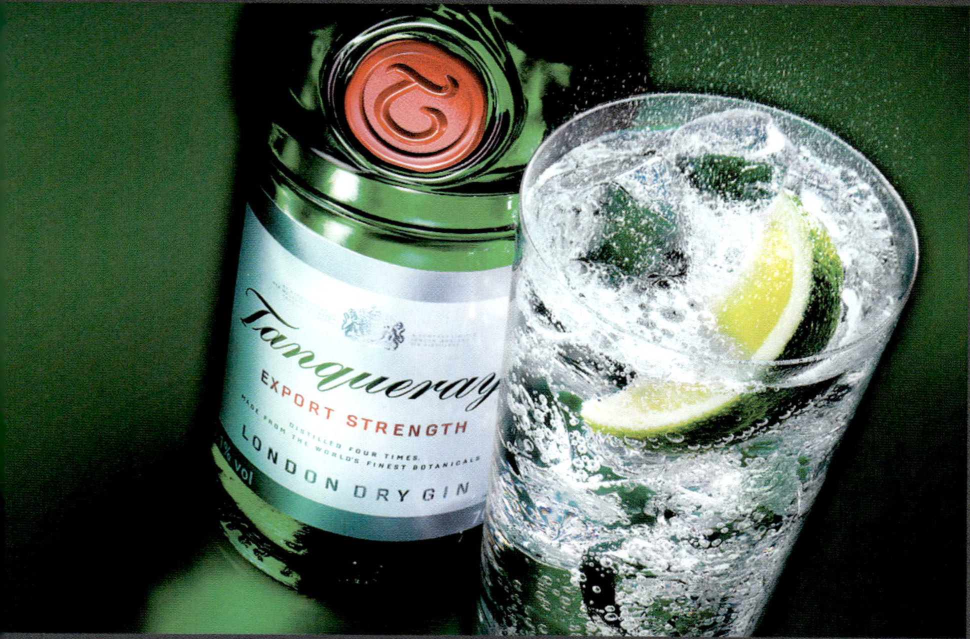

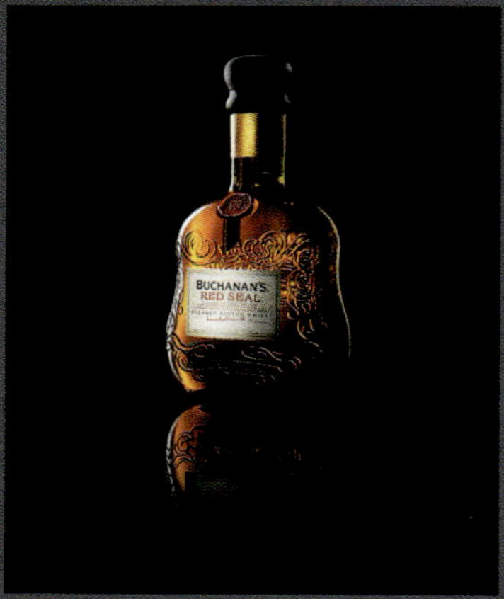

All images © Martin Wonnacott

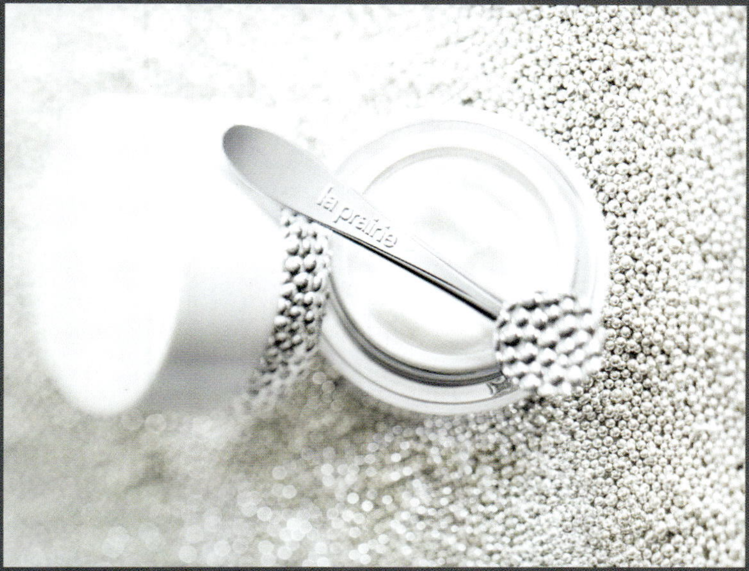
la prairie

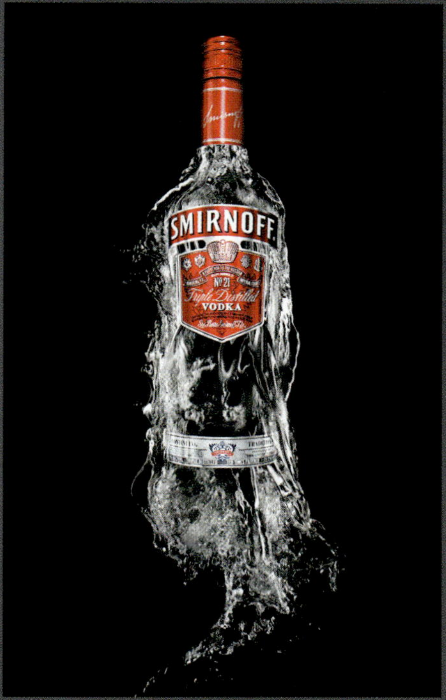
SMIRNOFF
Nº 21
VODKA

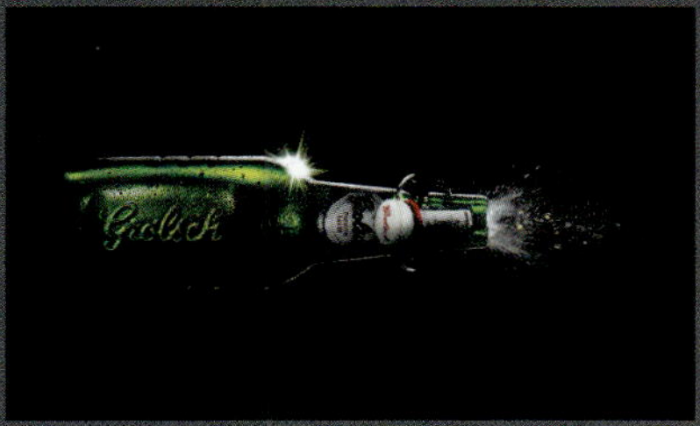

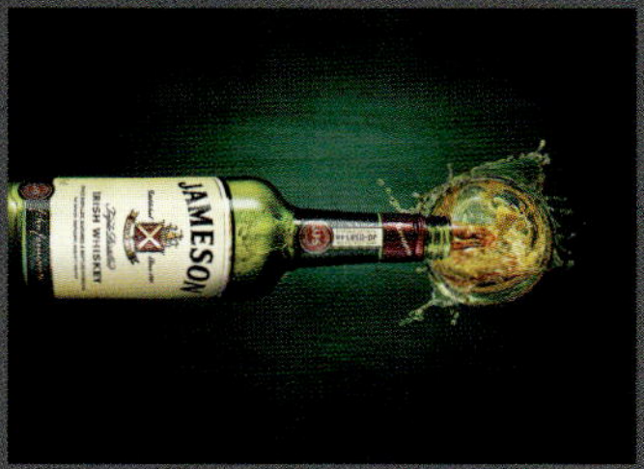
JAMESON

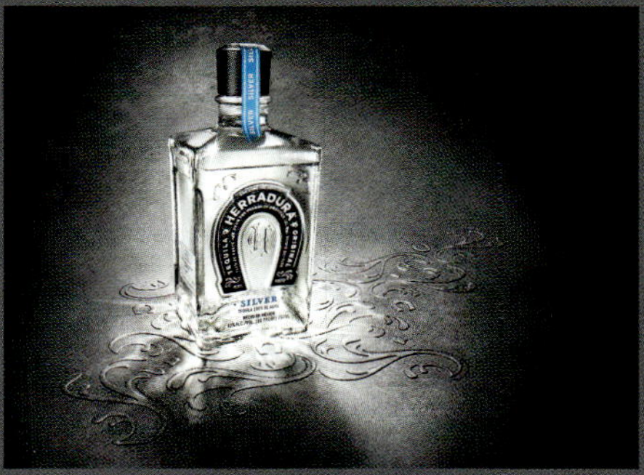
HERRADURA
SILVER

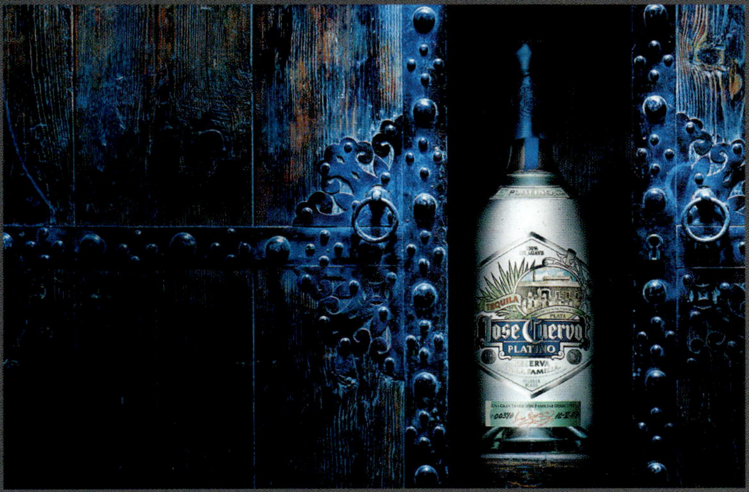
Jose Cuervo
PLATINO

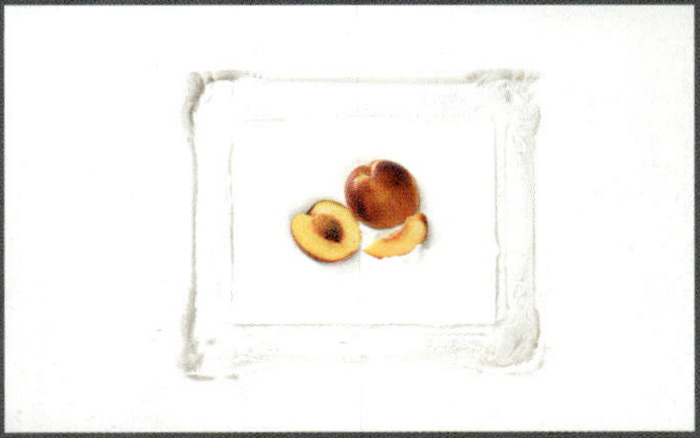

How long have you been a professional photographer?

I've been shooting full-time since I was 19 years old.

How did you get started?

I left high school at 17 years old and started assisting as a third assistant on a work experience program in England called a Youth Training Scheme. After the scheme ended, they employed me as a first assistant for one more year. At 19 I left and was hired to shoot products for another studio in London, and at 23 years old I went self-employed. I have had no formal education in photography whatsoever. In my personal experience this has been a bonus, but it's not for everyone.

Tell us more about your assisting experience.

I assisted a guy called Cliff Borlaise in England on the scheme; he was very old school but hilarious. He shot a lot of drinks ironically, which was a great inspiration to see. From an early age, I learned that socializing with clients was important. Everything was shot on 8 x 10 with no retouch, obviously. I had to process the film on an E6 hand line afterwards.

If you had to do it over, would you do anything different?

Move to NYC much sooner!

How would you define your lighting style?

Simplicity through attrition.

Is it important to be able to light using many styles of light, or do you think it's better to stick with one main style and refine it and adapt it to different subjects?

I think it's important to have an overriding style but not be rigid. In my case I don't like work that's "overlit," so I would start with one light and work with that till it can do no more. Only then will I add additional sources as required. Every subject is different, as are similar subjects such as bottles. They may both be bottles, but they will have unique and individual qualities that may require entirely front or entirely back lighting, as an example. Every subject should be observed thoroughly before even turning your lights on.

Do you have a favorite image of the ones that are featured, and if so why?

The Smirnoff liquid bottle shot—great fun to shoot, and the execution was fairly simple in reality.

What advice would you give to someone just starting out in the field?

It takes more than creating great photographs to be successful. Passion is a start but not enough. A good eye also helps but isn't enough. I've never employed anyone on the basis of his or her qualifications either.

Develop a style that suits your approach. Work fast. Remember that in the real world, you will have to literally "perform" on set with people hovering around you while you shoot. This may be frightening at first, but over time you will build your style and pace. Be aware of music, too; there should be a flow to the environment around you. Clients are people; never forget they get cold and hungry, too. Keep them watered. Think of them as seeds; one day they will move on and may commission you many years later for a huge job at a different company. It happens, trust me.

Professionalism, persistence, and personality will carry you further, especially if you are good with people. Build relationships. Repeat clients are key to success, which means making people comfortable, especially on a still life shoot. They will remember the experience of working with you more often than the images you created together.

Invest constantly in your work. Never be a diva. Never ever give up. Check your focus.

I assume many of these images have been composited. What's your take on trying to get the image in a single shot versus compositing elements together?

I will always try as far as is possible to shoot in camera. If it looks comped, then I've failed. I would rather rig something on set, then composite the least amount of elements as possible.

How about personal work?

I try and fit personal work into my diary as often as I can. Sometimes it's just for fun and it doesn't matter what comes out of it. Keeps you alive. It's better to show strong personal work in your book than second-rate commercial work when starting out.

Is there anything specific you would like to add?

There is a myth we hear often that all you need to do to be successful is find a great agent. An agent is something to be considered as you progress in your career, once you have a strong body of work and experience. They are an extension of yourself, so when that time comes choose wisely and appropriately for the path you want to follow.

Having a good agent will do nothing for you if you don't support your agent and build relationships with clients on your own, too. It's a team effort, and if you work together you can really go more places than you would on your own.

I founded cake-factory artist representation (cakefactory.com), which represents me and others, because I didn't find an agent I liked. That's another story.

There is no single way to success in this industry, so never stop working hard at your craft, be nice to everyone you meet always, stay hungry, be sociable, have fun. ■

INDEX

A

About-Me statement, 270
accessories, 135–140. *See also* equipment
  barn doors, 137
  booms, 136
  clamps, 136, 217, 244, 245
  diffusion panels, 138
  dots, 62, 216, 246
  fill cards. *See* fill cards
  fingers, 62, 246
  flags, 62, 215–216
  gobos, 62, 64–65, 215–216
  grips. *See* grip equipment
  light modifiers, 136–138
  light stands, 136, 214–217, 244, 246
  overview, 135
  radio slaves, 138, 139
  reflectors, 138, 139, 215, 278
  scrims, 11–12, 100, 138, 215
  softboxes, 39, 100, 138
  sync cords, 138–140, 212, 213–214
  umbrellas, 137
  weights, 136
Adobe Bridge, 110
Adobe Camera Raw, 152
Adobe Lightroom, 152
Adobe Photoshop, 56, 110, 111–112, 200
advertising, 264–274
  About-Me statement, 270
  branding, 264–266
  direct mail, 271
  email blasts, 271, 272
  mailing lists, 271
  overview, 264
  professional organizations, 247, 271–272, 279
  reaching your audience, 266–274
  social networking sites, 270–271
  websites, 270–271
Advertising Photographers of America (APA), 247
advertising/marketing, 264–274
Agency Access, 271
Air Remote, 277
American Society of Media Photographers (ASMP), 217, 247
angle of incidence, 60
angle of reflection, 60, 65
angle of view, 155
APA (Advertising Photographers of America), 247
aperture, 153, 171, 172, 178
aperture priority, 178
Aperture program, 152
Apple Aperture program, 152
applications. *See* software
ASMP (American Society of Media Photographers), 217, 247
auto exposure, 169
autofocus, 152
available light, 7, 169

B

backlighting, 29, 194–198
backlit scenes, 194–198
barn doors, 137
black foam core, 215
Blinkbid software, 247
blogs, 270
blurred images, 79
booms, 136
bounce board, 62
bracketing, 173–174
branding, 264–266
budgets
  clients, 217–218, 220–221
  considerations, 278–280
  determining rates, 217–218
  equipment, 276
  overview, 217–218
  software for, 247
  studio, 246–247
business cards, 271

C

camera axis, 8–9, 22
camera obscura, 147
cameras
  considerations, 161
  dgital backs, 157–158
  DSLR. *See* DSLR cameras
  large-format, 159–160, 176
  medium-format, 158–159
  other options for, 157–161
  SLR, 147
  view, 159–160
Capture One, 152
cards. *See* fill cards
careers. *See* photography career
CCD sensors, 150
center-weighted metering, 177
"chimping," 191
clamps, 136, 217, 244, 245
clients
  budget expectations, 220–221
  communications, 223
  considerations, 104
  finding, 218
  goals, 104
  moving to next level, 248
  studio visits, 219–220, 233, 274–276
  working with, 248–250
clipping, 189
clipping warning, 189
clouds, 9–11
CMOS sensors, 150
color aberrations, 201
color correction gels, 132–133
color temperature
  continuous lighting and, 130
  filtering and, 131–135
  gels and. *See* gels
  light painting and, 90
  modifying, 132–133, 150
  overview, 127–128
color temperature blue (CTB) gels, 133
color temperature orange (CTO) gels, 132–133
compositing, 228, 284
composition
  considerations, 84
  lighting and, 71–79
  subject hierarchy, 80–82
  traditional, 52
confidence, 219, 220, 224, 247
continuous lighting, 128–131, 172
contrast
  considerations, 79, 81, 87
  key light and, 59–60, 90
  LCD viewing and, 13
  light on dark, 26–27
  lighting ratios, 12
  warm vs. cool, 27–28
Coudron, Jennifer, 162–163

cropped sensors, 148–150
C-stands, 246
CTB (color temperature blue) gels, 133
CTO (color temperature orange) gels, 132–133

D

daylight lighting, 128
depth of field, 171, 173, 178
dgital backs, 157–158
diffused lighting, 9–12
diffusers, 210
diffusion baffle, 138
diffusion panels, 138
dimension, 8–18
direct mail, 271
distortion, 154
dome, 176
dots, 62, 216, 246
dramatic lighting, 30–37
DSLR cameras, 145–163
  basics, 147–153
  features, 150–153
  focus options, 151–152
  LCD. *See* LCD
  lenses. *See* lenses
  overview, 145
  quality settings, 152
  sensors, 148–150
  video features, 152–153
dynamic range, 167–168, 170

E

email blasts, 271, 272
emotional impact, 30, 33, 133
equipment, 121–143. *See also* accessories
  basics, 209–217
  black foam core, 215
  budget considerations, 276
  considerations, 220, 221
  continuous lighting, 128–131, 172
  dots, 62, 216, 246
  fill cards. *See* fill cards
  filtering, 131–135
  fingers, 62, 246
  flags, 62, 215–216
  flashes. *See* flashes
  generators, 124–125, 126, 240–242
  gobos, 62, 64–65, 215–216
  grips. *See* grip equipment
  high-end, 274–278
  as investment, 233
  light stands, 136, 214–217, 244, 246
  limitations, 219, 221
  miscellaneous, 217
  overview, 121–123
  for photography career, 209–217
  reflectors, 138, 139, 215, 278
  renting vs. buying, 153, 221
  scrims, 11–12, 100, 138, 215
  softboxes, 39, 100, 138
  speedlights. *See* speedlights
  strobes. *See* strobes
  studio, 233–246
  sync cords, 138–140, 212, 213–214
equivalent exposures, 171–173
exposure
  aperture, 153, 171, 172
  automatic, 169
  basics, 168–174
  bracketing, 173–174
  considerations, 168, 169
  equivalent exposures, 171–173
  high-key scenes, 192–194
  ISO settings, 150, 151, 169–170
  light painting and, 91
  low-key scenes, 194
  shutter speed, 126, 171, 172
exposure meters. *See* metering; meters
extension arms, 245

F

Facebook, 270
fashion photography, 163
files, image, 152
fill cards
  described, 61, 215
  gray card, 176, 192
  setting up, 60
  white card, 22, 61, 62
fill light, 61, 63
filtering, 131–135. *See also* gels
  color correction, 132–133
  creative, 133–135
  overview, 131–132
fingers, 62, 246
flags, 62, 215–216. *See also* gobo
flash duration, 125–127, 214, 241, 242
flash sync, 126
flashes, 123–128. *See also* strobes
  color temperature, 127–128
  modeling lamps, 124
  ring flash, 141
  shutter speed and, 126
  speedlights. *See* speedlights
flashlight, 87–91
fluorescent lights, 131
focal length, 154–157
focus options, 151–152
food photography, 94, 130, 232, 273
fotoQuote software, 247
Foveon sensors, 150
f-stops, 171, 172–173
full-frame sensors, 148–150

G

gels
  adding realism with, 113
  changing color temperature, 131–133, 135, 150
  color correction, 132–133
  creative, 111–113, 133–135
  overview, 131–132
generators, 124–125, 126, 240–242
gobo (go-between), 62, 64–65, 215–216
"good glass," 153
gray card, 176, 192. *See also* fill cards
grip equipment, 214–217
  booms, 136
  clamps, 136, 217, 244, 245
  described, 136, 214, 244
  dots, 62, 216, 246
  extension arms, 245
  flags, 62, 215–216
  gobos, 62, 64–65, 215–216
  light stands, 136, 214–217, 244, 246
  miscellaneous, 217
  must-haves, 244–246
  obtaining, 214
  resources for, 278
  upgrading, 278
  weights, 136

H

handheld light meters, 176–178
hero image, 24–26
hierarchy, 80–82, 91
high-key scenes, 192–194
high-key shots, 90
highlights
  blown out, 189
  detail in, 167, 189, 196
  specular, 11
  texture, 19–20, 21, 22
histograms, 185–203
  importance of, 191
  maintaining integrity, 198–201
  overview, 185, 187–190
  subject failure, 191–201
HMI (hydrargyrum medium-arc iodide), 131
Hosemaster, 85
hot lights, 129
hydrargyrum medium-arc iodide (HMI), 131

I

image files, 152
images
  blurred, 79
  compositing and, 228, 284
  composition. *See* composition
  critiquing, 33
  determining worth of, 217–218
  directing viewer's eye, 73–79
  emotional impact of, 30, 33, 133
  hero, 24–26
  high-key, 90, 192–194
  LCD vs. reality, 13
  low-key, 194
  message/concept, 49–53
  mood, 55
  previsualizing, 54–58
  quality, 152
  screen vs. prints, 201
  themes, 55
  visual metaphors, 50
in-camera light meters, 176–178
incident-light meters, 175–176
interviews
  Coudron, Jennifer, 162–163
  Mark, Brian, 202–203
  Oswald, Jan, 92–95
  Potts, Jake, 226–229
  Sokol, Howard, 38–41
  Wonnacott, Martin, 282–285
ISO settings, 150, 151, 169–170

J

Jones, Aaron, 85
JPEG files, 152

K

Kelvin, William, 127
Kelvin scale, 127
Kelvin values, 128, 150
key light, 59–60, 90

L

large-format cameras, 159–160, 176
LCD
  advantages of, 173, 191
  chimping, 191
  histograms and, 191, 201
  vs reality, 13
LED (light-emitting diode), 131
lenses, 153–157
  aperture/speed, 153
  distortion, 154
  focal length, 154–157
  long, 154–156
  normal, 154, 156
  overview, 153
  tilt-shift, 156–157
  wide, 154, 156
  zoom, 156
light meters. *See* metering; meters
light modifiers, 136–138
light painting, 81, 83–91
light stands, 136, 214–217, 244, 246
light-emitting diode (LED), 131
lighting
  addition, 58–61
  artificial, 123
  available light, 7, 169
  backlighting, 29, 194–198
  composition and, 71–79
  considerations, 73, 210–214, 237–243
  continuous, 128–131, 172
  daylight, 128
  diffused, 9–12
  dimension, 8–18
  distance to subject, 11
  drama, 30–37
  fill light, 61, 63
  flashlight, 87–91
  flat light, 9
  fluorescent lights, 131
  gels and. *See* gels

homemade options, 214
importance of, 7, 276–278
key light, 59–60, 90
main light, 59–60
multiple light sources, 128
natural light, 196
overview, 7–8
point source light, 9–12, 21
power, 129
previsualizing, 57
rim, 29
separation, 24–29
shadows. *See* shadows
single-source light, 39–40
subtraction, 58, 59, 62–65
sun, 9–11
temperature, 127–128
texture, 18–24
tungsten lights, 128, 129–133
upgrading, 276–278
lighting equipment. *See* equipment
lighting ratios, 12–18
Lightroom, 152
LinkedIn, 270
low-key scenes, 194

M

mailing lists, 271
main light, 59–60
Mark, Brian, 202–203
market value, 279
marketing, 264–274
About-Me statement, 270
branding, 264–266
direct mail, 271
email blasts, 271, 272
mailing lists, 271
overview, 264
professional organizations, 247, 271–272, 279
reaching your audience, 266–274
social networking sites, 270–271
websites, 270–271
matrix metering, 177, 178
Matthew's Dots and Fingers kit, 246
medium-format cameras, 158–159
metaphors, visual, 50
metering, 165–183
considerations, 167, 170, 174–175
dynamic range, 167–168, 170
exposure. *See* exposure
ISO settings, 150, 151, 169–170
overview, 165
meters, 174–179
handheld, 176–178
in-camera, 176–178
incident-light, 175–176
modes, 177–178
priority modes, 178–179
reflected-light, 175–176
mirrors, 61
modeling lamps, 124
models, 163, 191
monoblock strobes, 238–240
mood, 55
movies, 152–153
msegrip.com, 278
multisegment metering, 177

N

natural light, 196
Noble, Richard, 276
noise, 170, 201

O

Oswald, Jan, 74–79, 92–95
outdoor scenes, in studio, 113
overhead, 221, 276

P

parabolic reflectors, 278
personal style, 112, 176
photographers
  adaptability, 105
  comfort zone, 110
  local groups, 247
  personal style, 112, 176
  portfolio, 45, 110, 218, 267
  professional organizations, 247, 271–272, 279
  self-imposed standards, 247–248
  studio, 123
  style differences, 104
  vision, 103
photographer's assistant, 218
photographic gels
  adding realism with, 113
  changing color temperature, 131–133, 135, 150
  color correction, 132–133
  creative, 111–113, 133–135
  overview, 131–132
photographic subjects
  analyzing, 46–49
  considerations, 46–49, 104
  determining message, 49–53
  directing viewer's eye, 73–79
  heat considerations, 130
  hierarchy, 80–82, 91
  showcasing, 104–106
  subject failure, 176, 191–201
photography
  fashion, 163
  food, 94, 130, 232, 273
photography career, 207–228
  About-Me statement, 270
  advice, 40
  blogs, 270
  Brad's path, 268
  branding, 264–266
  budget issues. *See* budgets
  career path, 250
  character traits, 224–225
  confidence, 219, 220, 224, 247
  considerations, 207–209
  determining rates, 217–218
  equipment. *See* equipment
  expectations, 222–225, 247–250
  finding clients, 218
  Joe's path, 234
  limitations, 219
  market value, 279
  marketing. *See* marketing
  networking, 225, 271–272
  overhead, 221, 276
  portfolio, 45, 110, 218, 267
  reaching your audience, 266–274
  realistic goals, 222–224
  representation, 280
  resources, 225
  statement of career intent, 223, 224
  success in, 257–263
  support from family/friends, 225
  uncertainty factor, 259
photos
  blurred, 79
  compositing and, 228, 284
  composition. *See* composition
  critiquing, 33
  determining worth of, 217–218
  directing viewer's eye, 73–79
  emotional impact of, 30, 33, 133
  hero, 24–26
  high-key, 90, 192–194
  LCD vs. reality, 13
  low-key, 194
  message/concept, 49–53
  mood, 55
  previsualizing, 54–58
  quality, 152
  screen vs. prints, 201
  themes, 55
  visual metaphors, 50

Photoshop, 56, 110, 111–112, 200
Pinterest, 270
pixels, 187, 189, 200
PlusGreen gels, 133
point source light, 9–12, 21
portfolio, 45, 110, 218, 267
postcapture processing, 152
Potts, Jake, 226–229
power, 129
power packs. *See* generators
PPA (Professional Photographers of America), 247
previsualization, 54–58
prints, vs. screen, 201
priority modes, 178–179
professional organizations, 247, 271–272, 279
Professional Photographers of America (PPA), 247
Profoto equipment, 126
programs. *See* software
props, 57

R

radio slaves, 138, 139
RAW files, 152
reflected-light meters, 175–176
reflection, 60, 65
reflectors, 138, 139, 215, 278
representation, 280
rim lighting, 29
ring flash, 141

S

screen, vs. prints, 201
scrims, 11–12, 100, 138, 215
search engine optimization (SEO), 270
sensors, 148–150, 171
SEO (search engine optimization), 270
separation, 24–29
  backlighting/rim lighting, 29
  light on dark, 26–27
  warm vs. cool, 27–28
set construction, 57
shadows
  considerations, 11
  detail in, 167, 188, 189–190, 196
  texture, 19–20, 22, 23
shapes, 13–18, 26
shutter priority, 178
shutter speed, 126, 171, 172
SLR cameras, 147
social networking sites, 270–271
softboxes, 39, 100, 138
software
  Adobe Camera Raw, 152
  Adobe Lightroom, 152
  Adobe Photoshop, 56, 110, 111–112, 200
  Apple Aperture, 152
  Blinkbid, 247
  budget-related, 247
  Capture One, 152
  fotoQuote, 247
Sokol, Howard, 38–41
specular highlights, 11
speedlights
  benefits of, 125
  considerations, 123, 138, 242–243
  described, 242
  examples of, 213
  obtaining, 211–212
  vs. strobes, 123, 124–125
  sync cords, 138–139
  using, 212–214
spot metering, 177
stands, 136, 214–217, 244, 246
stress, 54
strobe heads, 124, 238, 240–243
strobe packs. *See* generators
strobes, 123–128. *See also* flashes
  benefits of, 124
  color temperature, 127–128
  considerations, 276
  vs. continuous light, 172
  flash duration, 125–127

generators, 124–125, 126, 240–242
light painting and, 81, 88, 90
modeling lamps, 124
monoblock, 238–240
overview, 123–125
radio slaves, 138, 139
reflectors, 138, 139, 215, 278
shutter speed and, 126
vs. speedlights, 123, 124–125
studio, 123–125, 138–139, 243
sync cords, 138–140, 212, 213–214
watt seconds, 125
studio, 231–255
appearance of, 274–276
budget issues, 246–247
client visits, 219–220, 233, 274–276
considerations, 209–210, 219–220, 233
deciding what to shoot, 210
examples of, 211, 237, 275
expectations, 219–220
importance of, 274–276
light painting in, 85–87
"outdoor scenes" shot in, 113
recommendations, 233–237
renting as needed, 236
sharing space, 236
studio lighting, 128–131, 172. *See also* lighting
studio photographers, 123
subject failure, 176, 191–201
subjects
analyzing, 46–49
considerations, 46–49, 104
determining message, 49–53
directing viewer's eye, 73–79
heat considerations, 130
hierarchy, 80–82, 91
showcasing, 104–106
sun, 9–11
sync cords, 138–140, 212, 213–214

T

temperature. *See* color temperature
texture, 18–24
controlling, 23–24
creating, 19–23
highlights, 19–20, 21, 22
overview, 18–19
shadows, 19–20, 22, 23
themes, 55
TIFF files, 152
tilt-shift lenses, 156–157
tonal values, 12
tungsten lights, 128, 129–133
Twitter, 270

V

video, 152–153
view cameras, 159–160
visual metaphors, 50

W

watch images, 113–117
watch project, 106–110
watt seconds, 125
websites
About-Me statement, 270
blogs, 270
social networking sites, 270–271
weights, 136
white balance, 128, 150–151
white card, 22, 61, 62. *See also* fill cards
wide-angle lenses, 154, 156
Wonnacott, Martin, 282–285

Z

zoom lenses, 156